POLITICAL LITERACY IN
COMPOSITION AND RHETORIC

POLITICAL LITERACY

IN

COMPOSITION

AND RHETORIC

DEFENDING ACADEMIC DISCOURSE AGAINST POSTMODERN PLURALISM

DONALD LAZERE

Southern Illinois University Press
Carbondale

18 17 16 15   4 3 2 1

Library of Congress Cataloging-in-Publication Data
Lazere, Donald.
Political literacy in composition and rhetoric : defending academic
discourse against postmodern pluralism / Donald Lazere.
    pages cm
Summary: "A critique of the postmodern pluralist faction in
composition and rhetoric that has led these disciplines to value
diverse student voices over the teaching of critical thinking and
writing, this book explains why political literacy is necessary and
how instructors may teach it"—Provided by publisher.
Includes bibliographical references and index.
ISBN 978-0-8093-3428-5 (paperback)
ISBN 978-0-8093-3429-2 (e-book)
1. Rhetoric—Political aspects. 2. Discourse analysis—Political
aspects. 3. Creative writing—Political aspects. 4. Literacy—Political
aspects. 5. Press and politics. I. Title.
P301.5.P67L39 2015
808.0071—dc23   2014049318

The paper used in this publication meets the minimum
requirements of American National Standard for Information
Sciences—Permanence of Paper for Printed Library Materials,
ANSI Z39.48-1992. ♾

CONTENTS

ACKNOWLEDGMENTS

This book is dedicated to Richard Ohmann and Gerald Graff. My intellectual and personal debts to both through several decades are evident on nearly every page, even when I air some of my disagreements with them. (Politically, I am somewhat to the right of Ohmann and to the left of Graff.) As editor of *College English* in 1977, Dick assigned me to guest-edit a special issue titled "Mass Culture, Political Consciousness, and English Studies," from which much of my subsequent work has developed. More recently, Jerry, whose model for teaching the conflicts I have long applied to the study of political rhetoric, has shown incredible fortitude in closely reading, to the point of line editing, two drafts of this book, with invaluable suggestions for shaping it. As for this book itself, I am grateful to Karl Kageff at Southern Illinois University Press for his patient encouragement over several years and for his encyclopedic knowledge of the field under study, and to the entire staff of SIU Press for their exceptional dedication and efficiency. Lynn Worsham as editor of *Journal of Advanced Composition* (*JAC*) has bravely published whole several of my more controversial articles, which I draw from here. Dean Birkenkamp at Paradigm Publishers has enthusiastically and swiftly published three versions of my textbook and generously granted me permission to draw here from sections of those as well. The many other colleagues and friends, some now departed, who have provided intellectual and moral support over the years, in several cases responding to sections of the book, include (first alphabetically and in my heart) Janet Atwill, followed by Marlia Banning, Dave Bartholomae, Jim Berlin, Cathy Birkenstein, Ed Corbett, Fred Crews, Karen Fitts, Alan France, Doug Gamble, Sandra Gilbert, Henry Giroux, Susan Searls Giroux, Teresa Grettano, Nina Gregg, Marlene Griffith, Jeanne Gunner, Michael Halloran, Joe Harris, Alan Hausman, Tom Huckin, Andrea Lunsford, Harriet Malinowitz, Charles Muscatine, Susan North, Irv Peckham, Steve Parks, Patricia Roberts-Miller, John Schilb, Ira Shor, Louise Smith, Gary Tate, Bill Thelin, Mary Trachsel, Jennifer Trainor, Myron Tuman, all the members of Rhetoricians for Peace in CCCC and of the Radical Caucus in MLA, and the faculty and administrations at Cal Poly, San Luis Obispo, and the University of Tennessee at Knoxville.

ACKNOWLEDGMENTS

None of the above bear any responsibility for my positions in this book, which have in fact provoked much disagreement and occasional outrage. I value many of the theorists I disagree with here as colleagues and friends, so I hope they will take my criticisms in the spirit of constructive conciliation of positions whose opposition is often based on misunderstandings. If I have misunderstood or misrepresented any colleagues here, I apologize and welcome correction.

PART 1

THE VIEW FROM
MIDDLE AMERICA

1

MARGINALITY AS THE NEW ORTHODOXY

Resolved, that the National Council of Teachers of English support the efforts of English and related subjects to train students in a new literacy encompassing not only the decoding of print but the critical reading, listening, viewing, and thinking skills necessary to enable students to cope with the sophisticated persuasion techniques found in political statements, advertising, entertainment, and news. (NCTE, "Resolutions")

The humanities lead beyond "functional" literacy and basic skills to critical judgment and discrimination, enabling citizens to view political issues from an informed perspective. . . . The entire secondary school curriculum should emphasize the close relationship between writing and critical thinking. . . . English courses need to emphasize the connections between expression, logic, and the critical use of textual and historical evidence. (Report of the Commission on the Humanities)

In this book I reaffirm the above goals expressed by the NCTE in 1975 and the Rockefeller Commission in 1980, while exploring the reasons they have largely been eclipsed in composition studies over the past four decades. Perhaps the wheel came full circle when the Governors' Commission of the States Common Core State Standards in 2010 (which were otherwise flawed in many ways) compensated against this gap in both K-12 and college education by giving primacy to instruction to "demonstrate the cogent reasoning and use of evidence that is essential to . . . responsible citizenship in a democratic republic" (Common Core 3). That passage recalled the account by the great historian of rhetoric Michael Halloran of the eighteenth-century American model of English studies, whose goal was to "address students as political beings, as members of a body politic in which they have a responsibility to form judgments and influence the judgments of others on public issues" ("Rhetoric" 108).

The present book forms part of my long-running, quixotic project for broadening college humanistic study, with rhetoric and composition at its center, to foster critical thinking about politics and mass media—thinking that is essential for a well-informed, progressive public in America.[1] I propose that our classes, mainly in units on argumentation in courses beyond first-year writing (FYW), instruct students in critical analysis of the rhetoric of partisan politics, propaganda, and public debates on issues like the environment, war and violence, health and nutrition, and above all, economic issues that impinge directly on every student's life, like the exponentially growing gap between the wealthy and the middle class and poor, with its consequences for college access and job availability. I further urge advanced-composition scholars themselves to act as public intellectuals speaking up for clear reasoning in these debates, which are rife with anti-intellectualism, logical fallacies, and deliberate deception—contributing to what Herbert Marcuse called "the systematic moronization of children and adults alike by publicity and propaganda" (Wolff, Moore, and Marcuse 83).[2]

My conceptual and pedagogical framework, delineated in chapter 3, is based on the discipline of critical thinking, as it incorporates argumentative rhetoric, general semantics, developmental psychology, sociolinguistics, Frankfurt School critical theory, and Freirean critical pedagogy (with some modification). In my approach to argumentative writing, political issues are introduced within semantic topics like denotation and connotation, abstract and concrete language, ambiguity and multiple viewpoints, including analysis of political terms and the complexity of labels like *conservative* and *liberal*; *left, center, and right*; *capitalism, socialism, communism/ Communism, Marxism, and fascism*—as opposed to their oversimplification in public usage. I apply rhetorical study to systematic analysis of opposing lines of argument on the right and left, patterns of fallacious or deceptive reasoning, psychological blocks to rational thinking, and the role of propaganda, special interests, and special pleading in the discourse of politics, news, and entertainment media, and of education itself.

For an audience here of scholars and teachers in *rhetcomp*, I try to account for the obstacles within our field itself to implementing such studies, both in curricula and scholarly journals, books, and conferences. A survey of those obstacles, developed in part 2, begins with the tendency in the profession since the 1980s to fixate on basic and first-year writing at the expense of more advanced studies in argumentative rhetoric. As a corollary, the production of students' personal writing (whether expressive or argumentative) has been privileged over the reading, analysis, and criticism of both academic texts and public rhetoric. My broader criticism of these trends in composition studies is that they are among the forces that have restricted the scope of composition as a discipline, toward isolation from the content and critical discourse of humanistic and other academic disciplines, especially the social sciences and communication, as grounding for critical study of public rhetoric. On the contrary, I immodestly conceive rhetoric and composition studies as the master discipline for application to every other academic field with the potential to foster civic literacy.

I further question some of the concepts that have dominated rhetcomp studies since the 1980s, reflected in keywords—applied both to subjects for study and to particular pools of students whose profile corresponds to these terms—like *diversity, discursive voices and sites, stories, contact zones, marginality* (or *liminality*), *difference, polyphony, subalternality, counterpublics, identity politics, multiple literacies, local communities and cultures.* Those who use those terms also tend to view the classroom, especially in first-year writing, either as a "safe house," a "comfort zone," a small community whose members are encouraged to feel good about themselves in sharing their common or diverse stories, or in one variation, Joseph Harris's model for study of argumentation: "a forum where students can articulate (and thus perhaps also become more responsive to) differences among themselves" (*Teaching* 123), and "where student writings . . . serve as positions in an argument whose blessings we can count and measure together, but whose final merits we can leave students to judge for themselves" (115).

In another variant, Bruce Horner and Min-Zhan Lu describe their basic writing (BW) classroom as a site of "conflict, contradiction, and tension" (*Representing* 133) in which students' diverse home cultures are a source of "discursive voices which conflict with and struggle against the voices of academic authority" (173), the latter being perceived as monolithically conservative. Despite the virtues of this conception, what often gets lost in all those voices and stories is more advanced, close study of reasoning and use of supporting evidence in both source readings and student writing. A corollary loss is study of fallacious or deceptive reasoning in sources— such as in politics and media—which students often uncritically replicate in their own voices. In fact, the limitless celebration of diverse voices, stories, and local "discursive sites" has tended to destabilize or even denigrate *any* common ground of academic discourse, factual knowledge, and vocabulary, including study of logic, critical thinking, and argumentative rhetoric. The previous sentence is a thesis statement for the object of my criticism throughout this book, which I label "postmodern pluralism" for shorthand, although it admittedly is not a label that all of the theorists I discuss would accept and does entail the risk of painting with too broad a brush.

By thus restricting my use of "postmodern," I hope to avoid sinking in the swamp of ambiguities in the vast body of theorizing about broad definitions of postmodernism and its relation to poststructuralism, deconstruction, antifoundationalism, social constructionism, multiculturalism, feminism, Marxism, postcolonialism, and more. Authors like Lester Faigley and Christian Weisser, who have courageously hazarded not only to sort out these relations but also to survey their applications to theory in composition and rhetoric, have soberly concluded that all these terms are so diffuse in their definitions and applications, so rife with disagreements among different varieties of theory, as to defy anything beyond minimal generalizations.[3] So I have attempted, undoubtedly with faltering success, to stick with my precise use of "postmodern" or "postmodern pluralism," and beyond that just to identify particular isms as they are explicitly invoked by the theorists I discuss.

The tendencies I am criticizing have enabled conservative culture warriors to allege, like Heather MacDonald in the *National Interest,* that "the only thing composition teachers are not talking and writing about these days is how to teach students to compose clear, logical prose" (70). This ceding of clarity and logic to the political right is one of several ways I will discuss in which some postmodern pluralists inadvertently play into the hands of conservatives.

The recent exaltation of pluralist theory also includes the many recent extensions of studies beyond the academy to community literacy projects and activism that have focused almost exclusively on diverse groups "on the margins," which I survey in chapters 5, 8, and 9 (the last focusing on pluralist resistance to national educational standards, most recently the Common Core State Standards). It's not that I find fault in these lines of study in themselves, as they have produced much worthy scholarship and teaching. It's that, paradoxically, they have largely eclipsed critical attention to mainstream, Middle American society and the kind of colleges and students that are precisely the demographic generally regarded as normative in American politics and culture. The margins have become the center, at least in English studies.

Some of the more doctrinaire advocates of these diverse literacy practices seem to me naïve in acting as though such practices in local classrooms and communities either can operate outside the influence of national and international centers of power or can somehow counteract them, so that the latter are virtually ignored as a subject of critique and action. The study of political economy on a society-wide and worldwide scale is simply off the radar of much postmodern theory and pedagogy. Thus, the insistence on unlimited proliferation of studies in localism and diversity is perversely contrary to the realities of an age of unprecedented concentration of economic ownership, political power, organs of propaganda, and social control by multinational corporations and the right wing in America (as I detailed in *Why Higher Education*). So the excess of diversity has had profoundly conservative consequences in dissipating the kind of coherent consciousness that progressive constituencies need to counteract the right—part of whose agenda is hostility toward collegiate liberal education and toward public education at all levels, which conservative lobbies would replace with for-profit educational corporations. Many such exercises in diverseology strike me as wistful revivals of the 1960s countercultural faith that if we all do our own thing, the military-industrial complex will just wither away. Thus Ellen Willis, in a 2005 article in *Dissent*, took issue with the tendency of some leftists toward "postmodern rejection of 'master narratives' and universal values," along with "the multiculturalists . . . celebrating 'diversity' and 'inclusiveness' within a socioeconomic system whose fundamental premises are taken for granted" (445–46).

As I survey in chapter 2, most of my own life history and teaching career have taken place in Middle American society, and most of my teaching and scholarship have been conceived in terms of critiquing it from within. My sense that it is now issues in mainstream society that have been "liminalized" has been confirmed by sympathetic responses to my work that I have received from colleagues with the same complaint, that they don't recognize in most recent English scholarship their own teaching situation at, as one correspondent put it, "football factories, party schools, and occupational diploma mills." These schools, then, are the precise site of the problems of political illiteracy that I address, and they are precisely the cultural center that those in the profession fixated on marginality often have been in denial about. (My specific points of reference are mainly Cal Poly, San Luis Obispo, where I taught for over twenty years, and the University of Tennessee at Knoxville, where I was a lecturer for a decade after retiring from Cal Poly.)

As I will illustrate in detail in chapters 2 and 3, many students at such colleges (often the majority in my own courses, polled anonymously) tend to be conservative, simply in the sense of uncritical conformity to the corporate capitalist-military status quo. (This sense, as I often need to reiterate, is distinct from the sense of an educated conservatism that can hold its own in reasoned debate with educated liberalism or leftism.) That conformity and their social homogeneity confound pedagogical strategies predicated on a rich polyphony of voices and diversity of social viewpoints in the classroom. In terms of social class, the identity of students at these schools, in my experience, is largely that of rural, small-town, or suburban whites fresh out of high school, in a range from the lower middle class to the new-rich lower-upper class, as distinguished from schools with large numbers from the blue-collar working class in poorer urban or rural areas, including working adults, or from elite colleges with more students from the old-rich and professional-managerial classes. (One of my criticisms of postmodern composition theory is that it has tended to ignore class analysis in general, and particularly in relation to pools of college students. The more judicious varieties of postmodern theory have problematized established definitions of class in valid ways, but much recent comp theory at least implicitly goes to the extreme of regarding the whole notion of class as outmoded, beyond studies of the working class as a subject of identity politics.)

The Lower Middle Class: Left Out of Identity Politics

With regard to lower-middle-class (LMC) students, Rita Felski's *PMLA* article "Nothing to Declare: Identity, Shame, and the Lower Middle Class" wittily argues that the lower middle class, as the stereotypical normative class in America and many other countries, is also the unmarked class, with "nothing to declare" in terms of identity politics. Indeed, much of the conservative backlash against the counterculture of the 1960s (counter, above all, to lower-middle-class-ness) and against today's multiculturalism can be attributed to this class's resentment against being left out of identity politics. No one chants, "I'm lower middle class and I'm proud." Members of the LMC also have tended historically to be conservative because of their frequent psychological need to feel superior to those beneath them on the social scale and to rationalize the power of—and aspire to join the ranks of—those above them. Whenever I point out to my LMC students the anomaly of their reluctance to criticize misbehavior by the super-rich and corporate executives, they answer almost in a chorus that their fondest dream is to become one someday and get their share of the booty. Furthermore, in Felski's account, the many intellectuals who grew up in the LMC but have determinedly gotten out of it, like her and me, tend squeamishly to try to identify with and approve of a wide range of more "authentic" identities—anything but the LMC, envisioned as the bastion of philistinism, babbitry, and reactionism. I suspect this tendency contributes to the avoidance of attention in our profession to the LMC and Middle American politics. In contrast, I would not deny that my own single-minded attention to LMC, Middle American students, politics, and culture might reflect a reaction formation against my deeply ingrained LMC-ness, from my upbringing in Des Moines, Iowa, recounted in chapter 2. If I am too hard on the LMC, it is not out of prejudice against an alien group but perhaps out of excessive closeness to it. (My concluding chapter continues this discussion in the context of a tentative sociocultural theory of the lower-middle and new-rich classes and its implications for critical teaching of students from these class segments.)

In my critique of Middle American politics and education, I break two apparent taboos in English studies: thou shalt not criticize students, and, thou shalt not criticize teachers or public schools (especially at the elementary and secondary levels). These taboos seem to be based on the supposition that the students or teachers referred to might be minorities, poor or working-class people, women, immigrants, or members of some other subaltern group, who are at least potentially progressive politically, so that to criticize them is to blame the victim, in the manner of conservative polemicists. However—and this is a point I will have to repeat perhaps to excess because my critics seem so bent on missing it—I am completely on the side of defending these groups against conservative prejudices. The students, teachers, and schools that are the object of my critique are exclusively those of relatively privileged classes. When I criticize some progressive champions of subaltern groups, here and in later chapters, it is only when they express doctrinaire attitudes that refuse to acknowledge the segments of education and politics that I focus on.

It is the cognitive patterns and political prejudices common (though not universal, to be sure) in this student demographic that have confirmed for me the validity of the theoretical schools I have drawn from and their profile of people with traits of oral versus literate thinking (traits that Mina Shaughnessy also associates with college basic writers), restricted versus elaborated cognitive-linguistic codes and lower stages of reasoning, the authoritarian personality and the culture of poverty (anomalously, in many solidly of the middle and even upper classes economically), and in the Frankfurt School's analysis, the one-dimensional language and thought transmitted by mass politics and commodity culture.

All of these theoretical schools have long been accused by critics on both the left and right of being flawed in their research methodology and prejudiced against people of lower classes, minorities, or women, who are erroneously alleged to embody the lower stages of psychological development. Part of my intention, developed mainly in part 3, is to show that many rejections of these schools have been equally erroneous or oversimplified, have attacked misappropriations of their ideas rather than the originals, and generally have been too quick to throw the baby of core truths in them out with the bathwater of their shortcomings and misappropriations. So, because either these theories or their misappropriations have in the past been turned toward disparagement of the working class and poor, minority or other cultures, and women, any positive reevaluation or reappropriation of them like mine is met with knee-jerk accusations of endorsing racial, class, and gender prejudice. I have been subjected to these accusations after conference presentations and in reviewers' reports on submitted articles and books making much the same arguments as those here. Those who make these accusations seem to suffer from irony-deficiency syndrome. They miss the central point in this book: *My object of study is not the supposed cognitive deficiencies of the working class and poor, minorities, or women, but exactly the opposite—the cognitive deficiencies most common to middle-class, conservative students, in their prejudices against those groups, and my attempts to devise pedagogical practices toward overcoming such prejudices.* My viewpoint concurs with that of University of Michigan philosopher Elizabeth Anderson defending college affirmative action in the *Chronicle of Higher Education*: "A largely homogeneous elite constituted by those advantaged by racial segregation thus suffers from cognitive deficits" (B13).

I agree with postmodern pluralists that members of subaltern groups tend to be more politically savvy in some ways, because they are apt to have more first-hand experience of harsh realities and the ironic disparities between those realities and the dominant representations of reality in American culture, which those in the middle class are disposed to accept at face value. Still, in "Pluralism and its Discontents," Henry Louis Gates Jr. lamented,

> The truth is that curricular changes in history or literature are irrelevant if a kid doesn't know how to read or write or add. And that's the real crisis in American education: a new generation of kids who are going to be functionally illiterate. Forty-four percent of black Americans can't read the front page of a newspaper. When we're faced with some brutal facts like that one, all the high-flown rhetoric about the "canon" becomes staggeringly beside the point. (138)

Even some faculty colleagues at Cal Poly and Tennessee have taken offense at my characterization of LMC students, but I have observed that few of them actually venture to find out, in writing assignments, how much their students know about political matters; the most common way to avoid finding out is just to steer clear of loaded political issues in assignments by taking refuge in the "safe house" classroom model. To colleagues who take umbrage at what I say here and who insist that it is sufficient for students to have "local knowledge," I pose the following questions. What is the minimal level of critical reading ability, vocabulary, and common knowledge needed for students—of all classes, ethnicities, and genders—to take an informed part in national and international affairs, for their own self-interest and for progressive social policy-making? (NCTE policy statements from the 1996 *Standards for the English Language Arts* to the 2012 *Framework for Success in Postsecondary Writing* have been sadly equivocal on this question.) Have you ever given your students a quiz on their understanding of newspaper reports and editorials, a journal of opinion at the level of the *Nation* and the *Weekly Standard*, a presidential speech or debate? Have you ever asked them to define the difference between *conservatism* and *liberalism*; *right wing* and *left wing*; *capitalism, socialism, communism, Marxism,* and *fascism*; the Republican, Democratic, Libertarian, Labor, and Green parties? Is there no cause for concern by college writing teachers in facts like the belief of over half the Americans polled in 2003 that all or at least some of the 9/11 hijackers were Iraqi and that Saddam Hussein was behind the 9/11 attacks— beliefs shared by about the same number of my sophomore students when I polled them? In a class of mine at Tennessee studying literature of antiwar protest, discussion turned to the recently waged Iraq War. After class, one student told me that in her small town, her family and teachers considered it improper to question what the government does in wartime. I asked if she had any personal contact with the Iraq War; she paused for a moment, then said she *thought* her uncle was stationed at some naval base in Cuba.

My own mode of remediation in these areas is to assign, in all of my writing and literary survey courses, regular supplementary reading in print or on the Internet of the *New York Times* and the *Wall Street Journal*, the *Nation* and the *Weekly Standard*, with emphasis on connections between class reading and writing assignments and the current issues therein. When local or national elections are taking place, we also devote time to discussing the campaign rhetoric. Would something like this be an unreasonable expectation for all college English teachers to adopt?

As an unreconstructed New Leftist, I identify with advocates of Freirean critical pedagogy more than with postmodern pluralists and will be delineating points of opposition between them. However, I will also be exploring the multiple problems in applying Freire to the particular sites of teaching I have worked in, with students who are mostly middle-class conservatives with little inclination to question their cultural assumptions and still less need to be liberated from political oppression—a pool of students sometimes acknowledged by Freireans but rarely by postmodernist celebrants of multiple cultures. (Apropos, critical pedagogy has been subjected to far more criticism in professional publications and conferences than postmodern pluralism has.) In chapters 4 and 5, I discuss Lu's criticism of Mina Shaughnessy for privileging academic discourse over students' home discourses. Lu says, "If it is the student's concern to align himself with minority economic and ethnic groups in the very act of learning academic discourse, the politics of 'linguistic' innocence can only pacify rather than activate such a concern" (Horner and Lu 115). However, in many classroom situations I have experienced, most students align themselves with *majority* economic and ethnic groups, so that "empowering" self-expression and pride in students' home cultures has only empowered them to flaunt the most prejudiced misconceptions that they have gotten from their home culture or Rush Limbaugh. Thus I argue that we need to reaffirm academic discourse and teachers' authority to convey information countering student prejudices through "the banking method," judiciously employed, in areas where we have far more knowledge or experience.

I also take issue (mainly in chapter 9) with some liberal or leftist scholars who argue against core curricula and rigorous academic and grading standards. Such scholars tend to be in denial about the extent of both political illiteracy and cultural parochiality among today's college students, at least at Middle American universities like those where I have taught. The consequence has been that these scholars, even when they have pursued admirably progressive projects in their own terms, have for the most part neglected the larger need for a common core of knowledge and advanced stage of cognitive development necessary to raise the level of American civic literacy as well as to empower a well-informed left. So I side with some *educational* conservatives, especially E. D. Hirsch and Diane Ravitch, in support of a nationwide, core curriculum for civic literacy, along with more rigorous course requirements and grading, in high schools and colleges nationwide. (I refer here to Ravitch's earlier, more conservative works, much in which she has reaffirmed in her most recent books while recanting her former support for aspects of conservative "school reform" like high-stakes testing, vouchers, and blaming of teachers and students.) I urge educators on the left and right to collaborate in seeking common ground here.

The Antiacademic Turn

In chapters 5 and 6, I further criticize the antiacademic, antirational tendencies in some theoretical defenses of subaltern cultures, oppositional discourses, and solecisms in reasoning that verge on rejecting reason altogether, such as theories of *l'écriture féminine* or tirades against "The Ruse of Clarity" (Barnard) and "The Tyranny of Argument" (2013 Conference on College Composition and Communication session title). These trends have often incongruously been wedded to the tendency of comp scholars to emulate the most abstrusely academic theory and jargon, in which rejections of rationalism are expressed in hyper-rational form. Not only would such formulations be incomprehensible to the marginalized peoples their authors champion but those authors also often seem oblivious to the quotidian realities of basic literacy education or, worse yet, they irresponsibly imply that their ideas can and should be applied at that level.

This disconnect between advanced theory and introductory writing instruction stems at least partly from the surprising quarter of some of our most admirable mentors, such as David Bartholomae and Anthony Petrosky, in their two joint books *Facts, Artifacts, and Counterfacts* (*FAC*) and *Ways of Reading* (*WOR*), and in Bartholomae's theoretical writings, collected in *Writing on the Margins*. My criticisms of Bartholomae and Petrosky (a professor of education at Pitt) previewed in this chapter are developed at greater length, and with more nuance, in chapter 7, where they are balanced with recognition of the many valuable aspects of their work. David has long been an inspirational, benevolent figure in comp studies, as a teacher, scholar, administrator, editor, and official in CCCC and the Modern Language Association (MLA). In all of these roles, he has contributed mightily to legitimizing composition theory, research, and teaching. But our esteem for his and Tony Petrosky's achievements might have impeded attention to their problematic aspects.

First, there is virtually nothing in either *Ways of Reading*, a popular FYW reader, or the earlier *Facts, Artifacts, and Counterfacts*, a teacher's guide for basic writing courses, about the direct study of argumentation and "clear, logical prose" in composition courses—beyond a vague, three-page section, "The Art of Argument," tacked on near the end of the ninth edition of *WOR*, which advises students, "You don't need technical terms for these assignments (like *induction* and *deduction*); you will be asked to develop your own terms, your own ways of describing the arguments you find" (764). This is less of a lapse in *FAC* than in *WOR*, with its more advanced, heavily argumentative topics and readings. *WOR* also inexplicably makes a "great leap" in developmental stages from the manageable, introductory college readings in *FAC* to university-press-level scholarly theory that I, at least, find far over the head of any first-year student, though perhaps excellent for more advanced courses in liberal arts colleges or graduate school. "Have your students talk back to Foucault," urges the jacket copy for the ninth edition. Why on earth should FYW students be expected to do that? Shouldn't they first learn how to talk back to Fox News and the Koch brothers, or to Barack Obama and MSNBC?

These lapses form part of a problem that I will be addressing throughout this book, centrally in chapter 4: a nationwide lack of clear delineation in writing curricula of developmental stages in course content from BW to advanced composition, including delineation of where and how instruction in reasoning and argument belongs. Chapter 4 foregrounds Mina Shaughnessy's authoritative formulation of "the vocabulary of logical relations" in BW (simply in creating cogency within and between sentences and paragraphs), along with her suggested sequence for further emphasis on argument in subsequent courses. But there is virtually no attention to either vocabulary building or syntactical logic in the versions of BW in Bartholomae and Petrosky or in Horner and Lu (who replace study of vocabulary and logical relations with conflicting "discursive voices"); and there is little consideration of development between their version of BW and later courses (like that for which *WOR* is conceived) in regard to vocabulary, reasoning, and argument. In fact, many of the theorists I discuss are quite vague about whether they are addressing basic writing, one or more terms of first-year writing, or advanced composition, and even vaguer about defining stages of development among them, as Shaughnessy or Russell Durst, discussed below, do. This vagueness—in which a one-term FYW course is in many cases the tacit culmination of writing instruction—is at the root of much confusion, not only about where study of logic, argument, or critical thinking belong, but about all the debates over critical pedagogy's and cultural studies' engagement with political issues—which I personally would limit mainly to advanced courses centrally about argumentative rhetoric, though I waffle on this and am sympathetic to some differing positions.

Bartholomae and Petrosky have also applied theories of subjectivity in reader response to the teaching of both BW and FYW, as when they stated in their introduction to *Ways of Reading* (third edition), "Student readers, for example, can take responsibility for determining the meaning of the text," urging them to avoid "timidity and passivity" and "take the responsibility to speak their minds and say what they notice" (7). Thus it never occurs to Bartholomae and Petrosky to consider how their ideas might be taken in the kind of homogeneously Middle American colleges where I taught for over three decades, where many students are far from timid in speaking their minds, projecting conservative political and religious doctrines parroted from their parents and Fox News onto "what they notice" and "describing the arguments you find" in readings, as I will illustrate in chapters 2 and 3. (Undoubtedly at colleges in heavily "blue-state" areas, teachers encounter some equally doctrinaire liberal or left students. All I can say is that I have had very few such undergraduate students where I have taught, other than as a graduate instructor at Berkeley, and a great many conservative ones.)

These passages in Bartholomae and Petrosky reflect the influence on Bartholomae in his theoretical works of antifoundationalist epistemology, concerning the subjectivity and social construction of knowledge, discourses, and especially reading response. In an interview with John Schilb in *College English*, he recalled that in the 1980s he was immersed in the study of these theories, but "I didn't really want to write *about* Derrida or Barthes or Foucault, but to put them to work, to imagine the discursive world of students in their terms" (Schilb 262). His way of putting them to work is epitomized in a sentence from Jonathan Culler's *On Deconstruction* quoted in the preface to *FAC*: "The claim that all readings are misreadings can also be justified by the most familiar aspects of critical and interpretive practice" (6).

Moreover, in Bartholomae's essay "Writing on the Margins: The Concept of Literacy in Higher Education," he curtly dismissed the whole body of scholarship applying developmental psychology to writing instruction, in which he claimed, "Basic writers, in other words, are seen as childlike or as uncultured natives. There is an imperial frame to this understanding of the situation of those who are not like us" (*Writing on the Margins* 114). I will discuss this passage more fully in chapter 7, but in brief, this and the other passages I cite here reflect several fallacies in the thought of Bartholomae, the kindred comp theorists I criticize, and indeed (as far as I can tell) the larger theoretical movements they emulate. Those fallacies begin with the apparent assumption that the theorized readers and writers are adults, with life experiences (especially like the "minority and special-admission students" Bartholomae and Petrosky describe teaching in *FAC*) that give them some authority to respond to readings and "speak their minds" in college-level classes, not late adolescents from sheltered, mainstream backgrounds and very limited knowledge of the world outside their parochial community and mass culture, like many of my students or myself when I entered college. Second, is Bartholomae's dismissal of developmental psychology meant not only to apply to unjustly labeled "childlike" young adults but also to actual children, at different ages, levels of education, social classes, and access to quality schooling? He has little to say about the relation of his theories to those of cognitive development in elementary education (as in Vygotsky, nowhere mentioned that I can find in Bartholomae's works) or the progression of that development in college, as analyzed by Perry, Kohlberg, Gilligan, and Belenky et al. Finally, although this is surely not Bartholomae's intention, passages like this edge toward a slippery slope from the acknowledgment that many of our first-year students (especially older ones from marginalized backgrounds) are more savvy than we had previously assumed, to the Rousseauan fancy that most, if not all students—whatever their age or background—are with proper encouragement sufficiently "like us" to handle college-level reading, reasoning, and command of factual knowledge, prepared in Horner and Lu's words to "conflict with and struggle against" academic discourse, *before they have even begun to acquire it.*

I note in chapter 7 that some influential antifoundationalists like Jacques Derrida and Stanley Fish make clear that they do not intend their ideas to apply to teaching children, adolescents, or even undergraduate students. I suggest, though, that Bartholomae, Petrosky, and others I criticize make an ill-considered inductive leap trying to apply these ideas wholesale to introductory college education, with reckless disregard for developmental or sociological/ethnographic variables in student bodies. In all these ways, then, these theorists and the teachers who follow their prescriptions both default on elementary political literacy at the levels I advocate and contribute to making comp studies a punching bag for conservatives like MacDonald ridiculing their foggy jargon.

Lu makes a revealing admission about one motive for bulking up composition studies with arcane theory: "This pedagogy could function as a relevant voice in our negotiation with colleagues and administrators over the conditions of our work because of its potential ability to mobilize the institutional authority of 'theory'" (Horner and Lu 189). She is surely right that composition teachers' professional status and conditions of work are inadequate for the scholarly level of studies demanded by the teaching of composition, but I submit that the level of theories I emphasize is more appropriate there than phenomenological philosophy.

Russell Durst's admirable *Collision Course: Conflict, Negotiation, and Learning in College Composition* presents a far more concrete delineation than Bartholomae and his associates of student ethnography, especially in conservative students. Durst, who based this study on his research as director of writing at the University of Cincinnati, states,

> I wanted to investigate the influence of class background on student performance. . . . As I was aware that the majority of students appeared to be fairly or very conservative, I wanted to see how they responded to a curriculum that was more liberal or even radical, that encouraged questioning of established ideas and beliefs. (2)

Even more valuably, Durst studies the developmental difficulties students have in going from a first-term course to a second-term one that introduces critical thinking, critical pedagogy, or cultural studies. He puts his finger

16

on the resistance of many students, especially conservatives, on being confronted, often for the first time, with the complex cognitive challenges of critical thinking and *simultaneously* with the left-leaning politics of critical pedagogy. The dilemmas posed by some extent of congruence between cognitive development at this level and liberal or leftist politics—or indeed of conservative politics at an advanced intellectual level—are crucial issues that I address throughout this book and *Why Higher Education*.

Another antiacademic tendency in comp studies is to deride traditional humanistic education at elite universities in America as a bastion of the ruling class and socioeconomic status quo. I maintain that this is only a half truth: these universities also are, and have been historically, bastions of dissent *from* that status quo, defended by Marxist sociologist Alvin Gouldner as essential sites of what he terms "the culture of critical discourse." For many students from the provinces like me, "elite" humanistic education meant liberation from parochialism and philistinism into cosmopolitanism, as well as a welcome initiation into both the culture of critical discourse and the political left. (By *cosmopolitan* here and throughout this book, I do not mean being superficially urbane or "stuck up," but having a global cognitive perspective and perhaps being active in organizations like Greenpeace or the International Socialist Organization.)

The convergence of postmodern-progressive anti-intellectualism here with conservatives' hostility to Ivy League–level universities, which they view as bastions of the liberal/leftist cultural elite, indicates the oversimplification on both sides, typical in the culture wars, of the complexity and internal conflicts of academic culture. It is an anomalous malfunction of capitalist society that oppositional education is accessible mainly to the privileged, whose class interests ultimately clash with oppositional consciousness. The best solution that I can conceive—in contrast to facile denigration of elite liberal education—is financial equalization of the whole American class structure and system of K-12, college, and graduate education, toward making preparation for such education accessible for all, as Jefferson envisioned his unrealized model of free public education at all levels, which would have "raised the mass of the people to the high ground of moral respectability necessary to their own safety, and to orderly government, and would have completed the great object of qualifying them to elect the veritable aristoi [meritocracy], for the trusts of government, to the exclusion of the pseudalists [aristocrats by birth]." Thus, "Worth and genius would thus have been sought out from every condition of life, and compleatly [*sic*] prepared by education for defeating the competition of wealth and birth for public trusts" ("To John Adams," *Writings* 1308). I would hope my

17

advocating this bottom-line solution confirms my allegiance to the political left, as proof against those readers of my previous writing who jumped to the conclusion that my criticisms of progressive pluralism reveal me to be a closet conservative.

Speaking of that Jefferson passage, one of the best indicators of the consciousness of students at the colleges where I taught was that whenever I assigned the passage, which clearly advocates public education as a counterforce to the power of the rich, many read it as saying that public education would enable anyone to *get* rich. When I asked them what in the text supported this reading, they interpreted "the trusts of government" not as entrustment of government office, but "trusts" in the sense of wealthy financial institutions. And in the second sentence, some read "defeating the competition of wealth" as defeating the competition *for* wealth! Thank you, Jonathan Culler, David Bartholomae, et al., for enabling what I have elsewhere described as right-wing deconstruction, through which these students expect to be praised for taking responsibility for "determining the meaning of the text." When I get such responses, I try patiently to support my interpretation within the context of Jefferson's letter and other works. Some students, though, still insist that their opinion of what Jefferson said is just as good as the professor's, and if they are graded down, that just proves the prof's PC prejudice against conservatives. On the larger political scene, conservative propagandists in America have mastered this ploy to bully the media and public into granting legitimacy to advocates for creationism, climate-change denial, and every other right-wing illusion.

Both-And, Not Either-Or, Solutions

To summarize these introductory remarks, for an academic field that is dedicated to the development of independent, nuanced thought in students, theory in writing instruction is little less captive to oversimplification, orthodoxy, fads, clichés, occasional fakery, and swings from one extreme to another than is American society in general. (I think it was literary critic Leslie Fiedler who observed that in America, the minute something is no longer banned, it becomes obligatory.) Over and over again, as I will show, the original formulation of theoretical positions by thinkers like Derrida, Lyotard, Foucault, Arendt, Freire, Gilligan, Belenky et al., Geertz, and the Frankfurt School gets vulgarized, watered down politically, and turned into dogmatic fiats that would be abhorrent to their originators. So we get Lyotard Lite (endless celebrations of "little narratives"), Marx-Free Freire, and Foucault à la mode, in Todd Gitlin's phrase. Historian Jackson Lears described the reduction of Foucault to "less a theorist of the surveillance state than an advocate of Nietzschean individualism, whose vision of 'heterotopia' celebrated myriad sites of resistance to repressive authority rather than any larger notion of commonweal.... No wonder the Right had such an easy time establishing its cultural hegemony" (32). "Heterotopia" is a perfect description of the postmodern-pluralist dogma. (Lu's chapter "Importing 'Science': Neutralizing Basic Writing" in *Representing the "Other"* astutely critiques this tendency to expurgate or shrink the political dimension of influential theorists like these—although I find the same tendency in some of her own and Horner's work.) It is particularly ironic that so many followers of the poststructuralist deconstruction of conventional binary oppositions, rather than seeking a nuanced reformulation of the oppositions I survey, have tended simply to privilege the previously undervalued pole in as one-sided, essentialist a manner as the other pole had conventionally been privileged. (To reiterate, these oppositions include personal writing versus argumentation and critical analysis of sources, nonacademic versus academic discourse and culture, multiculturalism versus the humanistic canon, women's versus men's ways of knowing, diversity versus commonality, localism versus cosmopolitanism.) Thus new sets are produced of what Ann Berthoff called "killer dichotomies." (Beth Daniell and Richard Miller also use this apt phrase.) Corrections of faults in the second sets of these binaries toward the side of the first sets, which indisputably are valuable to the extent of balancing the scales, get turned into Iron Laws, enforced with zero tolerance for any disagreement or deviation.

Once the theoretical winds shift, the previous orthodoxies, rather than being held up to judicious criticism, just disappear down the memory hole: "Why discuss old news? Nobody believes that stuff anymore." Like, what ever happened to tagmemic heuristics, problem solving, and *l'écriture féminine*? This amnesia guarantees against anyone ever having to admit they were wrong in their embrace of ephemeral trends, that they might still be embracing one, or that they may have been too hasty in dismissing some theoretical line when it has gone out of fashion. In part 3, I make a case in historical revisionism for revival of topics from social and developmental psychology and sociology—with particular emphasis on class analysis—that were influential in rhetcomp until the 1980s but are now regarded as *passé*, and I seek to rehabilitate to some extent the reputation of several scholars in those fields whose ideas have been too glibly dismissed by postmodernists, such as Ian Watt and Jack Goody, Walter Ong, Thomas J. Farrell, William Perry, Lawrence Kohlberg, Basil Bernstein, Richard Hoggart, Oscar Lewis, Seymour Martin Lipset, C. Wright Mills, the members of the Frankfurt School, and the book and topic *The Authoritarian Personality*, whose Frankfurt-ish perspective was indicated by Theodor Adorno being a coauthor. (Lo and behold, in September 2014, the *New Yorker* featured an article by Alex Ross declaring, "The philosophers, sociologists, and critics in the Frankfurt School orbit, who are often gathered under the broader label of Critical Theory, are, indeed, having a modest resurgence" [88].)

Poststructuralist/postmodernist theories have passed their own peak by now, and perhaps yet another paradigm shift has been building up over the past decade, amounting to a second wave of critical pedagogy. Confirmation came in a special issue of *CE* in July 2014, "Reimagining the Social Turn: New Work from the Field," edited by Jacqueline Rhodes and Jonathan Alexander, soon followed by a call for papers for a forthcoming special issue of *CCC* by Alexander, its new editor, announced as "The Political Economies of Composition Studies." In "Reimagining" the editors asserted: "An influx of new scholars and teachers, new theoretical models, and new reflections on practice has worked steadily to interrogate notions of identity-based politics and ask instead how writing might move beyond the articulation of difference to address questions of social inequity and social justice" (481). Works referred to in these two statements and kindred sources included *Living Room* by Nancy Welch, *Dangerous Writing* by Tony Scott, *Democracies to Come* by Rachel Riedner and Kevin Mahoney, and four collections: *Radical Relevance* edited by Laura Gary-Rosendale and Steven Rosendale, *Activism and Rhetoric* edited by Seth Kahn and Jonghwa Lee, *The Public Work of Rhetoric* edited by John Ackerman and David Coogan, and *Education as Civic Engagement* edited by Gary A. Olson and Lynn Worsham, gathered from *Journal of Advanced Composition*. I will return to some of these in chapter 8. They all moved, in the subtitle of Rosendale and Rosendale, "toward a scholarship of the whole left." They reached beyond locally based literacy studies and activism toward studies and action by students and faculty on national and international issues, preeminently neoliberalism, the environment, Islamophobia, militarism, and the national security state. I find this new wave quite heartening, beyond quibbles with its tendency to emphasize extracurricular activism and descriptions of upper-division, elective courses like Welch's "U.S. Literacy Politics" to the exclusion of lower-division, required courses, and with its exclusive assumption of progressive students and communities with little regard for the conservative teaching sites I am concerned with. My sympathy aligns most strongly with Henry and Susan Giroux's 2004 *Take Back Higher Education*: "Pedagogy as a critical practice should provide the knowledge, skills, and culture of questioning necessary for students to engage in critical dialogue with the past, question authority, and its effects, struggle with ongoing relations of power, and prepare themselves for what it means to be critically active citizens in the inter-related local, national, and global public spheres" (8).

In all of the disagreements discussed in this chapter, I reiterate that I am not trying to defend my own positions unilaterally and am only criticizing others that are posed exclusively, excessively, or with faulty reasoning. I side with those who seek *both-and* solutions, not *either-or* ones.

Coda: *The Fire Next Time* as Academic Discourse

Let me try further to avert likely misunderstandings of my political and theoretical position in this introductory preview, particularly in relation to sensitive subjects like race, by providing an exemplary case. In a key passage of Harris's *A Teaching Subject*, which I will examine further in chapters 4 and 5, Harris asserts in criticizing the limitations of academic discourse,

> We thus need to recognize that there are other Englishes, tied to other contexts or communities, which are not simply underdeveloped or less public versions of academic discourse, but that work toward different ends and whose use may express a competing or opposi-tional politics—as when, for instance, Geneva Smitherman draws on the forms and phrasings of black English throughout *Talkin and Testifyin*. (89)

I agree that critical intellectual operations can take place in nonacademic discourse communities and that we should always seek ways to connect them with academic discourse—but I assert that *only* the discourse of lib-eral education is (or ought to be) centrally dedicated to cultivation of these operations, so that college study presents a privileged space for students to grow beyond their home cultures.

My example comes from one of my favorite passages to teach (in both second-year argumentative writing and literary surveys—*not* in basic writ-ing or first-year writing, for which it is too hard), from James Baldwin's 1963 *The Fire Next Time*, a best-selling, book-length essay in the genre of intellectual and political journalism, partly first published in the *New Yorker*. Baldwin writes the following sentence about the historical amnesia of white Christians:

> They have forgotten that the religion that is now identified with their virtue and their power—"God is on our side," says Dr. Verwoerd— came out of a rocky piece of ground in what is now known as the Mid-dle East before color was invented, and that in order for the Christian church to be established, Christ had to be put to death, by Rome, and

that the real architect of the Christian church was not the disreputable, sun-baked Hebrew who gave it his name but the mercilessly fanatical and self-righteous St. Paul. (44)

The highly extended thought compacted in one sentence here, requiring multiple rereadings, includes the coordinate interjection in dashes and the three long "that" clauses that are the object of "forgotten." The sentence also exemplifies Baldwin's custom of tossing off highly provocative points in parenthetical, enigmatic phrases or epithets—"conundrum" is one of his favorite words—that need to be unpacked. These phrases include allusions to South African apartheid under Prime Minister Hendrik Verwoerd; "before color was invented"; "by Rome"; "the disreputable sun-baked Hebrew" (always a decentering shock for my students conditioned to visualize Christ as a haloed Anglo-Saxon!). For years, I read "by Rome" as a metonymy for the Roman Empire; then it dawned on me that in the context of the passage and the rest of the book, the probable meaning of "Rome" is more profoundly metaphoric: the Roman Catholic Church's "fanatical" doctrines put to death the message of universal brotherly love in Christ's life and teachings, perverting them into a rationalization for holy war, colonial conquest, slavery, and white supremacy. In another of Baldwin's subsequent, metaphoric variations on this central theme of his book, he writes, "God, going north, and rising on the wings of power, had become white, and Allah, out of power, and on the dark side of Heaven, had become—for all practical purposes, anyway—black" (46).

Baldwin's critique of the color-coded history of Christianity versus Islam was occasioned by the rise of the Nation of Islam in the 1950s as a rejection of American blacks' embrace of Christianity, so this passage and the rest of *The Fire* have acquired yet another dimension of resonance since 9/11 and the subsequent foregrounding in American consciousness of Islamic militancy. Timely passages jump out of the text now, like Baldwin's account of Nation of Islam leader Elijah Muhammed's prophecy, in a Chicago meeting between them, of "Allah's vengeance" against whites and Christians, which repulses the pacifist Baldwin, even though "I could see that the intransigence and ignorance of the white world might make that vengeance inevitable" (105). He has earlier said about the Cold War, "Russia's secret weapon is the bewilderment and despair and hunger of millions of people of whose existence we are scarcely aware.... Our power and our fear of change help bind these people to their misery and bewilderment, and insofar as they find this state intolerable we are intolerably menaced" (89–90). All we need do today is to replace "Russia's secret weapon" with "Islamic militants' secret weapon."

Smitherman might say that similar points to Baldwin's have been made by blacks in nonacademic, colloquial language—as in William Labov's oft-cited example of children's street talk, "Ain't no black god that's doin' that bullshit" ("Academic"). This is certainly true, yet Baldwin's elaborated-code version not only adds a devastating historical analysis and extended line of argument over 106 pages but is cognitively encrypted, as it were, in what by the standards of literacy in today's general readers is distinctly academic discourse. *The Fire* was a best-seller, yet I wonder how many nonacademic readers made the effort necessary to decipher passages like the ones I quoted. I never did myself until I had taught it several times. In class study, most of my black and white students alike have been stumped by the passage and the rest of *The Fire*, and peer-group discussions are little help. (Typically of student reading, most can follow the autobiographical narrative but not the historical and analytic sections.) The book demands frequent trips to the dictionary or encyclopedia and intensive decryption, based on a combination of research on world and American history of race and religion, study of theory on the social construction of race, and *explication de texte* by the teacher. When students finally "get it," however, most attest that they now consider the book a brilliant and inspiring classic in its plea for whites and blacks, Christians and Muslims, alike to overcome the blinding delusions of racism past and present.

As a corollary here, Harris and/or Smitherman seem to be lapsing into the fixation of *Students' Right to Their Own Language* (which I will discuss further in chapters 6, 11, and 13) on Black English versus Standard English dialects and colloquial speech with no examination of the substance of terms that Harris uses elsewhere like "critical or intellectual discourse," "a critical habit of mind," or "oppositional politics." These concepts go far beyond issues of different dialects or even "street smarts," as applied, say, to the difference between the children Labov quotes about "no black god" and Baldwin's elaboration. I would need to be persuaded that my criteria and dispositions of critical thinking in chapter 3 are significantly contingent on dialectal or vernacular differences, especially *at the level of college study* and in application to texts like Baldwin's. (However, Durst's *Collision Course* and Irvin Peckham's similarly admirable *Going North Thinking West: The Intersections of Social Class, Critical Thinking, and Politicized Writing Instruction* do make a case that study of critical thinking is *class biased*, a provocative position that I will return to in chapter 13.) One aim of education should be to enable youths with the background Labov describes to understand *The Fire Next Time* and perhaps to be inspired by that higher level of "critical or intellectual discourse" about racial and religious prejudice to advance an articulated "oppositional politics"—articulated both in the sense of persuasive expression and organized action. If Smitherman or Harris, then, were to essentialize *The Fire* as an example of academic discourse, which Harris defines simplistically as "the kinds of rarefied talk and writing that go on at conferences," versus "other Englishes," which "express a competing or oppositional politics," wouldn't this be another whopping killer dichotomy?

2

MY TEACHING STORY

Since composition theory in recent decades favors stories or Lyotard Lite "little narratives" (versus "grand" or "master" ones) over abstract analysis, I might best ground my arguments here in a brief account of my life experiences and teaching career, which seem to have taken place in a world apart from that depicted by the postmodern theorists I take issue with. I grew up, in the 1940s and 1950s, in a family of lower-middle-class shopkeepers and salespeople in Des Moines who had no political or intellectual inclinations. I do not see a lot of difference between the naïve political consciousness of my family's generation or my own and many of today's students at colleges where I have taught. My family was Jewish, and Iowa parochiality was compounded in the Jewish community of a few hundred families, most of whose founders had immigrated from Eastern Europe or Germany early in the century, by their division into Orthodox, Conservative, and Reform synagogues and a finely graded social hierarchy worthy of Proust. Des Moines culture in general was neatly skewered by another native, journalistic humorist Bill Bryson, who began his book *The Lost Continent: Travels in Small-Town America*, with, "I come from Des Moines. Somebody had to" (3). Among his whimsical claims for Des Moines as "the most powerful hypnotic known to man" (3) is that postcards there read, "We rode the escalator at Merle Hay Mall!" (8). This is not to denigrate my family and acquaintances personally; most were scrupulous, industrious, and good-hearted people who, like the small-town Iowans that Meredith Willson lovingly satirized in *The Music Man*, mocked "Shakespeare and Balzac and all them other hifalutin' Greeks," but would "give you our shirts, and the backs to go with them, if your crops should happen to die."

Social life for adults consisted largely of relatives and friends dropping in, often without warning, for interminable visits in which the main topics of conversation—ritualistically repeated over and over again—were the weather, the children, illnesses, and deaths, between or during card and board games. Multiple phone calls each day on the same topics filled in the gaps between visits. Gradually, however, these customs gave way to television as the prime means of filling up virtually every moment. I sympathize with the historical, tribal roots of the culture of visiting and the psychological necessity of clinging to quotidian community and regularity as a talisman against inexorable change. However, the consequence was a mentality that was fearful of solitude and precluded time by yourself to think or read, to develop the capacity for introspection and critical perspective on your circumstances, at any level of consciousness beyond the exigencies of everyday routines. Those routines were narrowly circumscribed, yet fraught with anxiety and bickering, as every molehill was magnified into a mountain—should we have macaroni and cheese or tuna casserole for dinner?—especially for the women, whose worldview was forcibly narrowed to the household and child-rearing. Growing up in this stifling atmosphere was one origin of my reservations about contemporary feminist and other cultural theories that privilege community bonds over autonomy and individuation. (From what I have seen recently about how people use cell phones, texting, Facebook, or Twitter, for many they seem to be a version, at a remove, of old-fashioned visiting as a means of filling time as a distraction from solitary thought.)

As a mostly pre-television generation, my family did read a newspaper, the *Des Moines Register*, but mainly for local news, trivia, and sports, and they were unaware of national papers like the *New York Times* and *Wall Street Journal*. Their magazines were *Reader's Digest*, *Look*, *Life*, and *Good Housekeeping*. Although one aunt, a theater fan, did subscribe to the *New Yorker* (whose conversational prose style I have emulated ever since, preferring it to academese) and gave me my love for musical comedy, they never heard of the *Nation* or the *New Republic* and would not have understood much in them if they did read them. They all declare not to understand a word or to have the attention span to read my own books and articles that I send them, even *Reading and Writing for Civic Literacy*, which I strove mightily to make accessible to general readers. (I recently e-mailed a younger cousin, now in Minneapolis, an 800-word column in the *Times* by Tom Friedman reminiscing about growing up there, but she replied that it was too long to read.) Their book reading consisted, and still does, of popular best-sellers in novels and nonfiction, along with some *Reader's Digest* abridged editions. They did vote in national elections, though their judgments of political candidates tended to be on the level of "Mr. X seems to be sincere" or "Mr. Y looks shifty-eyed." Comments like the latter were about the extent of their inclination to question the authority or credibility of government, military, or corporate officials. Their initial reaction to the protest movements of the late 1950s and 1960s was uncomprehending disapproval, though they did come around, fairly early, to approve of the civil rights movement and feminism, fairly late to disapprove of the Vietnam War.

In my public high school, Roosevelt, the most upscale and lily white in Des Moines, the important courses were driver training, typing, mechanical drawing, and shop for the boys, home economics (i.e., domestic consumerism) for the girls. Academic requirements were skimpy, especially in history and social studies, where courses were taught, somnambulantly, as a sideline by sports coaches—a widespread phenomenon now as then and perhaps the most telling symbol of American cultural priorities. Even today's students often refer to these courses as "a joke." In an example of the doctrinaire thinking of many academic progressives, an anonymous reviewer of a journal article submission of mine with similar phrasing charged that my denigration of such courses and teachers was "a cheap shot," and voted that the piece be rejected. The reviewer provided no explanation, so I can only conjecture that s/he must have had the preconception of high schools as being in poor or minority communities, where an account such as mine might indeed have been a cheap shot. But was it an inaccurate account of high schools like mine?

Alan Hausman, my life-long friend from Des Moines who is currently a philosophy professor at Hunter College, still tells a story from when he was president of the Roosevelt High debate club. He went to the principal to propose that the club become a team debating other high schools. After brief consideration the principal declined, on the grounds that such competitiveness would hurt the feelings of those who didn't make the team. He then excused himself because he had to go preside over a football pep rally. Alan gives a vivid account of the championship game against arch rival East High, in which our quarterback fumbled on a key play. The coach (yes, he was a social studies teacher—a lousy one) yanked him out of the game, lifted him in the air, and slammed him to the ground. Even in phys ed classes, teachers spent each class period working with varsity athletes while everyone else was consigned to running laps, presumably without hurt feelings.

In families like mine, it was assumed, as Calvin Coolidge said, that "the business of America is business," that going into business was what just about everyone did, and that going to college was about preparation to go into business, with intercollegiate sports spectacles and fraternity-sorority social life about equally important. My parents' main point of pride about their education at the University of Illinois was being there at the time of the football star "Red" Grange. (Football as the center of college life and the conflict between jocks and nerds have been staples of pop culture going back to early twentieth-century musical comedies like *Leave It to Jane* and *Good News* and silent films like Buster Keaton's *College*.) Whether Democrats or Republicans, their view of college, still maintained by their children and grandchildren, was occupational or preprofessional and social. They regarded liberal arts courses as peripheral and quickly forgotten, so they had little concept of college education as a site for either intellectual growth or skeptical questioning of dominant political and cultural norms. Those in my parents' age group are all dead now, and most of the small, personally managed businesses that they owned or worked for have been gobbled up by national or multinational corporations, a phenomenon beyond their comprehension. (I will say more about recent generational changes in Iowa in my concluding chapter.)

I was a scholarship student in college at Brown and Northwestern and in graduate school at Columbia and Berkeley, the kind of education that liberated me, like many others, from a provincial background. For five years after college in the early 1960s, I studied for an MA part time at Columbia while working in a succession of jobs on Madison Avenue in advertising, public relations, and celebrity journalism—an experience that exposed me to the more tawdry aspects of the upper circles of power and wealth in America. An advertising executive I worked for shrugged off the deceptiveness of a campaign for Westinghouse refrigerators by sneering, "There's no real difference between this year's model and last year's or the one five years ago, except for the slogans. But the average housewife is too stupid to know the difference." Experiences like that taught me that the liberal arts are among the few educational or occupational sites in America not subjugated to corporate control and dishonesty.

I moved to Berkeley for English doctoral study in the mid-1960s, at the height of campus protest, which was for me an inspirational challenge to the whole social order epitomized by Madison Avenue, a challenge epitomized in the eloquent speeches by twenty-two-year-old Mario Savio in the Free Speech Movement beginning in 1964, which built on his activism in the Mississippi Freedom Summer project earlier that year. That epochal summer of 1964 carried over into protest that fall against UC restrictions on campus recruitment for civil rights activism and against the broader corporate bureaucratizing and dehumanizing of both education and the larger society:

> In Mississippi, an autocratic and powerful minority rules, through organized violence, to suppress the vast, virtually powerless, majority. In California, the privileged minority manipulates the University bureaucracy to suppress the students' political expression. That "respectable" bureaucracy masks the financial plutocrats: that impersonal bureaucracy is the efficient enemy in a "brave new world". . . . America is becoming ever more the utopia of sterilized, automated

contentment. The "futures" and "careers" for which American students now prepare are for the most part intellectual and moral wastelands. This chrome-plated consumers' paradise would have us grow up to be well-behaved children. But an important minority of men and women coming to the front today have shown that they will die rather than be standardized, replaceable, and irrelevant. ("An End to History," in Cohen 329–32)

Savio's speeches reflected a revival of attention in the sixties to Marx's early writings on alienated labor. Similarly, in 1962, Students for a Democratic Society's founding manifesto, written mainly by Tom Hayden as an undergraduate at Michigan, asserted:

Some would have us believe that Americans feel contentment amidst prosperity—but might it not better be called a glaze above deeply felt anxieties about their role in the new world? And if these anxieties produce a developed indifference to human affairs, do they not as well produce a yearning to believe there *is* an alternative to the present, that something *can* be done to change circumstances in the school, the workplaces, the bureaucracies, the government? (Miller 330–31)

My goal in becoming a college teacher became to enable students to defend themselves against conformity and manipulation by corporations, media, and politicians. I wrote my dissertation, published by Yale University Press in 1973 as *The Unique Creation of Albert Camus*, about Camus's version of *la littérature engagée* integrating literature, language, and politics, both as a writer of fiction and drama and as a philosopher and political journalist. Thus his Nobel Prize acceptance speech and several essays addressed the political responsibilities of the literary artist. He asserted, "Because his vocation is to unite the greatest possible number of men, it cannot countenance falsehood and slavery, which breed solitudes wherever they prevail" ("Speech" 34). And, "How could an artist justify his privileges (if he has them) other than by taking part, on the level of everyone, in the long struggle for the liberation of work and of culture?" (*Essais* 1748, my translation). My book also dealt with Camus's affinities to American literature and the significance of his ideas for American society, especially in the influence of his pacifism and advocacy of nonviolent resistance on the New Left and civil rights movement.

In 1972, I was a TA for a section of English 1A, the first-year-writing course emphasizing critical writing from sources, in which the teacher was a full professor in classical and medieval literature and the central reading

Thucydides' *History of the Peloponnesian War*.[1] (Yes, each section of about twenty students was staffed by both a regular faculty member and a TA in that golden age, which has gone with the wind.) In case this course sounds like the epitome of the conservative, stuffy humanism rejected by postmodern pluralists, I should add that the secondary readings were the recently published *Pentagon Papers* (the secret State Department history of the Vietnam War, leaked to the press by Daniel Ellsberg) and Noam Chomsky's "The Responsibility of Intellectuals." The professor was Peter Dale Scott, an awe-inspiring though modest-demeanored polymath who was in his other personas a medievalist, a Canadian diplomat, a poet (whose book-length poem, *Coming to Jakarta*, indebted in form to Yeats and Pound, was about the CIA-engineered coup in Indonesia), and the author of several books of exposés, in the mode of Chomsky, of the nefarious international activities of the American military, intelligence agencies, and corporations from World War II through Iran-Contra to the later Iraq War. At about this same time he debated U.N. ambassador Arthur Goldberg on campus about the Vietnam War. The course was exceptionally rigorous and undoctrinaire in all its components—literature, history and politics, critical comparisons of Athens and the United States at war—incorporating research methodology, rhetorical analysis, and writing instruction including mechanics. It was obviously more centered on the teacher than the students, though they were hardly passive receptacles of banked wisdom, but contributed an impressive level of debate and critical research.

That high-intensity period at Berkeley also saw the first edition of *The Borzoi College Reader*, edited by the eminent Chaucer scholar Charles Muscatine (later a coauthor of the Rockefeller Foundation's *The Humanities in American Life*, cited here in chapter 1 as an endorsement of teaching for critical thinking applied to political literacy) and his student Marlene Griffith, later head of the English department at Laney College in Oakland.[2]

The Borzoi connected humanistic classics with writings on contemporary politics by Martin Luther King, Rachel Carson, James Baldwin, Albert Camus, Jane Jacobs, Erich Fromm, Aldous Huxley, Paul Jacobs, David Halberstam (on Vietnam), Norman Podhoretz, and Harvey Swados. The accompanying teacher's manual grouped readings and exercises by rhetorical and critical-thinking topics. I taught, and was so profoundly influenced by, this magnificent book that I said in my acknowledgments for *Reading and Writing for Civic Literacy* that it might have been titled *Child of Borzoi Reader*. This genre of liberal-arts reader, with its intellectual demands, has also largely gone with the wind. Other Vietnam-era, countercultural comp textbooks that came out of the Berkeley English department included

Starting Over: A College Reader, edited by iconoclastic literary and political critic Frederick Crews (my dissertation director) and scholar-journalist of Asian politics Orville Schell, and *Crisis: A Contemporary Reader*, edited by Peter Collier, who later converted to Reaganite conservatism along with his collaborator and fellow Berkeley English grad student David Horowitz.

Berkeley was distinctive as a public university, historically tuition free, but a selective one whose faculty were peers of the Ivy League and whose students tended to be high academic achievers, politically aware, and from moderate to affluent socioeconomic backgrounds. My later teaching experiences indicated that a pool of less-prepared students was less likely to "get" such a challenging course as Scott's or a textbook like *The Borzoi*. (That of course was in the 1960s and early 1970s; since that era, students in general have steadily retreated from politics, even at Berkeley.)

Sharon Crowley's generally astute *Composition in the University*, presents a typically oversimplified picture of the conservatism of elite universities, as I will argue further in chapter 5. Crowley cites a claim by Stanley Aronowitz and Henry Giroux that what the elite university degree "offers, that most others do not, is access to extremely powerful social and business connections as well as the social status that this association brings" (222). I regard Aronowitz and Giroux as superb cultural critics and long-time valued allies, and I know that neither of them have elite social or educational backgrounds. But I also know that both of them have become academic stars with prestigious professorships, and that they spend a lot of time palling around, as Sarah Palin would say, with high-status Marxist theorists at the most elite universities; likewise for my old *Radical Teacher* comrades Dick Ohmann, who became provost at Wesleyan, and Paul Lauter, who held an endowed chair at Trinity College. This is not in any way to impugn their political or intellectual integrity—their laurels are all totally merited—but only to highlight what Daniel Bell called the cultural contradictions of capitalism. One of my main arguments throughout this book is that stereotypes of literary, humanistic, and composition studies at elite universities as bastions of political and pedagogical conformity are complicated by cases like Giroux and Aronowitz, Ohmann and Lauter, Scott and Muscatine. To reiterate a key point from chapter 1, it is an anomalous malfunction of American education that oppositional education is accessible mainly to the privileged, whose class interests ultimately clash with oppositional consciousness. This clash is a constant factor in what Christopher Lasch termed the agony of the American left. Again, the best solution that I can conceive is financial equalization of social classes and the whole American system of K-12 and college education, toward making preparation for critical education accessible for all.

From Berkeley to San Luis Obispo

All of these anomalies about elite higher education were brought home to me in the contrast between the universities I had attended and taught at in graduate school and those where I worked subsequently, in settings that were more like the Middle America of my earlier years. I completed my doctorate in 1974—just in time to get caught in the collapse of the job market in English. I was chagrined to learn that my years of experience in nonacademic jobs and lectureships, plus a published book and several articles, rather than counting in my favor, made me overpriced for assistant professorships in the suddenly flooded candidate pool. During several years of desperately searching for a tenure-track job before and after finishing my PhD, I was an adjunct lecturer at Cal State Hayward and San Jose State. I also put in a gruesome semester teaching at an expensive private high school for problem children of affluent parents in the East Bay suburbs of San Francisco; the students drove BMWs to school and wore fashionable clothes, but their reading and writing were far below grade level, and several proudly flaunted their hatred of school and teachers. (The existence of a whole sector in American education of private K-12 schools and colleges catering to low-achieving children of wealthy families is another reality about which progressive pluralists tend to be in denial.)

I was on the brink of being terminally unemployable through overqualification when in 1977 Cal Poly had the largesse to hire me as an associate professor. While most other universities were languishing financially, Poly was booming from local prosperity and the increased demand for technological education and research, so the English department was able to grow—and recruit an excellent faculty from the reserve army of the unemployed—through providing service courses for tech majors in composition and general-education-and-breadth courses in literature, requirements that were beefed up in the 1960s when Poly was upgraded to a university and became part of the California State University system,. Poly's admission standards also became increasingly stringent, so the level of student achievement—and financial status—became one of the highest in CSU and UC, but almost entirely in science and math, while the level of achievement, and interest, in the humanities was far lower. Thus English and other liberal arts studies were considered the university's stepchildren, their faculty embattled against the prevailing vocationalism and conservatism, but also developing a collegiate *esprit de corps* among faculty members, who all taught both literature and composition. Our teaching load of twelve hours a quarter (four three-hour or three four-hour courses), with upward of thirty students per class and usually no grad-student TAs, guaranteed that we were more concerned with teaching than research, and we were evaluated accordingly, resulting in a salutary reduction of the petty egotism and status-seeking endemic to departments obsessed with publish-or-perish. (However, these conditions also virtually precluded being hired subsequently by any research university; one of the uglier truths of the English profession is the stigma attached to state and community college faculty, whose lack of time to do research—except sometimes about composition or teaching, subjects scorned by literary scholars—becomes a self-fulfilling prophecy, evidence of their innate inferiority.)

By that time, I had been labeled a composition specialist as a result of all those years teaching comp as an adjunct. I taught mainly the second-term course (typically taken by students in their second year or later) in critical thinking, argumentation, and writing from research sources, along with literary survey courses, occasional upper-division lit courses, and a master's level comp theory course, for the next twenty-two years at Poly.

For those not familiar with California's public higher-education system, more background may be needed here. It was reorganized in the 1950s, through a master plan to absorb the booming postwar college population, in three tiers. At the top in prestige and funding, the nine University of California campuses were heavy on graduate education and advanced research, and were most selective in undergraduate admissions. The second tier, mainly devoted to undergraduate education, with a heavier teaching load, consisted of nineteen California State Colleges; most of them were formerly teachers' colleges, though CPSLO had been an agricultural college. (In the 1960s they were all upgraded into the California State University, which mainly meant that a PhD became required for faculty and that more research was conducted, profiting from the ample funding then available from industry and government for the applied sciences.) The third tier consisted of over one hundred community colleges, with virtually open admissions. All three levels were close to tuition free and were amply funded by the state until Ronald Reagan was elected governor in 1967 and initiated tuition and reduced budgets as punishment for the protest movement at Berkeley and elsewhere. However, the student profile among the three tiers followed socioeconomic class lines and quality of secondary education, so more UC students were able to afford to major in liberal arts than in the other two segments. (These lines have intensified subsequently as UC tuition has far outstripped CSU.) The CSU campuses range from urban ones like San Francisco State and Los Angeles State, with the most diverse students ethnically, economically, and politically, to rural ones like CPSLO, with minimal diversity, even compared to its sister school Cal Poly Pomona, in the L.A. metropolitan area. So I went from one of the more liberal universities and areas in the country, Berkeley, to one of the more conservative.

San Luis Obispo is about two hundred miles from both San Francisco and Los Angeles, near the beautiful, mountainous coastline south of Big Sur, with scenic little harbors and vast beaches. When I arrived there, it still had vestiges of a reputation as a cow town and Poly as an agricultural school. San Luis Obispo County was lush in farm and ranch land (most owned by individual families), solidly Republican and white, especially by contrast to surrounding counties with large populations of Latino farm workers on agribusiness big spreads. Beginning in the 1970s, the county prospered from wine production, tourism, and retirees attracted by the scenery and temperate year-round climate from sea breezes and fog, all compounding the real estate boom throughout the state, so living there became increasingly pricy. Thus Poly became an attractive place for upscale students from areas like the arid Central Valley, Fresno, Bakersfield, and suburbs of the stressful urban centers. It was common knowledge that many middle-class parents wanted their children to go there to get away from multicultural urban populaces and their perceived dangers, and quite a few students had gone to virtually segregated private secondary schools.[3] I saw this pattern repeated at Tennessee with white students from heavily black Memphis who had gone to private schools. Tennessee has an equally scandalous history to Cal Poly of failure to recruit and retain minority faculty and students—except, of course, varsity athletes for the adored Vols. (Neither Poly nor Tennessee has a large number of adult students.)

This personal odyssey was what led me to the anomalous conclusion that political consciousness in faculty, students, and even administrators at elite universities like Berkeley and the Ivy League is often more liberal and multicultural, and tolerates a larger leftist presence, than at nonelite ones, and that the lower on the socioeconomic scale universities are, the more homogeneously conservative they tend to be. (To reiterate, major exceptions include working-class colleges in urban areas with large adult-student, unionized, and multicultural constituencies; colleges in minority or poor communities; and those in rural regions with a populist-left history.) One explanation is that in recent decades elite universities have had more financial resources for efforts toward student and faculty diversity, at least for recruiting and retaining the most promising minority and other nontraditional students and faculty. (According to a letter in the *New York Times* in 2012 from David Jones, president of the Community Service Society in New York, "Black and Latino enrollment at top CUNY colleges has plummeted

34

since the onset of the recession. . . . The percentage of black freshmen at Baruch College [6 percent] was lower than that of Harvard University [7 percent].") Similarly, Berkeley has the resources for a first-rate basic writing program housing the Bay Area Writing Project, aligned with the excellent Graduate School of Education, while CSU and the community colleges are cash-starved for basic writing programs, which their students need much more.

Another explanation is that it is mainly the leisure classes that have the money, time, and psychic energy to study liberal arts and critical thinking, and to have developed an elaborated-code psychology, extending beyond one's immediate locale, survival needs, and self-interest. The farther down the socioeconomic scale colleges go (again, with important exceptions), the more directly they tend to be dedicated to servicing business, with correspondingly conservative students, faculty, and especially administrators— and this pattern has intensified with fiscal shortages in the past few decades. At least until the 1980s, most UC top administrators were relatively liberal, distinguished scholars in the liberal arts, like Clark Kerr, president at the time of the Free Speech Movement, and their executive ethos tended to be collegial (rhetorically, if not consistently in practice—a sore spot for FSM protestors), while CSU administrators were more often conservative business executives or technocrats, enforcing a managerial mindset. In one of the key speeches of the FSM in 1964, Mario Savio lamented about UC—and Kerr in particular—that, "In California, the privileged minority manipulates the University bureaucracy to suppress the students' political expression. That 'respectable' bureaucracy masks the financial plutocrats" ("An End," in Cohen 329).[4] Savio may not have known it then, but compared to UC, CSU was bureaucracy and plutocracy on steroids, although in recent decades the managerial model has steadily gained more sway at all levels from the Ivy League and UC down.

All of these factors, then, have contributed to the reality that at Cal Poly, Tennessee, and the other colleges where I have taught, far fewer students are dedicated to liberal education than to job training, varsity sports boosterism and "school spirit," fraternity or sorority activities, and partying. More and more students—especially in the private schools where I have taught, and increasingly so in the public universities as poorer ones have gotten squeezed out—tacitly transmit the attitude, "My parents are spending a lot of money to buy me a degree, so you'd better make things easy and give me an A." The majority of women who have spoken out in my classes disavow feminism, which they often equate distastefully with lesbians and hairy legs, and they totally buy into the role of "the beauty myth." Many of them, far from feeling intimidated or silenced, view Ann Coulter as a role model and are quite unabashed in voicing and writing right-wing orthodoxies attained from her or their parents. The handful of minorities are mostly political and religious conservatives, and their previously small number has dwindled almost to zero in recent years, except for varsity athletes, as poorer students in general have been squeezed out by the economic crunch. Whenever the subject of labor unions arises, students most frequently respond with the most negative stereotypes. (This attitude was often colored in my farm-owning students at Cal Poly by their employment of immigrant labor and in Tennessee by that state's right-to-work law and other historical exploitation of cheap, non-unionized industrial labor, such in the several automobile factories that have moved there from Detroit; employees at VW's plant in Chattanooga voted against unionizing in 2014.) The international students and immigrants tend to come from middle-class families in their own countries and/or are avidly motivated to get rich in America. In literature courses, my students were inclined to regard Bigger Thomas and Meursault as menaces to society who got just what they deserved; Bartleby the scrivener and Gregor in "The Metamorphosis" as lazy bums who should have gotten off their asses and gone to work; Nora in *A Doll House*, Edna in *The Awakening*, and Sylvia Plath as disgraceful in abandoning their husbands and children; and Tom Buchanan as the hero of *The Great Gatsby*. (Who knows? Perhaps there is fertile soil here for a movement of right-wing canon revision.)

Among Cal Poly students—who were, it must be reiterated, on average among the most academically proficient (though far more in science than liberal arts) and financially affluent in the Cal State University system—political illiteracy and authoritarianism were rife, while reading and writing skills were often at junior-high level. In response to the unit in my argumentative writing course on political semantics, in which ideologies and lines of argument from left to right are defined, one quite pleasant-natured student wrote a paper about "facism"'s appeal to traditional values like patriotism, family, religion, military power, and obedience to strong rulers, saying all that sounded pretty good to her, though "facists might go a bit too far" in these policies. Another wrote, without any documentation, about how happy the Spanish people were under Franco and how miserable they have become under socialism.

One paper defended a Republican presidential cabinet member who was under fire for corruption. "I don't know why people have been so critical of the Secretary. They fail to realize that he must want what's best for the U.S., that's why he was elected." Another came out of controversies over the Diablo Canyon Nuclear Power plant near San Luis Obispo:

I am very interested on the topic of nuclear energy, probably because it is very controversial. On this type of issue there isn't much difference between the liberal and the conservative groups. Of course there are liberals who think only the best about nuclear power and say "nuclear power is needed and will soon be the only source of energy." Then there are the pro conservatives who may print leaflets.

Can you believe any authority? Take Dr. John W. Goffman M.D. Ph.D. a Nuclear Physisist for Lawrence Berkley Laboratories. Wow, pretty impressive huh. But if you read his book, "Poisened Power," you will realize that he is against nuclear power, therefore all his articles would be how bad nuclear energy is. Did you know Dr. Goffman is the co-discoverer for radioactive isotopes Uranium 135, 236, and 239. Why would a man be so against radioactivity when here he is a discoverer of radioactivity.

People talk about a cover up on nuclear energy. They say there has been fireing and stopping of governmental support to employees that are against nuclear power. But Mike Gravel, Senate Congressional Leader, has stated that he is very much against nuclear power and he is on paid salary by the U.S. Govt. How can people say there is a coverup on a subject, when nothing is printed and released to the public? We don't know everything that is covered up. Thats the whole reason for a coverup.

Such are the hazards when students who have been told by writing teachers that self-expression is more important than factual knowledge or cogent reasoning are asked to venture beyond thinking and writing about their personal stories. These examples, along with a few others in chapter 3, are typical of countless more from my students over the years, in which the most common traits are militant factual ignorance about political issues under discussion and enthymemic assumption of the generalization that those in positions of authority, power, or wealth always "want what's best for the United States," "know what they're doing," or "work hard and deserve every dollar they earn without being taxed to death." I have refrained from citing papers unabashedly voicing the ugliest bigotry against minorities, the poor, feminists, and homosexuals. I cannot understand why many progressive colleagues react with indignant denial of my claims here, when attitudes like these are so widespread in the general population.

One of my most traumatic teaching experiences was in a second-year literary survey course at Poly, a general-education requirement, where the most outspoken student was an agricultural management major who made it known to everyone that his family were wealthy ranchers in the Central Valley. (One day he went around the class distributing a copy of the student newspaper with a story about the campus polo team, of which he was captain.) He let me know early and often that he resented having to take any courses outside his major and that he particularly hated literature. He kept asking during class, in tones varying between derisive and belligerent, what the value of studying literature was. Once I tried, good-naturedly, to explain to him as I do to my classes in general, that studying literature and the other liberal arts can foster mental initiative and discipline, autonomous thinking, and a broad-ranging consciousness that are conducive to the capability for personal and professional responsibility. Indeed, I went on, that is why students at academically competitive, expensive colleges have historically studied liberal arts, and why their subject matter becomes common coin among their graduates. "Are you telling us," he snarled, "that we should study this stuff just so we can talk about it on the golf course?" (Not a bad point, actually.) In another class meeting, he got angry, ran at me from his seat, and stopped just short of slugging me. That this was not just an anomalous incident is confirmed by the increasing number of reports in recent years by college teachers—most often women—of similarly bellicose students.

I simply cannot conceive the relevance to students like these of the prescriptions of theorists like Richard Ohmann: "Respect the linguistic resources students have; make language a vehicle for achievement of real political and personal aims" (*Politics* 293). (In our long-running, friendly debates on this issue, I've gently suggested to Dick that this is easier to say at Wesleyan than at Cal Poly.) Or like Bartholomae and Petrosky, who affirm, "Student readers, for example, can take responsibility for determining the meaning of the text," and urge them to avoid "timidity and passivity" and "take the responsibility to speak their minds and say what they notice" (*Ways of Reading* 7). Or like Kurt Spellmeyer, sympathizing with students who might express "odious" opinions in the classroom:

> No attempt to change such people will succeed if it reinstates their experiences of radical powerlessness.... The only way that they can become worthy of freedom is to exercise real freedom.... And the solution must begin with restoring, somewhere and somehow, a measure of the freedom they have lost, if only the freedom in a composition course to think and write about their lives without coercion and disparagement. ("Culture" 295–96)

Well.... Where does one begin to apply these nostrums to students like my agricultural management major? Should I have tried to make my course a nurturing "safe house" for this bully, who was far from silenced, powerless, or deprived of freedom, beyond the liberty not to take any courses outside of his major? And this was a sophomore literature course, not basic writing or first-year composition. Would that make a difference to these theorists, and would it make a difference if it was an advanced writing course in argumentative writing and supporting arguments with research, on subject matter beyond "their lives"? Should I have deflected the student's belligerence toward me by asking, "What do the rest of you think about this? How about discussing it in small groups?" By that time, he had intimidated everyone else in the class from saying a word, whether they might have agreed with him or not (many probably would have, since resentment against general education and breadth requirements runs high in technical majors, often reinforced by faculty advisors). I do not doubt that on some level he might have had some legitimate grievances, say, toward agribusiness corporations and the global economy squeezing out family businesses like his, or toward students in liberal arts colleges with higher cultural and political capital, or even perhaps toward the reasonable question of whether students like him should need a four-year bachelor's degree from state universities requiring a general education component rather than having access to the kind of agricultural college Cal Poly was before its admission into the CSU system. A critical pedagogy perspective might have pursued the arbitrariness of college credentialing and its role in our political economy. If I had the ingenuity of a teacher like my old friend Ira Shor, I might have been able to tread through these issues successfully. But should I have tried, especially since this effort would have led the class farther and farther away from the literary topics the student was distracting us from? As it was, after that class period, I said I would be glad to discuss these issues further with him and any other students outside of class, but that I was going to limit class discussion to the assigned texts. Was that overly coercive and disparaging? As Mark Twain would say, I dunno.

No matter how vehemently I labor these points, I do not expect those with the mindset of these theorists to get them. Nor do I expect to convince the composition journal editor who sternly disapproved of my implication in a submission that some of my students were, as he put it, "rich dummies." I would wager that he and many teachers reading this have had as many as I have, whether they admit it or not. The issue for me is whether and how critical pedagogy can be adapted to effective teaching of students who, while not necessarily either rich or dummies, are inclined to "resist and transgress" critical questioning of their comfortable social status and cultural assumptions.

In recent years I have foregrounded as topics for student debate in my argumentative writing course at Tennessee and (in a visiting appointment) Iowa the issues of the increasing cost of college and student loans, the declining availability of scholarships, and the shift in lottery-funded scholarships from need-based ones to merit-based ones favoring families who can afford better secondary preparation. I was initially baffled about why so few students seemed to consider these trends a bad thing—until I figured out that most of them were the winners in this "survivor" scenario. So the main thrust of my inquiries throughout this book is where to start and how to proceed with such students in ways that persuade them of the value in humanistic and civic education as a process of critical self-questioning, without being coercive or disparaging, on issues like their possible shortsightedness in not being able to think beyond their ethnocentric self-interest about the consequences for American democracy of restriction of higher education to the wealthy and its role in the widening gap separating the wealthy from the middle class and poor.

On the Upside

So I am indeed breaking the taboo against criticizing both students and teaching colleagues who enable complacent students like those described above with classroom approaches justified by a "nurturing" ethos rather than one challenging their prejudices. Making my case has of course necessitated presenting the worst-case scenario of teaching experiences, those that keep us all awake at night and cause falling hair and rising blood pressure. But I do not want to leave the impression that my experiences have been entirely or even mostly bad. Please keep in mind that I have taught almost exclusively undergraduates, mainly in lower-division writing and literary-survey courses that students take as general-education requirements, so that most students who take my classes do not choose me as the teacher or know what to expect from me. What many of my students expect is the "feel good about yourself" ethos they tell me they have gotten in most English courses; what they get instead is one along the lines of a recent Harvard faculty report: "The aim of a liberal education is to unsettle presumptions, to defamiliarize the familiar, to reveal what is going on beneath and behind appearances, to disorient young people and to help them to find ways to reorient themselves" (*Guide*). My approach is, what's good for Harvard students is also good for those at Cal Poly or Tennessee, even if the resistance is stronger.

In spite of these daunting circumstances, four decades of teaching these courses has not diminished my love of teaching them, my—and students'—constant discovery of new insights into long-familiar texts, and the gratification of watching the process of students becoming attuned to academic discourse and critical consciousness. I compare the trajectory of my courses from beginning to end with the myth of Sisyphus. Every semester starts with pushing that damn rock up the mountainside against the resistance of student incomprehension and resentment of intrusion into their safe space and of intellectual demands beyond their comfort level. By about mid-semester, however, most have readjusted to the different wavelength, and from then on, many show a quantum leap in rhetorical, research, and writing skills that surprises me and them alike. Then it's back to the bottom of the mountain the next semester.

I hope that what I say in the following will not be perceived just as vanity but as evidence that students have appreciated in my teaching—as inadequately achieved as I know it is—the attempt to fill a vast gap in the education most of them have received through high school and college. The available evidence, in the form of course evaluations and correspondence from students after grades have been entered, indicates that the large majority of students have liked my courses a lot; many took more of them and have said they were the most valuable they'd ever had, in terms of being exposed to information and viewpoints they had never gotten in any other course and being challenged to question the opinions they had absorbed from their families and peers. Some of my most cordial relations have been with conservative students who have studied some political theory and are able to support their arguments with reputable sources and cogent reasoning; they typically have said after the course that they greatly appreciated having a professor engaging their views respectfully, challenging them to refine those views against opposing ones, and grading them positively for their efforts in this process.

I received two outstanding teacher awards at Poly and was very fortunate in the early 1980s to be awarded two year-long research fellowships for undergraduate teachers, one from the National Endowment for the Humanities (NEH), the other under the Mina Shaughnessy Scholars Program of the Fund for the Improvement of Post-Secondary Education in the U.S. Department of Education, whose support toward the long process of writing this book I tardily express gratitude. (Andrea Lunsford and Lisa Ede were fellow scholars in that blissful year, which was one factor in enabling them and me to publish more, about teaching-based issues, than most other writing teachers.) Both of these programs were killed off by William J. Bennett as head of the NEH and secretary of education under President Reagan—never to be resurrected to this date, alas. I also received visiting appointments as the Cardin Chair in the Humanities at Loyola of Maryland and as a senior lecturer teaching two honors sections of Iowa's great first-year rhetoric course combining written and oral argument.

Quite a few students have testified, long after the fact, that my courses were a life-transforming experience. A few years ago I got an e-mail from a student twenty years earlier at Cal Poly, who wanted to let me know that my argumentative writing course had prompted her to go to law school and devote her career to public interest law and community organizing. More recently, I got another e-mail from a student several years ago at Tennessee:

> I took one of your rhetoric courses a few years back, and I just wanted to thank you for opening my eyes to a world that I knew nothing about. During my time in your class I began to develop a great interest in the state of American education and the achievement gap that is still plaguing our society. At the beginning of this year I applied for a teaching position with Teach for America. I can't help but pay great thanks to you and your vigorous teaching style. So thanks again for giving me the true gift of knowledge, because without the things I learned in your class I would not be the person I am today and probably still clueless to what is going on around me.

And still more recently, this from another Tennessee student, who got a PhD in education and now works in a literacy center at the University of Mississippi as a consultant to an impoverished, 98 percent black elementary school:

> You were the first to really challenge my indoctrinated familial conservative beliefs. I have since gotten so much flack from my family for being a "damn liberal" and my Heritage Foundation supporting, incredibly wealthy grandfather has more or less threatened to rescind any inheritance of which I might be the beneficiary. I'll take the critical thinking skills instead and feel just as wealthy.

On the other hand, I do occasionally get responses like this posted on Facebook a few years ago:

> I am in English 222. It is a literature class and the professor teaches it like it was a liberal indoctrination course. He says that liberal values were a key focus of the 17th century Enlightenment; therefore, his

class will reflect those values. This man is an admitted socialist and a spin doctor of the worst sort and needs to be held accountable and teach the literature, drawing on his beliefs to interpret it instead of teaching politics, using literature to support it. In short Dr. Lazere needs to be fired.

If it weren't for the relatively constant, successful outcomes of my courses through the years, reactions like this and the traumatic early weeks every year would have driven me to give up on this approach decades ago. I should also note, though, that I know I have been able to persevere in this high-wire act every semester only because I could exercise the powers of a tenured, white, Ivy League male, and I know that adjuncts, women, and others without security like mine will be taking far more risks trying it—among the reasons I would not recommend my approach to *anyone* teaching basic or first-year writing. I can only hope that teachers and other readers who are in sufficiently secure positions and who identify with the problems I address will be encouraged to read this book with an open mind and to advance further professional and public dialogue on these problems.

Reaffirming Critical Thinking

Chapter 3 sums up the conceptual framework that I developed over the years in response to my teaching experiences, and *Reading and Writing for Civic Literacy* applies it more fully. The backstory to chapter 3 involves the adjustments I had to make between teaching at Berkeley and three CSU schools. My first year at Poly, 1977, coincided with the publication of Mina Shaughnessy's *Errors and Expectations*. It quickly became apparent to me that the learning problems of the inner-city basic writers Shaughnessy discusses were strikingly similar to those of my mostly affluent students at Poly, and that Shaughnessy's use of scholarship in sociolinguistics and developmental psychology was equally applicable to critical-thinking instruction there. My early years at Poly also coincided with the implementation of critical-thinking instruction throughout CSU, other colleges, and K-12 education in California and elsewhere, as described in chapter 3. I incorporated this concept of critical thinking into my argumentative writing course (along with a dose of Freire and Frankfurt School critical theory), served on state and national task forces for development of critical-thinking instruction, and for a decade was a board member of the annual summer institute at the Center for Critical Thinking and Moral Critique at Sonoma State. In 1987, I published an

ERIC Digest titled "Critical Thinking in College English Studies," and my 1992 article in *College Composition and Communication*, "Teaching the Political Conflicts: A Rhetorical Schema," was based on my model of critical thinking.

Ray Kytle's *Clear Thinking for Composition* was the textbook that I found most useful for argumentative writing at Cal Poly, and I taught from it regularly until I expanded on it—and snitched from it, with acknowledgment—in my own book. It was first published in 1969 and really more a text in critical thinking and informal logic than writing. I also used *Logic and Contemporary Rhetoric: The Use of Reason in Everyday Life*, by Howard Kahane and Nancy Cavender, which was primarily a philosophy text though adopted in some second-term comp classes. Kytle and Kahane/Cavendar both had a 1960s political and psychological dimension, emphasizing the need for middle-class students to question culturally conditioned assumptions and prejudices, to study viewpoints that challenge their ethnocentrism. Kytle wrote,

> Because you live in a particular country, in a particular part of the world, in a particular age; because you were raised in a particular class and educated in a particular educational system by teachers who were also in many ways the product of their culture, *you possess a large collection of attitudes and values whose accuracy, truth or merit, you have never questioned.* (37; emphasis in original)

I still think little was added to this succinct formulation by subsequent decades of tortuous theoretical deliberations on "social constructionism" or "formations," "subject positionality," and "interpellation." But Kytle was pretty much of a solitary voice in composition, and his book is now generally, but unfairly, considered *passé* because of the profession's neglect of argumentation in favor of the composing process, personal expression, and polyphonic voices.

Alongside Kytle, I taught *The Borzoi College Reader* my first few years at Poly, but found that it was over the head of most students there in its level of historical and cultural literacy, and attendant vocabulary. (In chapter 7, I find a similar problem in Bartholomae and Petrosky's *Ways of Reading*, whose difficulty is an intrinsic virtue but a drawback for use in FYW.) But I also gave up on using any readers and the hodgepodge of topics they try to encompass, which I concluded only reinforces the atomized consciousness of the larger culture. Instead I turned toward a more limited and coherent range of critical thinking and political topics, along the lines of "Teaching the Political Conflicts" and "Teaching the Conflicts about Wealth and Poverty."

In any case, critical thinking as I conceive it has been bypassed in the mainstream of composition studies over the past few decades. My analysis of how this has happened and my case for reversing the resulting negative consequences for political literacy constitute the rest of this book. At this writing, there were signs of a revival of attention to critical thinking in several studies that lament the lack of learning in critical thinking, argumentation, and civic literacy in both American K-12 and college education. These included Richard Arum and Josipa Roksa's *Academically Adrift*, the Common Core State Standards Initiative of the National Governors' Association, the National Task Force on Civic Learning and Democratic Engagement's *A Crucible Moment: College Learning and Democracy's Future*, and Martha Nussbaum's *Not for Profit: Why Democracy Needs the Humanities*. Nussbaum wrote,

> If a nation wants to promote . . . democracy dedicated to "life, liberty and the pursuit of happiness" to each and every person, what abilities will it need to produce in its citizens? At least the following seem crucial: The ability to think well about political issues affecting the nation, to examine, reflect, argue, and debate, deferring to neither tradition nor authority . . . (25)

Unfortunately, neither Nussbaum nor these other sources discuss at any length the disciplinary and curricular context in which these subjects are, or should be, taught; none are very specific in defining elements of critical-thinking instruction, and they have received much criticism from composition scholars on methodological, political, and pedagogical grounds. I only address these criticisms in passing, but instead outline my own model in chapter 3, in terms that I hope will resist similar criticism.

3

CRITICAL THINKING FOR POLITICAL LITERACY

Around 1980 American educators began to identify critical thinking as a subject that needed increased, explicit emphasis in our high schools and colleges, and as an essential element in civic literacy. The Rockefeller Foundation's Commission on the Humanities reported in 1980,

> The humanities lead beyond "functional" literacy and basic skills to critical judgment and discrimination, enabling citizens to view political issues from an informed perspective.... Educational policy makers at all levels should define critical thinking as a basic skill and recognize the value of the humanities for developing it.... The entire secondary school curriculum should emphasize the close relationship between writing and critical thinking.... English courses need to emphasize the connections between expression, logic, and the critical use of textual and historical evidence. (*The Humanities in American Life* 12, 22, 44)

Also in 1980, Chancellor Glenn Dumke announced the requirement of formal instruction in critical thinking throughout the nineteen California State University campuses, serving some 300,000 students. The announcement read:

> Instruction in critical thinking is to be designed to achieve an understanding of the relationship of language to logic, which should lead to the ability to analyze, criticize, and advocate ideas, to reason inductively and deductively, and to reach factual or judgmental conclusions based on sound inferences drawn from unambiguous statements of knowledge or belief. The minimal competence to be expected at the successful conclusion of instruction in critical thinking should be the ability to distinguish fact from judgment, belief from knowledge, and skills in elementary inductive and deductive processes, including an understanding of the formal and informal fallacies of language and thought.

Similar requirements were soon adopted by community colleges and secondary schools throughout California and elsewhere. Here is the list of "Basic Critical Thinking Skills" in the California State Department of Education's Model Curriculum for Grades 8–12 in 1984.

1. *Compare similarities and differences*
   The ability to compare similarities and differences among two or more objects, living things, ideas, events, or situations at the same or different points in time. Implies the ability to organize information into defined categories.
2. *Identify central issues or problems*
   The ability to identify the main idea or point of a passage, argument, or political cartoon, for example. At the higher levels, students are expected to identify central issues in complex political arguments. Implies ability to identify major components of an argument, such as reasons and conclusions.
3. *Distinguish fact from opinion*
   The ability to determine the difference between observation and inference.
4. *Recognize stereotypes and clichés*
   The ability to identify fixed or conventional notions about a person, group, or idea.
5. *Recognize bias, emotional factors, propaganda, and semantic slanting*
   The ability to identify partialities and prejudices in written and graphic materials. Includes the ability to determine credibility of sources (gauge reliability, expertise, and objectivity).
6. *Recognize different value orientations and different ideologies*
   The ability to recognize different value orientations and ideologies.
7. *Determine which information is relevant*
   The ability to make distinctions between verifiable and unverifiable, relevant and nonrelevant, and essential and incidental information.
8. *Recognize the adequacy of data*
   The ability to decide whether the information provided is sufficient in terms of quality and quantity to justify a conclusion, decision, generalization, or plausible hypothesis.
9. *Check consistency*
   The ability to determine whether given statements or symbols are consistent. For example, the ability to determine whether the different points or issues in a political argument have logical connections or agree with the central issue.

10. *Formulate appropriate questions*
    The ability to formulate appropriate and thought-provoking questions that will lead to a deeper and clearer understanding of the issues at hand.
11. *Predict probable consequences*
    The ability to predict probable consequences of an event or series of events.
12. *Identify unstated assumptions*
    The ability to identify what is taken for granted, though not explicitly stated, in an argument.

The fields of developmental psychology, sociolinguistics, and composition theory itself have provided supplements to such criteria with other skills of analysis and synthesis that distinguish advanced stages in reading, writing, and reasoning (sometimes termed "higher order reasoning"). These include the abilities to reason back and forth between the past, present, and future, cause and effect, the concrete and the abstract, the personal and the impersonal, the local and the global, the literal and the figurative, the explicit and the implicit ("reading between the lines"), the actual and the hypothetical or between what presently exists and conceivable alternatives. Also, the abilities to retain and apply material previously studied and to sustain an extended line of argument in reading, writing, and speaking, incorporating recursive and cumulative thinking (the abilities to refer back to previously covered material and to build on that material in developing stages in an argument). Still further skills involve understanding (within personal, historical, and political contexts), complexity and multiple levels of meaning or points of view, and to recognize irony, paradox, and ambiguity in disparities between what is said and meant, between appearance and reality (especially between what people say and what they do), and between intentions and results.

Some scholars such as Robert Ennis make a further distinction, between critical thinking *skills*, related formally or informally to traditional logic, and *dispositions* that foster or impede critical thinking within the broader context of psychological, cultural, social, and political influences. Dispositions that foster critical thinking include the development of open-mindedness, autonomous thought, and reciprocity (Piaget's term for ability to empathize with other individuals, social groups, nationalities, ideologies, etc.). Dispositions that act as impediments to critical thinking include defense mechanisms (such as absolutism or primary certitude, denial, and projection), culturally conditioned assumptions, authoritarianism, egocentrism

48

and ethnocentrism, rationalization, compartmentalization, stereotyping, and prejudice.

In a corollary to these skills and dispositions emphasizing open-mindedness, reciprocity, and multiple viewpoints, Richard Paul, a leading theorist of critical thinking, asserts that a setting which facilitates the exchange of free dialogue between opposing views is essential to any authentic exercise of critical thinking (Walsh and Paul). This dialectical dimension of critical thinking is obviously linked to central precepts in rhetoric, composition, and literature from the Platonic dialogues to modern theorists like Bakhtin and Camus. In composition theory, it is evident in models for cognitive development from writer/speaker-based to reader/listener-based writing and in methods like Rogerian argument and Peter Elbow's "Believers and Doubters," which help us to get outside our own egos and empathize with others' viewpoints.

Many of these critical-thinking skills and dispositions coincide with ideas that have been generated since the 1930s by the International Society for General Semantics and its journal *et cetera*, still published by the renamed Institute for General Semantics. The society's Institute for Propaganda Analysis, which flourished from 1937–42, produced a list of the kind of logical fallacies that has become standard in argumentation textbooks, although most now present these fallacies as unintentional lapses rather than as propaganda devices. A general semantics approach to rhetorical analysis was implicit in Dumke's reference to "the relation of language to logic" and "an understanding of the formal and informal fallacies of language and thought"—suggesting questions of denotation and connotation, euphemism, jargon, deception and lying—as well as in the skills in the California guidelines distinguishing fact from opinion and identifying stereotypes, "partialities and prejudices in written and graphic materials," bias, propaganda, semantic slanting, different value orientations and ideologies, and the disposition of facility in perceiving ambiguity and multiplicity of meanings or points of view.

Several important figures in general semantics (GS) were scholars in English or related fields like linguistics and speech communication, including Benjamin Lee Whorf, S. I. Hayakawa (whose classic 1940 textbook *Language in Thought and Action* has been in its fifth edition since 1991), Irving Lee, Kenneth Burke, I. A. Richards (*The Meaning of Meaning*), Stuart Chase, Wendell Johnson (whose son Nicholas, a media critic and FCC commissioner, has also incorporated a GS perspective in his books like *How to Talk Back to Your Television Set*), and Neil Postman (a great editor of *et cetera* from 1976–86 and author of *Amusing Ourselves to Death*, which definitively anatomized the cognitive destruction wreaked by televised discourse and politics). The work of two GS-oriented psychologists, Carl Rogers and Gordon Allport, has been incorporated into English studies through Rogerian argument and the theoretical and research model in Allport's *The Nature of Prejudice*. Literary historian Richard Altick's *Preface to Critical Reading* was also influenced by GS, and certainly deserves a revival, as does the perspective of the entire movement, despite the quirks of some of its members and affiliations. Orwell's newspeak and doublethink in *1984* and "Politics and the English Language" were indebted to GS, as were Marcuse's *One-Dimensional Man* and other works on the closing of the linguistic universe of discourse. I was always puzzled, in the heyday of structuralist and poststructuralist theory, that no one seemed to discuss its relation to GS, and that Saussure and his followers eclipsed Korzybski, Whorf, Richards, Burke, and others. (For a good review of the rise and decline of GS, and of Burke's relation to it, see Nicotra.)

General semantics further influenced, via Orwell, several NCTE resolutions on language and politics in the 1970s, such as the one in the epigraph to chapter 1 in this book, and the following, "On the Relation of Language to Public Policy," in 1971: "RESOLVED, That the National Council of Teachers of English find means to study the relation of language to public policy, to keep track of, publicize, and combat semantic distortion by public officials, candidates for office, political commentators, and all those who transmit through the mass media" (quoted in Dieterich x). These resolutions in turn gave rise to the NCTE Committee on Public Doublespeak, which thrived from the mid-1970s into the 1990s, followed by a few unsuccessful efforts to continue or revive it. It was most widely known through its annual Doublespeak Award for abuse of public language and Orwell Award for scholarly or journalistic works critiquing doublespeak. The committee declined as these awards lost their novelty for fickle mass media, which were more willing to publicize humorous examples of jargon and euphemism than of "dishonest and inhumane uses of language," in another NCTE resolution's words (Dieterich x). The committee also produced a regular column in *College English* under Dick Ohmann's editorship, the *Quarterly Review of Doublespeak*, as well as two collections published by NCTE—*Teaching about Doublespeak*, edited by Daniel Dieterich, and *Beyond Nineteen Eighty-Four: Doublespeak in a Post-Orwellian Age*, edited by William Lutz—and several textbook rhetorics and readers like *Language Awareness*, edited by Paul Eschholz, Alfred Rosa, and Virginia Clark. Hugh Rank, its first chair, self-published two excellent little guides, *The Pitch: How to Analyze Ads* and *Persuasion Analysis: A Companion for Analysis*. (His "Intensify-Downplay

Schema" formed the basis for my "Semantic Calculator for Bias in Rhetoric" and "Predictable Patterns of Political Rhetoric" in "Teaching the Political Conflicts: A Rhetorical Schema.")

The whole panoply of critical-thinking terms surveyed here contained the potential for providing a new, unifying disciplinary framework for studies in composition, rhetoric, literature, and cultural studies—a framework that could also make English courses the gateway and master discipline for critical thinking in virtually all academic studies. Many of these skills and dispositions provided a warrant for the application to English studies of Frankfurt School, Freirean, and other Marxist, feminist, multicultural, and postcolonialist theories critiquing authoritarianism, ethnocentrism, and mass-media stereotyping (see Adorno's "Television and the Patterns of Mass Culture"). The references to value orientations, ideologies, and multiple viewpoints further warranted a cultural-studies perspective examining ideological implications and subject positions in a wide range of cultural practices and texts, as in James Berlin's social-epistemic rhetoric: "the study and critique of signifying practices in their relation to subject formation within the framework of economic, social, and political conditions" (77). Unfortunately, both the study of semantics and critical thinking in general have waned in rhetcomp over recent decades, for reasons I will explore in part 2.

Critical Thinking and Cultural Literacy

Much debate in educational circles has centered on the relative importance of learning critical-thinking skills versus factual knowledge related to specific disciplines like history, social science, or the natural sciences. This debate seems to me a classic either-or fallacy, since common sense dictates that both are indispensable and inseparable in practice. The leading recent advocate of increased emphasis on factual knowledge in American education, E. D. Hirsch, in his 1987 *Cultural Literacy: What Every American Needs to Know*, agrees:

> The old prejudice that facts deaden the minds of children has a long history in the nineteenth and twentieth centuries and includes not just the disciples of Rousseau and Dewey but also Charles Dickens who, in the figure of Mr. Gradgrind in *Hard Times*, satirized the teaching of mere facts. But it isn't facts that deaden the minds of young children, who are storing facts in their minds every day with astonishing voracity. It is incoherence—our failure to ensure that a pattern of shared, vividly taught, and socially enabling knowledge will emerge from our instruction.

The polarization of educationists into facts-people versus skills-people has no basis in reason. Facts and skills are inseparable. There is no insurmountable reason why those who advocate the teaching of higher order skills and those who advocate the teaching of common traditional content should not join forces. (133)

I will say more in defense of Hirsch against his critics in the English profession and elsewhere subsequently. For now, suffice it to say that Hirsch simply reiterates the obvious truth that factual knowledge of history and of the contemporary world are foremost among the fields of knowledge essential for critical thinking—*not* for the purpose of rote memorization of dates and names, but for the purpose of reasoning back and forth between the past, present, and future, of being able to understand present conditions in comparison and contrast to past conditions and in a sequence of causal analysis explaining how conditions have evolved to their present state; and for the purpose of reasoning from the personal to the impersonal, from the local to the global. As *The Humanities in American Life* put it:

The humanities do not impose any single set of normative values, whether moral, social, or aesthetic; rather, as a record of the ideals that have guided men and women in the past, they give historical perspective. Students made sensitive to what it might be like to live in a different time, place, or culture can make value choices without automatically assuming that contemporary reality has no precedent, or that quick scientific or humanistic prescriptions can remedy every problem. The humanities bring to life the ideal of cultural pluralism by expanding the number of perspectives from which questions of value may be viewed, by enlarging young people's social and historical consciousness, and by activating an imaginative critical spirit. (30)

And, on the relation of English courses to history and other humanistic disciplines:

High schools should concentrate on an articulated sequence of courses in English, history, and foreign languages. Courses in these disciplines should not divorce skills and methods from knowledge of content and cultural context. . . . English courses need to emphasize the connections between expression, logic, and the critical use of textual and historical evidence. (44)

One of my persistent arguments throughout this book (and particularly in chapter 4) is that study of "the critical use of textual and historical evidence" has largely been elided from the discipline of rhetcomp in recent decades as writing instruction has been isolated from the context of academic discourse.

The most important link between critical thinking and cultural literacy is the vocabulary of words denoting mental operations, rhetorical terms, and factual knowledge that constantly expands over the course of our education and varied life experience. In *Errors and Expectations* (1977), Mina Shaughnessy, whose work inspired many followers including Hirsch and myself, summed up the kinds of words that college students are being introduced to and that constitute what she termed "the vocabulary of general literacy," though she might equally well have referred, as she sometimes did, to the vocabulary of "critical thinking," "cultural literacy," or "academic discourse."

1. Words that allude to events, places, and people that are assumed to be commonly, if but vaguely, known (Gandhi, the French Revolution, the Nile, etc.).
2. Words that serve as formal equivalents to concepts already familiar to the student in different words (as *atheist* is the equivalent to "someone who doesn't believe in God").
3. Words that serve to identify complex historical movements (Renaissance, Marxism, evolution, etc.).
4. Words that, although part of the nomenclature of certain fields, are also used in the wider culture with variant meanings (in literature, for example, such terms as *fiction, drama,* or *novel*).
5. Words that are intended to initiate highly specific academic activities (*define, compare, generalize, document, illustrate, prove, summarize, interpret,* etc.).
6. Words that are used in deliberately ambiguous ways in order to enrich or refine meaning (*irony, figures of speech,* etc.).
7. Words that articulate relationships such as addition, negation, condition, or causation (*moreover, therefore, however,* etc.).
8. Words that represent Latin- or Greek-based synonyms for familiar words (i.e., *initiate* or *commence* for *begin*) and that tend to give an academic flavor to the writing and speech of teachers. (217)

All of the previous critical-thinking skills and others contribute to the abilities to make connections between diverse experiences, ideas, and subjects studied, through multiple varieties of analysis and synthesis, including those incorporated in standard textbook surveys of modes of discourse or exposition. Reading or writing extended arguments incorporates modes of analysis that can consist of identifying and interpreting key issues and elements in them; of establishing relationships between events or facts (frequently through analogy, equation, or comparison and contrast); of breaking a subject down into components through defining, grouping, or ordering them; or of making reasoned logical, moral, or evaluative judgments of ideas, arguments, or actions, including analysis of fallacies.

Cumulativeness, Recursiveness, and Levels of Meaning

In reading others' texts and writing one's own, recursiveness involves the process of rereading as many times as necessary to decode the author's full, complex meaning (or to encode your own), to follow the development of theme or thesis and of the reasoning (or lack thereof). Good writing requires such rereading and holds up, or even appears better than before, under many rereadings, but poor writing falls apart thematically, stylistically, or logically under closer scrutiny. In one's own writing, the counterpart to rereading is *revision (re-vision)*. About this process, Orville Schell, the polymath Asia scholar, journalist, and dean of the Graduate School of Journalism at Berkeley, writes:

> Nine-tenths of good journalism is writing a piece over and over until you get it right. I would love to teach a course in which each student writes one article and spends the whole semester editing it over and over, which is maybe not something you can always do in the real world but which builds an awareness that good writing is not a question of getting it right the first time, it's a question of sticking with it until you can get it to sing. (*San Francisco Examiner*, June 16, 1996, B-9)

Conversely, cumulativeness refers to the continuous building and retention by the writer or reader of knowledge, ideas, and reasoning throughout a particular work, and from that work to future ones. The entire process of general education, from kindergarten to graduate school and beyond, depends on this steady accumulation. In teaching, the sequence of individual course assignments and the structure of a complete course can be organized cumulatively and recursively to help foster these abilities. Thus I often assign a series of short papers and exams in a continuous sequence, which are then assembled, with recursive revision, into a term paper or final, comprehensive essay exam. I also give daily notes assignments on readings, make comments and raise questions on them, and ask students to respond to them and resubmit, to maintain continuity. These and all other assignments throughout the term are saved in a portfolio, which I review with each student at the end of the semester to arrive holistically at the final grade.

Critical thinking necessitates not only reading or writing recursively and cumulatively, on a linear or horizontal plane, so to speak, but also stopping frequently to process varieties of information stacked or compressed "vertically" in a text, through the whole repertory of rhetorical and stylistic techniques.

These three processes are summed up in the diagram.

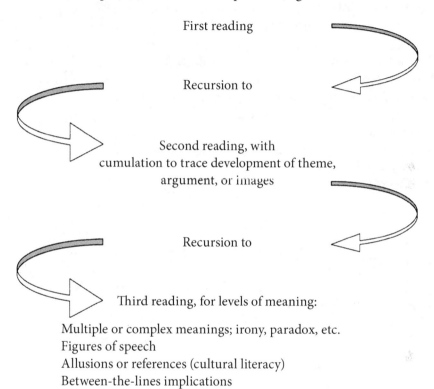

First reading

Recursion to

Second reading, with
cumulation to trace development of theme,
argument, or images

Recursion to

Third reading, for levels of meaning:

Multiple or complex meanings; irony, paradox, etc.
Figures of speech
Allusions or references (cultural literacy)
Between-the-lines implications
Words to look up in a dictionary
Facts to look up in reference works
Citations to check for accuracy and further information

Literature for Critical Thinking

Teachers of literature will be quick to make connections between all these aspects of critical thinking and their favorite literary works, as I did throughout the years when I found constant congruence here between my literature and writing courses. Space here does not allow my indulging many of my literary examples, although I did so throughout *Reading and Writing* and in the concluding chapter of *Why Higher Education*, titled "The Radical Humanistic Canon," a survey of the centrality in the Western literary tradition of skepticism toward authority and conformity in religion, government, economics, race, and gender roles. Here is just one, small sampling from a master of critical thinking in literature, Marcel Proust.

In Proust's *Swann's Way*, the narrator recalls that when he was a boy, he was accustomed to see three church spires in the same formation from his house, until one day he went on a ride around them in a carriage, when they appeared disconcertingly to be spinning around each other. He was intrigued by the experience, but not until years later was he able to make sense of it in terms of cognitive mapping, relative point of view, Heraclitean flux, and the contingency of habitual thinking—central themes throughout Proust in multiple contexts, such as the narrator's shifting perceptions on the various characters he knows, as he acquires new information about them and as they change over time. Thus reading *Remembrance of Things Past* is the ultimate exercise in recursion and cumulation. An excruciating dramatization of egocentrism, rationalization, and denial is the scene in which the Duke de Guermantes gets more upset when he notices that his wife's shoes don't match her dress than he does when their best friend Charles Swann tells them he is fatally ill—both events delaying the Guermantes's departure for a party, but the shoe-change taking priority over time to console Swann, who is brushed off with an evasive assurance that they'll talk about it some other day. Proust's summation of art as the ultimate in Piagetian reciprocity comes near the end of *The Past Recaptured*: "Only by art can we get outside ourselves, know what another sees of his universe, which is not the same as ours and the different views of which would otherwise have remained as unknown to us as those there may be on the moon" (1013).

Negative Social Forces on Critical Thinking

Research suggests a correlation of television watching (and consumption of mass culture in general) to a tendency toward literalness in thought. . . . Put succinctly, children of all social classes . . . seem unable to penetrate beyond the surfaces of things to reach down to those aspects of the object that may not be visible to the senses. . . . The problem of abstraction becomes a major barrier to analysis because students seem enslaved to the concrete. Finally, teachers notice that many have trouble making connections between two objects or sets of concepts that are not related to each other in an obvious manner. . . . The critical project of learning involves understanding that things are often not what they seem to be and that abstract concepts such as "society," "capitalism," "history," and other categories not available to the senses are nonetheless real. This whole critical project now seems in eclipse. (Stanley Aronowitz, "Mass Culture and the Eclipse of Reason: The Implications for Pedagogy" 467)

Writing, the clearest demonstration of the power of analytical and sequential thinking, seems increasingly to be an alien form to many of our young, even to those who may be regarded as extremely intelligent. . . . The electronic information environment, with television at its center, is fundamentally hostile to conceptual, segmented, linear modes of expression; thus, both writing and speech must lose some of their power. Language is, by its nature, slow-moving, hierarchical, logical, and continuous. Whether writing or speaking, one must maintain a fixed point of view and a continuity of content; one must move to higher or lower levels of abstraction; one must follow to a greater or lesser degree rules of syntax and logic. . . . Every word contains the possibility of multiple meanings and therefore of multiple ideas. . . . The young in particular are experiencing an acute inability to make connections, and some have given up trying. The TV curriculum, we must remember, stresses the fragmented and discrete nature of events, and indeed is structurally unable to organize them into coherent themes or principles. (Neil Postman, *Teaching as a Conserving Activity* 74, 78)

Critics of contemporary American society and culture like Aronowitz (a sociologist following in the line of Frankfurt School Marxism) and Postman make the case that many individuals' development of analytic and synthetic skills—indeed their capacity to make connections between events and ideas at all—has actually been impaired by the atomizing "sound bites" and low reasoning level of mass political discourse and media—and that, in a vicious circle, the diminished level of the public's reasoning skills is pandered to by politicians and media "giving the people what they want." Note the echo of Thoreau's "our vision does not penetrate the surface of things" (*Walden* 87) in Aronowitz's "children . . . seem unable to penetrate beyond the surfaces of things."

These cultural critics consider the atomized discourse of television and politics foremost among these forces, but the structures of education itself in many ways work against cognitive accumulation. College students typically take four or more courses each term, few of which have much continuity with the others or with others they have taken earlier or will take later. Many individual courses are structured as a sketchy sequence of modular units with little sense of building on what has been learned previously. Assignments and tests cover only the current unit, and students are conditioned into the attitude that studying consists of cramming for each day's assignment and then forgetting it to go on to the next one. So even when class discussions are lively, it is hard to retain enough from last week's or yesterday's to continue it today. And with all the pressure put on "getting the grade," short-term efforts to do so naturally take precedence over motivation to truly learn. So education is reduced to a sequence of jumping through hoops, doing no more than what is needed to finish each day's assignment, to pass the exam, to get the grade, to get the diploma, to get the job—with the result that in the end students are apt to have retained little of what they have studied at all. When I raise this analysis in class, most students readily agree with it, though they tend to be reticent about doing the kind of assignments calculated to counteract cognitive atomization.

A Case Study in Obstacles to Critical Thinking

Here is an example from my argumentative writing course that illustrates several obstacles to critical thinking including the social forces identified by Aronowitz and Postman—especially students' "trouble making connections between two objects or sets of concepts that are not related to each other in an obvious manner." I assigned the following passage from "The Age of Irony?" by Susan Searls Giroux in *Journal of Advanced Composition* 25:2 (2002):

> Currently, the Bush administration is planning yet another wave of tax cuts to benefit the wealthiest Americans in the name of "economic stimulus," even as . . . mayors of every major city in the country are left to negotiate deficits—as high as thirty-eight billion dollars in California—entirely on their own.
>
> In addition to a massive tax restructuring that has starved social programs for the benefit of the very rich, we've also seen the stagnation of wages for working people. . . . The pay gap between top executives and production workers grew from 42:1 in 1980 to a staggering 419-1 in 1998 (excluding the value of stock options), according to *Business Week*'s "Forty-ninth Annual Executive Pay Survey." The same report notes that "Had the typical worker's pay risen in tandem with executive pay, the average production worker would now earn $110,000 a year and the minimum wage would be $22.08" instead of the current wage of $5.15. And how does this wage figure in terms of

yearly salary? A 40-hour week at $5.15 per hour "nets a pre-tax annual income of $10,300, or about $6,355 below the official 1998 poverty line for a family of four." In contrast to these poverty wages, "the average large company chief executive was paid $10.6 million, a 36 percent jump over 1997." (970–71)

The first time I gave the assignment, I asked students to write their personal responses to these data, as present or future workers, in an attempt on my part to prompt making connections between the abstract and the concrete, the impersonal data and their personal significance for each student. Here are two responses.

> STUDENT A: The wealth gap is increasing every day, but is that all bad? I think not. Giroux's article outlines how the rich are getting richer and the poor are getting poorer, but is comparing a minimum wage worker to a big chief executive fair? This is like comparing diamonds to rocks.
> STUDENT B: For many years there has been a wealth gap in America, but it looks as though there is not really a way to fix this gap. Raising taxes is not the answer. People should be able to work and reap the benefits of their hard work. Corporate executives work hard and deserve to keep every dollar they earn without being taxed to death. Most poor people dropped out of school along the way and in return for their lack of motivation have lived in poverty. I don't care for the fact that my taxpayer money goes towards welfare to support them.

The next time I tried the assignment, the following year, I included Student A's and B's responses and asked the class to evaluate their reasoning and their relevance both to Giroux's data and to my request that students respond "as present or future workers." Both times around, it was evident that almost all the students evaded relating the topics to their own situation, and I was rather chagrined to find that most said the responses were quite relevant, with explanations like, "Both Giroux and A and B are talking about the wealth gap," while few found any fallacies in the reasoning. I pursued in-class and personal discussions with the student writers, including A and B, who said their families were lower middle class, that they had worked for minimum wage and saw their future as workers, not executives, and that they had just written the first thing that came into their mind, along the lines of things they had heard from their parents. I subsequently arrived at the following speculations:

- Students generally have difficulty absorbing academic writing like Giroux's because they are used to reading a passage once over, hurriedly, and responding off the top of their head. They did not read her passage several times over to register the sequence of reasoning in it. Statistical arguments seem especially distant and abstract.

- Students are accustomed to regarding academic reading as unconnected to them personally, and writing about it as BS. Many are also extremely reluctant to write about sensitive areas of their own lives, or about disturbing information like Giroux's, and are inclined toward impersonal BS as a defense mechanism. (I have modified the wording of questions like these to give students the option of either writing about themselves or "most people you know." I also state in the syllabus that they are not obliged to write on any subject that they feel is an invasion of their privacy.)

- Many students have rarely or never thought about the connections between what executives and their employees make. Student A explained to me that the "diamonds and rocks" analogy was not intended to be a value judgment (although some students reading it interpreted it that way and found it prejudiced), but as a claim that corporate executives and workers function in wholly separate realms, so that "apples and oranges" might have been a more apt comparison. When I put it this way to the class, many agreed, and it took a lengthy exposition to convey the notions that the salaries of both come out of the same pool, that as one makes more, the others must make less, and that the relative share is not determined by impersonal, uncontrollable forces but by the exercise of power by human agents whose policies are subject to alteration through means like collective bargaining or government legislation.

- Similarly, many students do not understand or accept Giroux's argument because they have never thought about the cause-effect relation between taxation and funding of public services like education, national defense, police, and infrastructural staples like the levees in New Orleans that collapsed in Hurricane Katrina. This mindset obviously has been fostered by the past thirty years of antitax, antigovernment conservative rhetoric, which has led Americans to rationalize, or wishfully believe, that they can have adequate public services while paying greatly reduced or no taxes for them. The same lapse is evident in the lengthy explanation that it takes to enable students to understand the causal sequence between cutting of taxes, government budget cuts for education, and increases in college tuition accompanied by decreases in financial aid other than high-interest loans. Although many students are aware that tuition has increased and financial aid other than loans has decreased, their tendency is to think about these as though they are inevitable acts of God, not political policies that are contestable; regarded this way, such policies are somehow more acceptable, obviating the responsibility of possible action by students, for whom inert conformity to the status quo is a comfort zone. A related compartmentalization is evident in student discussion and writing about Adolph Reed's article in *Reading and Writing for Civic Literacy*, "Majoring in Debt," arguing that excessive government spending on war, particularly the Iraq War, has drained billions that could have gone to student financial aid. Several students deny that there is any causal relation or anything that might be subject to change here, because "spending for defense and education come out of separate areas of the federal budget."

- The thinking of students like A and B about issues like these tends to be formulaic and ahistorically static. Statements like "Corporate executives work hard and deserve to keep every dollar they earn" disregard Giroux's data about the growing disparities since the 1970s (to say nothing about other possible factors such as increased corporate power over government legislation and unions). In a more tangibly personal line of argument, students often say, "My parents got out of poverty into the middle class through hard work and intelligence, so anyone can." While I acknowledge to student writers the rhetorical value of the specific example here, I also ask them to consider whether cases like this are the rule or perhaps the exception in the general population, contingent to some extent on factors like geography, race, gender, or sheer luck, and whether the odds that were favorable to their parents might have worsened today.

- Many students predictably rationalize whatever executives and rich people acquire, out of authoritarian awe and class prejudice exalting the wealthy and denigrating the poor or rank-and-file workers ("diamonds and rocks"). When I raise the question in class of why so many poor or middle-class people are eager to defend executives and the rich, the response is invariably that they fervently believe they have a chance to reach that level themselves—a reflection of the "winner take all"/*Survivor*/*The Apprentice* conception of democracy and "equal opportunity" in recent decades: Everyone has a chance to win the lottery. Welfare recipients have become a favorite scapegoat, going back to President Reagan's apocryphal stories about affluent "welfare queens." Thus Student B evades Giroux's arguments about tax cuts favoring the rich and causing cuts in "social programs" like education, by reducing social programs to welfare payments coddling loafers who presumably are the major beneficiaries of taxes and the largest category of poor people, in disregard of Giroux's data about declining wages and those who work full time or more below the poverty level.

- In light of students' notorious tendency to psych out what they think the teacher wants—which is universally assumed to be liberal in politics—and to perform accordingly, it is curious that students like A and B seem oblivious that they are writing belligerently conservative arguments. Some conservative intellectuals suggest that such students may be slyly demonstrating Foucauldian resistance and transgression against liberal pedagogical authority. I am dubious, however, considering most students' slavish obsession with "the grade" and their quickness to shift ground once their positions are exposed to criticism or a low grade. My inference is that they show a combination of egocentric lack of sense of writing to an audience and of elementary lack of knowledge about the ideological differences between liberals and conservatives on these issues; what they have heard from their parents is just assumed to be common knowledge. (The latter inference has been confirmed many times over after I have given students my "Glossary of Political Terms and Positions," and they have responded with gratitude for information they say they have never been taught systematically before.)

- There *are* more complex, legitimately debatable issues implicit in Giroux's assertions that the rich are the prime beneficiaries of recent tax cuts, that the cuts have contributed to the wealth gap, and that they have caused reductions in federal and local government budgets. Conservative politicians and publicists argue that all classes benefit equally from flat-rate tax cuts, that the revenue lost from tax cuts from the rich is offset by revenue generated from their greater earnings, which also "trickles down" to employees, and so on—arguments that many students like A and B have at least distantly heard and assume to be valid. Evaluating substantive arguments and evidence on opposing sides of this debate involves extensive study of sources and data that can take up the greater part of an argumentative writing course, as indicated by a sequence of two chapters on this topic at the end of *Reading and Writing for Civic Literacy* presented as a model for generating a term paper. (The economic issues here, incidentally, are addressed at the level of mass political and media discourse, not that of specialized economics.)

After I read students' initial responses to A's and B's take on Giroux, and with these speculations in mind, I asked them to do the assignment over, but this time to list Giroux's arguments point by point, and then to list A's and B's arguments point by point and judge on each point how directly and relevantly they were responding to Giroux. This time around, through recursion, most of them were able to pinpoint the inadequacy of the responses. I also added an exercise, along the lines of the California Department of Education's critical-thinking criterion of "Predict Probable Consequences," asking them to predict the likely consequences of the gap between executives and employees continuing to grow over their lifetimes at the same ratio as in the past three decades, and asked, "Where do you draw the line?" between when growing inequality would be acceptable or not. This worked effectively to overcome their tendency toward static, ahistorical thinking.

Was I thus "coercing" students into a predetermined conclusion, as I suspect some of them felt, and as conservative critics claim about liberal or leftist professors? I raised this question with the class, and tried to explain that all I was coercing them to do was to think more carefully and rationally about the topic and readings. Whatever conclusion they came to, on one side or the other, should have been defensible through reasoning and evidence. Once they acknowledged the inadequacy of A's and B's arguments, I encouraged them to go on to explore what other, better arguments against Giroux might be made, so long as they did so through sound reasoning and supporting evidence from research sources. (If, for example, they were inclined to agree with Student B that welfare is a major area of tax expenditure, or that most welfare recipients and other poor people are drop-outs with "lack of motivation," they should be able to provide supporting data and refutations of contrary evidence.) So the entire unit of study became an illustration of the dialogic, infinitely expanding, continuous, and open-ended nature of critical thinking.

At the same time, this case study illustrates the dilemma of college English teachers trying to foster critical reading, writing, and thinking within the vacuum of many students' civic or cultural literacy. Much of the factual knowledge on the issues here should have been acquired before students reached a second-term college writing course, and the expectation that we should have to provide remediation in an entire civic education (along with students' frequent resentment at being expected to have some such background knowledge for a writing class) is enough to give the feeling that we are sinking in quicksand. Nevertheless, in the present circumstances, I see no alternative to our educating ourselves to teach civic topics and doing the best we can to provide such remediation.

PART 2

THE EXCESSES OF POSTMODERN PLURALISM

4

WHAT EVER HAPPENED TO CRITICAL THINKING?

In recent decades, many rhetoric and composition scholars have continued vigorously to pursue the goals of critical thinking and political literacy—in my definition of critical awareness of national political and economic issues, including through academic study of political rhetoric. These have included most visibly the Conference on College Composition and Communication caucus Rhetoricians for Peace, the *Radical Teacher* group, and advocates of Freirean or Marxist-inflected critical pedagogy like Henry Giroux, Susan Searls Giroux, Ira Shor, Stanley Aronowitz, bell hooks, James Berlin, John Trimbur, Richard Ohmann, Karen Fitts and Alan France, James Seitz, Teresa Ebert, Dale Bauer, Nancy Welch, Mark Bracher, Cathy Chaput, Seth Kahn, Jonghwa Lee, William Thelin, Paul Tassoni, Marc Bousquet, and Tony Scott. (See the survey of recent examples toward the end of chapter 1.)

Others similarly engaged with political literacy, though not directly identifying themselves with critical pedagogy, include Jonathan Kozol, Mike Rose, Glenda Hull, Shirley Brice Heath, James Zebroski, Susan Jarratt, Lynn Worsham, Gary Olson, Patricia Bizzell, Bruce Herzberg, Patricia Roberts-Miller, Ellen Cushman, Henry Louis Gates, Lester Faigley, Linda Flower, Myron Tuman, Kathleen McCormick, Gerald Graff and Cathy Birkenstein, John K. Wilson, Stephen Parks, Eli Goldblatt, Deborah Meier, Lisa Delpit, Jennifer Trainor, Marlia Banning, John Ackerman, and David Coogan. However, there has also been another prominent tendency—in rhetoric/composition courses, professional journals, conferences, scholarly books, and research—to marginalize or even to disdain such goals. In the next six chapters I will trace the complex of developments in the profession that have converged toward this tendency, to analyze some of the excesses in these developments, and to advocate the reaffirmation of the earlier goals throughout the field.

As I emphasize throughout this book, probably the most significant development is the isolation of writing courses from academic discourse in general and particularly from subject matter and critical thinking in the social sciences and communication, as applied to analysis of political rhetoric and media. A related development is the privileging of the production of students' personal writing (whether expressive or argumentative) over analysis and criticism of either academic texts or public rhetoric, with the personal dominating conceptions of first-year writing and the analytic and critical being bumped to advanced courses or other disciplines, which receive relatively little attention in our field's scholarship.

Another related development is the tendency toward anti-intellectualism and antirationalism in some advocates of pluralistic alternatives to academic discourse, along with dismissals of study of factual knowledge (Hirschean cultural literacy), "masculinist" modes of argumentation, and the humanistic tradition in liberal arts colleges. A final development is celebrations of diversity and difference over cultural commonalities and unifying political causes, in tandem with emphasis on local and identity politics, communities, and cultures to the exclusion of national and international politics and cosmopolitan culture. As noted in chapter 1, at the risk of painting with too broad a brush, I use the term *postmodernism* as shorthand for these various tendencies.

To pick up from the history in chapter 3 of the critical-thinking movement in the 1980s, critical thinking has never gained much of a foothold in English studies. In California and elsewhere, college philosophy and speech departments waged more aggressive turf wars to teach the new critical-thinking courses, and the main research centers, such as the Center for Critical Thinking and Moral Critique at Sonoma State University (now reconstituted without university affiliation as the Foundation for Critical Thinking in Tomales, California) and the Centre for Research in Reasoning, Argumentation and Rhetoric at the University of Windsor, Ontario, have been philosophy centered. The main professional organization that remains active in the field is the Association for Informal Logic and Critical Thinking (AILACT), consisting almost entirely of faculty in philosophy and education departments. Scholars associated with AILACT have produced a valuable body of empirical research, formulations of critical-thinking criteria, curricular models, and learning-assessment measures, which few of us in English have drawn from (for instance, Ennis, Hatcher and Spencer, Possin). Most textbooks based extensively on the above models of critical thinking are also intended for philosophy courses, in contrast to the English texts that use the term only as a vague buzzword for conventional composition instruction. Unfortunately, even in philosophy, critical thinking has remained an orphan, with little recognition as a field of graduate study, faculty hiring, scholarly publication, or even teaching—so that basic critical-thinking courses tend to staffed in the same irresponsible way as FYW courses in English. The tendency, in a discipline that prioritizes formal logic and other advanced modes of philosophy, is to disdain critical thinking as "baby logic," and to claim that "all our courses teach critical thinking," the same claim made by literature professors who insist that critical-thinking courses *per se* are unnecessary, but who fail to understand critical thinking as a distinct discipline in the way I have been delineating it.

English studies have defaulted on critical thinking on several fronts. For example, in 1979, *CE* published Andrea Lunsford's "Cognitive Development and the Basic Writer," and *CCC* published her "The Content of Basic Writers' Essays" in 1980, applying the stage-developmental theories of Lawrence Kohlberg and William Perry. But then along came Carol Gilligan's *In a Different Voice*, and *Women's Ways of Knowing* by Belenky et al., which judiciously corrected for the gender bias in Kohlberg and Perry (see chapters 6 and 11). These corrections were quickly turned by some feminists into a dogmatic killer dichotomy between women's and men's ways of knowing, and the very notion of stage development of moral or intellectual reasoning was dropped like a hot potato in English studies. Terms like "higher order reasoning" were banished as masculinist, Eurocentric, elitist, hierarchical, essentialist, and "logic chopping." So when recent scholars like Marcia Curtis and Anne Herrington dare to revive developmental ideas, they are highly defensive: "Does the notion of personal development carry any credence at all in a time when notions of person and self have become so problematic?" ("Writing Development" 70). These and other varieties of anti-intellectualism and antirationalism that have sidetracked the study of critical thinking will be explored throughout this and the next five chapters.

The Divorce of Writing Instruction from Factual Knowledge and Critical Reading

The famous paradigm shift that began with the Dartmouth Conference in 1966 has led away from the previous model of composition as a mode of response to academic readings, toward process instruction and successive spin-offs including expressivism, narrative "stories," collaborative and community-based writing, and the conception of classrooms as argumentative "contact zones." A corollary to this history is the increasing emphasis in the discipline on basic writing and FYW and de-emphasis on advanced composition, especially in critical reading and argumentative writing. Although we continue to pay lip service to "reading, writing, and reasoning" as the realm of our discipline, the mainstream of composition theory has privileged writing instruction as an autonomous discipline, with reduced attention to the development of skills in reading, vocabulary, reasoning, and argumentation—at a level geared to prepare students for academic study in other disciplines or for the critical reading of media or public discourse like journalistic periodicals, books, speeches, debates, and political deliberations. When readings *are* discussed these days in professional circles, they are often limited to a multicultural diversity of "discursive voices" and narrative "stories," which are used as prompts for students in "negotiating meaning," with little attention to negotiating academic, journalistic, and political readings that are outside students' own experience. A serious consequence is that the profession of college English has pretty much washed its hands of responsibility for, or even recognition of, the fact that students graduate from most American high schools with deficiencies in reading, reasoning, vocabulary, and world knowledge, especially in political literacy, at least as grave as those in writing.

Reports in the 1980s by the National Assessment of Educational Progress indicated that there is a difficult stage-developmental step between reading or writing self-expression or narration and critical analysis and argumentation. While some recent compositionists have sought pedagogical means for facilitating that step, many others have taken the easiest path by sticking with personal writing (even in argumentation) as the be-all and end-all of composition instruction. If college composition courses *must* privilege personal over critical writing, why can we not at least recognize the need for required, college-level advanced courses in critical analysis of arguments in readings?

A prototypical formulation of the expressivist view of composition was Maxine Hairston's "Diversity, Ideology, and Teaching Writing," in the May 1992 *CCC*. As a member of the University of Texas English department, Hairston was writing in opposition to rhetoric colleagues' controversial effort to introduce political controversies in FYW there (the only required writing course). Hairston asserted:

> First, students' own writing must be the center of the course. Students need to write to find out how much they know and to gain confidence in the ability to express themselves effectively. *They do not need to be assigned essays to read so they will have something to write about—they bring their subjects with them. The writing of others, except for that of their fellow students, should be supplementary, used to illustrate or reinforce.* (186; my emphasis)

Even within the confines of a one-semester freshman English course, one might object that Hairston's expressivist view was overly restrictive. Elsewhere in the article, she did pay lip service to the role in such a course of "critical thinking" (which she didn't define) and acknowledged, "In this kind of classroom not all writing should be personal, expressive writing. Students need a broader range of discourse as their introduction to writing in college. The teacher can easily design the kinds of writing assignments that involve argument and exposition and suggest options that encourage cross-cultural awareness" (191). But her only examples of sources for that "broader range of discourse," "argument and exposition," and "options that encourage cross-cultural awareness" were the supposedly diverse backgrounds of other students in the class. Her statements here and elsewhere provoked much criticism in *CCC* (including my "Teaching the Political Conflicts," juxtaposed to her article in the same issue), and it has been superseded by broader conceptions of writing courses, but much in her position has been reiterated by recent, influential theorists like Joseph Harris, Min-Zhan Lu and Bruce Horner, and Kurt Spellmeyer, in his defense of students' "freedom in a composition course to think and write about their lives without coercion and disparagement" ("Culture" 295–96).

In correspondence with me, Harris has objected to being associated with Hairston; my point is that, although Hairston favored teaching expressivism and "comfort zone" nurturing while Harris in *A Teaching Subject* favors argumentation and negotiation of conflict, Harris shares Hairston's view that students "do not need to be assigned essays to read so they will have something to write about—they bring their subjects with them." His version is "a classroom where student writings . . . serve as positions in an argument whose blessings we can count and measure together, but whose final merits we can leave students to judge for themselves" (115).

Our very conception of writing as an autonomous academic subject in America is symptomatic of a larger problem that has been little acknowledged in the profession. In most other contemporary democracies, reading, writing, and reasoning instruction is integrated far more into courses in academic subject areas in both secondary and college education. This split in America lets faculties in other disciplines off the hook from teaching English skills and lets English teachers off the hook from connecting their courses to other disciplines. The concept of writing across the curriculum is an admirable but insufficient attempt to remedy the damage when it is already too late. (I think it also works against my concept of English as the master discipline for critical thinking across the curriculum.)

One statement in support of my arguments here was in *The Humanities in American Life* in 1980:

> High schools should concentrate on an articulated sequence of courses in English, history, and foreign languages. Courses in these disciplines should not divorce skills and methods from knowledge of content and cultural context. . . . English courses need to emphasize the connections between expression, logic, and the critical use of textual and historical evidence. (44)

71

Another supporting statement, from a surprising source, appeared in Gary Olson's *JAC* interview with none other than Jacques Derrida, who sounded much like E. D. Hirsch:

> Q. Most European universities do not offer courses in writing. Is composition taught in French universities? If not, do you think that formal courses in writing should be taught there?
>
> A. No, there is no such instruction in France. We don't teach composition, as such. Of course, through the teaching of French and literature, there has been, or there should be, the concurrent teaching of composition. The teacher of French literature, for example requires students to write correctly, elegantly, and so forth. There are grammatical and stylistic norms. . . . There should be parallel teaching of composition everywhere: in the teaching of French literature, of history, and so on. . . . Of course, the minimal requirements in grammar, clarity of exposition, and so on can be addressed everywhere. . . .
>
> Q. In fact, there's a model here that we call "writing across the disciplines" in which all or many of the academic departments are involved in the teaching of writing.
>
> A. I don't know what your feeling is, but is it possible to teach writing without being competent in the content of a discipline? You can't teach writing simply as a formal technique. Each technique is determined by the specific content of the field. (125–26)

I would expand Derrida's last point to say that specific, exigent topics that prompt one to write about them determine technique. I have always found organization to be the most difficult part of writing to teach or to practice oneself. Consider the technique of organizing an essay for effective coherence, continuity, and comprehensibility, a technique that cannot be taught through generic formulas, without a specific substantive context— though this is what many English teachers and textbooks try to do, through all-purpose models like the funnel-shaped essay or argumentative schemas like tagmemic heuristics, the Toulmin Model, or stasis theory. I have struggled for years to wrestle the extensive subject matter of this chapter and the rest of the book, with their wide scope of ideas, academic disciplines, and sources, into a cogent exposition—a feat that I have not wholly succeeded in, as I am sure critics will be quick to point out. No formula whatsoever has been useful—only multiple drafts, endless experiments in cutting and pasting, and feedback from colleagues familiar with the subject matter. Students likewise depend on feedback from the teacher, preferably with more knowledge of the subject matter, and from peers *who have studied the same material.* So we may be able to help a student or colleague at the stage of assembling and evaluating sources, and again in revising after the fact, at which point we might apply general analytic guidelines, but only in the specific context of the topic. Every task of substantial writing is unique, not only in organization but in style and tone, all shaped by the distinct challenge of the subject matter and the rhetorical situation of the writer. That is why I am sympathetic to Hirsch's argument that teaching of reading and writing skills at all levels is most effective within the study of disciplinary, factual knowledge, and to his model curricula, textbooks, and tests based on this principle, although they also need to be integrated with critical-thinking and rhetorical perspectives. It also goes without saying that this concept of writing instruction cannot work at all in large, assembly-line classes taught by overworked graduate students or adjuncts.

A 1991 National Endowment for the Humanities report titled *National Tests: What Other Countries Expect Their Students to Know* presented academic high school graduation and college entrance exam questions from Europe and Japan. The British General Certificate of Education exam in history consists of four essays in three hours, with this preface:

> Ensure that you pay close attention to the specific wording of the question, answer all its aspects and maintain strict relevance to its requirements.
>
> *When writing an essay, it is necessary to frame an argument and to use information as evidence to support your case; descriptive or narrative material is of limited value.* [My emphasis.] Appropriate references to historical sources will be credited.
>
> You are reminded of the necessity for good English and orderly presentation in your answers. (59)

The essay questions in American history include, "'It was necessary to free the slaves to win the war; the war was not fought to free the slaves.' Discuss this judgment of the Civil War" (59). Also, "Examine the causes and consequences of the black migration from south to north in the inter-war period" (60). And "To what extent does the conduct of American foreign policy, 1954–74, offer evidence for the existence and influence of a 'military-industrial complex'?" (60). The other countries' exams expect a comparable level of writing and critical-thinking abilities *and* factual knowledge about the United States—in addition to far greater knowledge about their own countries. It is essential to recognize, however, that the questions on exams like this and the French *bac* are based on topics that students have been directly studying in their courses, a notion that Hirsch has recently advocated for application here.

Such international comparisons are, of course, complicated by many variables. It was often argued in the past, for example, that the pool of students admitted to universities was far more restricted than in America. This may have been true in the past, but much evidence suggests that the disparity has been narrowed, and even reversed, in recent decades when other countries have made a concerted effort to prepare more students and provide more financial support for college. According to one recent report, the United States declined from first place a decade earlier to thirteenth in 2000 in percentage of the population that goes to college (Gomstyn). Such variables, however, seem to me beside the main point. Shouldn't the United States be willing and able to educate *all* high school graduates to the level of these exams? Shouldn't every high school (and college!) graduate be able to analyze the causal relation between slavery and the Civil War, the causes and consequences of black migration to the North, and disputes about the military-industrial complex? And shouldn't we college educators be lobbying to bring about the public policies needed to raise primary and secondary education nationwide to that level?

National Tests was commissioned by Lynne Cheney as chair of the NEH in 1991. I admit to being bemused about agreeing with Cheney, with whom I have clashed on other matters, in endorsing this report. (See my "Ground Rules for Polemicists.") I can only surmise that implementation of the standards in the report that she advocated would have been intolerable to Cheney, other Republican leaders, and their mass base, both in the liberal implications of many of the exam questions and in their level of difficulty, since implementing them would cost vastly more public funds for education than would ever be supported by Republicans, whose perennial calls for higher standards are rarely matched with comparable calls for increased spending. Republican ideologues like Cheney and William J. Bennett also waffle between calling for rigorous, impartial academic or intellectual inquiry and demanding pro-American indoctrination. It is an anomaly of the American culture wars that the defense of these realms of learning has been conceded to conservatives, while progressives have figured, if the right supports it, it must be bad. However, it is obvious from the kind of essay topics in *National Tests* that a substantial bank of historical, geographical, and political facts is necessary (though not sufficient in isolation from critical thinking) for enlightened progressive forces.

So I think that conservatives like Cheney, Diane Ravitch and Chester Finn (in *What Do Our Seventeen-Year-Olds Know?*), and especially E. D.

Hirsch, in spite of some dubious positions, have been on the right track in their emphasis on deficiencies in American schooling for a common base and minimal standards of factual knowledge and vocabulary concerning civic literacy and its integration with reading and writing instruction. Perhaps the most important aspect of Hirsch's *Cultural Literacy* has been virtually ignored by composition scholars: the empirical research, confirming the earlier National Assessment of Educational Progress (NAEP) reports, showing that college students whose reading and writing skills function well in dealing with personal experience and knowledge often are stymied when they encounter academic discourse and readings with vocabulary or elementary historical or cultural allusions outside their personal knowledge. One example Hirsch gives is a reading passage that assumes minimal knowledge about the facts of the Civil War, along similar lines to the question in *National Tests* applying critical thinking, specifically causal analysis, to the relation of slavery to the war.

Hirsch's emphasis in *Cultural Literacy* on the primacy of factual knowledge in learning rankled many progressive educators, as though he was a Gradgrind forcing "rote memorization" of lists of facts on students. This impression was prompted by his subtitle, "What Every American Needs to Know" and its infamous accompanying list of facts. What they misunderstood was that the subtitle and lists were not prescriptive but descriptive and empirically derived, of the vocabulary needed to understand "the information that is assumed without explanation in magazines like the *Atlantic* and general circulation books" (136). Is it outlandish to expect all Americans to be educated to read at that level, or that of the *Wall Street Journal*, *New York Times*, the *Nation*, and *Weekly Standard*, which I assign in all my courses? His list of terms was not intended as complete, immutable, or sufficient in itself for learning, but only as a tentative and partial foundation for the knowledge that is *necessary but not sufficient* to build on toward a common culture that transcends identity politics. (Obviously, as Hirsch acknowledges, the nature of this knowledge is always somewhat in flux and open to additions, most recently of a multicultural nature.) What Hirsch actually says, as opposed to straw-man accounts, poses a crucial question that multiculturalists have evaded: what minimal factual knowledge and level of reading performance are needed by all Americans, regardless of their identity group, in order for them to act in their own interests in the public sphere and in order for democracy to function? (I will return to the issue of progressive educators' resistance to national standards and core curricula in chapter 9.)

In addition, Hirsch's lists of terms were not just to be memorized but taught within the context of subject-area courses and integrated with critical thinking, along lines that Hirsch and his associates have developed in their Core-Knowledge schools. He has refined and described applications of this approach in recent works like *The Making of Americans: Democracy and Our Schools* and a spin-off column, "Reading Test Dummies," in the *New York Times* in 2009:

> The schools have long imagined that reading is merely a "skill" that can be transferred from one passage to another, and that reading scores can be raised by having young students endlessly practice strategies on trivial stories. Tragic amounts of time have been wasted that could have been devoted to enhancing knowledge and vocabulary, which would actually raise reading comprehension scores. . . . Let's imagine a different situation. Students now must take annual reading tests from third grade through eighth. If the reading passages on each test were culled from each grade's specific curricular content in literature, science, history, geography and the arts, the tests would exhibit what researchers call "consequential validity"—meaning that the tests would actually help improve education. Test preparation would focus on the content of the tests, rather than continue the fruitless attempt to teach test taking.

Hirsch adds, "Our current reading tests are especially unfair to disadvantaged students. The test passages may be random, but they are not knowledge-neutral." He cuts through the Gordian knot of cultural bias in testing by proposing that all tests be directly based on course content that has been the common ground of all students—as is the practice in many other countries. That might seem only to shift the cultural bias from testing to course content, but Hirsch anticipates this objection in *The Making* with extensive models of courses that reconcile cultural differences with common-core knowledge, whose content has been democratically negotiated in communities and whose mastery is agreed by the diverse community representatives to be to the advantage of every cultural group. (The main problem I see in this policy is how it could be implemented in the kind of homogeneous, white-bread communities in which I grew up. In other words, Hirsch's proposal inadvertently avoids the issue of segregated school communities, which is an obstacle to implementation of *any* unbiased curriculum.)

Confusion over Academic Vocabulary, Logic, and Argumentation

Hirsch has been one of the few university-level English theorists in recent decades to emphasize academic vocabulary building—mainly in K-12 but with obvious implications for college study—though Gerald Graff's *Clueless in Academe* has a welcome chapter on bridging the gap between student and academic vocabularies, and Bartholomae and Petrosky also address the problem, though from a very different perspective, as we will see in chapter 7. Hirsch's positions on the relation of vocabulary and factual knowledge to academic discourse are close to Mina Shaughnessy's in *Errors and Expectations*, the *locus classicus* on this nexus. (Hirsch was one of Shaughnessy's many devoted colleagues and disciples.)

Champions of multiculturalism and diversity have tended to view vocabulary expansion as a zero-sum game, in which students must choose either academic vocabulary and discourse or their own "discursive voices which conflict with and struggle against the voices of academic authority" (Horner and Lu 173)—the former viewed as politically conservative and the latter progressive. In writing on Shaughnessy, these theorists have tended to ignore, if not to denigrate, her analysis of academic vocabulary and discourse in basic writing courses, as well as the importance she placed on them in her germinal 1977 article in *CCC*, "Some Needed Research on Writing":

> We need above all else to take a closer look at vocabulary, which is of course critical to the development of complex concepts, the maturation of syntax, and the acquisition of an appropriate tone or register. This is probably the least cultivated field in all the composition research, badly, barrenly treated in texts and not infrequently abandoned between the desks of reading teachers and writing teachers. We lack a precise taxonomy of the academic vocabulary that might enable us to identify those words and those features of words that would lead themselves to direct instruction or that might enable us to hypothesize realistic and multi-dimensional timetables for vocabulary growth. . . . In short, the territory of academic rhetoric—its vocabulary, its conventions, its purposes—is waiting for an Aristotle. (320)

In *Errors and Expectations*, published the same year, Shaughnessy herself became that Aristotle, in a forty-page chapter on "Vocabulary" and a fifty-page chapter on "Beyond the Sentence," constituting about a third of the book. These passages also present a more cogent general account of the role of academic discourse, logic, and argument in writing courses *at different levels* than do any of these recent theorists. Shaughnessy uses both the phrase "academic discourse" (237) and a variety of other phrases including "the dominant code of literacy" and "the general dialect of literacy" (13), "the code that governs formal written English" and "the dialect of formal writing" (45), "academic language" (187), "the vocabulary of general literacy" (237), "the idioms of academic prose" (287), and "the vocabulary of logical relationships" (205), which I will emphasize here. Her categories in the vocabulary of general literacy that basic writers need to master, cited above in my chapter 3, incorporate elements of Hirschian cultural literacy (for example, *Gandhi, the French Revolution, Marxism*), logical and critical-thinking terminology (*generalize, document, prove, causation, condition*), modes of discourse (*define, compare, summarize, interpret*), and literary-rhetorical terms (*irony, figures of speech, fiction, drama, novel*).

She further argues, most significantly, that academic discourse is "the language of public transactions—educational, civic, and professional" (125) and "the common language not only of the university but of the public and professional world outside" (187). In other words, academic discourse is, or should be, the groundwork for both participating in and critiquing public argument—for students of all classes, races, and genders. As for the objection that not all social groups have equal power to acquire academic discourse and participate in pubic argument, I do not see the solution as being to denigrate academic discourse but to make our first priority enacting socioeconomic policies equalizing access to it.

Shaughnessy brilliantly analyzes the difficulties that students' lack of facility in vocabulary and other components of academic discourse lead to in critical-thinking operations like reasoning between cause and effect, the personal and impersonal, abstract and concrete, generalizations and cases, literal and figurative, past, present, and future; or like sentence-level or whole-essay coordination and subordination, cumulation and recursiveness in exposition or argument. (For examples, see her p. 240.) Shaughnessy relates development of a sense of time to use of tenses and historical perspective, as well as to reading or writing complex passages, which requires suspension of the normal flow of time in the continuous present orientation in which we are immersed during most of our life (especially in the thrall of mass media's fixation on continually disposed sound-and-visual bites), and necessitates stopping to process coordinate and subordinate ideas (as in this sentence itself), multiple levels of meaning, allusions, figures of speech, irony and paradox. This is the same process Neil Postman describes in contrast to "The TV Curriculum" that I cited in chapter 3.

Shaughnessy soberly recognizes that this whole panoply of academic vocabulary, grammatical, organizational, and logical issues cannot be "covered" in any single course, especially basic writing, though it can be brought to BW students' consciousness as the goal to be pursued throughout college study and the rest of one's life.

The responsibility for vocabulary development must be shared by all teachers and not isolated in the "remedial" wing of a college, as if vocabulary were a prerequisite course rather than the medium of instruction in all courses. Here the possibility of combining skills and content instruction offers the skills teacher a real vocabulary world to work in and the content teacher expert help in assessing vocabulary difficulty and developing vocabulary materials. (225)

In her concluding chapter, Shaughnessy also suggests a three-semester developmental sequence of eight broad topics for writing courses, two beyond BW, though the boundary lines are flexible; a unit on vocabulary is fifth and "Order and Development," including "Combined patterns in argument and analysis," is sixth—both obviously in the second or third term. The genres culminate with the complete essay, reviews, and the research paper (285–86), which form the basis for the kind of second-term or advanced comp courses I have mainly taught. Coming back to the limits of BW, she next outlines a possible one-term course, mainly on grammar, syntax, and spelling, which culminates with "Vocabulary—prefixes, suffixes, roots, abstract-concrete words, precision" (289). She then adds:

The student is ready by the second semester to take up assignments that will increase his power to sustain commentary over longer and longer units of discourse without losing his or his readers' bearings. . . . Reading now becomes a major source of data for the development of ideas, and the structures of essays should become more elaborate. (290)

Errors and Expectations remains a monumental accomplishment, both as a virtuoso synthesis of interdisciplinary scholarship toward delineating basic writing as a subject of advanced academic study and as a compendium of practical guidance for teaching. I would only take issue with Shaughnessy, or focus on ideas that are (perhaps necessarily) not fully developed, at a few relevant points here. Her chapter "Vocabulary" includes a section titled "Reading" (222–24), which touches on different views about the role of reading in writing courses, but only concentrates on the relation between the reading and writing process, without delving into the possible uses of different kinds or levels of readings in BW. (As she rightly says on 290, extensive use of readings probably is best deferred to second-semester and advanced courses.) Everything in my experience indicates that the most important variable for acquiring academic discourse in beginning college writers is the amount and quality of the reading they have done in the years prior to college, with the natural assimilation of reading into writing. As

Shaughnessy says, "More important than remembering the forms and definitions of words is having the judgment to use them in appropriate ways, a judgment that comes not from the study of vocabulary lists but from having been a steady reader of the kind of writing people do in college" (188). (I would phrase it, "a steady reader of approximately the kind of texts studied in college.") How to make up that difference at the late stage of beginning college is the dilemma. Perhaps a course in basic reading in addition to basic writing? Bartholomae and Petrosky's *Facts, Artifacts, and Counterfacts* was a bold attempt to build on Shaughnessy in integrating basic reading and writing in a single BW course, to which I will return in chapter 7.

There is much equivocation among composition theorists between the multiple meanings of the word *logic* (a point I return to in chapter 6), which even Shaughnessy perhaps slips into. On pages 236–37 of "Beyond the Sentence," she addresses faulty logic in student writing, which she says often leads teachers to conclude "that thinking rather than writing ought to be the focus of his instruction, that in fact once the student has 'learned to think,' the task of writing down his thoughts will come easily." She rejects this conclusion because "it assumes that because thoughts, once they have been generated, can be shown to reflect various patterns of logic which can be analyzed and reproduced, it is possible to generate thought through the analysis of logic." She adds, "We can observe in many students over the course of their training in college an increase in their specifying and generalizing powers, but we cannot link this growth to particular forms or subjects of instruction." I question several points here. First, perhaps Shaughnessy's point was relevant to BW courses, but surely not to subsequent courses in argumentative writing, which centrally include study of at least informal logic. Wilfred Stone and J. G. Bell's excellent first-term handbook *Prose Style*, first published in 1968, used the apt phrase "The Logic of Argument," and that was preceded in 1963 by *The Logic and Rhetoric of Composition*, by Harold C. Martin, James Wheatley, and Richard M. Ohmann (long a beacon of lucidity in composition, currently going strong in his eighties). Other textbooks on rhetorical approaches to writing also incorporate elements of logic with greater or lesser distinction between logic and rhetoric in the manner of Plato or Aristotle.

Furthermore, Shaughnessy's dismissal of teaching *logic* here is based more on the philosophical study of formal logic than on informal logic, aka "critical thinking," a phrase that she does not use, at least in the sense of a distinct discipline, but whose components she employs copiously—for instance, she includes as part of "the vocabulary of general literacy" and "the vocabulary of logical relationships" words like "*generalize, document, prove, causation, condition*." The California State University mandate for critical-thinking instruction, issued in 1980, just three years after *Errors and Expectations*, put more emphasis on "the ability to distinguish fact from judgment, belief from knowledge, and skills in elementary inductive and deductive processes, including an understanding of the formal and informal fallacies of language and thought" (Dumke). An interesting historical study might be made of the exigencies that produced *Errors* and these guidelines at nearly the same time, and of the different cognitive emphases between the two.

Nor does Shaughnessy explicitly consider logic in the context of cognitive and moral-reasoning development during college education, which is central to many models of critical thinking, in a manner like that of William Perry's 1970 *Forms of Intellectual and Ethical Development in the College Years*, though she does cite Piaget and Vygotsky on childhood stages of development like moving from the concrete to the abstract and from egocentrism or sociocentrism to reciprocity and reader-based writing. Perry, and later Lawrence Kohlberg, describes elements of critical thinking though not of formal logic (see chapter 11). (Andrea Lunsford's previously noted articles "Cognitive Development and the Basic Writer" in 1979 and "The Content of Basic Writers' Essays" in 1980 supplemented Shaughnessy on Perry and Kohlberg.) Shaughnessy, again, applies some principles of cognitive development cited in my summary above, but not as directly as Kytle in *Clear Thinking for Composition*, whose central section on "Blocks to Logical Thinking" drew from developmental psychology in identifying obstacles to college students' reasoning about politics, such as absolutism ("primary certitude"), authoritarianism, ethnocentrism, rationalization, and compartmentalization, along similar lines to critical thinking scholarship surveyed in my chapter 3.

I also take mild issue with Shaughnessy's (and many other composition theorists') denial that "because thoughts, once they have been generated, can be shown to reflect various patterns of logic which can be analyzed and reproduced, it is possible to generate thought through the analysis of logic." First, this denial elides the issue of logical fallacies that students commit in their own thought and writing, which in turn often stem from immature stages of development in moral reasoning, which in turn often reflect sociopolitical conformity, dualism, or authoritarianism. (Think of my student who wrote about charges of corruption against a presidential cabinet member that "only wants what's best for the U.S., that's why he was elected.") Isn't pointing out these fallacies and discussing how they might be corrected an important means of generating thought?

Finally, concerning Shaughnessy's and other theorists' exclusion of the analysis of logic from writing courses, shouldn't evaluating the logic *in source readings* be an essential part of critical reading and writing instruction, at least in an advanced course in argumentation and the research paper that includes critical analysis of sources? Such analysis can be foregrounded within course units on inductive and deductive reasoning, fallacies, semantic slanting, refutation, and psychological blocks to critical thinking—preeminently in application to analysis of political advocacy or propaganda, advertising, and other sources and techniques of deceptive reasoning. Howard Kahane and Nancy Cavender's *Logic and Contemporary Rhetoric* was strong in this focus (though as previously noted, it was mainly a philosophy/critical-thinking textbook). Gerald Graff and Cathy Birkenstein's more recent *They Say, I Say* is based on rhetorical "templates" for rebuttal that the authors have usefully expanded, in editions after the first, into a broader mode of critical analysis of readings on politics, economics, and mass media, though in an ad hoc manner that does not incorporate an overview of the logic of argument or the rhetoric of public discourse.

Shaughnessy's Critics

All these complex issues raised by *Errors and Expectations* have been muddied by postmodernist critics' distortions of Shaughnessy. Harris in *A Teaching Subject* egregiously misreads Shaughnessy's concluding chapter by focusing only on the section on the first-semester course and ignoring the rest of her proposed sequence, which is in turn based largely on her two longest chapters, "Vocabulary" and "Beyond the Sentence." On the basis of this bit of cherry-picking he claims the book "remains, again, after everything else is said about it, a book on teaching grammar" (80). And, "Her measures of good writing . . . centered on fluency and correctness at the almost total expense of meaning" (81). Everything I have cited from Shaughnessy here contradicts this calumny; her central focus is on how exactitude and correctness in vocabulary and syntax serve to *construct* cogent meaning. Even in that first semester, mastering the logical relationship of elements within the sentence and beyond is vastly more difficult, more foundational for academic discourse and civic literacy, than Harris and other critics like Min-Zhan Lu recognize.

Lu's 1991 article "Redefining the Legacy of Mina Shaughnessy: A Critique of the Politics of Linguistic Innocence" takes Shaughnessy to task for "innocence" and "essentialism" in assuming the political neutrality of academic discourse and failing to take account of it as an agent of cultural imperialism oppressing students coming from marginalized discourse communities.[1] As noted in chapter 1 above, Horner and Lu's postmodern notion of education as "a site of conflict, contradiction, and tension" pits students' discursive voices against the voices of academic authority, which support what they earlier term "the dominant social and political forces" (xiii). But for Shaughnessy, "academic discourse" enables critical thinking, which in turn enables critical engagement with the dominant social and political forces, so formulations like Horner and Lu's pose a disastrously false binary. (Don't "the voices of academic authority" include all of us scholars and public intellectuals who encourage social conflict and struggle for justice—such as Horner and Lu?) In chapter 5, I examine some of Lu's criticisms of specific passages in Shaughnessy, which I find labored and petty. None of her arguments seem to me to present evidence that any of the passages in Shaughnessy surveyed above about either vocabulary, the logic of syntax and continuity of exposition and analysis, or the logic of argument itself (though she only indirectly addresses it) are intrinsically biased culturally—excluding any American social groups from learning them, given a supporting environment, or opposed to their political interests. Are Gandhi, the French Revolution, and Marx agents of the dominant social and political forces? Nor can these bodies of factual knowledge and reasoning be reduced just to discursive "voices" or "sites of conflict." Advancing such arguments against Shaughnessy leads toward some of the wilder versions of antirationalism and dismissals of logic itself that I address in chapter 6.

In my earlier discussion of the tacit presence in Shaughnessy of principles of developmental psychology in relation to informal logic, I mentioned that Andrea Lunsford's articles in 1979 and 1980 supplemented Shaughnessy in applying Perry and Lawrence Kohlberg to BW. Alas, soon thereafter, the more doctrinaire postmodern pluralists declared that the very notions of cognitive or moral development and higher order reasoning are a Eurocentric, masculinist snare and delusion, a mere tool of Foucauldian surveillance, punishment, or "gatekeeping" in writing courses—rather than a potential opening of the gate (for all races, classes, and genders) to autonomous thinking and self-defense against political demagogy, propaganda, and commercial mass media, *which always aim at "lower-order reasoning."*

Again, it is true that not all social groups have equal opportunity to acquire academic discourse and its access to developing higher stages of reasoning and participating in public arguments. However, I do not see the solution as denigrating academic discourse, but as making our first priority to enact political and economic policies equalizing access to it—a view that has been shared by leftists like Karl Marx, Leon Trotsky, Antonio Gramsci, and our contemporaries like Jonathan Kozol, Stanley Aronowitz, Susan Searls Giroux, and Henry Giroux.

Even the usually undoctrinaire David Bartholomae, citing Lunsford in her 1979–80 articles among other developmentalists, rejects their view, in which he claims, "Basic writers . . . are seen as childlike or as uncultured natives. There is an imperial frame to this understanding of the situation of those who are not like us." Here Bartholomae comes close to the postmodern-pluralist position that college education should be just a carnival of diverse discourse communities and discursive voices, with no clear-cut demarcation line in levels of cognitive development between basic writing students and professors, which I think is coyly Rousseauan. (Bruce Horner follows the same antidevelopmentalist line in "Mapping Errors and Expectation," a chapter in *Representing*.) But consider the several student papers I discussed in chapters 2 and 3, such as students A and B, who rebutted Susan Giroux's article about the wealth gap. Would Horner and Lu praise these students' "struggle against the voices of academic authority," here the voice of Giroux? Would Bartholomae consider it "an imperial frame" to consider their thinking to be at an ethnocentric, dualistic, or authoritarian stage of development in moral reasoning, or to point out the dizzying number of fallacies and signs of sheer factual ignorance? (See my discussion in chapter 11 of Lunsford's study of different developmental levels of reasoning and factual knowledge in papers expressing students' opinions toward capital punishment.)

One other, related source of semantic confusion, which I develop more fully in chapter 6, is ambiguity in the meaning(s) of "affect" and "emotion," as privileged by some feminist and other theorists against "reason" and "rational argument." When I oppose rationality to irrationality, the latter refers to "emotional appeal" as the classical logical fallacy, in varieties like "appeal to fear" and "appeal to pity," precisely the manner of demagogues and propagandists who always appeal to lower-order reasoning, such as zealotry, bigotry, ethnocentrism, and xenophobia. Nothing I say disparages personal testament and justifiable emotion as means of supporting a rational argument, nor is this nexus necessarily tied to gender or cultural differences. David Coleman, director of the Common Core State Standards, provoked ire within English circles by writing about their aim: "People really don't give a sheet about what you feel or what you think." But his next sentence was, "What they instead care about is can you make an argument with evidence, is there something verifiable behind what you're saying or what you think or feel that you can demonstrate to me?" (*Introduction*).

Still another variant on the reason/emotion binary appears in *Women's Ways of Knowing* by Belenky et al., which makes a thought-provoking distinction between the words *knowledge* and *comprehension*; the authors suggest that the former can imply a purely rational, impersonal way of knowing—with masculine inflection—while the latter can have the different, female-inflected meaning of understanding, inclusion, and compassion. The authors admirably avoid turning this distinction into a killer dichotomy, as some of their followers have done, but instead pose the two modes as complementary, sensibly just calling for more recognition by men as well as women of this "feminine" dimension of knowledge. I return to their distinction within a context of developmental psychology in chapter 11, but here I just want to identify it as one of the many praiseworthy sources that have been misappropriated toward false formulations of opposition between reason and emotion or affect.

Marginalizing Logic and Argument in the Profession

All the confusion over these aspects of logic and argument has resulted in their being minimized in the mainstream of recent scholarly composition books, journals, and curricula. In journals, for example, among the very few recent articles studying argumentation in *CCC*, A. Abby Knoblauch's "A Textbook Argument: Definitions of Argument in Leading Composition Textbooks" in December 2011 is mostly limited to discussion of *argument* versus *persuasion* and of Rogerian argument versus the Toulmin Model, with no mention of analyzing arguments, political or other. Marilyn M. Cooper's "Rhetorical Agency as Emergent and Enacted," in the February 2011 *CCC*, reads like a parody of Alan Sokal's famous parody of poststructuralist jargon in *Social Text*. Its ostensible concrete example, Barack Obama's 2008 speech on race, gets swamped by a theoretical disquisition "drawing on neurophenomenology" (421) and pondering issues like the "'carceral model of subjectivity,' as a nonporous, inflexible category into which subjects are interpellated by ideology and determined by discourse'" (423). (Although Cooper is a past editor of *CCC* and teaches composition at Michigan Technological College, this article seems to me more suited to a journal in phenomenological philosophy than to one for college writing teachers, especially at schools like Michigan Tech or Cal Poly, where I taught.) I discuss Ian Barnard's antilogic tract "The Ruse of Clarity" from February 2010 in chapter 6. The only recent article I could find that actually models analysis of arguments was "Rhetorical Numbers: A Case for Quantitative Writing in the Composition Classroom" by Joanna Wolfe, a refreshingly clear call for rhetorical analysis of current economic statistics, in stark contrast to Barnard's article in the same issue.

I surmise that the hole in the curriculum is a combined byproduct, once again, of the fixation on students generating their own ideas or arguments, rather than on analyzing others' (even in some textbook anthologies in which readings on a vast array of subjects are typically framed as prompts for students' own responses or emulation), and the lack of national consistency within writing programs of a clearly defined, developmental sequence of writing courses, along the line suggested by Shaughnessy, from BW to FYW, to a second term of FYW or advanced courses on critical thinking, argumentative rhetoric, and evaluation of sources. Even the many excellent rhetorics and readers in argumentation or critical reading are bafflingly diffuse in organizational principles, topics of readings, and course levels; many state that they are intended mainly for first-year writing courses, without specifying whether this assumes a one-term or two-term course, and if for one term, how the massive contents of such books can conceivably be incorporated with everything else usually expected to be covered in that term. Pressures applied by the major textbook publishers present additional impediments, as they seek to maximize their market by keeping the wording vague about what kind and level of courses books are designed for, and as they squeamishly steer authors away from foregrounding political controversies. Another curiosity about textbooks is that while many of their recent editions have incorporated more political and economic issues, there has been far less attention to such issues in the main composition journals, again with the exception of *JAC*. And while this development in textbooks presents important issues for theoretical considerations such as those I pursue here, there is a policy against reviewing textbooks in the major English journals, and they get very little attention as topics for scholarly articles, books, and conference papers.

Sharon Crowley's *Composition in the University* presents a powerful critique of the impossible expectations that have been piled onto one-semester FYW courses, but it gets somewhat vague in addressing the place of argumentation and logic in them. In a section criticizing current-traditional rhetoric, Crowley notes that argument was one of four genres covered by that school, but, "The current-traditional course of study can hardly be called practical in the sense that it prepared students to engage with issues, since it never addressed the quality of a student's argument or its suitability to a given rhetorical situation" (94–95). In the context of a survey of the shift from current-traditional pedagogy to process instruction, she notes, "While many programs say they move students into the composition of argumentative or persuasive writing in the second course, they actually focus on composition of a research paper, which is a current-traditional exercise in exposition rather than in argumentation" (220). But she does not delineate what approaches to argumentation would be preferable. Her other references to the teaching of argumentation tend to be similarly noncommittal or negative. In critiquing the 1993 edition of *The Bedford Guide for College Writers*, she says, "Under the topic of 'revising and editing,' the authors give their students a short course in the detection of logical fallacies, another inheritance from the current-traditional theory of discourse" (212). This unit in the *Bedford* only applied to students revising to detect their own logical fallacies, not detecting those of sources as a central activity—but Crowley doesn't pursue this point either, even to the extent of saying whether she thinks detection of logical fallacies both in sources and one's own writing is a useful practice, in either a first-term or more advanced course.

In the same section Crowley criticizes Lad Tobin's summary of a 1992 conference on the writing process: "Now, traditional opponents of process pedagogy argue, is the time to get back to the basics: that is, back to grammar, usage, logic, argumentation, belles lettres, great literature" (213). But throughout Crowley's history of twentieth-century composition courses, logic and argumentation appear to have played a scant role in them, and she does not comment on Tobin's inclusion of them as "basics" or on the support by other composition traditionalists she criticizes, for their emphasis on logic and argumentation, a cause that has also recently been picked up by political conservatives. If those traditionalists and conservatives want to get back to course requirements (beyond FYW) in the basics of eighteenth- or early nineteenth-century argumentative rhetoric—whose goal Michael Halloran describes as to "address students as political beings, as members of a body politic in which they have a responsibility to form judgments and influence the judgments of others on public issues" ("Rhetoric" 108)—I count myself among them. (I will come back in chapter 6 to the attempt by conservatives in the culture wars to champion logic and argumentation against their widespread abandonment by academic pluralists.)

In the final section of her book, "Writing Beyond Freshman English," Crowley does laudably sketch out what a "vertical" or full curriculum in rhetoric might include, with "a commitment to understanding and teaching public discourse" and to "influencing the course of cultural and political events" (263). Unfortunately, so much of her book has been devoted to detailing her case against requiring FYW that these few pages at the end are left sketchy. Nor does she connect her analysis with her own viewpoint as coauthor with Debra Hawhee of an argumentation textbook, *Ancient Rhetorics for the Contemporary Student*, which applies extensive sections on logic to current political rhetoric—the central topic of ancient rhetorics, as Crowley and Hawhee emphasize. That book is a worthy successor to Edward P. J. Corbett's *Classical Rhetoric for the Modern Student*, though Corbett in my opinion had the advantage of more emphasis on fallacies and refutation. (Its first two editions included a reading by John Illo, "The Rhetoric of Malcolm X"—emphasizing Malcolm's expert use of classical tropes and refutations of white delusions—which I consider a perfect model for analysis of political rhetoric, but which unfortunately got dropped in the third edition.) I assigned Corbett in my master's-level comp theory class at Cal Poly, and that also seems to be the most appropriate level for Crowley and Hawhee, although it has been adopted in some FYW courses.

Two significant research projects have recently been devoted to the issues addressed in this chapter. Andrea Lunsford and Karen Lunsford's 2008 survey in *CCC*, which compared the topics most often currently taught in FYW to twenty years earlier, indicated, "Emphasis on personal narrative has been replaced by an emphasis on argument and research" ("Mistakes" 793). "Researched argument or report" is first on their list, and "Close reading and analysis" is third, with "Argument with very few or no sources" second. Their study confirms my point that the paucity of recent professional articles, books, and conference sessions on either researched argument or close reading indicates a strange disconnect between topics privileged in theory and those applicable to most current courses.

The Citation Project is a multi-institutional research effort whose initial aim was to study plagiarism in college student papers but whose scope has widened to study students' critical uses of research sources. The *Chronicle of Higher Education* featured its work in an article by Dan Berrett, "Freshman Composition Is Not Teaching Key Skills in Analysis, Researchers Argue" (30 March 2012, A29), based on presentations at the 2011 and 2012 CCCC and on interviews with two of its directors, Rebecca Moore Howard, professor of writing and rhetoric at Syracuse, and Sandra Jamieson, professor and chair of English at Drew, concerning their research on "the process by which students find, evaluate, and use the sources they cite." The project focused on research paper assignments in first-semester courses and students' problems with them, about which Howard is quoted as saying, "It's very clear that they don't know how to analyze their sources." Jamieson offered an example of a student paper on eating disorders for which the author quoted uncritically from sources including a best-selling diet book by an agent for a modeling agency and a trade-association press release. According to Jamieson, "The problem is that this is a site that provides secondhand data at best and with a commercial slant. It's the lack of critical thinking that says, 'Wait, can I trust this source?'" Howard and Jamieson concluded that the research paper should be scrapped altogether and replaced by shorter papers throughout the course, for which students "are trained to read, analyze, and synthesize their sources, so that they can identify the argument and sort through the evidence." Howard added, "On the most basic level, it's reading comprehension: finding claims and finding evidence. Then you get to the much more interesting issues of analysis, which is how the writer is persuading the readers of claims."

Dramatic confirmation of the Citation Project's account of these shortcomings in comp courses was provided in reactions in English circles to the emphasis in the 2010 Core Curriculum State Standards (CCSS) Initiative on evidence-based writing in K-12 (more about which in chapter 9). A progress report on CCSS in NCTE's *Council Chronicle* in September 2013 noted,

> Teachers who have asked students to complete reading-writing tasks similar to those being developed for CCSS assessments report that their students are initially unable to produce the kind of evidence-based writing required for these assessments. However, with a rich diet of literacy development, including daily reading and writing, increased emphasis on informational texts, and explicit instruction in strategic reading, students later wrote significantly better. (14)

So these projects by Lunsford and Lunsford and the Citation Project, along with CCSS, might be an indication that the pendulum is swinging back toward the neglected areas of study that I am advocating here.

5

DEGREES OF SEPARATION FROM
ACADEMIC DISCOURSE

Several degrees of separation from Shaughnessy's (and my) conception of academic discourse and critical thinking can be marked in theorists since the 1980s. (As suggested in chapter 1, Bartholomae and Petrosky are key figures here, so it might make the most sense to discuss them at the outset; however, their case is a complex one, demanding lengthy consideration, so I have decided to bump it to chapter 7, where comparisons and contrasts with the others I consider here will also become clearer.) Harris's discussion in *A Teaching Subject*, on pages 88–90, begins with questions about "the workings of the academic discourse community," "the specific conventions of college writing," and the "conceptual and rhetorical problem" in "a stress on specifically academic writing." (In other passages, Harris hints at a broader notion of "critical or intellectual discourse" and "a critical habit of mind," but does not develop it.) Harris next asserts that "this view of academic discourse as a limited and specific *use* of language," despite having some pedagogical value, can "cast its advocates in the role of simply teaching a professional jargon." Harris himself casts them in this role, agreeing with Richard Rorty, who ridicules the notion of teaching freshmen "distinctive disciplinary jargon." There is a serious slippage here from the language and subject matter of liberal education to the specialized discourse of disciplinary scholarship. Harris compounds the slippage in his next chapter: "While I don't mean to discount the effects of belonging to a discipline, I think that we dangerously abstract and idealize the workings of 'academic discourse' by taking the kinds of rarefied talk and writing that go on at conferences and in journals as the norm" (106–7). Thus Harris casually skips over the level of academic discourse that constitutes the entire liberal arts curriculum—along with Shaughnessy's expansion of it into the *lingua franca* not only of the university but of the civic and professional world outside.

Harris's following development only widens these gaps in his position:

> While I almost always ask undergraduates to write on texts and ideas, I rarely ask them to do the sort of reading through the relevant academic

> literature that I would routinely require of graduate students (who *are* training to become professional intellectuals), and I don't spend much time on issues of citation, documentation, and the like. (I rarely even teach anything like the "research paper.") I'm more interested in having students read the work of others closely and aggressively, and to use their reading in thinking and writing about issues that concern them. (89)

Again, isn't there abundant "relevant academic literature," along with journalistic sources about political controversies, accessible to *undergraduates*, not just graduates?

Harris's diminishing of academic discourse simultaneously diminishes the role of politics in writing courses:

> How do writers negotiate among themselves and respond to the voices of others? How do they forge a sense of self among the languages available to them? Such an approach shifts attention from politics as a set of issues one writes about to the politics of writing itself—to questions of style, authority, autonomy, stance. It also suggests that one measure of the politics of a teacher might be the range of voices and perspectives that she helps students take on. (96)

Note the glaring equivocation on the meaning of "politics" here.

In Harris's later *CE* article "Revision," he takes issue with critical pedagogy, particularly in Ira Shor's teaching emphasis on the content of political readings (environmental ones here) for writing assignments, to the neglect of process instruction, and presents as a preferable alternative an emphasis on the revision process in students' writing, supposedly about political issues. But the examples Harris gives from his own courses involve mainly reading fictional stories dealing marginally with social class, while the kind of revision he emphasizes is in the mode of writing-about-literature, and the student writing is again based purely on personal experience and opinions, producing predictable platitudes to the effect of, Dr. Jekyll is rich and has everything he could desire, but it seems like money doesn't buy happiness. Couldn't students go on to write and revise papers about argumentative readings for general readers on social class, like sociologist Stanley Aronowitz's *How Class Works* or literary scholar Benjamin DeMott's *The Imperial Middle: Why Americans Can't Think Straight about Class*?

The culminating example in *A Teaching Subject* of Harris's classroom practices is a discussion of student writing responses to the differing views on racial conflict in Spike Lee's film *Do the Right Thing*, articulated in the film by allusions to the opposition between Martin Luther King and Malcolm

X. These responses were apparently based purely on students' personal experience and opinion. There is no indication that this assignment was extended, as it might well have been, to reading some history of the civil rights movement and urban ghettos, the speeches of King and Malcolm, and *The Autobiography of Malcolm X* or James Baldwin's *The Fire Next Time*, two books that I have frequently taught as great models for the movement in cognitive development from personal narrative to extended, complex argument—though, as noted in chapter 1, many students fixate on the narrative elements and need considerable prompting from the teacher in coping with the difficult vocabulary and syntax of the argumentative sections. A further challenge would be to evaluate these books against recent conservative arguments about race by authors like Thomas Sowell and David Horowitz.

The jacket copy for *A Teaching Subject* says it is about first-year writing, but like many other recent theorists, Harris fails to specify whether he intends passages like those above also to apply to advanced courses, especially in argumentative writing incorporating researched sources, or how his pedagogy would carry over to them, without leaving large gaps between them. Even in first-term FYW, remember, Lunsford and Lunsford reported in 2008 that the most frequently assigned papers are currently "researched argument or report," and the most common student errors are in these processes—although as I have argued, I believe incorporating these subjects in a single, already overburdened FYW course, mostly taught by overburdened adjuncts, is problematic. Harris and others here just evade this whole, thorny issue.

Harris does actually conceive his FYW course as one in argumentation, but with a distinctively postmodernist spin that views "the classroom as a contested space where many discourses and cultures may meet and struggle with each other" (*A Teaching* 117), Much of this kind of praise throughout Harris and other theorists of "contact zones" between different discourse communities, of "polyglot" or "polyphonic" classroom interactions, assumes some approximation of parity, or commensurability, in scope of knowledge and reasoning between students' various community discourses and academic discourse, narrowly construed. But in the broader senses of the term, the claim by these theorists of equivalence in the interaction between academic and nonacademic communities becomes a comparison of apples to oranges, as their proponents ignore vast areas of thought distinctive to academic discourse—as in my example from *The Fire Next Time* in chapter 1. By contrast, consider the components in my model of critical thinking, Shaughnessy's and Hirsch's enumeration of essential factual knowledge and vocabulary, the Rockefeller Commission's "connections between expression, logic, and the critical use of textual and historical evidence," Gouldner's "culture of critical discourse," or Stanley Fish's "In the classroom, the gathering of evidence on the way to reaching a conclusion is the prime academic activity" (*Save* 70) and, "The goal is to establish, by argument and evidence, the superiority of one analysis or description or prescription over its (intellectual) rivals" (*Save* 173).

The postmodernist, multicultural model of argumentation has been favored in *College Composition and Communication* since Harris's editorship in the 1990s, when it was often articulated in opposition to Freirean critical pedagogy and cultural studies—most prominently in the October 1996 issue, where it was reiterated in Susan Wells's "Rogue Cops," Fishman and McCarthy's "Teaching for Student Change" ("Conflict must always occur within the context of appreciation for cooperative inquiry and the virtues that sustain it" [344]), and preeminently Spellmeyer's malicious review of *Left Margins: Cultural Studies and Composition Pedagogy*, edited by Karen Fitts and Alan France. That collection, applying critical pedagogy to writing courses, included my "Teaching the Conflicts about Wealth and Poverty," which described the courses I have discussed in chapters 2 and 3.

In his review and in the exchange about it between Spellmeyer, France, and me in the May 1997 *CCC*, Spellmeyer singled me out in savaging the contempt that its contributors allegedly show toward students' home cultures and personal sensitivities, along with such teachers' alleged attempts to coerce students into submission to academic discourse and their own leftist, cosmopolitan view. I dredge up this ancient feud only because it involved the central issues that I have pursued in this chapter and book, issues that Spellmeyer evaded in using the review to grind his axe against the whole scope of European-influenced cultural studies and the academic left, whose point, he charged, "is not to learn about the everyday world from face-to-face encounters" (427) or from "lived realities that no citation from Gramsci or [Raymond] Williams could have prepared us for" (431). (Ironically, I agree with much in his critique of abstract, esoteric theory, and my article was not based on theory but on my lived realities with the kind of students I have described in chapters 2 and 3.) As noted in chapter 2 above, he defended students' "freedom in a composition course to think and write about their lives without coercion and disparagement." He assumed the course I described was FYW, which he conceived on the "safe house" model, but I had made clear that it was an advanced course in argumentative writing. None of his subsequent writings that I have seen, some of which are excellent, address a developmental sequence between basic or first-year-writing and later courses, and how that sequence should move beyond expressivism.

Ignoring my detailed account of my method for adapting critical pedagogy to affluent, often arrogant conservatives, he denounced my and other critical teachers' "scarcely veiled contempt" for our students, adding, "I must confess that I find Lazere's political thinking quite naive, and I'm sure that some of his students must have felt the same embarrassment for him that I feel myself" (427–28). That's all he wrote. No explanation of what in my thinking was naïve or cause for embarrassment by my students. Did he think they were really adept in following extended political arguments and knowledgeable about opposing theories on tax policy? Or that these topics were unimportant, or too elementary for a second-term argumentative writing course? Or what? How could he be so "sure" that he knew my students better than me after my years of face-to-face encounters with them, when he was writing from across the continent as a writing director at Rutgers, in urban New Brunswick, with totally different student demographics? He contrasted my and other critical teachers' "profound loathing for ordinary people" ("Culture" 295) with the sympathetic studies of poor students and their "multiple literacies and mul- tiple cultures" affirmed by Shirley Brice Heath and Mike Rose ("Out" 431). His account epitomizes those theorists I criticize who have made pluralist populism into the new dogma and who, like Harris celebrating classrooms "where many discourses and cultures may meet," seem unable or unwilling to acknowledge more homogeneously Middle American teaching sites.

What Spellmeyer twisted into critical teachers' loathing for ordinary people was simply, at least in my case, an attempt to make Middle Amer- ican students aware of precisely such loathing by those like my boss on Madison Avenue declaring, "The average housewife is too stupid to know the difference." (Once at CCCC I asked Spellmeyer if he had never worked in a large corporation or mass media, and he said no. So much for "lived realities.") As my citation of Dwight Macdonald in chapter 1 indicated, Spellmeyer's deceptive move here has long been common in the motives of both conservatives and liberals who try to reverse leftist intellectuals' or teachers' critiques of political and corporate "Lords of Masscult" into contempt for the "ordinary people" who are their prey. An extension of this line that has become a staple of postmodern pluralism is to argue, as Spellmeyer implicitly does, that ordinary people are not so easily taken in by efforts at mass manipulation and often are capable of agency through devising ingenious modes of resistance and transgression. This line surely has some validity, but it often has led down a slippery slope to the conclusion that the mechanisms of political or corporate propaganda and social control are no longer a problem at all and need not be a central subject for critique in education. See chapter 6 about a feminist variant on this line.

In sum, I see several limitations to the whole concept of the argumentative writing classroom as a site of negotiating differences among students. First, few of its proponents indicate use of an argumentation textbook or other direct study of informal logic. Second, how can students "articulate differences among themselves" about issues like James Baldwin's history of racism in Christianity, or the wealth gap, political elections and legislation, the military-industrial complex, the global economy, Middle Eastern geopolitics, or even the increasing cost of college without sufficient prior factual knowledge, which few in a first-year English class might have? A similar problem arises with attempts at student-centered literature courses, which often founder because few students have adequate critical reading skills or background knowledge of readings' historical and other context. Third, in the kind of homogeneously Middle American colleges I have described, isn't it the responsibility of teachers to "coerce" students into confronting topics, readings, and data that challenge their ethnocentric consensus, and to "bank" with them a base of factual knowledge and analytic know-how that we have and they don't? (In other colleges where the socioeconomic mix of students is the opposite and the consensus is liberal, the teachers' responsibility would be to compensate by presenting conservative viewpoints.) Fourth, what about the conservative students I have discussed who emulate the bellicose manner of Rush Limbaugh, Ann Coulter, and Bill O'Reilly, attempting to intimidate liberal students, and even teachers, into silence, with zero "appreciation for cooperative inquiry" or "cross-cultural awareness"? Some of these students belong to the networks created by Republican-front organizations including Young Americans for Freedom, Young America's Foundation, the Leadership Institute, the Collegiate Network, and the Intercollegiate Studies Institute, which fund, train, and coordinate college conservatives as classroom provocateurs (see Colapinto). Will those like Harris, Spellmeyer, and Fishman and McCarthy, who are so solicitous about respecting student sensitivities, please tell us how teachers are supposed to deal with these classroom bullies without being coercive or domineering?

Contact-zone theorists like Harris and Spellmeyer, and even some social constructionists, tend to be ingenuous in regarding students' home communities and discourses as free from influence by social-class hierarchies or political propaganda and ideology, as channeled through the communication media that inundate students every day of their lives. (Granted, poor students and minorities may be somewhat less influenced by mass media than the Middle Americans I have taught; this is a good topic for empirical research.) Liberal arts courses are virtually the only place that many students might ever encounter critical questioning of this indoctrination.

Further Degrees of Separation

Other recent rhetcomp scholars have been even more dismissive of academic discourse than Harris. For Ellen Cushman, it is "the production of legitimate (read specialized, publishable, esoteric, academic) language, which gains material, cultural and symbolic capital by implicitly devaluing nonstandard (read colloquial, vernacular, common, vulgar) language" ("The Public" 334–35). For Beth Daniell, it, along with the entire institution of "schooling in the United States as well as in the Third World is a class-based enterprise, serving the status quo and making few allowances for students whose home experiences with language and literacy deviated from middle-class 'ways with words'" ("Narratives" 399).

Min-Zhan Lu's 1991 article "Redefining the Legacy of Mina Shaughnessy: A Critique of the Politics of Linguistic Innocence" discusses a section in *Errors and Expectations* where Shaughnessy praises a revision of a paper written by an inner-city student late in the term, though she identifies points at which the writing could still be improved. The paper is about the oppression of people like the writer's family by politicians and the need for those people to educate themselves and organize in their defense. Lu quotes Shaughnessy saying this writer might be "struggling to develop a language that will enable him to talk analytically with strangers, about the oppression of his parents and his own resolve to work against that oppression" (*Representing* 110). Lu criticizes the presumptions of teachers like Shaughnessy, in passages like this, to understand the psychology of their student "others." Yet Lu herself here, as in many other passages, imperialistically projects into the mind of the student: "To this writer, these 'strangers' are people who already belong to what Shaughnessy calls the world of 'public transactions—educational, civic, and professional' (125) a world that has traditionally excluded people like the writer and his parents. In trying to 'talk analytically,' this writer is also learning the 'stranger's' way of perceiving people like his parents" (110). The implication is that talking analytically, or knowing something about the French Revolution, Marx, and Gandhi, should be shunned. Moreover, these particular "strangers," hapless teachers of basic writing (most likely grad students or beleaguered adjuncts, many of them political progressives), are lumped together indistinguishably with the corporate ruling class as discursive oppressors, wielding the billy club of *talking analytically*. This verges on being a parody of Foucauldian notions of the panopticon of discursive power, eclipsing all hierarchies in capitalist political economy, about whose larger power structures Lu and Horner show relatively little concern in their pedagogical model.

Lu charges that Shaughnessy's "essentialist view of language also seems to have kept her from noticing her own privileging of academic discourse" (113), as though Lu does not privilege academic discourse throughout her own writing. The writings of Lu and Horner (students of Bartholomae and Harris at Pitt) are founded on postmodernist notions like reconceiving education as a site of "conflict, contradiction, and tension," and "a fluid, shifting sense of identity which flies in the face of what Harris calls 'the myth of the autonomous, essential self'" (Horner, *Representing* 135).[1] Yet they never consider that they are perpetuating exactly the kind of essentializing binary that postmodernists reject in depicting conventional college instruction and academic discourse as monoliths of oppression, rather than prime sites throughout their history of internal conflict and contradiction.

Is academic discourse really the monolithic, exclusionary evil that such killer dichotomies suggest? If it is, as Shaughnessy termed it, "the common language not only of the university but of the public and professional world outside"—the common language of national and international political discourse, of books, newspapers, and magazines whose audience is college educated—and if, as Beth Daniell claims, "restricting access to literacy is an effective way to deprive particular groups of power" (399), are we doing a service to members of communities traditionally deprived of college education by telling them that their own culture is just as good as academic culture and that they shouldn't want the kind of education that *we* have been privileged with? Shouldn't we instead be doing everything we can to enable them to gain access to academic discourse for their own empowerment?

Sharon Crowley reduces the first-year-writing requirement to the familiar stark metaphors of "gatekeeping" and Foucauldian "surveillance," "disciplining," and "policing": "This is the instrumental service ethic of the required composition course: to make student writing available for surveillance until it can be certified to conform to whatever standards are deemed to mark it, and its authors, as suitable for admission to the discourses of the academy" (253). Is that all there is to it? Academic discourse cannot be as exclusionary and oppressive as Lu, Daniell, Cushman, and Crowley claim, as is evidenced by its having been accessible to *them* and its other critics within the academy, as well as to many like me, for whom college education and its introduction to cosmopolitan culture served as a liberation from a stiflingly provincial local culture, and later from the conformity of working on Madison Avenue. Again, in few of these writers that I have read is there much acknowledgment of other influences on the discourse communities of students (even inner-city, foreign, or rural-poor students), like consumption of mass media and commodity culture, conservative religion, worship of the rich, or demagogic right-wing ideology and its authority figures on talk radio and Fox News—discourses toward which academic discourse affords one of the few oppositional influences they may ever encounter. In this respect, Lu and others seem to have it upside down in their sweeping account of conventional college education as an agent of "the dominant conservative ideology of the 1990s" (55), rather than a site of challenge to that ideology *as many students themselves champion it.*

This leads to the most important, and what should be the most obvious, point here—that the academic and intellectual worlds are far from being the monoliths of domination depicted by these critics. The history of Western universities, intellectual culture, and the facilely derided literary canon has been variegated and contested, between dominant cultural forces and those of dissent, reform, and even revolution. Marx, Engels, Trotsky, Goldman, Gramsci, Fanon, Ho Chi Minh, Castro, Guevara, and Allende were intellectuals, most university educated. Trotsky wrote *Literature and Revolution*, defending the canon and its value for the proletariat, echoing Big Bill Haywood of the International Workers of the World declaring "Nothing's too good for the proletariat" (though this was his tongue-in-cheek defense against criticism of his smoking expensive cigars). Yes, this culture has always included its prejudices, but it has also incorporated opposition to them. Indeed, I think a preferable phrase to "academic discourse" is Alvin Gouldner's "the culture of critical discourse" (see chapter 13). This phrase signifies that academic and intellectual discourse are a unique site for the fostering of all aspects of critical thinking, aspects which are necessary (though not sufficient in themselves) means for challenging the mainstream social forces of authoritarianism, ethnocentrism, and conformity. How could such an oppressive institution as the American university produce Toni Morrison, Edward Said, Noam Chomsky, Edward Herman, bell hooks, Howard Zinn, Richard Ohmann, Henry and Susan Giroux, and legions of others who have merited right-wing attacks on the academic world as the bastion of adversarial politics? A moment's thought makes it evident that countless leaders of domestic and colonial revolutions, women's, blacks', and workers' liberation have drawn strength from their acquisition of the culture of critical discourse—even when, like Frederick Douglass and Malcolm X, they were denied access to formal education and struggled to learn basic English on their own.

It is equally evident that all the postmodern attacks on academic discourse are written in that same discourse, yet few of their authors pause to consider the implications of this fact. The ultimate anomaly here is the frequent evocation of deconstructionist theory in such attacks. In the words of Jacques Derrida himself, interviewed by Gary Olson in *JAC*:

I think that if what is called "deconstruction" produces neglect of the classical authors, the canonical texts, and so on, we should fight it.... I'm in favor of the canon, but I won't stop there. I think that students should *read* what are considered the great texts in our tradition—even if that's not enough, even if we have to change the canon, even if we have to open the field and to bring into the canonical tradition other texts from other cultures. If deconstruction is only a pretense to ignore minimal requirements or knowledge of the tradition, it could be a bad thing. (131)

If vulgar deconstructionists followed the implications of their dictates, they wouldn't even be able to read Derrida or to articulate their own theories.

Once again, this is not to deny that nonacademic communities are also frequently sites of critical thinking and oppositional culture, but only to defend against killer dichotomies that position the two sites as mutually exclusive. Cushman, to her great credit, in "The Public Intellectual," does say she wants to overcome this dichotomy and successfully connects the two sites in her description of a graduate course she taught in which the students combined academic studies in literacy theory with participatory research working with children in an inner-city literacy program.

Invasion of the Theoryspeakers

To pursue my earlier point that all of these assaults on academic discourse self-deconstruct by being written in that very discourse, preeminently in the form of poststructuralist/postmodernist theory, I find it especially anomalous that so many works praising nonacademic, local communities and discourses are written in the most pompous academic jargon—clogged with "interpellation," "imbrication," "inscription," "instantiation," "oppressive formations," and "discursive interventions"—not remotely comprehensible to the peoples they champion or to students in lower-division writing courses. Why is there a need to approach immediate problems in American society and teaching circuitously, by slavishly imitating the most opaque European philosophy, obscuring the trees with a dense forest of "theorizing"? I draw from some theory too, as did Shaughnessy, but a distinction can be made between theories that help deal with concrete issues like those this book addresses and those that are just indulgences in abstract philosophizing. Various schools of Marxist theory range from incomprehensible jargon (Althusser, late Adorno) to quite lucid, materialist studies in history, political economy, class relations, high and mass culture (early Adorno). (For a survey, see my general and section introductions in *American Media and Mass Culture: Left Perspectives.*) Many theoryspeakers sound like they are in a trance where all they can speak or write is endless permutations of the above words and hackneyed catchphrases, epitomized in the title of Lu's *CCC* article "Professing Multiculturalism: The Politics of Style in the Contact Zone." When such colleagues whose conversations are perfectly intelligible get up to speak in conferences, it's like hearing the squawking noises coming out of Donald Sutherland's mouth after he succumbs to the invasion of the body snatchers, in the 1978 version.

In *Into the Field: Sites of Composition Studies,* a 1993 collection published by MLA and edited by Anne Ruggles Gere, Brenda Deen Schildgen's "Reconnecting Rhetoric and Philosophy in the Composition Classroom" repeats "fore-meaning" and "foreconception" (anything like "preconception"?) thirteen times on two facing pages. In "Composition Studies and Cultural Studies: Collapsing Boundaries," James Berlin (whose later writing and public speaking sadly became increasingly entangled in jargon) uses "signifying practices" or "discursive practices" eleven times in four pages, and is also fond of "imbrication," "inscription," and "intervention." In editor Gere's six-page introduction, every other word seems to have an *-ize* or *-ity* suffix arbitrarily tacked on. Passages like these recall Orwell's "Politics and the English Language": "As soon as certain topics are raised, the concrete melts into the abstract and no one seems able to think of turns of speech that are not hackneyed: prose consists less and less of *words* chosen for the sake of their meaning, and more and more of *phrases* tacked together like the sections of a prefabricated henhouse" (250). And, "Modern writing at its worst . . . consists of gumming together long strips of words which have already been set in order by someone else, and making the results presentable by sheer humbug" (254).

Not only authors are blameworthy here, but also the editors of professional journals and books who have been too intimidated by the seeming erudition of such writing to exercise a blue pencil (or track editing) to prune prolix or repetitive passages and to declare a moratorium on all the catchphrases that are both pretentious and clichéd by overuse. Dick Ohmann and I edited articles by Fredric Jameson and Stanley Aronowitz for an issue of *College English* on mass culture and had to clarify some impenetrable passages, with no complaints from the authors.

It is not necessarily the pedagogical aims of these theorists that I take issue with, but the vagueness with which they embody those aims (or should I say, "instantiate their praxis"?). It has frequently struck me that the source authors invoked here are more clear and concrete than their emulators. Lu and Horner flog Foucauldian tropes like "discursive practices" more drearily

100

than does Foucault, who, while no means a lucid writer, does have a more vivid style and grounds his key terms in describing specific historical and social situations on a far larger scale than anything in Lu and Horner. (Their book unfortunately did not include Lu's 1987 *College English* article "From Silence to Words," which grounded her theoretical perspective in the autobiographical context of her education in China.) They say they are doing Marxist "cultural materialism" in the mode of Raymond Williams, but lack the specific details of Williams's studies of structures of feeling or of ideology in media like television, or those of his colleagues Richard Hoggart and Basil Bernstein on class and culture, and E. P. Thompson's working-class history. (Thompson's book *The Poverty of Philosophy* is an attack on poststructuralist theory.) Lu and Horner pay lip service to Shirley Brice Heath and Mike Rose, but Heath and Rose draw inductive conclusions from empirical, ethnographic studies of student populations, rather than starting from theoretical *a prioris*. Gloria Anzaldúa's *Borderlands/La Frontera* is another favored text, but she is a gifted prose poet of personal experience, not a theoryspeaking academic. In her critique of Lu's "Conflict," Barbara Gleason shrewdly observes, "A curious feature of poststructuralist theories is the prioritizing of the theoretical perspective over the object under analysis" (886).

Horner and Lu's two-hundred-page book, mainly a collection of their previous articles, consists largely of theoretical ruminations and their application to critiquing the pedagogical practices described by other teachers, primarily Mina Shaughnessy. The authors' rote use of Marxist concepts like historical situation and genealogy, cultural materialism, and praxis is applied in the extremely narrow terms of the role they allegedly play in the discursive practices of basic writing students in relation to academic discourse. While the sources they dutifully cite like Bernstein, Gramsci, Foucault, Jameson, Williams, and Ohmann are centrally concerned with the dominant structures of power in capitalist society, Lu and Horner seem wistfully to believe that the realm of linguistic "conflict and struggle" in BW courses—for instance, opposition to "talking analytically"—can be a significant challenge to capitalist society at large. About this limitation, Gleason asks, "Are language conflicts to be privileged above all of the other sorts of internal and external conflicts that beset students who are often working, providing for families, and surviving in difficult home situations and neighborhoods?" (889). Lu and Horner never really explain why they consider discursive theory and practice to take precedence over study of, say, political economy, criticism of mass culture, or propaganda analysis; in this respect their work is the ultimate in what leftist historian Harvey Kaye has criticized as "the jargon and 'the linguistic turn' of the postmodernists" (234).

Not until 174 pages into a 210-page book do we get a detailed pedagogical application by Lu of all these theoretical abstractions, in the aforementioned "Professing Multiculturalism," her *CCC* article from 1994. Even then, the main case study is drawn from what sounds more like an ESL class than BW, in which the students discussed are Chinese speakers from Malaysia and Vietnam, writing about a textbook reading of an essay by a Hawaiian historian, Haunani-Kay Trask, analyzing her identity conflicts. It is disconcerting that for all of Horner and Lu's postmodern insistence on precise differentiation of the identities of students and sites of teaching, she neglects to tell us anything about the situation of this class. At what college was it taught, and when? What was Lu's rank and workload as a teacher, allowing for the incredible amount of time she must have put into this class? How old were the students, and what was the stage of their proficiency in reading and writing, or other education, in their native languages? I have a personal interest here, because I presume the course was at Drake University, where Lu and Horner were teaching then, which happens coincidentally to be just a few miles away from my home and high school in Des Moines, in a neighborhood that in my day was quintessentially Middle American, as was Drake; so I would have loved to hear about the progress of multiculturalism in Des Moines between the 1950s and 1990s. Actually, in a critique of Lu in *College English*, Patricia Laurence pointed out that Drake in the 1990s only enrolled 10 percent minorities and 3 percent international students (Laurence 881). So Lu and Horner give no indication of the relevance, if any, of their approach to the large majority of students there.

The ESL situation skews Lu's central analysis of "errors" in these students' papers concerning their use of the phrase "can able to" in place of either "can," "be able to," or "be allowed to," which she attributes to difference in usage between their native tongues and English, as well as to the difference in English between "can" and "may." This avoidance of the situation of native speakers of English and their home cultures, none of whom are mentioned here, is compounded as Lu goes on for three pages with her own conjectures about both Trask's text and the student papers on it, concerning the assumptions, implicit in "can able to," of different cultures about sociopolitical agency, abilities, and mobility. Thus,

> I explore with the class how and why this passive voice might be read as indicating that the student writer is approaching Trask's ability from the perspective of the external circumstances of Trask's life— using "can" in the sense of her having the "permission to" become a native Hawaiian historian—as well as from the perspective of her having the qualifications to argue as an historian. (177)

It "might be read" that way, but mightn't it also be read as indicating that the student simply needs to learn the difference between active and passive voice, along with the verb form "to be able" and difference between "can" and "may" in English usage—and might even have *wanted* to learn them in signing up for a BW course? This analysis, like most of the section, appears to be, as Gleason suggests, Lu prioritizing her own academically derived theories, not students' initiatives. She assures us, "Once I feel that the students have a sense of how to go about enacting such a process, I encourage them to practice the method on their own, and I use conferencing and workshops to help individual students further that line of exploration" (181). I'll take her word for it, although I can also envision some students being utterly in the dark on what she was talking about and feeling as controlled and browbeaten as in more conventional courses.

Since much in Lu is based only on her speculations about what students are thinking, I offer an alternative speculation concerning her passage beginning, "I explore. . . ." It seems to me that she is attributing to these students a level of cognitive development that entails the capacities for introspection, critical distance from one's cultural assumptions, and connection between concrete experience and abstractions from it—in other words, "trying to 'talk analytically.'" However, developmental psychologists and sociolinguistics like Bernstein suggest that precisely such capacities mark a cognitive stage that may be beyond these students' present level. When Lu says, "I explore with students . . . ," she is priming the pump toward transition to that stage, probably with the initiative on her part more than the students' and from the subject position of one who has attained that stage. I approve of this endeavor and am only suggesting that she inadvertently gives more weight to academic discourse (that of developmental psychology here) and the teacher's authority than she says she does.

This section and others in Lu contain similar inconsistencies. At the outset she says:

> I am most interested in doing three things: (1) enabling students to hear discursive voices which conflict with and struggle against the voices of academic authority; (2) urging them to negotiate a position in response to these colliding voices; and (3) asking them to consider their choice of position in the context of the sociopolitical power relationships within and among diverse discourses and in the context of their personal life, history, culture, and society. (Horner and Lu 173)

She further stipulates, "I would have already introduced my definition of 'the conditions of life' in previous assignments and class discussions, a definition that includes a whole range of discursive sites, including that of race, ethnicity, gender, sex, economic class, education, religion, region, recreation, and work" (178). Whoa! This sounds like a desperation move to make up for the absence of this curriculum full of crucial issues—all reduced here to "discursive sites"—everywhere else in her and Horner's work.

Furthermore, Lu echoes Hairston and Harris as well as Bartholomae, who she says "has recently reminded us that there is no need to 'import "multiple cultures" [into the classroom, via anthologies]. They are there, in the classroom, once the institution becomes willing to pay that kind of attention to student writing'" (173). Yet Lu says her assignment discussed above was based on a reading in the popular anthology *Rereading America*, and Bartholomae also edited a reader for writing classes. While this assignment might conceivably become a Freirean generative theme toward critical study of the political topics she lists, she gives no indication of how all these dots might be connected in a single course, especially within the limitations of what students new to college can be expected to know strictly from their life experience. Surely, knowledge of the topics she lists cannot be acquired solely through familiar "discursive sites" for most such students, but requires an entire curriculum in the academic discourse that postmodern pluralists disdain, supplemented by wide journalistic reading. How can students "struggle against the voices of academic authority" if they haven't reached the level of studying them in the first place? Once again, I can't remotely imagine myself as an ingenuous freshman at Brown, from a shopkeepers' family and white-bread high school in Des Moines—whose life experience hadn't extended much beyond riding the escalator at Merle Hay Mall—considering my "choice of position in the context of the sociopolitical power relationships . . . ," any more than I can imagine the Middle American students I have taught doing it. Thus her whole line of argument self-deconstructs as she "innocently" reenacts ("re-inscribes"?) the role of the teacher as authority on and guide to the full array of academic discourse that she dismisses as oppressive: "I would have already introduced my definition of 'the conditions of life' in previous assignments and class discussions. . . ." I sympathize with this dilemma, but don't see how it can be avoided.

In sum, although I admire Lu's intentions and ingenuity, as well as the lengthy time she describes devoting to individual conferences and workshops with students, they are surely impossible to apply in *any* single course, let alone one in BW, which is also supposed to address fluency in syntax and coherence (at the levels of the sentence, paragraph, and whole essay), usage, punctuation, spelling, and so on. Lu herself recognizes the stark external limitations imposed on most teachers of BW. Nor do I find at all convincing the attempts by her and other recent theorists (like Paul Butler, discussed in chapter 6) to elevate problems in basic writing into a realm of creative, stylistic options by student writers who might just not have learned to translate their natural speech into the forms of written English. (How could one explain to students why I did not put a comma after "writers" in the last sentence, in terms other than grammatical correctness concerning restrictive versus nonrestrictive modifiers? With a comma, the subject would be all student writers, while I meant to restrict it to particular ones.) Her few examples of such attempts are so circuitous and time-consuming that it would seem more efficient just to teach some conventional grammar—of course within the context of actual student writing, as most of us have long done—which she herself ends up doing in another case study, involving punctuation of possessives (*Representing* 182–84) and as Horner does.

After being rather harsh here about Lu and Horner, especially Lu's own contributions, I must give credit to one exceptional chapter in *Representing*, Lu's previously unpublished "Importing 'Science': Neutralizing Basic Writing." Here Lu, much along the lines I pursue throughout this book and in other works, anatomizes the depoliticizing of leftist, especially Marxist, thought as part of the American cultural Cold War beginning in the 1950s. She frames this process as the substitution of pseudoscientific, or specialized disciplinary, perspectives for political ones in "amputated" adaptations of leftists like Bernstein, Freire, Vygotsky, Ohmann, and Kenneth Burke. She is quite brilliant here, and her application of this critique to the history of basic writing theory and pedagogy is audacious and thought-provoking, though I am not completely convinced by her application of it to Shaughnessy's work, which I find more amenable to progressive ideological uses than Lu does.

Moreover, at the risk of sounding nitpicky about Lu's stimulating chapter, I find a strange disconnect between it and the rest of *Representing*. That is, while this one chapter champions Marxists like Bernstein, Freire (along with his American followers), Vygotsky, and Ohmann against the American "amputation" of their ideas, she and Horner make virtually no use of those ideas in their applied pedagogy. There is little more incorporation of Vygotsky's class-conscious developmental-social psychology, Bernstein's class-inflected progression from restricted to elaborated codes (and Ohmann's critique of it, addressed in my chapter 13), or Freire's generative themes, than in the work of their mentor Bartholomae. Exactly how does Lu's labored account of "can able to" apply Marxist "cultural materialism"?

Lu and Horner's teaching prescriptions sound quite a bit like what has long been amply practiced (though not widely in BW) by Freireans like Ira Shor, who, like Freire himself, only receives passing mention in their book, beyond "Importing 'Science.'" Plowing through Lu and Horner's prolix linguistic theories makes one long for that viscerally greasy fast-food hamburger that Shor brought to class (in *Critical Teaching*) as a generative theme for academic study of capitalist mass culture. Now that's cultural materialism! A wealth of similarly concrete practices has been described over the past four decades in *Radical Teacher*, none of them couched in theoryspeak, but they are rarely cited by postmodern theorists in the thrall of the latter-day courtly muses of Europe.

There is a history here, going back to the 1970s when leftists in MLA divided between the Eurocentric, theory-oriented Marxist Literary Group and those of us in the Radical Caucus, publisher of *Radical Teacher*, which came out of Freirean critical pedagogy, the civil rights movement, New Left campus and antiwar activism, Marxist materialist history and political economy (as practiced by writers like Zinn, Chomsky, and C. Wright Mills), and the traditions of American popular radicalism and labor unions. Since the inception of the Radical Caucus, its most eminent leaders have been Ohmann, Louis Kampf, and Paul Lauter, authors of a rich body of left criticism wholly free from, and opposed to, theoretical jargon.[2]

Are Literary and Rhetorical Education Intrinsically Undemocratic?

I earlier argued that the history of Western universities, intellectual culture, and the literary and humanistic canon, so facilely derided by postmodernist populists, has been variegated and contested, between dominant cultural forces and those of dissent, reform, and even revolution. Crowley's *Composition in the University* raises a significant related issue. She argues that the entire humanistic tradition is intrinsically bound up with aristocratic prejudice and exclusion of lower classes on the grounds of their supposed aesthetic incapacities. This section of her book forms part of the arc she traces by which composition has been steadily more separated from rhetorical, humanistic, and literary education, and reduced to the lowly turf of FYW. Along with many other scholars who have traced this history like Graff, Berlin, Bartholomae, Elbow, Brereton, and Agnew, she assumes as givens several dichotomies that I want to question here, beginning with that between college-level reading and writing instruction. Through that dichotomy, virtually all these scholars equate reading with literature or humanistic classics rather than either basic reading achievement (including vocabulary building and critical comprehension) of college-level nonfictional prose such as news and opinion media as well as works like *The Fire Next Time*, so that problems of basic cultural, media, and political literacy (Hirsch's realm) are skirted. Within *that* dichotomy, literature is equated with *belles lettres* in the sense of aestheticism rather than with other approaches such as romanticism, realism, naturalism, or existentialism. And within *that* dichotomy, varieties of aestheticism that are most detached from politics are emphasized rather than those with a political dimension. For examples of the latter, Oscar Wilde is widely regarded as the ultimate aesthete, but in *The Soul of Man under Socialism*, he argued, much like Marx, Trotsky, and Gramsci, that only under socialism could poverty and cultural deprivation be eliminated, thereby enabling everyone to fulfill their artistic potential. The force of *The Fire Next Time* as a democratic political polemic is inextricable from its complex poetic style and canonical allusions. Likewise, Mario Savio's rebellious speeches as a student in the Free Speech Movement at Berkeley were rich with allusions to authors like Herodotus, Thucydides, T. S. Eliot, Aldous Huxley, Albert Camus, and the transcendentalists, as was Tom Hayden's Students for a Democratic Society manifesto "The Port Huron Statement."

In Crowley's valuable survey in *Composition in the University* of the history of Western humanistic, literary, and rhetorical education, she reiterates Michael Halloran's account of the shift in nineteenth-century American rhetorical education "away from civic virtue and toward the bourgeois project of self-improvement" (34) but also toward *belles-lettristic* aesthetics. Her account of the role here of changing conceptions of taste is especially significant. She cites a Scottish tradition whose

> theorists defined taste as that capacity, or faculty, which permits persons to discriminate the good from the bad in works of art as well as the virtuous from the vicious in the realm of morality. In this tradition, which probably stems from the work of Frances Hutcheson, the exercise of taste was directly connected to the exercise of public responsibility. (37)

She views Hugh Blair as continuing this tradition in the United States: "By the mid-nineteenth century, however, Blair's firm connection of taste to civic virtue had all but disappeared from mainstream school rhetoric texts" (37), being supplanted by more literary, aestheticist definitions of taste, associated with the refined sensibility accessible only to an aristocratic leisure class or autonomous "bourgeois subject." But couldn't she make a case for the possible reaffirmation of advanced composition courses as a humanistic *and egalitarian* site "to discriminate . . . the virtuous from the vicious in the realm of morality" (and of politics), a preparation for the *democratic* "exercise of public responsibility"—a conception that could also incorporate elements of literary study? Once again, of course, a precondition for that conception would be legislating equal financial access for all to K-12 preparation for this level of study. I think Crowley would agree with most of what I say here, since it accords with her central argument that impossible burdens have been placed on FYW and that it ideally should be abolished and replaced by a whole curriculum of rhetorical study, or what I term a core curriculum for civic literacy.

A related killer dichotomy implicit in Crowley's claim that humanistic education historically excluded the lower classes lies in her neglect of progressive humanistic elements in the Enlightenment and American Revolution, European romanticism beginning with Rousseau, and American transcendentalism, with their affirmation of democratic culture and education. Jefferson's (unfortunately unrealized) model of free public education from elementary school through graduate study is quoted in my chapter 1. The ultimate American expression of cultural democracy was Emerson's "The American Scholar" in 1837:

> I read with some joy of the auspicious signs of the coming days, as they glimmer already through poetry and art, through philosophy and science, through church and state.
>
> One of those signs is the fact that the same movement which effected the elevation of what was called the lowest class in the state, assumed in literature a very marked and as benign an aspect. Instead of the sublime and beautiful, the near, the low, the common, was explored and poeticized. . . . The literature of the poor, the feelings of the child, the philosophy of the street, the meaning of household life, are the topics of the time. (77–78)

Defending Teachers' Authority

So teachers can and should steadily recuperate the progressive elements in the humanistic canon. (See chapter 10, "The Radical Humanistic Canon," in my *Why Higher Education*.) Postmodernists who disparage that canon, along with the authority of teachers who teach it at least partially through the banking method, often seem blind to the obvious truths that we know a lot more than our students do about many important subjects, that we are more experienced and traveled in realms outside of most students' scope, that we are more adept in the culture of critical discourse, and that, consequently, we have, or should have, the right and responsibility to convey what we know to them, in classroom practice that must go beyond "a forum where students can articulate . . . differences among themselves." Today's challenge is to explore means of conveying that knowledge through pedagogy that is, to every reasonable extent, not mere "banking" but dialogical, interactive, and respectful of students' own realms of knowledge—means that have been modeled by various Freireans and other theorists like those mentioned previously. (I must again pay tribute here to Ira Shor, who for over a quarter century has been conducting an awesomely scrupulous, ingenious exploration of these problems, even though he reduces the authority of teachers more than I am comfortable with.)

Nevertheless, neither postmodern pluralists nor Freireans in general have realistically acknowledged that a sound education, especially at the elementary and secondary levels, necessitates a certain level of banking of factual knowledge, standards, and coercion, if you will, by authorities in selection of subjects studied, and that it always will, unless we are ready to abandon the ideal of universal public education—a prospect whose most enthusiastic backers would be Christian conservatives, voucher advocates, and schools-for-profit privatizers. We just need to assert ourselves to become the authorities in implementing progressive standards. (I see those standards including factual knowledge of basic political vocabulary and opposing ideological or partisan positions, knowledge that needs to encompass the complex ways in which ideology and partisanship bias the definitions of terms and points of opposition themselves. Such a base of factual knowledge must precede any effective cultural/political critique, for as Graff observes, many students don't feel coerced by leftist teachers so much as baffled by what they're talking about.) These truths are taken for granted by most educators, including leftists, in most other countries and other academic fields. Why is it only American scholars in English who work themselves up into excesses of anti-intellectualism and self-hatred in their phobia of factual knowledge and their perceived collusion in domination, coercion, and elitism?

These are some of the reasons I am inclined to share conservatives' disapproval of turning required writing courses at the basic level into political consciousness raising—although I would be glad to see it in an elective, advanced writing course or one titled something like "Negotiating Multicultural Discourses." I likewise feel that Freirean experiments in student-controlled coursework belong more in a separate, elective course rather than in required, BW or FYW classes—though I am open to persuasion otherwise.

6

DOWN WITH "CLEAR, LOGICAL PROSE"?
CEDING REASON TO CONSERVATIVES

The only thing composition teachers are not talking and writing about these days is how to teach students to compose clear, logical prose. . . . Composition has abandoned correctness because grammatical errors signify the author is politically engaged. (Heather MacDonald, "Why Johnny Can't Write" 70, 71)

We progressive academics have allowed conservatives to beat up on us by posing hypocritically as the champions of clear language and thought. MacDonald's view was echoed in a 2009 report of the American Council of Trustees and Alumni (ACTA), founded by Lynne Cheney, which argued against politicizing composition on the grounds that first-year writing should be "an introductory college writing class, focusing on grammar, style, clarity, and argument" (ACTA 10).[1] I share E. D. Hirsch's distress, in *The Making of Americans*, that liberals, among whom he counts himself, have let themselves be pigeonholed as being indifferent, if not hostile, to clear writing, thinking, and academic standards—indeed as believing that both academic laxity and jargon-riddled theoretical writing promote progressive politics. (MacDonald's cheap shot about grammar and politics was a travesty of the actual widespread notion that political consciousness is more important than grammar, in itself another either-or fallacy, to be sure.) On the contrary, as I have argued throughout this book, both of these tendencies on the left entrench the power of the right wing by default of reasoned opposition. MacDonald's piece appeared in the *National Interest*, a journal edited by Irving Kristol, who was the master architect of neoconservative doublethink in simultaneously championing high, impartial intellectual standards and promoting anti-intellectual, demagogic Republicans—precursors in Kristol's time to Sarah Palin, Michelle Bachmann, Rick Perry, and Herman Cain ("We need a leader, not a reader"), along with media like talk radio (Kristol praised Rush Limbaugh, in *Neoconservatism* 383) and Fox News, where Kristol's son William, a Harvard PhD, is a regular talking head as a Republican spokesperson. I believe above all that we on the left need persistently to employ logic to refute such self-contradictions and other logical fallacies in conservative political and corporate propaganda. But discussions about logic are bedeviled by equivocal definitions, self-contradictions, and inconsistencies by those on both the right and left.

In relation to disputes about whether this role of reasoned opposition to conservative propaganda leads inevitably toward advocacy of unreasonable, PC dogma, the erstwhile antifoundationalist Stanley Fish has recently, in his *New York Times* blog and 2008 book *Save the World on Your Own Time*, ostensibly sided with the conservatives defending the basics and opposing critical pedagogy. This has been a slightly sticky position for Fish, whose wife, Jane Tompkins is a feminist literary critic and author of the celebrated, quasi-Freirean "Pedagogy of the Distressed" in *College English*. Moreover, I find his position quite equivocal in relation to our deliberations here on teaching argument and logic. He begins by rejecting political advocacy outside of a legitimate academic context: "*To academicize a topic is to detach it from the context of its real world urgency, where there is a vote to be taken or an agenda to be embraced, and insert it into a context of academic urgency, where there is an account to be offered or an analysis to be performed*" (27, author's italics). He explains:

> This is not to say that academic work touches on none of the issues central to politics, ethics, civics, and economics; it is just that when those issues arise in an academic context, they should be discussed in academic terms; that is, they should be the objects of analysis, comparison, historical placement, etc.; the arguments put forward in relation to them should be dissected and assessed *as* arguments and not as preliminaries to action on the part of those doing the assessing. The action one takes (or should take) at the conclusion of an academic discussion is the action of rendering an *academic* verdict as in "That argument makes sense," "there's a hole in the reasoning here," "the author does (or does not) realize her intention," "in this debate, X has the better of Y," "the case still is not proven." (25–26)

Fish has earlier said:

> College and university teachers can (legitimately) do two things: (1) introduce students to bodies of knowledge and traditions of inquiry that had not previously been part of their experience; and (2) equip

those same students with the analytical skills—of argument, statistical modeling, laboratory procedure—that will enable them to move confidently within those traditions and to engage in independent research after a course is over. (12–13)

Putting aside for a moment the vagueness about how these goals might fit into the specific context of English studies, let's take Fish at his word here. Regarding his first suggestion, the kind of students prevalent in the colleges where I have taught for over three decades are quite unlikely to have previously experienced leftist bodies of knowledge and traditions of inquiry (Marxism and other varieties of socialism, feminism, multiculturalism, and environmentalism). Nor can these bodies of knowledge, with large traditions of intellectual and literary champions, be dismissed as beyond the fringe of legitimate scholarly study, as Fish rightly dismisses creationism and Holocaust denial. Concerning his second suggestion, consider Fish's statements about teaching analytic and argumentative skills quoted above, as well as these: "In a classroom, the gathering of evidence on the way to reaching a conclusion is the prime academic activity" (70). "The goal is to establish, by argument and evidence, the superiority of one analysis or description or prescription over its (intellectual) rivals" (173).

I totally agree. So suppose that instead of advocating or attempting to indoctrinate students into left political views, a teacher says, as I habitually do, "This leftist source makes this argument, supporting it with this reasoning and evidence," and then that teacher goes on to compare and contrast this argument fair-mindedly with conservative counterparts, with the comparison resulting inductively in "establish[ing] by argument and evidence, the superiority of one analysis or description or prescription [the leftist one] over its (intellectual) rivals." To borrow a page from Fish's well-known defense of antifoundationalism, this simple rhetorical move would seem to readmit to legitimate academic discourse, at a stroke, the whole body of political content and advocacy (of superior prescriptions) that Fish has banished. Simply academicize pro-and-con arguments, in the manner of Gerald Graff's "teaching the conflicts."

Fish does not recognize an inconsistency between his above passages and another one, trashing Mark Bracher's "Teaching for Social Justice: Re-Educating the Emotions through Literary Study" in *JAC*. Fish rejects out of hand Bracher's claim: "What right do we have to impose our view...—our 'liberal' or 'progressive' ideology—on our students? We have the right . . . because the evidence supports . . . our ideology" (175). Well, if Bracher or any other teacher can empirically establish that the evidence supports left ideology (against conservatives' best shots in rebuttal), then shouldn't he or she be squarely in Fish's academic ballpark? In another formulation, Fish says,

> The only advocacy that goes on in the classroom is the advocacy of what James Murphy has identified as the intellectual virtues, "thoroughness, perseverance, intellectual honesty," components of the cardinal academic virtue of being "conscientious in the pursuit of truth." . . . If you're not in the pursuit-of-truth business, you should not be in the university. (20)

Leaving aside Fish's voluminous writings on the problematic nature of truth and its pursuit, let's again pursue the consequences of his arguments here. Suppose we take as a subject of academic study the obstacles posed to the pursuit of truth in a society in which public opinion is manipulated by political and corporate forces spending billions of dollars annually to produce propaganda, deception, outright lies, and other more-or-less toxic forms of "spin." (When Fish and other theoretical deep thinkers like Barbara Herrnstein Smith or Jonathan Culler address the subject of truth, it is almost invariably on an abstract epistemological level, avoiding the epistemology of deliberate lying, propaganda, and stupefaction.) Shouldn't those of us in the pursuit-of-truth business devote a major part of our teaching and scholarship to dissecting and assessing all these sources of fallacious argument, *as a purely academic enterprise*? Shouldn't we also perhaps take an advocacy position—opposing "systematic moronization"? In other words, might not the advocacy of "intellectual honesty" take on the force of the kind of moral imperative that Fish claims to eschew, in the manner of Emerson's exhortation to the American Scholar: "See it to be a lie, and you have already dealt it its mortal blow" (75), or Chomsky's "Intellectuals are in a position to expose the lies of government, to analyze actions according to their causes and motives and often hidden intentions" (1)?

Also suppose, just hypothetically, that "the superiority of one analysis or description or prescription over its (intellectual) rivals"—say, the intellectual superiority of one major political party or ideology in America over the other, which constantly flaunts its anti-intellectualism, derision toward "the cultural elite," and science—can be established by "argument and evidence"? Isn't this endeavor also in Fish's academic ballpark?

Fish's failure to consider all these questions at any length is surely "a hole in his reasoning here." An even more gaping hole is left by his failure to say anything about how the very kind of academic deliberation on political and moral issues that he prescribes and practices here, or the kind of questions that I raise in response, could be centrally incorporated into the liberal arts curriculum, individual courses, and pedagogical practice—particularly in English. All his support of studying analytic skills, "coherent and persuasive" argument, and "the canons of argument and evidence" leaves us rhetoric scholars nodding, yes, yes, of course. And yet, the sum of Fish's attention to the teaching of rhetoric, and particularly argumentative writing, as the academic discipline in which his prescription for academicizing political argument might best be embodied, or to the long history of the academic study of political rhetoric and possible ways of returning it to a central place in the humanities as one means of reversing the universally lamented decline of political literacy in America, amounts to—zero. Indeed, he bans any such concerns from his FYW course, in which, "We don't tell each other what we think about anything—except about how prepositions or participles or relative pronouns function" (40). I find this failure to champion a revival of the critical study of political argumentation in composition especially disappointing for someone with Fish's influence as a theorist, administrator, and public intellectual.

Students' Right to Illogic?

It is quite perplexing that the issues I have raised here have received so little attention in recent composition theory or curriculum design. Moreover, as noted in chapter 4, there has been a great deal of confusion by theorists even in defining *logic, argument*, and *clarity*, and in distinguishing their role in different levels of writing instruction. Even more confusion is reaped by some recent theorists who sweepingly belittle the goals of study of logical reasoning, clarity, and even argumentation altogether in writing instruction.

Paul Butler's 2008 *JAC* article "Style and the Public Intellectual: Rethinking Composition in the Public Sphere," attempts to defend composition studies from attacks by journalists and politicians—specifically Heather MacDonald—some of whom have a conservative agenda and know little about the discipline, and laudably affirms that composition scholars "could profit by clearly articulating a public position" (65). Unfortunately, in attempting to refute charges like MacDonald's, Butler only exemplifies the lack of clear articulation he calls for and confirms MacDonald's charge.

My first problem with Butler is that he spends four introductory pages surveying different theories of grammar and instruction in it (he doesn't include Shaughnessy's), concluding, "Because the field has adopted various rhetorical approaches to grammar that fall more accurately under the rubric of style, my discussion of the field's response to grammar—to the extent I discuss it here—relates to the study of style" (68). But as far as I can tell, the extent to which the rest of the article illustrates the relation of grammar to style, in any specifics, is virtually zero. My second problem is that Butler sets out to refute MacDonald's charge that we fail to teach students "to compose clear, logical prose," but then zooms in on criticism of the word "clear" throughout the rest of the article, to the exclusion of the whole subject of logic and its role in writing instruction. For instance, as Shaughnessy put it, there is the logic of grammar and syntax—in matters like punctuation, the relation among elements in a sentence, subject-predicate agreement, coordinate and subordinate clauses, the use of conjunctions and adverbs in linking sentences, and the continuity of ideas between sentences or paragraphs. Then there is informal logic, central to courses in critical thinking and argumentative writing, including precise definition and usage of terms, cogent reasoning and rhetorical strategies, avoiding logical fallacies (or identifying them in others' arguments as a mode of refutation), and showing sufficient knowledge of the facts about which one is writing. These vast realms are ignored by Butler along with the many current theorists who limit comp studies almost exclusively to basic writing or FYW courses that exclude systematic study of these subjects.

Further confusion in Butler's account results when he changes the subject from clarity in student writing to that of scholars like Victor Vitanza. With the latter's gnarly prose as an example, Butler argues that lack of clarity may be a justifiable choice toward creative, complex, or only apparently "opaque" ideas—ideas that Butler views as highly rational, although he elsewhere seems as indifferent or even hostile toward "logical prose" as are feminists like Elizabeth Ellsworth and Lisa Langstraat, discussed below. Butler's whole discussion of style here waffles between its common meaning of deliberate craft or rhetorical options—as in his discussion of Vitanza's prose—and the different equation that Butler makes, of style with grammar, syntax and usage *at the level of the basic learner*, which he fails to support at all. Thus he dodges the issue of unclear reasoning in student writing.

Ian Barnard's "The Ruse of Clarity" in *CCC* (2010) largely clones Butler. Barnard portentously seeks to deconstruct the sinister "ideological work done in the name of clarity" (434). Both he and Butler argue that clear language can be a tool for the oversimplifications of conservative indoctrination, without the qualification that it is not *always* that, and indeed that clear thinking is essential for identifying oversimplification as well as exposing verbal mystification, as in NCTE's call "to enable students to cope with . . . sophisticated persuasion techniques." Barnard continues, "We also need to think about how insistences on clarity [*always?*] restrict ideas and thinking and might make impossible for students the kind of complex thinking to which critical theorists aspire" (445). There are, however, lines to be drawn in levels of complexity. In chapter 1, I showed how explication of a complex passage in *The Fire Next Time* enabled students to understand and be inspired by it. But should we really expect our BW or FYW students to aspire to, and be inspired by, *Of Grammatology*?

Thus both Butler and Barnard make an inductive leap from the value of complexity in scholarly theory to its alleged value in beginning college writers, without responsibly considering the limited developmental level of much student reading, writing, and reasoning. Both discuss clarity and opacity mainly in terms of style rather than of logic and argumentation. All Barnard says on the latter is, "Why pretend that we aren't sometimes entranced by writing that is mysterious or enigmatic or illogical?" The more illogical, the more entrancing, right? Glenn Beck must be Barnard's favorite writer. Notice how dizzyingly Barnard, like Butler, lurches between being entranced by hyper-rational theory and by student writing "over which the writer or reader does not always have under complete control" (446). Of course, one's mind is boggled at MacDonald's implication that the present-day Republican Party is the defender of clear, logical prose, but aren't Butler and Barnard examples of how ingenuous progressive academics can be in providing ammunition for conservative culture warriors?

When Butler does discuss stylistic clarity in student writing, it is only to agree with *Students' Right to Their Own Language*: "In every class there are examples of writing which is clear and vigorous despite the use of non-standard forms . . . and there are certainly many examples of limp, vapid writing in 'standard dialect'" (69). Of course this is true, but it is another false dichotomy; there are equally many examples of writing by students—of all dialect groups, ethnicities, and social classes—that is simply incoherent in syntax, punctuation, diction, reasoning, or any comprehensible meaning. I ask students who write such passages what they meant, and they usually reply that they just hadn't thought about it carefully. Or I ask them to read one of their grammatically incoherent sentences out loud, and they stop halfway through it, shake their head and mutter, "Wait, that's not what I meant to say." I think this problem in students who can speak quite coherently involves their unfamiliarity with the conventions, complexities, and fixedness of written English, which needs to be learned like a foreign language if it has not been a part of one's home culture. One reason for this unfamiliarity is that, as Shaughnessy noted, they simply have not formed the habit of reading a lot, so their writing problems parallel their reading ones. There are obvious ways of identifying these problems and helping students to deal with them, as Shaughnessy amply showed. "Correctness" and "error" need not be pejorative, "disciplining" terms, but can just describe success or failure in communicating a comprehensible meaning. But nothing that either *Students' Right* or Butler says helps much toward such learning.

Butler also seems to be among the many compositionists who have fetishized the 1963 NCTE statement against the teaching of grammar isolated from application in student writing, and who have tumbled down a slippery slope to the conclusion that grammar need not be taught at all (or even learned by teachers) or that it can just be folded into instruction in style—far easier said than done. An opposing view was recently expressed by Hirsch in *The Making of Americans*, discussing common confusions between subject and object pronouns like *I* and *me*:

> One has to know the difference between a subject and an object, so it is important to understand what phrases and clauses are and to know something about sentence structure. To impart such knowledge it is convenient to teach young students a vocabulary about language— such words as *subject* and *object, singular* and *plural, past, present,* and *future, sentence,* and *clause,* as well as the parts of speech: *noun, adjective, adverb, article, pronoun, conjunction, preposition.* American teachers are told that research shows such grammar instruction to be harmful or useless, but it is this spurious research that is questionable, not intelligent instruction in the grammar of the standard language. Teaching a few simple things about the parts of speech—not exclusively, not ad nauseam, not to the detriment of writing—is no more harmful than teaching the basic parts of plants. And for the child's future it is enormously more important. (122–23)

I might put it more in terms of grammar potentially being a useful, and even interesting, subject of student study quite apart from direct writing instruction, although Shaughnessy, Hirsch's one-time colleague and mentor, once again cut through this Gordian knot by showing how explanation of grammatical principles can be helpful for student writers in identifying and overcoming problems in expressing what they mean.

Hirsch ultimately launches a frontal assault on the Rousseauan and vulgarized-Deweyan mindset of college composition teachers who believe that reading and writing can be naturally acquired and primarily centered in students' personal experience, and who believe that composition should be an autonomous discipline, isolated from the acquisition of vocabulary, factual knowledge, and aspects of critical thinking in the context of a curriculum in basic academic subjects like history, government, literature, and science. Over three decades Hirsch has amassed a large body of research in cognitive psychology and comparative curricular practices in support of his position.

I have not thoroughly studied his evidence, but my own experience in four decades of teaching predominantly white, middle-class, conservative students makes me sense that, despite some disputable specifics, he is on the right track. Right or wrong, we at least have a professional obligation to evaluate his research findings evenhandedly rather than denigrating them out of hand.

Antirationalism in Feminist Rhetoric

Many feminist theorists since the 1950s have revolutionized our thinking about a whole world of social and cultural topics in which assumptions of male supremacy have long clouded our vision. I have found *In a Different Voice* by Carol Gilligan and *Women's Ways of Knowing* by Mary Field Belenky et al., among the most stimulating works of feminist theory, in their reformulations from women's perspective of William Perry's and Lawrence Kohlberg's models of development in moral reasoning, which were based on study of male Harvard undergraduates in the 1970s. (See chapter 11 for an extended survey of developmental psychology and its feminist revisions.)

Similar issues to those in Gilligan and Belenky have been addressed by several brilliant literary critics like Jane Tompkins, whose *Sensational Designs* made the case that the "objectively" determined canon of nineteenth-century American writers has not only been in constant flux but has been male biased, and she reaffirmed the importance of women writers like Harriet Beecher Stowe who had long been disdained by male authors and critics for excessive sentimentality. While not demeaning the greatness of Mark Twain, she raised a quite reasonable question about the "universal truth" of *Huckleberry Finn*: how would Huck's adventures have differed if he had been a girl of the same age, and what range of male privilege, even among poor people, does the novel inadvertently reflect? Tompkins's *West of Everything* presents an equally astute feminist perspective on the western. So Tompkins and many other feminist critics have made us aware of the failures of the male imagination (and prior assumptions about it in developmental psychology) to incorporate women's experience and sensibility.

Unfortunately, as with the other fields I have been addressing, the most salient feminist ideas have also been misunderstood, vulgarized, and pushed to untenable extremes by some scholars. Conservative polemicists jump on these extreme versions to make straw-person arguments against the more cogent versions (see the example of Lynne Cheney's account of Elizabeth Ellsworth below). Conservative critics had a field day especially with the antirationalism of some experiments in *l'écriture féminine* when it was trendy some twenty-five years ago; even progressive feminists like Lynn Worsham stopped short of endorsing them in her survey on the subject in MLA's 1991 collection *Contending with Words: Composition and Rhetoric in a Postmodern Age*, and since then they have dropped off the feminist radar screen. The phrase and its advocates were absent in Worsham and Susan Jarratt's 1998 *Feminism and Composition Studies*. In a definitive chapter of *No Man's Land* on the subject, "Sexual Linguistics," Sandra Gilbert and Susan Gubar take down Hélène Cixous, Luce Irigary, and Julia Kristéva, who "seem almost immoderately mystical in their straining to 'invent the other history'" (23).

Another source of confusion in recent theories about the binaries rationality/irrationality and objectivity/subjectivity has been misunderstanding of the Frankfurt School and New Left critics of university education in the 1960s. Their central idea was that the Platonic, Renaissance, and Enlightenment ideals of reason and scientific objectivity have over the past three centuries been corrupted into "instrumental reason" that recruits intellectuals to administer the efficient functioning of dehumanizing technology, economics, and politics. In the New Left critique, the modern "multiversity" has been debased into yet another branch of Marcuse's "totally administered society," as a service station to business, government, and the military. Faculty and students have, consciously or not, become technocratic servants rationalizing these ruling forces; much of the faculty's ostensibly scientific research makes a false claim to objectivity that masks its ideological biases and subservience to special interests—for example, research in military weaponry and strategy, or class-biased social-science research. That this entire social and educational order was explicitly or implicitly male-dominated and instrumental in multiple forms of discrimination against women is now more obvious than then, as feminist critics since the 1960s have called attention to many specific manifestations of sexism in it. So, in my view, the imperative of the Frankfurt and New Left critique (incorporating feminist perspectives) was to reaffirm the progressive elements in Platonic, Renaissance, and Enlightenment ideals of authentic, impartial reason, in opposition to "irrational" or rationalizing, instrumental reason and false objectivity. I see this project as quite consistent with the imperative in *Women's Ways* to "value both subjective and objective strategies for knowing." My understanding of Lyotard's *The Postmodern Condition* is that he was belatedly making the same critique of instrumental reason made by American New Leftists and of the tyranny of totalizing ideologies ("grand narratives") made in the 1960s by thinkers like Daniel Bell in *The End of Ideology* and Albert Camus in *The Rebel*. His ideas, however, have been vulgarized and pushed to extremes in similar ways.

Unfortunately, the Frankfurt School, New Left, and Lyotardian critique of the perversion of Enlightenment reason and objectivity toward oppressive aims was misinterpreted by some feminist and other theorists as a rejection of reason altogether—a classic case of throwing out the baby with the bath water. I find a convergence here between two quite different varieties of antirationalism: Paul Butler's and Ian Barnard's rejections of "the ruse of clarity" in favor of opaque though putatively rational language, and this strain privileging emotion or affect over reason. A prime example was a widely cited and reprinted *Harvard Educational Review* article in 1989 by Elizabeth Ellsworth, "Why Doesn't This Feel Empowering? Working through the Repressive Myths of Critical Pedagogy," singled out by Lynne Cheney as representative of anti-intellectualism in current academic theory (Cheney, *Telling* 1995: 11–12)—which made Cheney a strange bedfellow with the leftist critical teachers attacked by Ellsworth. Ellsworth, dubiously conflating the New Left line with poststructuralist theory, claims:

> Poststructuralism . . . has facilitated a devastating critique of the violence of rationalism against its Others. It has demonstrated that as a discursive practice, rationalism's regulated and systematic use of elements of language constitutes rational competence "as a series of exclusions of women, people of color, of nature as a historical agent, of the truth value of art." In contrast, poststructuralist thought is not bound to reason, but "to discourse, literally narratives about the world that are admittedly *partial*." (96)

Ellsworth cites Stanley Aronowitz, a prominent New Left theorist, as the author of the quoted fragments in the second and third sentence cited above. However, she takes both quotations out of his context, which is to summarize lines of poststructuralism *that he finds faulty*. It is the *false* claim to reason, impartiality, or objectivity that he says has served exclusionary purposes, not rationality itself. Far from equating rationality with false impartiality in the piece cited, Aronowitz is appealing to reason to demystify the inauthentic facsimiles of impartiality and scientific objectivity that are conventionally used to rationalize the hegemony of dominant groups, and he is criticizing poststructuralism and postmodernism from the viewpoint of the Frankfurt School's highly rationalist mode of Marxist cultural critique (see Aronowitz, *Politics of Identity* 258). Another Aronowitz article, "Mass Culture and the Eclipse of Reason: The Consequences for Pedagogy," first published in *College English* and cited in chapter 3 above, laments the destructive effects of mass culture on reasoned discourse. Aronowitz and Henry Giroux later pointed out Ellsworth's misunderstandings in *Postmodern Education* (132–33).

Ellsworth's writing is also choked with the dreary, redundant jargon—"as discursive practices"—that makes many postmodernist/poststructuralist theoryspeakers unreadable, enabling rightists like Cheney and MacDonald to claim the high ground as the champions of clear language and thought. Last but far from least, she falls into the common fallacy that speculative theories "demonstrate" truths—in an appeal to exactly the scientific rationalism she renounces in the same breath. Indeed, she seems oblivious of the fact that her article itself is a model of the same rational "discursive practice" that she ostensibly rejects.

To the contrary of those like Ellsworth who simplistically view reasoned discourse as an agent of oppression, it is precisely higher order reasoning (aka critical thinking) that is needed to refute the logical fallacies in sexist, racist, class-biased, or jingoistic rhetoric, manipulating appeals to sociocentric emotions in the dominant culture such as lauding of "church, kitchen, and children," among other stereotypical realms of supposed female sentimentality. These are the perennial appeals of right-wing demagogues. Hitler and Mussolini compared the fickle masses to women, incapable of intellect or reason and submissive to the superior male mind. Current masters of such appeals to irrationalism like Rush Limbaugh and Glenn Beck sound much like postmodernists, claiming to champion plain-folks common sense against the logic-chopping, liberal cultural elite, while they themselves amass wealth and power in the Republican Party elite.

In recent years we have largely been spared earlier postmodernist orthodoxies to the effect that you can't use the master's tools to tear down the master's house, or that reasoned discourse and polemical argument are no more than a masculinist snare and delusion. Somewhere along the line it must have dawned on even the most zealous exponents of this trope, like Ellsworth, that in the very process of voicing it they were refuting it. Writers like Frantz Fanon and James Baldwin have been powerful critics of Eurocentrism, but they have mastered the master's tools to tear down his house. Nor have injunctions against phallogocentric modes of argumentation deterred the whole galaxy of great political, journalistic, and academic female polemicists in our time. A substantial cohort of feminist scholars in our field supports (and practices) agonistic argument, including Gilbert and Gubar, Dale Bauer, bell hooks, Teresa Ebert, Susan Jarratt, Patricia Roberts-Miller, Karen Fitts, Patricia Bizzell, Kathleen McCormick, Andrea Lunsford, and Cathy Birkenstein.

Is Mass Culture Feminist?

A similar, bizarre twist in recent composition and cultural studies theory seems to be based on a misreading of mass-culture critics like Tania Modleski and Andres Huysmann. It follows a deductive line of reasoning something like the following. First premise: Rationalistic, male intellectuals condemn mass politics and culture for their irrational manipulation of the populace. Second premise: The same intellectuals charge that such propaganda partially aims its irrational appeals to women and/or uneducated lower classes. Conclusion: Therefore, feminists and progressive populists should defend mass politics and culture for their irrationality, against those intellectuals. The first confusion here is in thinking it is the intellectual critics who scorn audiences' supposed female irrationality, rather than the politicians or media they *criticize* for doing so, in the manner of the advertising executive I worked for on Madison Avenue who sneered about deceptive commercials, "The average housewife is too stupid to know the difference." The second confusion is between popular or populist culture, as created by and for common people, and mass culture produced by the culture industry for maximum profit or mass politics engineered by propaganda agencies, which appeal to the lowest common denominator of rationality. Thus Sharon Crowley, whose own reasoning is usually quite cogent, falls into a version of these confusions:

> Professional literature from the early 1950s displays humanist contempt for mass media and popular culture. . . . Humanists fear popular texts because they address the current, the common, and the practical. . . . Humanists also seem to dislike the lack of discipline they perceive in popular culture, where no one seems to be in control of either language or taste. (106)

Those like Crowley who fall into these confusions are generally politically liberal, but they echo conservative polemicists who perpetuate the same confusions in alleging that liberal critics of "plain-folks" conservative demagogues like Sarah Palin and Glenn Beck are the ones who are contemptuous of the masses, rather than the conservative demagogues themselves.

Both of these confusions are typified at length in a 1996 article in *Composition Forum* titled "'Hypermasculinity' in Cultural Studies and Composition: Mapping a Feminist Response," by Lisa R. Langstraat, which concludes, "The phallocentric impulses compositionists have inherited from cultural studies' feminization of mass culture limit the potentially powerful effects of our pedagogies. It is vital to recognize and challenge these impulses if feminist teachers are to become our own cartographers, mapping change on our own terrain" (13). Drawing from sources like Modleski and Huysmann, Langstraat traces the history since the nineteenth century of male, highbrow critics and literary modernists who disdain both the social masses and popular culture, often coded as feminine, and who claim as males the prerogatives of "autonomy, individual consciousness, . . . mastery . . . high art and the power of production" (4–6). She extends this history to argue that much recent cultural-studies theory is similarly male biased. So far, so good, except that she tends to slip into the above confusion attributing to critics themselves the scorn for the alleged feminine traits that they condemn in political demagogues and mass media manipulating those traits. Is the problem "cultural studies' feminization of mass culture" or mass culture's feminization of its audience? (Sometimes she seems to make this distinction, sometimes not.)

Langstraat goes farther off the track when she acknowledges, "The terms 'popular culture' and 'mass culture' are similarly contested. I use the terms interchangeably, assuming that both represent those cultural forms which are traditionally associated with 'low' or 'folk culture'" (13). Her failure to make this distinction muddles her whole discussion of mass media and their reception by audiences. With the political ingenuousness that I take issue with in so much of American cultural studies, she acknowledges the biases in popular media but shows little awareness of the material realities of their manufacture by giant media corporations that cynically calculate every second of screen time (whether in entertainment or political reportage) for emotional appeal to audiences, often subconscious, that is congenial to consumption of the products advertised by sponsors, and more broadly congenial to the passive consent engineered by the entire corporate and political power structure, with its apparatuses of market research, polling, advertising, public relations, spin doctors, and cognitive saturation.

Like many other second-wave cultural-studies scholars, Langstraat celebrates instances of classroom exercises in which students watching popular TV programs "use the texts in creative ways, making their own meanings in excess of popular media's ideological constraints, and in the process, the writers become more critical about their affective identifications with popular TV shows" (11–12). (Langstraat identifies such activities as a mode of "the feminist response" in opposition to study of supposedly phallocentric, impersonal cultural criticism.) It is all very well to begin a study with students' personal experiences and responses, but Langstraat and many others who advance this line of argument seem to believe, contrary to Modleski and Huysmann, that such moments of creativity or resistance are a sufficient substitute for studying the larger critique of the culture industry. Why shouldn't such first steps toward critical consciousness in students be used as a Freirean generative theme toward study of academic or journalistic critics who present a wider view of the politics of media, like the Frankfurt School, Naomi Wolf's *The Beauty Myth*, Jean Kilbourne's film series *Killing Us Softly*:

Advertising's Image of Women, or Herman and Chomsky's *Manufacturing Consent*? It seems to me that the causes for this limitation are, first, the killer dichotomy coding critical texts like these as masculinist, even when written by women; second, the theoretical dogma banishing such academic texts (providing "intellectual distance") from writing courses and limiting content only to material that directly relates to students' immediate lives and knowledge; third, the confused notion that discussion by critics of the scorn for audiences shown by media corporations or politicians reflects this scorn in the critics themselves.

Langstraat can also be taken as representative of the lack of clarity in these debates about definitions of key terms that have ambiguous meanings, like "reason," "affect" or "emotion," and even "critical thinking," which leads to further confusion in so much recent theory. She criticizes "masculinist" composition theorists who "require a position of intellectual distance as a precondition for critical thinking and writing" (9). I simply do not consider any of the criteria and dispositions for critical thinking and cognitive development in my own definitions in chapter 3 to be gender specific or to exclude the personal, emotive, or communal; my criteria include skill in connecting "the personal and the impersonal, the local and the global." Maybe I should add "the emotional and the rational."

Langstraat says, "Cultural studies pedagogues should help students understand that reason, like common sense, can be deployed as a structure of power. Writing teachers must not only acknowledge 'the existence of different rationalities, but the importance of the irrational and a-rational in human life' (Grossberg 25)." The citation is to Lawrence Grossberg's *We Gotta Get Out of This Place: Popular Conservatism and Postmodern Culture*, and her first sentence paraphrases one in Grossberg preceding the direct quotation: "Cultural studies does not reject reason but acknowledges its limits and its deployment as a structure of power." Langstraat significantly cuts "does not reject reason," although I find Grossberg's passage nearly as murky as her version; nor does the surrounding context in Grossberg clarify or develop his point. Both seem to be attributing the deployment of reason exclusively to ruling powers and ideologies (in similar manner to Ellsworth, whom Langstraat cites, and with similar equivocation in definition of "reason"). Hasn't *antirationalism* more often been deployed as a means to gain power, and hasn't reason also been deployed through the ages by intellectuals to "speak truth to power"? In any case, that passage in Grossberg is quite a subsidiary one in a four-hundred-page book, whose central theme, ignored by Langstraat, is announced on the same page cited: "the appearance of a certain structure of depoliticization which is moving the nation into a new conservatism" (25). So Grossberg's larger point and his support for it are quite similar to mine in this book, and he is equally critical of the excesses of the politics of identity and diversity in dissipating progressive opposition to the new conservatism, as surveyed in chapters 4 and 5.

Langstraat's advocacy of "affect" and "emotion" is equally equivocal. She says, "Social-epistemic rhetorics tend to configure affective investments as mere effects of ideological formations. . . . Hence, rarely do our pedagogies account for the complex affective investments and the structures and economies of feeling that enable ideology to take root and have meaning in our lives" (7). As a counterexample, she discusses a paper by one of her students about the culture of tanning salons, based on her own use of them, which is certainly a good kind of assignment for connecting large social forces with personal experience. The student admits, "Our whole society is based on looking good or trying to fit in to what other people think looks good. If other people like our tan, we may keep tanning no matter how bad we think it is for us" (9). Langstraat notes that the student still kept going to the salon after writing this, yet Langstraat rejects theories that would explain this only in terms of false consciousness and resistance to critical pedagogy: "Because cultural studies compositionists, as well as other researchers and teachers who explore the socially constructed nature of subjectivity, have in great part excluded or offered reductive theories about affect, we have little vocabulary to discuss and understand Amy's, and our own, affective ways of knowing" (9). Exactly why, however, would it be reductive to account for the student's behavior with terms like false consciousness, conformity to cultural conditioning and peer pressure, "lack of intellectual distance" and of development to a stage of (supposedly male) mental autonomy? We can hope that critics like Langstraat might develop a vocabulary to discuss affective ways of knowing, but wouldn't it probably be expressed in much the same vocabulary of cultural critique that she rejects as phallocentric?

"Clear Language and Simple Words Are the Only Salvation"

In conclusion to this chapter, when theorists like Elizabeth Ellsworth, Lisa Langstraat, Paul Butler, and Ian Barnard discuss "reason," "logic," "clarity," "affect," and "emotion," without defining which of the several senses of such words they have in mind, their positions become indefensible. In criticizing them, I have used common terms in informal logic or rhetorical analysis to identify unclear or fallacious arguments—such as vague or equivocal definitions and usage, inaccurate quotations, false dichotomy, inconsistency, failure to draw the line (leading to a slippery slope), and the variety of emotional appeal in which emotion is approved of without differentiating justifiable from unjustifiable forms of or appeal to it. I distinguish between *pathos* as emotion or appeal to it that is justified by empirical facts and reasonable moral qualities like justice, and *pathos* which reflects or manipulates ignorance of such facts and qualities to express or incite blind irrationality.

Likewise, I define clear writing and reasoning as that which is free from these fallacies as well as just being comprehensible and coherent. If no one can understand what a writer, especially a student, is saying, sometimes even including the writer, isn't that sufficient evidence of lack of clarity? Now, would these theorists accept the validity of this concept of reasoning in general (though not necessarily in my particular judgments) or dismiss out of hand the very criticism of logical fallacies or incomprehensibility as masculinist logic-chopping? Doing the latter would not only exempt the most nonsensical writing from criticism but would preclude criticism of demagogues in politics or media who manipulate the ignorance of their audience through misinformation, obfuscation, and appeal to the emotions of prejudice, ethnocentrism, xenophobia, and jingoism. (Consider right-wing claims that Barack Obama—"Obama/Osama, middle name Hussein"—was not born in the United States and is an Islamic jihadist or stealth third-world revolutionary through his father's blood.)

Paul Butler in responding to my critique in *JAC*, wrote:

> While Lazere seems to define clarity primarily in terms of what he sees as the lack of logic and coherence in some student writing, that narrow definition assumes a limited view of what it means for students to write clearly based primarily on what Lazere calls their "unfamiliarity with the conventions, complexities, and fixedness of written English, which needs to be studied like a foreign language if it has not been a part of one's home culture." This sounds to me very much like the inflexible, drill-and-kill approach to learning grammar and other aspects of language that gave rise to negative perceptions of current-traditional rhetoric. ("Revisiting" 320)

Butler's first sentence is grammatically unclear—it needs a comma or dash between "clearly" and "based" to indicate that the "based" refers to my definition, not what student writing is based on. QED. I leave it to readers to judge whether here or anywhere else in this book I equate clarity, logic, and coherence with "drill and kill." If Butler has a different definition of these traits and ways to teach them to basic writers, he fails to indicate them in either his article or response.

I have pointed to the tendency of Butler, Barnard, and other defenders of difficult, even "opaque," writing to equivocate between writers whose

126

difficult language creatively departs from previously mastered basic clarity, and those students who have not yet mastered the basics. There seems to be a failure to distinguish here between writing that is logical though unclear in style and that which is unclear because it is illogical, vague or misinformed, like my student in chapter 2 writing about nuclear power, "Then there are the pro conservatives who may write pamphlets," or because it is illogical, like the same student claiming that the opposition of one senator to nuclear power, who was "on paid salary by the U.S. Govt.," disproves claims that there was a government cover-up of nuclear dangers—by unelected officials in other governmental branches. And these are only a few of the mind-boggling factual and logical errors packed into the student's brief sentences.

In addition, I have not seen much effort by these theorists to indicate what minimal degree of comprehensible reasoning is desirable in all writing and even in writing addressed to fellow initiates in opacity or emotionality. Would they at least accept the principle that writers should choose the simplest words and sentence structures or the clearest reasoning that accurately convey their meaning, rather than indulging in either opacity or irrationality for their own sake? Wouldn't they allow that in their own writing, they seek to be understood and judged cogent by an audience of writing teachers, and that if a moderately informed peer, like me, can't understand them, they have failed? Even those whose conception of deconstruction is to destabilize conventional conceptions of clarity, reason, coherence, and comprehensibility must believe in them enough to write to be understood by *someone* or to be explicable to those who don't understand them. Otherwise why would they write at all? If opacity, like emotionality, is uncritically fetishized, there can be no way of discerning cases in which writers may just be confused or lazy about what they mean to say, are of unsound mind, or even are faking it. (Sartre admitted as much about some of his philosophical ramblings that he wrote on amphetamines.)

Finally, none of these defenders of opaque language whom I have read seem aware of the admonitions of many modern writers like Orwell and Camus against the manipulation of such language by politicians seeking to obfuscate and obstruct, who use language "for concealing or preventing thought," in the manner of doublespeak and newspeak, rather than expressing it (Orwell, "Politics" 259). In Camus's 1948 play *State of Siege*, a government bureaucrat explains the purpose of an edict in legalistic doubletalk: "It's intended to get them used to the touch of obscurity which gives all government regulations their peculiar efficacy. The less these people understand, the better they'll behave" (165). By contrast, Orwell says, "Good prose is like a window-pane" ("Why I Write" 248), and Camus asserts, "Every ambiguity, every misunderstanding, leads to death; clear language and simple words are the only salvation from this death" (*Rebel* 283–84). Weigh Orwell's and Camus's admonitions against the line of argument, most familiarly associated with Judith Butler's defense of Adorno's cryptic late work (and reiterated by Paul Butler and Barnard), that the debased, "clear" language of political propaganda and mass culture can only be counteracted by language that is incomprehensible to the masses (even when it claims to speak in the interest of the masses!). I counter this line by distinguishing the false clarity of propaganda—which is calculated to lie to and manipulate the masses through illogical oversimplifications and "feminine" emotional appeal—from logically "clear language and simple words" employed by public intellectuals of both genders, whose responsibility, as Chomsky famously put it in the *New York Review of Books*, is "to tell the truth and to expose lies" ("Responsibility" 1). Those who defend or write in language that is either opaque or irrationally emotive, when clearer, reasoned language is possible, seem to me either incapable of clear writing or just self-indulgent and seeking prestige among those who equate incomprehensibility with profundity. An apt postscript here is to salute Judith Butler, who in recent years has replaced arcane philosophizing with lucid polemics and self-endangering activism on behalf of the Palestinians.

7

BARTHOLOMAE AND PETROSKY'S
DEPOLITICIZED WAYS OF READING

David Bartholomae, in his theoretical essays collected in *Writing on the Margins* (*WOTM*) and in his two classroom-oriented books with Anthony Petrosky, *Facts, Artifacts, and Counterfacts* (*FAC*) and *Ways of Reading* (*WOR*), is in many ways distinct among the rhetcomp theorists I have been criticizing. He is a solid intellectual, whose writing mostly, though not entirely, eschews the antiacademic tendencies of some of his prominent students whom I have criticized, who have vulgarized his ideas. He is admirably devoted to integrating reading with writing instruction and to making basic writing and first-year writing gateways to academic discourse. He has carried on Mina Shaughnessy's legacy in making BW an academically substantial course and subject of scholarly study. He has lent prestige to that effort throughout a long, distinguished career as a regular teacher of BW and FYW; mentor of graduate students and administrator at Pitt; official of CCCC, MLA, and other professional organizations; and coeditor of the University of Pittsburgh Press's outstanding *Series in Composition, Literacy, and Culture*. In 2011 *College English* editor John Schilb, introducing an interview with him marking the twenty-fifth anniversary of "Inventing the University," called it "perhaps the most often cited and discussed essay in composition studies" ("Reconsiderations" 260). Although Bartholomae has been influenced by poststructualist/postmodernist theory in ways that I find fault with here, his own writing is generally free from theoretical jargon. His ethos as both an author and individual has consistently been sensible and benevolent. All that being said, several aspects of his work have been influential on trends in the profession that I find unfortunate, in ways I will detail here, I hope sympathetically and constructively, and I invite him to respond in kind.

The course of Bartholomae's professional career was similar to mine, when after undergraduate and graduate education as a literature major, he switched to being a composition specialist, while seeking to link the two realms. In *WOTM* he cites as his ideal course a fabled one that Richard Poirier, his graduate-school mentor at Rutgers, had earlier taught at Harvard: Humanities 6, "The Interpretation of Literature," which combined close reading, influenced by the New Criticism, with critical writing. He explains, "This course began on a different campus as the sophomore follow-up to the Amherst freshman course," one of whose founders, Reuben Brouwer, "carried the course with him when he went to Harvard" (248), where it was taught by leading junior faculty members in English including Peter Brooks, Paul de Man, and Neil Rudenstine (future president of Harvard). That course obviously has played a similar role in Bartholomae's psyche as Peter Dale Scott's English 1A course—for which I TA'd at Berkeley—has in mine, as a touchstone (for me, anyway) for the cultural and political anomalies of elite versus nonelite universities, teaching of literature and composition. My ultimate argument here is that *WOR* is in effect an ideal textbook for courses like these at Amherst and Harvard, rather than the widely adopted FYW reader it has been established as.

Bartholomae and Petrosky's 1986 *Facts, Artifacts, and Counterfacts* largely extended Shaughnessy's *Errors and Expectations* in its model of an experimental BW course at the University of Pittsburgh, designed "to teach young adults how to read and write. Ours were students outside the mainstream, students unprepared for the textual demands of a college education. Most of them were minority or special-admissions students" (4). In the course description and commentaries on it by other faculty members and PhD students who taught it, which constitute most of the book after a forty-page introduction, Shaughnessy and her sources are invoked several times, especially in the concluding chapter by Glynda Hull, who would go on to distinction as a professor in the Graduate School of Education and administrator of Subject A and the National Writing Project at Berkeley, and whose own students in the program in Literacy, Writing, and Culture there have included Ellen Cushman and Jennifer Trainor.

The preface to *FAC* explains that the BW class it describes was "an exemplary course—a small seminar where students met to read, write and talk about a single problem or subject—and to provide the additional time and support they needed . . ." (n.p.). The course counted for six credits, and graduate tutors worked closely with students. And,

> Our work on the course began several years ago when Bob Marshall, the dean of our college, asked if we could design a course for the increasing number of students who were unprepared to do the work of the standard curriculum. . . . It should be rooted in an existing department. It should be taught by regular faculty. It would be the kind of course for which students could receive full academic credit. . . . The dean who prepared the way for the course taught a section in our first semester . . . and he continues to teach a section each semester. (n.p.)

While the conception and implementation of this course, along with the accounts of it in *FAC*, were wholly admirable, its particular situation was problematic in several ways, especially in light of the audacious statement in the preface: "The course presented here can stand as an example of any first- or second-year course in the liberal arts" (n.p.). This course was offered at a research university in a middle-class urban neighborhood, where it was obviously well-funded and implemented by high-ranking administrators like Marshall, Bartholomae (a Rutgers PhD in literature, tenured professor, and eventual English-department chair), and Petrosky (a SUNY Buffalo Doctor of Education, accomplished researcher, and dean in the School of Education). It was team-taught by them and their top PhD students, who contributed chapters to *FAC*. All of their accounts confirm that the class was small and they had time to devote a great deal of individual attention to student writing and revision. As for the students, most of them are identified as minority or special-admissions students, but few details are provided about their age, ethnographic profile, financial support, and so on. Their selection or self-selection in these circumstances would seem likely to produce a BW student pool with more-than-average preparation, motivation, and liberal political leanings (to the limited extent that the course addressed politics, and in comparison to the parochially conservative students in my courses). Without meaning in any way to diminish the accomplishment of the Pitt course as an ideal laboratory for reading and writing instruction, I cannot help believing that if anything like these conditions were available for K-12, BW, FYW, and other general education and breath courses in all the less privileged regions of American education, like state and community colleges with their assembly-line writing programs, the results would be similarly positive, whatever the pedagogical approach might be. (For such an influential figure in the profession, Bartholomae has written only marginally about the curricular, funding, and staffing inequities in writing programs nationally.) I am inclined to see the course as confirmation of my recurrent argument about the anomaly that elite colleges and research universities are in many cases more supportive of critical literacy than nonelite colleges. So without looking the gift horse of *FAC* in the mouth, one message I take from it is that courses of the quality of this one at Pitt should be made available to less privileged students everywhere, beginning in K-12.

In the description of the course on which *FAC* is based, the primary readings were autobiographical or fictional narratives like *I Know Why the Caged Bird Sings*, *Hunger of Memory*, and *Catcher in the Rye*, although there is a development of the course theme of adolescence later in the term to Margaret Mead's *Coming of Age in Samoa* and Edgar Friedenberg's *The*

Vanishing Adolescent; one instructor assigned *The Autobiography of Malcolm X.* The syllabus states, "We will give you a list of books recommended by former BRW students, and this includes novels, science fiction, romances, biographies, books on sports, 'self-help' books and books on careers. The only restrictions are these: you cannot read magazines, textbooks, books from other courses or 'how-to-do-it books'" (51). Likewise, throughout Bartholomae's theoretical essays in *WOTM*, virtually all the numerous student papers analyzed are based on subjects within their personal experience, or on readings about personal experience, rather than academic or journalistic readings that deal with controversies in the public sphere. Although this limitation may be justifiable within a BW course, Bartholomae's theoretical perspective on BW, including the ignoring of developmental psychology and student ethnography, has little discernible carryover into the problems that I have been raising in more advanced courses—foremost problems in reasoning and argumentation. To find any more-or-less direct attention to these problems, we need to look at *WOR*, to which I will return.

The influence of postmodernist theory is evident from the beginning of *FAC*, which depicts students

> shuttling . . . between their understanding of what they have read and their understanding of what they must say to us about what they have read. (Our language is the language of written academic discourse, including the peculiar spoken version that passes as "talk" in disciplined classroom discussion). . . . We want students to learn to compose a response to their reading and, in doing so, to learn to compose (a reading) within the conventions of the highly conventional language of the university classroom. (4–5)

A later passage describes reading and writing "simultaneously an imitative act and an individual performance" (40). Similarly, at the outset of Bartholomae's celebrated "Inventing the University" (1985), he says, "The student has to learn to speak our language, to speak to us as we do, to try on the peculiar ways of knowing, selecting, evaluating, reporting, concluding, and arguing that define the discourse of our community" (*WOTM* 60). The student "has to invent the university by assembling and mimicking its language while finding some compromise between idiosyncrasy, a personal history, on the one hand, and the requirements of convention, the history of a discipline, on the other. He must learn to speak our language. Or he must dare to speak it or carry off the bluff" (61).

The postmodern language here—"peculiar spoken version," "conventions of the highly conventional language," "mimicking," "an imitative act," "an individual performance," "carry off the bluff"—implies that academic discourse is no more than an artificial, arbitrary social construct at which to play-act, the argot of one discourse community among others over which it has no substantive superiority. As I understand this general approach, its primary goal is to enable students to assimilate the content, vocabulary, form, and style of various academic disciplines, then to appropriate or challenge them from their personal viewpoint—but all in an ad hoc, instance-by-instance manner. In Harris's account of Bartholomae and Petrosky, "students are asked both to take on the method or ideas of other writers *and* to draw on their own experiences in responding to what these writers have to say, to use what they read for their own ends. . . ." (*A Teaching* 38–39). The process of learning, then, seems to be one of osmosis, immersion, and mimicry, comparable to the Rosetta Stone style of learning foreign languages. Nowhere do Bartholomae and his colleagues explicitly delineate their "conventions of language" or distinguish them from mastery of Shaughnessy's "vocabulary of general literacy" as it incorporates both the lexicon *and substance* of factual knowledge, reasoning, and critical evaluation. (These are some points on which the analogy with foreign-language acquisition breaks down.) My own alternative to those "conventions" is delineated in my survey of traits of critical thinking and cognitive development, in relation to subject matter, in my previous chapters.

The Dismissal of Developmentalism and Sociology

Bartholomae's theoretical justifications are scattered throughout the essays of *WOTM*, as in this, from 1987, the fuller version of the passage cited in chapter 1:

> We have not looked [sufficiently] at the borderlands, comparing the actual work of students who are newly in the mainstream with those who are caught on the margins. This is where we are stuck, and we are stuck because we have begun to imagine the problem as an abstract problem and because we have chosen to define the problem—this relation of one style to another—within the language and methods of developmental psychology. Basic writers, we are asked to imagine, work with a style that is preacademic. They are caught at some earlier step in cognitive development (at the level of concrete rather than formal operations, for example), or they belong to a culture that is pretextual (an oral culture, like those that preceded the development of alphabetic writing) and that hinders the cognitive development required for literate participation in a textual culture. . . . Basic writers,

in other words, are seen as childlike or as uncultured natives. There is an imperial frame to this understanding of the situation of those who are not like us. We define them in terms of their separateness. We do not see ourselves in what they do. (114)

A footnote on page 127 identifies some of the developmentalists Bartholomae disagrees with, including Frank D'Angelo, Thomas J. Farrell, David Olson (whom he nonetheless cites favorably elsewhere in *WOTM*), and Andrea Lunsford ("Cognitive Development and the Basic Writer"). This passage also alludes, without naming them, to Piaget, Vygotsky, and orality/literacy theorists like Havelock and Ong. In support of his position here, he identifies with Patricia Bizzell's account in "Cognition, Convention, and Certainty" (1982), of her shift in sympathy from cognitive psychology and problem solving in composition studies (in the mode of the early work of Linda Flower and John Hayes, associated with process theory) to social constructionism and discourse communities. However, Bartholomae blurs the important shift that Bizzell also made from cognitive to developmental psychology, which is socially contextualized in a different manner than social constructionism. (Flower has also shifted toward sociological, community-based literacy studies.) And nowhere in *WOTM*, whose essays run up to 2005, does he acknowledge Bizzell's later changes in position traced in *Academic Discourse and Critical Consciousness*—published in the series that Bartholomae coedited at Pittsburgh University Press—which supported William Perry's developmental model, Paulo Freire's and other Marxist critical pedagogy, and an affirmation of academic discourse, teachers' authority, and Hirsch's *Cultural Literacy*. Bartholomae's only discussion of Hirsch that I can find is a brief couple of pages in 1986 (*WOTM* 55–59) noncommittally acknowledging his formulations of cultural literacy prior to his 1987 book. This absence is regrettable, since I see Hirsch's position as diametrically opposed to Bartholomae's and would have liked to see them debate.

Bartholomae comes close, in the postmodernist manner, to reducing the difference between basic writers and mainstream students or even professors, to a matter of different discursive "styles," and to reducing pedagogy to negotiating the contact zones between those styles. (The further vulgarization of this reduction is seen in works like Paul Butler's "Style and the Public Intellectual" and Ian Barnard's "The Ruse of Clarity.") As suggested in chapter 1, a large realm of complications is evaded here. For applied college-level teaching, to what exact extent are young adults, for example, who have not gone to or finished high school—for whatever reason—"like us"? Are those *equally* like us who have received the best primary and secondary education and/or have assimilated literate discourse through extensive reading and those who have received a lower quality education and not been acculturated in reading—whether because of poverty or because of the lassitude of middle-class schools that my students deride as "a joke" and of families who raised their children on TV, video games, and social media instead of reading? Don't these variables impinge on students' preparation for college work and cognitive obstacles to it, even at the basic writing level? Is it an "imperial frame" to take realistic account of these sociological factors that prepare some kinds of students much more than others to negotiate the contact zones? To reiterate, progressive educators often argue that "disadvantaged" students, and adults, may possess more visceral experience and street smarts on some subjects than more academically privileged ones; I quite agree, but this evades the issue of preparation to read and write about subjects outside the realm of personal experience or at an abstract cognitive level, like *The Fire Next Time*.

Barthomolae and Petrosky similarly reflect what I find to be the astounding absence in much poststructuralist and postmodernist theory, of attention not only to developmental psychology but its relation to sociology and sociolinguistics. Thus these theories ignore scholarship in sociological and ethnographic variables influencing both K-12 and college students' reading and reasoning in college courses, like class socialization and quality of secondary education, along the lines of Basil Bernstein, Richard Hoggart, Pierre Bourdieu, Claus Mueller, and Ohmann, which I survey in part 3. When these scholars *are* cited, it is often out of their sociological and political context (especially the context of Marxist critique).[1] Bartholomae quotes Bernstein in an epigraph to "Inventing the University": ". . . the text is the form of the social relationships made visible, palpable, material" (60), but fails to discuss this passage—whose context, of *class socialization*, is quite different from anything in Bartholomae—or to mention Bernstein anywhere else in this essay or *WOTM*. Bartholomae does not discuss Bourdieu at all, and other American postmodern critics have paid far more attention to his theoretical works than his sociology on class reproduction in education and culture, including his collaborations with Bernstein. Likewise, American attention to abstruse Althusserian philosophy has eclipsed Althusserian sociology like that of Étienne Balibar and Armand Mattelart.[2]

In chapter 1, I questioned Batholomae's and others' judgment in applying poststructuralist theory to teaching basic or first-year writing. On the rare occasions when masters like Derrida and Fish switch gears from high-flown theory to basic pedagogy, they sound like fuddy-duddy foundationalists. Derrida, in his 1991 interview with Gary Olson in *JAC*, lamented the recent

decline of traditional French academic standards, in which "the pedagogy
... was very rigorous, and the social authority of the teacher was enormous.
This meant that there was an ethics of spelling, of *orthographe*, and every
transgression, every misspelling was a crime" (126). So much for poststructuralist transgressiveness!

In *Save the World on Your Own Time* Fish describes the course description for FYW that he taught at UIC:

> We don't do content in this class. By that I mean we are not interested
> in ideas—yours, mine, or anyone else's. We don't have an anthology of
> readings. We don't discuss current events. We don't exchange views
> on hot-button issues. We don't tell each other what we think about
> anything—except about how prepositions or participles or relative
> pronouns function. (40)

Fish's recent *How to Write a Sentence and How to Read One* is more in the
mode of Strunk and White than Fish's more abstruse theories. And, as indicated in chapter 6, Fish's prescription in *Save* for "academicizing" hot-button
issues in teaching is to approach them through quite conventional standards
of evaluating reasoning and evidence. Is this Stanley Fish, the guru of an-
tifoundational skepticism? What then, after all, is the use of all this arcane
theorizing that has held literary and rhetcomp scholars in thrall for decades,
when its own mentors reveal it is irrelevant to undergraduate teaching?

Bartholomae quotes as an inspiration on several occasions, including
at the very beginning of his and Petrosky's *FAC*, a passage from George
Steiner's *After Babel* that includes statements like these:

> The potentials of fiction, of counter-factuality, of undecidable futurity
> profoundly characterize both the origins and the nature of speech.
> ... Through language, we construct what I have called "alternities of
> being." To the extent that every individual speaker uses an idiolect,
> the problem of Babel is, quite simply, that of human individuation.
> ... To move between languages, to translate ... is to experience the
> almost bewildering bias of the human spirit towards freedom. (3)

As our students would say, I may be dumb, but I don't have the foggiest idea
what Steiner is talking about in all this *ity*-speak or what conceivable relevance it has to teaching writing to either K-12 or college students, in the context of the problems I have delineated. Nor are Steiner or Culler very relevant
to the succeeding portions of *FAC* or Bartholomae's other works that deal
with actual student writings, whose considerable value seems to me largely
autonomous from all the theoretical scaffolding. Neither Bartholomae nor

any of the other theorists I have discussed from what might be called the Pittsburgh School devote any sustained attention to factual ignorance, fallacious reasoning, or political prejudices in student reading. Nor do any of them consider the need for a foundational study of critical thinking to provide a framework for students in evaluating readings and analyzing arguments. Such concerns occasionally show up in the written interchanges between students and teachers transcribed in the later portions of *FAC*, but again just on an ad hoc basis.

Reading and Argument

Bartholomae's "The Argument of Reading," a 1996 piece in *Writing on the Margins*, attempts to bridge the gaps between literary criticism, argumentation, composition instruction, and politics in quite an idiosyncratic way. His aim here is "to think about literature and composition, about competing definitions of 'argument,' and about the usual sources called on to authorize instruction in logic and argument as part of the English (as opposed to the philosophy) curriculum" (250). (I must intervene here to ask, don't many of the poststructuralist/postmodernist sources Bartholomae and other current literary theorists call on belong more in the philosophy curriculum than English?) He regrets here that in CCCC, the influence of the disciplines of rhetoric and linguistics in recent decades "made it inevitable that composition should turn toward philosophy and rhetoric for its models of argumentation" (253) rather than toward literary criticism. I find this last distinction highly provocative, but it demands more development than Bartholomae provides here or anywhere else, to my knowledge. It is also somewhat of a false dilemma, or has been turned into that by the profession. For example, would Bartholomae exclude analysis of opposing political arguments in sources or fallacious reasoning about them in student writing because those subjects belong in philosophy or rhetoric, or political science, courses (usually not requirements like FYW)? Maybe so, given his own lack of attention to these realms in the student papers he analyzes throughout his work.

Perhaps what most distinguishes his model of argumentation is a shift of emphasis from critical analysis of public cultural texts to ad hoc analysis of students' own writings as cultural texts, distributed to the whole class for collective discussion and suggestions for revision.

> Students learn to read their writing closely not to make corrections but to ask how the language works or doesn't work. . . . By teaching reading, the writing course, as I am imagining it [not clearly identified here as BW, FYW, or advanced], can teach students to engage

in a complex, revisionary argument with the culture as it is present
in their own sentences and paragraphs, in their shapes and sounds
. . . (*WOTM* 252)

This sounds good, but I would need to see more examples than those Bartholomae or Joseph Harris, who advocates the same method, provide in any
of their work of the way this sophisticated mode of cultural critique and
pedagogical practice might work. (Nor are Min-Zhan Lu's similar efforts
described in chapter 5 very convincing.) The main problems I have with it
are that its success would seem to depend on exceptionally astute teachers
and peer students, versed in knowledge of cultural criticism (and with much
more time for reading papers than is commonly available), and that they
almost unavoidably, like Freirean teachers, will bring their own ideological
judgments to bear on what they call attention to in the papers they read and
in their prompts for revision. I have no objection to this, but it does mean
that student writers might have less agency and latitude in this process than
its advocates like to think. Finally, this method seems subject to the same
limitations of the classroom as a contact zone surveyed in chapters 2 and 5,
concerning different pools of students, such as doctrinaire conservatives.

In the same article, Bartholomae for once overtly defends the evasion
of leftist politics implicit throughout his thought. He first cites his mentor
Richard Poirier praising his former Harvard Humanities 6 colleagues, for
whom the teaching of close reading "should never be broken off because of
some vague feeling that the activity of reading is not sufficiently political or
socially beneficial. It should be understood as a lonely discipline that makes
no great claims for itself" (249).[3]

Bartholomae agrees:

Those who work on reading and writing in introductory courses can
easily be seen to be working with very little in comparison to colleagues whose students, at least putatively, are dealing with the "big"
questions (say) of race, class, and gender. . . . This, to me, is why the
meeting of composition and cultural studies has been such a great
disappointment. The cultural studies course has been quick to teach
the critique of commodity capitalism; it has shown almost no interest
in teaching students how to work with words (turning them this way
and that) as a form of critical practice. (249)

This killer dichotomy was especially puzzling because Bartholomae himself
had devoted an entire textbook, *WOR*, then in its third edition, to merging
these two aims.

Another of Bartholomae's mentors in "The Argument of Reading" was F. R. Leavis, whose mode of literary criticism as the close reading of texts Bartholomae distinguishes from that of the American New Critics (and implicitly Poirier):

> For a generation that had learned through World War I and during the period between the two world wars to understand propaganda and the effect of control through mass media, there was as much at stake in teaching students to understand from the inside how language worked and to discriminate between "good" uses of language and "bad." Close reading became a means of investigation, a way to exercise discrimination in the face of commercial, political, and cultural interests with a previously unheard-of power to penetrate daily life and produce the "common sense" of the citizenry. (251)

Even the American New Critics at their best, Bartholomae stipulates, in their emphasis on close reading, "were polemicists and their interest in the classroom and its methods was political." He explains:

> The pedagogy was designed to make visible those productions of selfhood and society, those forms of reading, writing, and imagining produced by contemporary mass culture through literature, radio, film, and advertising. Students, by reading, engaged in an argument with interests and points of view and habits and seductions latent in the words on the page. (252)

I cannot think of any New Critics who practiced this Marxist-sounding kind of ideological critique, but it would be pretty to think they did. Here Bartholomae himself, though, helpfully suggests a resolution to the dichotomy he previously set up between close, literary reading and "critique of commodity capitalism" in cultural studies. Again, however, few of the examples of student writing throughout his works illustrate the process he advocates here.

Aside from these points, his passages about mass culture coincide closely with my own conception of the application of literary study to the critique of arguments in mass media and political ideology. Bartholomae does (seemingly with approval) acknowledge about the Leavis "tradition of argument," "You can trace it through the development of British and American cultural studies (both as a critical practice and as a classroom practice) . . ." (252). This acknowledgment would seem to contradict his dismissal of cultural studies above and of critical pedagogy in several other works, as well as his claim that rhetcomp has been influenced more by philosophy and rhetoric than literary study, which includes the Leavis tradition and other connections to political/cultural criticism such as *Partisan Review* (which Poirier, himself a political activist, edited in its later years).

Unfortunately, instead of pursuing the passages in "The Argument of Reading" favoring criticism of mass culture anywhere else in *WOTM*, Bartholomae gets sidetracked endorsing epistemological theories like Culler's, Steiner's, and Gadamer's about the subjectivity of reading response, which seem to assume that "misreading" results only from differing subjective perceptions between writer and reader, without consideration of misinformed writers and readers or the possible intention to deceive by writers or speakers, especially in mass politics and media, as emphasized by Leavis and Orwell among many other critics. So there is little consideration in Bartholomae or the current theorists he favors of the epistemology of stupefaction, propaganda, lying, and doublethink—which Orwell explicitly defined as "reality control," the deliberate obfuscation of fixed, objective truth.

The paraphrases from Leavis and the New Critics in "The Argument of Reading" resonate (except for obvious differences in political position) with all the recent varieties of analysis of ideology in mass culture by Marxist-influenced literary critics. However, Bartholomae for whatever reason fails to make the connection with leftist literary critics including the Frankfurt School, Raymond Williams, Terry Eagleton, Fredric Jameson, Jane Tompkins, Richard Ohmann, Robert Scholes, Ariel Dorfman, Susan Willis, Tania Modleski, and Gerald Graff, who argued in *Beyond the Culture Wars*, "A neo-Marxist analysis of Vanna White's autobiography, *Vanna Speaks*, one that emphasized, say, the commodification of the self under postmodern capitalism, might be more challenging than any number of analyses of weightier tomes than Vanna's" (100). *WOR* partially compensates for this lack by including an ample contingent from this body of criticism, yet it is strangely absent from Bartholomae's own essays. Along the same lines, one might think Bartholomae would acknowledge the affinities between his ways of using student writings to generate cultural critique and those of Marxist/Freirean critical teachers, but he, like Harris and Spellmeyer, is consistently dismissive toward critical pedagogy, which receives no more attention in *WOTM* than one perfunctory footnote, on page 59, citing *Critical Teaching and Everyday Life* by Ira Shor (whose name is misspelled) and another pair of authors in Shor's collection *Freire for the Classroom*.

Nor does Bartholomae advocate more elementary critical studies, along the lines of the NCTE resolutions in the 1970s, of the language of political and economic persuasion. Such studies need not have a leftist inflection; I actually am more critical of him for neglecting such studies than neglecting leftist ones. A significant sidelight—here it is that Walker Gibson, who is one of the heroes in Bartholomae's and Poirier's account of the course in literary criticism at Amherst, helped initiate those Leavis-like NCTE resolutions and the Committee on Public Doublespeak, along with Ohmann, an equally prestigious, elite-college literary and cultural critic. Benjamin DeMott and Leo Marx were two other Amherst literary scholars who wrote criticism on politics and mass culture, as in DeMott's *The Imperial Middle: Why Americans Can't Think Straight About Class* and his textbook *Created Equal: Reading and Writing about Class in America*, and Marx's *The Machine in the Garden*.

I am not centrally making a brief for Marxism in this book, but in this context, I must call attention to a remark by Bartholomae nearly at the end of his interview with John Schilb, in the course of praising the essays in Schilb's and Patricia Harkin's *Contending with Words*: "I thought Pat Bizzell was exactly right about the absence of Marx in our thinking and writing" (279). That's all—one sentence, with no further *mea culpa* for the absence of Marxism, in relation to literary criticism, mass culture, or critical pedagogy, and for the snide remarks about Marxists, throughout his own thinking and writing. (That one essay by Bizzell was also about the extent of *her* attention to Marxism throughout her large and influential body of work, aside from a rather marginal chapter about Freire in *Academic Discourse*.) In this same interview, Bartholomae is quite nasty toward "Jim Berlin or others who were promoting a critical pedagogy. (Where one course in the first year was to overcome a lifetime of training in the American Way—and prevent students from buying designer jeans)" (272). He continues:

> My own feeling was (and is) that revision is the primary tool in a critical pedagogy. In a strict materialist sense, the one thing we can change in a writing class is sentences. If revision is something more than fixing up a paper or shoring up an argument (getting rid of the contradictions by pretending they don't exist), it can be a way of enacting critique. A revision can, say, feature the contradictions rather than hide them. (272)

But isn't the express goal of *WOR* to teach, in one first-year course, "reading against the grain" of training in the American way, through close reading, writing, and revising, about texts critiquing commodities like designer jeans, by Marxist mentors of critical pedagogy and cultural studies such as John Berger, Susan Willis, John Fiske, Mark Crispin Miller—and Freire himself? Dare I say that what I am writing, after lengthy reading and revision of thought about Bartholomae, features the contradictions in his thinking about these issues?

Difficulty in, and with, *Ways of Reading*

This brings us at last, frontally, to *Ways of Reading*.[4] It is in many ways a wonderful book, which audaciously advances aspects of critical thinking instruction that I have emphasized here. The readings are considerably longer, more complex, and politically progressive than normal in FYW anthologies, and the editors have bravely resisted the predictable pressures to shorten and dumb it down over nine editions since 1987. The prompts for reading are similar to my model in chapter 3 for recursion, cumulation, and multiple levels of meaning, with suggestions for continuous sequences of study that counteract the typical atomized units that detract from both academic study and modern public discourse. The selections are drawn from some of the most important contemporary critics and creative writers, and I have been engrossed for hours in reading them myself. Ay, there's the rub.

From the extreme of theorists like Hairston and Harris who would largely exclude academic readings from writing courses, *WOR* goes to the opposite extreme. It makes a quantum cognitive leap beyond *FAC* and BW, skipping over the level of most undergraduate liberal education and critical reading of day-to-day public discourse, to many readings at the level of a graduate seminar—or at least of Humanities 6 at Harvard. Despite the jacket-copy claim that it is designed for FYW and has been adopted at over four hundred colleges, much of the book is way over the heads of most lower-division students that I have ever had, and it has not been widely adopted anywhere I have taught. I fear that many instructors at those four hundred schools adopt it mainly because it affords an opportunity to inflict their graduate studies in cultural theory on hapless freshmen, in the same manner that past instructors have turned FYW into a course on their more orthodox graduate-school specialties, or because it affords them a misguided sense of self-importance in teaching what many departments disdain as a lowly course.

Indeed, the preface reveals, "These are the sorts of readings we talk about when we talk with our colleagues. We have learned that we can talk about them with our students as well" (vi). Many of the readings come from university press books or scholarly journals, but there is no explanation for why readings whose audience is professional scholars should be considered of pressing interest, or worth the extensive effort to make accessible, to first-year students—especially when such readings take precedence over possible alternatives addressing issues in liberal arts and the public sphere at a level more meaningful to undergraduates taking courses for general education and breadth. It is ironic that *WOR* recalls precisely the approach criticized by Bartholomae's colleague Joseph Harris as "this view of academic discourse as a limited and specific *use* of language" that can "cast its advocates in the role of simply teaching [freshmen] a professional jargon."

WOR makes an unqualified virtue of difficulty in academic texts. "We wanted to avoid pieces that were so plainly written or tightly bound that there was little for students to do but 'get the point'" (vi). In rejecting the question frequently posed to them, "whether the readings aren't finally just too hard for students" (ix), Bartholomae and Petrosky claim, "It is not hard to convince students they ought to be able to speak alongside of (or even speak back to) Clifford Geertz, Adrienne Rich, or Susan Willis" (ix). It *isn't?* They do not acknowledge that many texts are just too hard or distant from even avid students' intellectual maturity and world knowledge in a first-year course. I remember early in college giving up on certain books and authors as over my head; one was Proust, and it was not until I reread *Swann's Way* in my late twenties, in a graduate seminar with Justin O'Brien at Columbia, that I found out, as in Alain de Botton's title, *How Proust Can Change Your Life*, and was inspired to read nonstop the rest of *Remembrance of Things Past*.[5]

"Have your students talk back to Foucault," exhorted the jacket copy for the 2011 edition of *WOR*, which includes "Panopticism," replacing "The Body of the Condemned" in earlier editions. (The Foucault line was dropped from the 2014 jacket.) I have never gotten much out of Foucault myself, certainly not for teaching him in a first-year writing course, before most students have even taken an introductory course in philosophy or history. So it strikes me as sheer folly to expect that students of mine, like the one described earlier who referred to her uncle stationed at some naval base in Cuba, could or should reach the level of advanced philosophical discourse to talk back to Foucault, or to Judith Butler, whose *Undoing Gender* (only marginally easier than her infamously unreadable *Gender Trouble*) was added to the 2011 edition.

To compound an excess of difficulty, the immersion-and-imitation method of learning in *FAC* is applied to the far more difficult level of readings in *WOR*, with a vengeance. The book might be titled *Inventing Academic Discourse—On Your Own*. Though it is pitched at a much higher level of student than those idealized by the other postmodern pluralists I discuss, it just ups the ante in Platonic-Rousseauan faith in innate learning ability. The preface to *WOR* states:

> You will notice that there are few "glosses" appended to the essays. We have not added many editors' notes to define difficult words or to identify names or allusions to other authors or artists. We've omitted them because their presence suggests something we feel is false about

reading. . . . Good readers do what they can and try their best to fill in
the blanks; they ignore seemingly unimportant references and look
up the important ones. There is no reason for students to feel they lack
the knowledge necessary to complete a reading of these texts. (viii–ix)

The 1993 edition included a brilliant but highly theoretical Marxist-feminist
article, "Work(ing) Out," by Susan Willis, from her book *A Primer for Daily
Life*, whose ironic title belies the fact that it is an erudite, scholarly book
published by Routledge. The editors' gloss instructs, "As you reread, see if
you can develop working definitions of terms like 'commodified practice'
and 'gendered subject'" (725). Then, "Write an essay in which you explain
Willis's argument about women and their bodies under capitalism. It might
help to imagine that you are writing to someone who is interested but who
is having trouble understanding the arguments in 'Work(ing) Out.' You get
a chance to be the teacher here" (727). This is the editors' idea of respecting
and empowering students, but I can only envision my freshman agriculture
majors at Cal Poly or Tennessee reading this and stampeding to drop the
course in fear and loathing.

Bartholomae and Petrosky's negligence of developmental psychology
is again apparent in statements like, "Good readers do what they can and
try their best to fill in the blanks," with no distinction in readers' age or
stage of achievement, prior to and throughout college, at Amherst and
Harvard, at state and community colleges, or after they are long out of
school. Nor do they explain how beginning college students are expected
to know what references are or are not important—a large impediment to
reading at this level, as E. D. Hirsch has confirmed. There are considerable
glosses before and after readings, making some attempt to explain authors'
more difficult ideas and terminology and to encourage further research as
a general principle, but students are left on their own about how to select
from a virtual infinity of sources in the Google age. Mightn't the editors
at least recommend readings for each selection known to provide useful
background information at a comprehensible level?

The 2011 edition of *WOR* added a lengthy piece by Edward Said from
After the Last Sky: Palestinian Lives, a book of critical reflections prompted
by photographs of Palestinian refugees by Jean Mohr. This is a powerful
reading but more literary than argumentative in style, and it presupposes
that readers know something of the history and politics of the Middle East.
An exercise following it says, "The essay is filled with references to people
(including writers), places, and events that are, most likely, foreign to you.
Choose one that seems interesting or important, worth devoting time to

research" (576). Would footnote glosses really impair the unmediated reading experience? And wouldn't it be more helpful to precede study of this piece with a research assignment on the basics of the Israeli-Palestinian conflict, then evaluating texts on it with opposing arguments, including some of Said's clearly written journalistic polemics and those of his critics? (As noted earlier, Judith Butler has also written lucid political journalism on the Middle East, which might be assigned to supplement her theoretical work.) For that matter, mightn't a more definitive introduction to Said and to the postcolonialist theory underlying this selection be taken from *Orientalism* or *Covering Islam*?

Bartholomae and Petrosky seem insufficiently concerned, then, to distinguish, as most teachers and anthologists try to do, what level of difficulty in general-education readings is worth the trouble and what isn't in different pedagogical circumstances. We learn by trial and error. As much as I loved teaching the *Borzoi College Reader* at Berkeley, I gave up on assigning it at Cal Poly after a few years. In teaching Baldwin's *The Fire Next Time* year after year, I figured out that passages like the one discussed in chapter 1 about the role of race in the history of Christianity and Islam were incomprehensible despite a reasonable amount of student rereading and peer discussion, but that lecturing to explicate them and providing further references was well worth the effort to unravel their significance for all Americans today. I was surprised when I first assigned "The Age of Irony?" by Susan Searls Giroux, thinking that at least the passages I quote in chapter 3 would be significant to second-term FYW students and not just teachers reading *JAC*, because of Giroux's poignant account of "the frightened reactions of the besieged" current citizens, and implicitly students, who have been too overwhelmed by economic and educational deprivation to understand the political forces driving that deprivation, let alone to take arms against them. But I found that many students, in a grim confirmation of Giroux's point, not only were turned off reading her because the ideas were at a level of abstraction and syntactic complexity that they could not connect with personally, but because they misread it in small and large ways, for the variety of reasons analyzed in chapter 3, and it took considerable explication in my teaching and revision of assignments to overcome these obstacles. So I cannot envision any amount of effort that might make Foucault, Kuhn, Geertz, Butler, Willis, or Said comprehensible and important to students like mine, and I would prefer to look instead for provocative readings at the intermediate level of Baldwin and Giroux, or at a more journalistic level.

WOR is in large part a reader on cultural studies, but its principle is not to select texts that apply criticism of "those forms of reading, writing, and imagining produced by contemporary mass culture," in the manner of many FYW textbooks, such as *Rereading America*, but to enable reading of advanced cultural theory. The resulting problem can be seen in the selection of Freire's "The 'Banking' Concept of Education" and the exercises following it, such as: "If you think of Freire as your teacher in this essay, does he enact his own principles? Does he speak to you as though he were making deposits in a bank? . . . Look for sections in the essay you could use to talk about the role Freire casts you in as a reader" (221). But this essay, from *The Pedagogy of the Oppressed*, is one of Freire's more erudite works, with quotations from Beauvoir and Sartre (in French), Husserl, Niebuhr, and Fromm—emphatically not addressed to an audience of first-year college students. Surely, more accessible readings could have been selected from Freire and his American mediators, such as his conversations with Ira Shor, Donaldo Macedo, and Henry Giroux, or their own works describing classroom applications for an audience of teachers, like Shor's *Critical Teaching and Everyday Life* or Jane Tompkins's "Pedagogy of the Distressed." Freire's and his followers' teaching practice typically does not begin with academic texts at all, but with students' own experiences and spontaneous discussion or writing, which can then lead to relevant readings and writing instruction. This is something like what Bartholomae, Petrosky, and Harris say they are after too, but they don't demonstrate it as concretely as Shor and other Freireans do.

Sidestepping around Marxism

Bizzell astutely criticizes the way recent textbooks incorporate leftist political readings, specifically referring to *WOR*, and with implicit relevance to the entire "Pittsburgh School":

> We often leave the choice and handling of this material entirely up to the students, with the result that they are often stunningly successful at normalizing or defusing material that we might have thought was politically explosive. . . . This really should not surprise us, since leaving so much up to them sends the message that what one does with politically explosive material is entirely a matter of personal choice. One's ideological conditioning, the intertextuality of interpretations, seems to be allowably left outside. ("Power" 66)

An even more pointed critique of the equivocal use of political readings in *WOR* was made by Alan France in *Composition as a Cultural Practice*, which provided an illuminating Marxist critique of recent composition studies, with extensive attention to the third edition of *WOR*. (Alan's death from cancer at fifty-seven in 2001 silenced a much-needed voice in theory of composition and rhetoric.) France made the intriguing point that in *WOR*, the editors' "sidestepping of Marxist criticism—even when a reading they were discussing was hardly explicable without it—was remarkable" (15).

Indeed, Marxist theory is prevalent in these readings, but without any direct explanation of why, in a historical or even theoretical context. One indirect explanation may be found at the outset of Bartholomae's celebrated "Inventing the University" (1985): "The student has to learn to speak our language, to speak to us as we do, to try on the peculiar ways of knowing, selecting, evaluating, reporting, concluding, and arguing that define the discourse of our community" (*Writing* 60). (Couldn't he just have said that college teaches critical thinking, regardless of "discourse communities")? Thus Bartholomae would reduce Marxism to being a mode of professional jargon rather than a call, not to study the world but to change it, the tacit inspiration for texts like "The Port Huron Statement," expressing students' "yearning to believe there *is* an alternative to the present, that something *can* be done to change circumstances in the school, the workplaces, the bureaucracies, the government." (I teach this text under the mode of critical thinking that enables us to envision alternatives to our "culturally conditioned assumptions.")

A related problem is again indicated in the exercises for the Freire reading: "Freire uses two terms from Marxist literature: *praxis* and *alienation*. From the way these words are used in the essay, how would you define them? And how might they be applied to the study of education?" (220). Most of my students would be clueless in defining these complex terms just from the context, and even the theoretical "study of education" is beyond the cognitive radar of some at that age—though they can certainly "get" more visceral demonstrations of it like Shor's comparison between the teacher's spacious, free-standing desk or authority to stand up and the students' regimented rows of cramped seating. (Ira is reputed, back in the headstrong early 1970s, to have picked up a student desk in class and smashed it to show how tacky it was.)

Similarly, Susan Willis's "Work(ing) Out" is introduced:

Willis brackets in her critique even the utopian dimensions of mass culture (resisting, for example, the image of the physically strong woman as a sign of liberation or resistance). This image, too, becomes part of a general process by which a woman's body is commodified: "The liberatory impulses are in every instance contained within the larger capitalist system which gives the lie to the notion of feminized production." (703)

For all the editors' calling of attention to style, they seem unconscious that almost every word in their own passage here and other exercises on Willis, as well as in her own phrases like "commodified practice" and "gendered subject," is couched in the vocabulary and syntax of Marxist theoryspeak, a foreign language to anyone without some grounding in Marxism. France suggested about this selection in *WOR*, "Students might begin with further readings from Willis' *Primer*, particularly Chapter 1 ('Unwrapping Use Value'), which is an accessible introduction to the elements of Marxist criticism" (15–16).

The sidestepping around a direct exposition of Marxism is apparent in phrasing like this, about a group of readings under the rubric of "Reading Culture":

> Most of the readings that follow ask you to imagine that you are the product of your culture; that your ideas, feelings, and actions, your ways of thinking and being, are constructed for you by a large, organized, pervasive force (sometimes called history, sometimes called culture, sometimes called ideology). You don't feel this to be the case, but that is part of the power of culture, or so the argument goes. (828)

Or, a degree more directly, about Willis's article:

> Behind her argument is the assumption that our usual ways of thinking and speaking are determined in advance by a history of patriarchy and capitalism (ways of thinking and speaking about gender and work that *produce* the world that seems to be simply and naturally there). To learn to read, then, is to learn to read against the grain of these conventional systems of representation. (818)

Fine, but the M-word is still not mentioned or defined here, and students are left to puzzle out the meaning of *ideology, patriarchy, capitalism,* and *systems of representation.* For that matter, these passages do not delineate a distinctly Marxist position but are only another prolix variant on Kytle's non-Marxist "culturally conditioned assumptions."

By the 2011 edition of *WOR*, Willis's article had been replaced, perhaps as a concession to readability, by Susan Bordo's "Beauty (Re)Discovers the Male Body," which is a somewhat more accessible study of sex roles in mass culture (though Bordo is followed by Judith Butler on gender issues, which is more abstract than Willis). However, Bordo puts less emphasis than Willis does on the relation of gender issues to capitalist ideology and economics. A further retreat from Marxism in the 2011 edition may be signaled by the disappearance of overtly Marxist analyses like John Fiske's "Madonna" and Mark Crispin Miller's *Boxed In: The Culture of TV*, with no comparable replacements. The loss of that dimension in these authors is especially regrettable in light of the already disproportionate emphasis in the earlier editions (indeed as in American cultural studies generally and the culture itself) on issues of gender and race over those of class and political economy, including the culture industry, which have scarcely appeared in any edition of *WOR*, except for the Rodriguez-Hoggart sequence, which, as previously noted, actually emphasizes the narrative of family relations and ethnicity more than Hoggart's incisive class analysis.

I sympathize with the dilemma that Bartholomae and Petrosky faced, of anthologizing Marxist critics and concepts at the level of FYW without being able to devote adequate space to explanatory background. I faced a similar challenge in editing a collection at a more advanced level, *American Media and Mass Culture: Left Perspectives*, which grew out of the issue of *College English* in 1977 that Ohmann, then its editor, commissioned me to put together on "Mass Culture, Political Consciousness, and English Studies." Developing it into a six-hundred-page book necessitated a long general introduction including a historical survey and definition of terms, plus explanatory introductions to eight sections of readings and recommended further readings, grouped as "Media and Manipulation," "Capitalism and American Mythology," "Moments of Historical Consciousness," "The Mass-Mediation of Popular and Oppositional Culture," "Ideology in Perception, Structure, and Genre," "Media, Literacy, and Political Socialization," "From the Halls of Montezuma to the Shores of Tripoli: Cultural Imperialism," and "Alternatives and Cultural Activism." This was a scholarly collection, mainly in the mode of literary criticism, but with a selection of articles for maximum readability, avoidance of jargon, and focus on application to undergraduate teaching and activism. It has been adopted for some graduate and upper-division courses in cultural studies or media criticism, and I used it myself for one such upper-division course at Cal Poly, assigning only the most accessible articles, like Ohmann's "Doublespeak and Ideology in Ads: A Kit for Teachers," Louis Kampf's "A Course in Spectator Sports," Tania Modleski's "The Search for Tomorrow in Today's Soap Operas," Christopher Jencks's "Should News Be Sold for Profit?," Ariel Dorfman's "The Infantilizing of Culture," and Neil Postman's "The Teaching of the Media Curriculum." Postman's is the only article that I recall ever trying to teach in even the second term of FYW, in its relation to critical thinking noted in chapter 3 here.

For purposes of FYW, however, it seems to me that *WOR* could select challenging readings and issues at a more accessible level of political literacy, that of journals like the *Nation* and the *New Yorker*, books by authors like Postman, Barbara Ehrenreich, James Baldwin, David Cay Johnston, Wendell Berry, Eric Schlosser, and Tamara Draut (*Strapped: Why America's 20- and 30-Somethings Can't Get Ahead*). I would recommend for future editions of *WOR* Naomi Wolf's *The Beauty Myth*, which is implicitly in the mode of Marxism that France advocates as "cultural materialism," but without jargon like Willis's on the same subject. Wolf incisively pulls gender and economic issues together, piercing to the heart of what Bartholomae disdains as "the critique of commodity capitalism." "Why is it never said that the really crucial function that women serve as aspiring beauties is *to buy more things for the body*. Somehow, somewhere, someone must have figured out that they will buy more things if they are kept in the self-hating, ever failing, hungry and sexually insecure state of being aspiring 'beauties'" (66). And,

> Powerful industries—the $35-billon-a-year diet industry, the $20-billion cosmetics industry, the $300-million cosmetic surgery industry, and the $70-billion pornography industry—have arisen from the capital made out of unconscious anxieties, and are in turn able, through their influence on mass culture, to use, stimulate, and reinforce the hallucination in a rising economic spiral. (17)

Wolf is not expressly a Marxist, and she is a journalist rather than a scholar or theorist, but teaching her analysis can serve well to exemplify a material Marxist perspective.

Again, however, in this book I am not primarily pleading the cause of any variety of Marxist criticism or teaching, which I am not convinced has a legitimate place in BW or first-term FYW, though some Freireans and other leftists make substantial arguments to the contrary. I am pleading for a more basic level of instruction for political literacy that is a necessary *precondition* for student understanding of Marxism and leftist thought in general. That level could begin with the introduction of Marxism, socialism, communism, and other left concepts as part of the vocabulary of cultural literacy, in the way Shaughnessy and Hirsch include them, and could continue with explanation of them in the critical-thinking context of semantics—their complex denotations, connotations, accurate and inaccurate usage. (In *Reading and Writing for Civic Literacy*, see "Socialism, Communism, and Marxism" 270–71, and "Conservatives, Liberals, Socialists, Libertarians" 277–79). The basic theoretical issues could then include the Marcusean closed universe of discourse that excludes public debate and education in these very subjects, through the economic and ideological hegemony of corporations that marginalizes left voices. Finally, that basic level of education would apply study of principles and practices in argumentative rhetoric to opposing texts (conservative, liberal, libertarian, *and leftist*) on our most urgent political and economic disputes.

The absence of these more fundamental levels of critical study in *WOR* again highlight its peculiar "sidestepping," this time of the vocabulary of logic and argument—which finally got just a perfunctory nod in the 2011 edition, in a four-page section on "The Art of Argument." In spite of all its virtues, then, in entirely skipping over more elementary ways of "reading against the grain," *WOR* is a massive case of putting the cart of advanced theory before the horse of basic political literacy, thus contributing to en-couragement (or intimidation) of novice FYW teachers to pitch their courses above the head of many, perhaps most, students at non–liberal arts colleges.

8

ACTING LOCALLY, THINKING LOCALLY: THE SHRINKING OF THE PUBLIC SPHERE

As previously indicated, the recent developments in English studies that I see as distracting from effective instruction in critical thinking and civic literacy include unqualified celebrations of identity politics, diversity, and difference instead of emphasis on cultural commonalities and unifying political causes; fixation on local and identity politics, communities, and cultures to the exclusion of national and international politics and cosmopolitan culture; and resistance to any movement toward national curricular standards. In spite of the unquestionable intrinsic value of all these diverse literacy practices, some of their more doctrinaire advocates, whom I call *diverseologues*, seem to me ingenuous in acting as though such practices in local communities either can operate outside the influence of national and international centers of power or can somehow counteract those centers, so that the latter are virtually ignored, and sometimes denigrated, as a subject of critique and action. Thus, although most of the advocates of these theoretical lines consider themselves and their causes as politically liberal or progressive, their insistence on unlimited proliferation of localism, diversity, and identity politics—coincident with an age of unprecedented concentration of economic ownership, political power, and social control by multinational corporations and the political right in America—has had profoundly conservative consequences in obstructing the scale of studies that are educational preconditions for the unified opposition that progressive constituencies need to counter the right.

My arguments about English studies coincide on a larger political scale with those of other leftist critics like Walter Benn Michaels's *The Trouble with Diversity: How We Learned to Love Identity and Ignore Inequality*, Todd Gitlin's *The Twilight of Common Dreams*, Elizabeth Fox-Genovese's "The Claims of a Common Culture," Benjamin Barber's *An Aristocracy of Everyone*, and the contribution by historian Jackson Lears to a recent forum on "Intellectuals and Their America" in *Dissent*, partially cited in chapter 1, where Lears writes about identity politics:

One unintended consequence of the quest for alternative identities was that it created a new kind of fragmented, interest-group politics, unmoored from any larger vision of the good society. . . . The regnant modes of theory shifted as well. Cultural Marxism fell into disuse. There were many new theorists on the block, but the most influential across disciplines was Michel Foucault. . . . For many left academics, he became less a theorist of the surveillance state than an advocate of Nietzschean individualism, whose vision of "heterotopia" celebrated myriad sites of resistance to repressive authority rather than any larger notion of commonweal. All of this comported well with the emerging cultural politics of the academy, which in many ways constituted a mirror image of free-market individualism. From the mid-1980s on, it was possible to discern a kind of left-wing Reaganism among academics in the humanities and social sciences, most visible in the postmodern tendency to celebrate consumer culture as an area of choice, liberation, and self-creation. Fearful of seeming to be puritanical killjoys, left intellectuals backed away from environmentalist critiques of heedless consumption. No wonder the Right had such an easy time establishing its cultural hegemony. (32)

Similarly, Fox-Genovese had asserted in 1986:

At some point the attack on the received canon shifted ground. Increasingly, the attack has been waged in the name of the individual's right to education as a personal history, a parochial culture, and a private epistemology. The worst of it is that the "radical" critics of the purportedly irrelevant canon have sacrificed the ideal of collective identity that constituted its most laudable feature. To settle for education as personal autobiography or identity is tacitly to accept the worst forms of political domination. (1986: 133)

I see two other main sources of current theory favoring local cultures and discourses over cosmopolitan ones. The first line seems to derive, directly or indirectly, from sources including Jean-François Lyotard's *The Postmodern Condition*, Hannah Arendt's *The Human Condition*, and Clifford Geertz's *Local Knowledge*, while pushing their ideas to extremes never envisioned by their authors; for example, these authors champion local communities, but not to the point of condoning indifference to, or ignorance of, national and international politics in literacy education, as some postmodernists seem tacitly to do.[1]

Thus Beth Daniell, after making a persuasive critique of the oversimplified killer dichotomies grounding the "great leap" theory of orality versus literacy, advocates in their place the trend toward studies in "little narratives [that] almost all examine literacy in particular local settings," conducted by scholars who "seldom make theoretical statements that claim to be valid for literate persons in general or literate cultures in general" (403). But is a theory of literacy that would make accessible to all Americans the culture of critical discourse, in higher education and knowledge of international and national politics, economics, and serious journalistic media, an invalid one, no more than a "grand narrative" to be shunned by our students in favor of being restricted to their local culture? Isn't Daniell creating yet another killer dichotomy?

In a *College English* article, "Service Learning and English Studies," Aaron Schutz and Anne Ruggles Gere outlined a theoretical justification for an argumentative writing course Schutz taught, keyed to service learning and community activism, with the culminating example of students collaboratively researching and writing about campus issues like a case of racial discrimination in their student union. I wrote a comment in a later *CE* admiring their approach while offering a "friendly amendment" suggesting extending such assignments to national politics and offering the example of an assignment I gave at Loyola College in Baltimore in 1997, in which students collaborated on communicating with their representatives in Washington and with national journalists concerning disputes over a part of the recent Republican Contract with America's Orwellian "Personal Responsibility Act" that reduced funds for the federal school lunch program. (Republicans claimed they were in fact increasing them, just at a reduced rate of growth, though Democrats claimed this amounted to a net loss after inflation.) The students pooled their results—which clearly showed Democrats telling the truth and Republicans equivocating or stonewalling—and they individually wrote op-ed columns to submit to local newspapers. Schutz and Gere's response was churlishly doctrinaire, insisting on the superiority of their approach.

> Schutz's class encouraged students to work toward a discursive intervention into the larger community . . . and not just write about it for a teacher. . . . In addition, Lazere's project appears to have been designed to engage students more as individuals than as collective groups. . . . Finally, Lazere presents his project as an effort that moves beyond the limited "local" nature of Schutz's class. In his effort to address national issues, however, Lazere appears to have avoided exploring the impacts this policy change might have on actual people in particular local contexts. (358–59)

Never mind that I said most of the students at this private college actually lived in affluent local contexts unaffected by cuts in school lunch subsidies, and that the main result of the assignment was to shake their faith in the credibility of Republican rhetoric. Didn't Schutz and Gere come across like cultural commissars in dictating that American college students cannot benefit from individual engagement with national and international issues without immediate reference to their own communities? There is, once again, a tinge of smugness in scholars like this who claim to champion marginalized people while remaining oblivious to the inapplicability of their dogmas to mainstream students and society.

All this Rousseauan romanticizing of local cultures glosses over the fact that now and in the past, they have as often been politically reactionary as progressive. They are currently the "red state" electoral bedrock of the Republican Party. For those raised in such cultures, exposure in college and elsewhere to cosmopolitan views is an avenue toward decentering their ethnocentric prejudices. If empowering conservative, provincial bigotry is part of postmodern localists' agenda, they should at least be straightforward about it. Would Shutz have helped the College Republicans make a "discursive intervention" in support of racial discrimination on campus?

In *Arts of Living*, Spellmeyer asserts,

> In a genuine democracy, all politics become local politics because the decision making that matters most occurs at the local levels. By the same token, a democratic culture will not teach us to look beyond our actual lives for the solution to our problems; it will remind us instead that solutions of some sort always lie at hand, even when our hands have been tied. (9)

The untenability of this position is inadvertently exposed later in Spellmeyer's book when he proposes an agenda for contemporary humanistic studies that would address "central problems of our time—globalization, the environmental crisis, the growing split between the haves and have nots, the erosion of well-defined cultures, the disappearance of the transcendent" (20). He also praises a faculty proposal for curricular reform he had a hand in at Rutgers that "acknowledged openly what everyone knew but seldom vocalized: that college students across the United States graduate without an adequate understanding of their society, their world, and their times." The committee recommended, "instead of a core curriculum . . . courses designed around 'dialogues' on the issues of consequence to society as a whole. The idea was to give students the intellectual tools—the information and the interpretive paradigms—to explore both the problems of the coming century and their possible solutions" (242–43). Spellmeyer never acknowledges the contradiction between these opposing positions, nor does he explore possible ways of reconciling them—as Freireans and Graff, both of whom Spellmeyer sneers at, have done.

By 2012, in an eloquent article for *College English* titled "Saving the Social Imagination: The Function of the Humanities at the Present Time," the protean Mr. Spellmeyer had abandoned localism and expressivism in rhetcomp theory for a return to the global vision of leftists like the Frankfurt School and Bourdieu critiquing one-dimensional society, thought, and language in the neoliberal age, and he reaffirmed the intellectual discourse of academia, as well as socialist political economy, as cognitive alternatives.

> For generations of Americans, college was a special place, and they saw their professors as the embodiment of values that challenged the servitude which ruled everywhere outside. The academy's other-worldliness was actually the source of its greatest strength, and the bleakness of the world today makes that otherworldliness essential to our shared pursuit of a better life. (585)

Now if Spellmeyer would only acknowledge that the position he affirmed here is much the same as that of the left cultural critics he ridiculed in his review of Fitts and France's *Left Margins*.

A second line of theory privileging the local derives from discussions of terms "public discourse," "public intellectual," and "the public sphere." Several postmodern theorists praise Michael Halloran's 1982 "Rhetoric in the American College Curriculum: The Decline of Public Discourse." Christian Weisser summarizes Halloran's case that the eighteenth-century American origins of modern English studies consisted of educating secondary and college students for oratory and debate on political issues, and he notes Halloran's qualifier, "rarely were the topics of discussion limited to subjective or local matters" (44). Weisser briefly cites Lester Faigley's endorsement of Halloran's project of restoring the rhetoric of national public discourse into our studies, and then turns to several other recent theorists who cite Halloran and/or Faigley, preeminently Susan Wells in "Rogue Cops" (to which I will return). Weisser fails to register, however, that these theorists no sooner pay homage to Halloran and Faigley, than they switch from their national scope to "local matters." This unexplained slippage from the national to the local can be seen, for example, in Cushman's "The Rhetorician," which begins with a citation from Halloran, then states, "One way to increase our participation in public discourse is to bridge the university and community through activism" (7). However, Cushman's examples of activism and service learning, both here and in "Public Intellectuals," (though irreproachable in themselves, as noted above) are all local. Likewise, in the chapter "Community" in *A Teaching*, Harris, without citing Halloran, discusses other recent thinkers' use of the term *public* "in theorizing a *large scale* [author's emphasis] form of democracy, as a key (if troubled) means of bridging the interests of local communities and individuals with those of a state or nation" (108). But rather than pursue this "bridging," he immediately and thenceforth throughout his book shifts the focus to local civic and classroom communities. Again, it is perfectly justifiable to turn academic attention to previously neglected local communities, but not to the unwarranted exclusion of national and international communities or issues.

A more combatively delineated dichotomy is expressed by Linda Flower in *Community Literacy and the Rhetoric of Public Engagement*. Flower describes the shift in rhetcomp theory from expressivism, as well as from her own early, cognitivist approach to problem solving (criticized by leftists like James Berlin and Alan France), to leftist "social-process" theory. The latter

> offered students a formidable set of literate practices that allowed them to *speak against something*—against the media and ideology, against their own assumptions and inclinations as well as against institutions, oppression, and power. . . . But what these paradigms— that so strongly influence teaching and scholarship—do not do well is teach how to *speak with* others across the chasms of difference. (78–79)

These chasms of difference, however, are not, as one might suppose, between the political left and right, but between academics and local communities. While Flower does not expressly deny the intrinsic value of critical pedagogy and asserts her leftist bona fides with references to Saul Alinsky and Paulo Freire, the recent flood of local studies along the lines she advocates and admirably describes in this book and elsewhere, such as her work with the Community Literacy Center in Pittsburgh, has largely eclipsed critical studies of "media and ideology."

"The public sphere" is mainly associated with Jürgen Habermas, whose *The Structural Transformation of the Public Sphere* has prompted many appropriations in rhetcomp studies, most of which take issue with Habermas's focus on national public spheres and posit instead a diversity of smaller, local publics and "counter-publics." (The jacket copy of Flower's *Community Literacy* says she "articulates a theory of local publics and explores the transformative potential of alternative discourse and counter-public performances.") Wells's "Rogue Cops," a much-cited example, is eloquent and compelling in many ways, but I remain puzzled over several key points in it that typify this line of postmodern theory. First, without any explicit justification for this, Wells's examples of "public literate action" nearly all are local rather than national ones. They include a Temple student who wrote a complaint after being brutalized by Philadelphia police, and the conversation at a neighborhood meeting between whites and blacks about crime. It would be patronizing to suggest that people engaged in such community struggles should or could find the energy to connect their local problems with pertinent national political policies, but mightn't scholars who become involved in struggles like these provide a useful service by drawing on the resources of academic discourse to contribute those connections?

The only national case Wells devotes substantial space to concerns the rhetorical problems facing President Clinton in trying to sell his national health insurance plan to the public. Wells says, "In spite of Clinton's palpable desire for a broad public debate, and the force with which he expressed it in the health care speech, we had no debate, no health care reform" (331). Her analysis of this situation is restricted to the complexities involved in addressing a fragmented public sphere, and while conceding that "the failure of health care reform was not primarily rhetorical" (331), she says nothing about what the primary cause *was*—the Republican attack machine, in league with the HMO and pharmaceutical lobbies, conducting a campaign of lies and deceptions like the "Harry and Louise" commercial. If this campaign was not a prime subject for academic rhetorical study, I cannot imagine what a more valid one would be.

Unlike Fishman-McCarthy's and Spellmeyer's articles in the same *CCC*, Wells's does support critical pedagogy and cultural studies, but with some qualifications and somewhat marginally. She says about Faigley's endorsement of cultural studies in writing courses, "Faigley advocates the analysis of literacy rather than public literate action. . . . Cultural studies has made invaluable contributions to political pedagogy, but it does not answer the question of how students can speak in their own skins to a broad audience with some hope of effectiveness" (334). This is a valid point, and I accept it as a limitation in my own work, although I find more value than she does in individual classroom writing assignments like her example of a student writing on gun control, which she describes as writing in a vacuum, "since there is no place within the culture where student writing on gun control is held to be of general interest" (328). Isn't researching, synthesizing, and analyzing opposed arguments on this topic into a paper a valuable learning experience, which might well be subsequently applied to influencing legislation, working with gun control organizations, and so forth?

Wells goes on to say, "Given the intractable fragmentation of our own public sphere, it is likely that the representations of the public we offer students beyond the classroom will be provisional; we will look for alternate publics and counter publics" (335). But is the public sphere really that intractable, and do alternate publics need to be invented from scratch? Don't plenty already exist, *nationally and internationally,* in oppositional electoral and legislative politics, parties like the Greens and Labor Party (and even the currently marginalized democratic wing of the Democratic Party); the national communitarian movement, activist groups for environmentalism and peace and against globalization; civil-, women's-, and gay-rights organizations, Internet political and media activism groups; labor unions (including those of teachers, regular and contingent college faculty, and graduate students); the journalistic circles of the *Nation, In These Times,* the *Progressive, Mother Jones, Dissent,* Fairness and Accuracy in Reporting, and Pacifica Radio? These activist arenas can all be linked to composition instruction and other realms of university activity. Wells neglects the corporatized university itself as a site of national political struggle and, even as it is presently constituted, as a base for counterpublics, as was manifested in the campus protest movement of the 1960s. Even in composition studies, CCCC has several activist contingents, including Rhetoricians for Peace, a Labor Special Interest Group, and most prominently, a Working Class Special Interest Group, led by activist scholars like Ira Shor and Steve Parks.

So I find the whole discussion of the public sphere in Wells, Schutz and Gere, and other postmodern theorists (as well surveyed by Weisser) disconcertingly vague, convoluted with theoryspeak, and oblivious to the most glaring political and economic realities dominating public discourse in America today. (I also wonder why Habermas's *Structural Transformation* has received more attention than his more Frankfurt-ish books on mass culture and communicative rationality.) One looks in vain for any extensive concern with these "grand narratives" in recent rhetcomp professional journals (*JAC* being the most prominent exception), conferences, or books. (Do, however, note the recent signs of a New New Left with international scope, surveyed in chapter 1.) I reiterate that I am not denigrating the many wonderful community literacy projects in recent decades, conducted and written about by scholars like Shirley Brice Heath, Steven Parks, Eli Goldblatt, Glynda Hull, Mike Rose, Linda Flower, and others discussed below. I only take issue with such scholars when they themselves ignore or belittle academic cultural critique or attention to national and international politics rather than trying to link them with their projects.

In one local situation near my present home, Highlander Research and Education Center, located a few miles east of Knoxville, since 1932 has been a classic site for working-class, multicultural community education and organizing. Its most inspirational leader was Myles Horton, a scholar and graduate of Union Theological Seminary, whom James Bevel called "The Father of the Civil Rights Movement," and who coauthored with Paulo Freire *We Make the Road by Walking: Conversations on Education and Social Change*. Highlander has always linked local activism with national and international perspectives, most prominently as a base for civil-rights organizations like the Southern Christian Leadership Conference and leaders like Martin Luther King, Rosa Parks, and Guy and Candy Carawan. Many University of Tennessee students and faculty members have worked with Highlander; former UT political sociologist John Gaventa, a renowned scholar of community power movements, was its director in the 1990s. Starting in 1999, Highlander affiliates, local and national union leaders, and UT staff, student, and faculty activists all collaborated in organizing a nonacademic workers' union, United Campus Workers, and in campaigning, partially through a campus teach-in, for a living wage for all campus employees. UCW has steadily grown, incorporating contingent faculty and graduate TAs, and affiliating with Communication Workers of America. The oratory at the teach-in and rallies by the nonacademic workers, many earning minimum wage, was magnificent; I will never forget their speeches outside the office of a lavishly paid administrator calling for a face-to-face meeting, which they got, though their wage demands were only partially met and still continue. They provided a great lesson for scholars of rhetoric, otherwise absorbed in their esoteric theories.

Also in Appalachia, University of Illinois Press in 2012 published *Transforming Places: Lessons from Appalachia*, a powerful collection on regional activist movements where "in frequently localized battles, issues of global scale and the future of fossil fuels, from militarization and the expansion of the U.S. empire to the production of local foods and sustainable economies—are being contested" (Fisher and Smith 2). The volume was edited by Stephen Fisher, founder of the Appalachian Center for Community Service at Emory and Henry College in southwest Virginia, and Barbara Ellen Smith, professor of women's and gender studies at Virginia Tech in Blacksburg; its contributors include a mix of community activists and academics (several being both participants in and analysts of the projects they describe), with Highlander Center again a common link for many.

Two Books on Activism and Rhetoric, Local and Global

Two fine scholarly collections that do seek to link local with national and international, academic and extra-academic, rhetorical issues appeared in close order in 2010 and 2011, *The Public Work of Rhetoric: Citizen Scholars and Civic Engagement*, edited by John M. Ackerman and David J. Coogan, and *Activism and Rhetoric: Theories and Contexts for Political Engagement*, edited by Seth Kahn and Jonghwa Lee. My sympathies lean more toward *Activism*, which came out of Rhetoricians for Peace in CCCC, than toward *Public*, which came out of the Alliance of Rhetoric Societies. (I have been active in both RFP and Rhetoric Society of America, an eclectic mix of classical rhetoricians and current critical theorists.) There is some crossover of contributors and topics in the two books. (Ellen Cushman appears in both with articles eloquently relating her academic studies to her life and work in the Cherokee Nation.) The differences, however, begin with Gerard A. Hauser's foreword to *Public*: "Most of it finds its inspiration in the work of Jürgen Habermas" (x) and other variants on public sphere theory, which are amply cited throughout the readings. On page 1 of *Activism*, Kahn and Lee avow, "At the 2006 National Communication Association conference, Jeffrey St. John of Ohio University contended that too much current rhetorical theory is 'tweaking' Habermasian public sphere theory, instead of breaking any new ground. We agree." There is only one other, dismissive mention of Habermas in the readings, while Freire, scarcely mentioned in *Public*, is the most frequent inspiration.

Some key parts of *Public* bring to mind Barbara Gleason's illuminating comment on Min-Zhan Lu's writing: "A curious feature of poststructuralist theories is the prioritizing of the theoretical perspective over the object under analysis" (886). Thus Ackerman and Coogan's introduction concentrates on surveying academic perspectives on rhetoric related to recent political history, with the theories taking precedence over the history. It is heavy with theoryspeak jargon: "We begin by returning to rhetoric's pursuit of epistemic relevance but turn less inward toward academic expertise and more outward to the *phronesis* of the street, as a physical and figurative placeholder for publicity" (3). And, in a sentence rivaling the most unintelligible of Judith Butler: "Rhetoricity ad infinitum will not completely erase rhetoric from discourse and communication—it joins the class of logocentric, theoretical tropes that include limitless signification, interconnectivity in the heteroglot, and 'literariness'" (6). (The sentence, and the quoted last word, derives from Jonathan Culler's *On Deconstruction*, also a favorite of David Bartholomae.)

The rhetorical perspective and language in *Activism* are more expressly that of the New Left, deriving, as Philip C. Wander puts it, from "the great popular movements of my youth, civil rights, anti-war, environmental" (xiv), as well as politicized college studies in the 1960s. The three introductory essays and several other chapters evoke Students for a Democratic Society's "Port Huron Statement" more than *The Transformation of the Public Sphere* or *On Deconstruction*. Thus the contributions have mostly been generated empirically out of particular political-economic, educational, or media disputes. For example, a touching memoir of "a Middle-Class Activist" by the hardy veteran education theorist and founder of RFP Charles Bazerman includes his account of teaching in a black elementary school in Brooklyn during the fierce battle over community control there in the 1960s.

Beyond these distinctions, however, and if one just skips over Ackerman and Coogan's introduction, the fifteen chapters in *Public* and eighteen in *Activism* present an equally stimulating variety of concrete analyses connecting academic study to community and broader politics, including Ackerman's own "Rhetorical Engagement in the Cultural Economies of Cities" and Coogan's "Sophists for Social Change." Ackerman's richly situated examination of the politics of city planning in Kent, Ohio (where he taught at Kent State), is prefaced, "As soon as civic engagement jumps the track from experiential learning for the causes of progressive education to planning and political spheres, it is implicated in global economic policies" (77). Now you're talking! Coogan describes his involvement in an extraordinary project in Richmond, Virginia (modeled on an earlier one in Chicago and similar to that of Steve Parks and Eli Goldblatt in Philadelphia), creating an inner-city teen center and series of publications written by black youths refuting the negative stereotypes propagated by mainstream media. Coogan, however, cannot resist a swipe at "critical pedagogies . . . that allow classroom theorizing about social change to take the place of community action" (159). He does not criticize the opposite exclusion, which I have witnessed more often in recent decades. Contrast his comment with Kahn's in *Activism*, "Our intention isn't to binarize academic and non-academic activism; instead, we believe that the chapters move from the global to the local . . . and that, for most of us, the most local issues we work on are campus/academy-oriented" (3).

Public does in fact contain several good chapters based on strictly academic study, such as M. Lane Bruner's "The Public Work of Critical Political Communication." It includes a section titled "Theorizing Critical Political Communication"—but why theorize it, instead of just practicing it? Bruner does the latter well in addressing instances of mass-cultural propaganda, misinformation, and Guy DeBord's "society of the spectacle," with apt reference to *The Matrix* and *The Truman Show* (63–64). Ralph Cintron's "Democracy and Its Limitations" is a brilliant critical analysis of shrinking democratic rhetorical possibilities in global politics over recent decades, exemplary in its scope from South Chicago ward politics to ethnic conflict in Kosovo (he has done ethnographic research in both); he alludes to poststructuralist/postmodernist theory without allowing it to overwhelm his own lucid style. Closest to my own approach, however, in seeking subjects for classroom study that counteract the dominant conservative culture, are "Finding a Place for School in Rhetoric's Public Turn" by David Fleming and "A Place for the Dissident Press in a Rhetorical Education" by Diana George and Paula Mathieu.

Those last two articles would fit equally well in the ample sections on "Activism within Academic Institutions" and "Activist Pedagogy" in *Activism*. Included there is one of Matthew Abraham's several impassioned accounts of suppression of pro-Palestinian spokespeople and activism on American campuses. Kahn's "(Re)Politicizing the Writing Process" recounts his work as a professorial rhetorician-in-residence for a peace organization in West Chester, Pennsylvania, where he practiced Freirean situated writing. "Breaking News: Armchair Activists Access Their Power," by two young scholars in English, Shelley DeBlasis and Teresa Grettano, reaffirms the tradition of education in leftist media criticism, in detailed cases unclouded by theoryspeak. Marxist composition and rhetoric scholar Catherine Chaput describes her highly informative chapter, "The Role of Communism in Democratic Discourse": "Interested in how capitalism has become the sole signifier for democracy, a semiotic pairing that precludes the possibility of democratic practices outside of capitalist structures, this chapter explores the World Bank as it financially and discursively helps to establish the parameters of democracy" (81).

A similar Marxist perspective is developed in my favorite chapter in *Activism*, "Speaking Power to Truth: Observations from Experience," by Lee Artz, a professor of media studies who helped develop Loyola University of Chicago's Communication and Social Justice Program and whose books include *Marxism and Communication Studies* and *Global Power and Media Hegemony*. A former union spokesperson as a machinist and steelworker, a teacher in inner-city Detroit, and a civil-rights and peace activist before he became an academic, he writes in an unabashed pre-post-Marxist style and analytic mode. Thus he boldly declares, "My experience informs my understanding, my knowing, and places me against the stream of the post-structuralist, post-modern rhetorical turn" (51). He offers instead "a materialist-based rhetorical analysis" (51), which "begins with recognition of capitalist class relations in all their contradictory manifestations" (47). His examples of such materialist-based analysis include the complex role of class relations in the overthrow of Somoza by the Sandinistas in Nicaragua, as well as in the 2003 Iraq War, in which "the US invasion and occupation of Iraq creates different issues for different social classes—without regard to their identification or agreement with any particular political argument" (48). Artz concludes:

> Rhetoric and activism? Three things. First, recognize the material conditions of our lives, especially the social relations of capitalism and its class contradictions expressed in neoliberalism, consumerism, and individualism, two-party elections, and the quality and inequality of life. Second, identify those human agents capable of making fundamental social change. . . . Finally, present a rhetoric for new consensual social power that underscores the truth of capitalist inequality, favors the building of participatory communities, and expresses the potential for new democratic social relations—in Gramscian terms, advance a new hegemony by demonstrating the benefits of a new socialist culture. (53–54)

Whether one agrees or disagrees, Artz's directness of language and social vision exposes by contrast how remote from any such concerns are the esoteric ruminations of the theoryspeakers I have been criticizing. In fact, few of the other readings in either of these collections focus centrally on class relations and the dynamics of power.

Kevin Mahoney's "You Can't Get There from Here: Higher Education, Labor Activism, and Neoliberal Globalization" in *Activism* addresses much the same subject matter as Artz does, but less successfully. Mahoney sketchily discusses the political pressures on composition instruction, then jumps to faculty unions, then to other unions, thence to economic globalization, attempting to find a common theme in advocating rhetorical "engagement with political theory" (153). Fine, but instead of aiming at the fundamental level I have advocated, he looks to *Empire* by Hardt and Negri—yet another ponderous exercise in postmodern exegesis, lacking the incisive polemics of works like Henry Giroux's *Youth in Revolt* and, with Susan Searls Giroux, *Take Back Higher Education*. Mahoney's sketchy account of labor issues reflects the skimpiness in both these volumes on rhetoric in labor struggles, in contrast to its central role in *Transforming Places: Lessons from Appalachia*. (Mahoney's viewpoint was developed much more successfully in his book coauthored with Rachel Riedner, *Democracies to Come: Rhetorical Action, Neoliberalism, and Communities of Resistance*.) Both of these collections would have benefited from chapters on the Center for Working Class Studies at Youngstown State, the Cornell University School of Industrial and Labor Relations, and other university labor studies programs, as well as union-sponsored educational projects like the AFL-CIO Organizing Institute in Washington, which published *Faculty@Work: Inspiring Activism and Supporting Working Families*; another useful supplement would have been the special issue of *College English* in November 2004 on "Social Class and English Studies" (Linkon et al.). As a postscript, I must grumpily point out the sparse attention in both collections to my pet causes like coping with conservative students and arguments, devising curriculum and pedagogy in political literacy, and asserting the responsibility of academics, in the classroom and the public sphere, to engage with political rhetoric.

9

THE RESISTANCE TO NATIONAL STANDARDS:
COMMON CORE STATE STANDARDS
AS THE PERFECT STORM

All of the excesses of postmodern pluralism that I have surveyed contribute to reflexive anathematizing in many progressive circles of anything associated with the multivalent words *standard* or *standards*, especially when prefixed by *national*, such as criteria of academic or aesthetic quality, standardized curricular content, and/or standardized testing, along with Standard English versus multiple dialects—all of which should be considered separately, not be lumped together as they too often have been. Worse yet, controversy in all of these cases has been polarized between the political right and left in the culture wars, and in the heat of these controversies, various ones of these discrete issues have often been fallaciously conflated, entailing tragic confusions and obstacles to good-faith negotiation. In the 1970s and 1980s, canon revision and the celebration of previously marginal cultures by progressives, while making many valuable contributions, sometimes went to the extreme of leveling all standards of quality and banning words like *excellence, great,* and *classic.* This extreme was both provoked and exploited by Republican Party conservatives, who proclaimed themselves the champions of educational, intellectual, and aesthetic standards, producing projects like the National Commission on Excellence in Education (which wrote *A Nation at Risk* in 1983) and journals with names like the *New Criterion* and the *Weekly Standard.* Leftist critics have long argued that the conservative position has typically masked a campaign to roll back egalitarianism and retrench hegemony by the socioeconomic elite, corporate interests, and segregationists; another left line of argument has been that this championing of high standards by the American right is grotesquely belied by its practices. I have developed these arguments in *Why Higher Education.* The waters in these debates have been muddied further by the growth since the 1970s of a conservative educational-industrial complex, with large corporate investments in private school systems (in both K-12 and university ones like Phoenix and massive open online courses, or MOOCs), "high-stakes" standardized testing, textbooks, curriculum models, and lobbying efforts toward "school choice." That phrase has been a code word for vouchers, charter schools, and other incremental steps toward destroying quality public education and replacing it with corporatized schools that would serve the multiple purposes of producing large profits, replacing liberal educators' ideological control with that by corporate conservatives, and encouraging middle-class parents to remove their children from inner-city or rural schools, leaving them in segregated squalor. (See Saltman, *The Failure of Corporate School Reform*.)

This complex has exercised large influence over every presidential administration, Republican and Democratic, from Reagan to Obama, most recently visible in Secretary of Education Arne Duncan's "Race to the Top" program. In a powerful chapter of *The Death and Life of the Great American School System* titled "The Billionaire Boys' Club," Diane Ravitch traces the history of corporate foundations in the educational-industrial complex, with emphasis on powerful recent players like the Gates, Walton, and Broad foundations, about which she says, "Unlike the older established foundations, such as Ford, Rockefeller, and Carnegie, which reviewed proposals submitted to them, the new foundations decided what they wanted to accomplish, how they wanted to accomplish it, and which organizations were appropriate recipients of their largesse" (199). Ravitch acknowledges that Bill and Melinda Gates's foundations are more progressive than most and that they have poured billions into worthy international and domestic projects (along with several more self-interested ones), but she insists, "There is something fundamentally antidemocratic about relinquishing control of the public education policy agenda to private foundations run by society's wealthiest people" (200).

Because the educational-industrial lobby cloaks its real aims in appeals to "excellence," "standards," "choice," "reform," and "accountability," liberals and leftists have good cause to distrust any such appeal, but they often overreact in doing so. Ravitch has devoted four informative though depressing books to these problems: *National Standards in American Education, Left Behind: A Century of Battles Over School Reform, The Language Police: How Pressure Groups Restrict What Students Learn*, and most recently *The Death and Life* (in which she recants her previous support for school choice, vouchers, and high-stakes testing, but continues to support national standards and a core curriculum, along the same lines as Hirsch), and *Reign of Error: The Hoax of the Privatization Movement and the Danger to America's Public Schools*, which follows similar lines.

In *National*, Ravitch recounts a series of episodes in which distrust and misunderstanding between liberals and conservatives stymied any progress toward national standards in the 1980s and 1990s. She reports that after the 1992 presidential election, the departing Bush administration awarded funds to create English standards to a consortium of NCTE, the International Reading Association, and the Center for the Study of Reading at the University of Illinois.

> In March 1994 the Clinton administration canceled the contract, citing a lack of progress. When the Department of Education placed a notice in the Federal Register about its plans to rebid the award, several members of the organizations that participated in the original project wrote to express their fear that the department would seek standards based on "traditional English," [an allusion to the *Students' Right* dispute?] and to warn that they would not cooperate with any other standard-setting project. (*National* 209)

Kenneth Goodman, past president of IRA, wrote a column in *Education Week* titled "Standards, NOT!" in which he told the Clinton DOE, "I believe your office has already decided to award this contract to right-wing ideologues and enemies of children and teachers" (Goodman 39).

In another episode, Secretary of Education Lamar Alexander in 1991 persuaded Congress to establish a National Council on Educational Standards and Testing, whose aim was "to create a broad bipartisan consensus about national standards and testing" (*National* 139). According to Ravitch (who was a DOE official backing the project), the council's recommendations unfortunately perpetuated the common failure to separate the issues of curricular standards and standardized testing or "accountability," but it also contained some progressive aspects. She recounts:

> The debate about delivery standards was strongly influenced by Jonathan Kozol's best-selling book, *Savage Inequalities*, which argued passionately for equalization of resources between rich and poor schools. NCEST never fully defined what it meant by delivery standards but described them in its report as "a metric for whether a school 'delivers' to students the 'opportunity to learn' well the material in the *content standards*. . . ." Some members of NCEST argued forcefully that it would not be fair to expect students to meet high content standards so long as there were glaring inequalities among schools and school districts. (143)

Nevertheless, on the same day in 1992 that the report was released, fifty prominent, liberal educators including Theodore Sizer, Marion Wright Edelman, John Goodlad, and Donna Shalala issued a statement opposing it, which concluded, "Any policy to establishment benchmarks for achievement without creating equity in the educational resources available to children would be a cruel hoax" (quoted in *National Standards* 143). Their failure to acknowledge that NCEST had at least attempted to address this vexing issue led Ravitch to infer that the authors hadn't even read the report. As further evidence, she argued,

> The statement indirectly demonstrated the difficulty of engaging in informed debate about national issues. Its primary point was to oppose a national test, but NCEST had not recommended a single national test. The statement criticized the inappropriate use of norm-referenced, standardized test scores, yet NCEST had not recommended such tests. (144)

Ravitch added that the authors of the statement opposing NCEST echoed another familiar progressive refrain: "Any assessment, they held, should be developed at the local level, expressing the values and standards of the local community" (143). Ravitch did not pursue my lines of criticism of the pitfalls of localism, but this is a classic case of the naïveté of progressives who fail to anticipate that their position will be preempted to justify reactionary policies, or just Middle American, sports-worshipping, educational lassitude, in "red" states and communities. Over and over again, the chickens have come home to roost in localistic statements like the 2012 platform of the Republican Party of Texas:

> We oppose the teaching of Higher Order Thinking Skills (HOTS), values clarification, critical thinking skills and similar programs that are simply a relabeling of Outcome-Based Education (OBE) (mastery learning) which focus on behavior modification and have the purpose of challenging the student's fixed beliefs and undermining parental authority. (Republican)

And the Texas Board of Education in 2010 approved "a social studies curriculum that will put a conservative stamp on history and economics textbooks, stressing the superiority of American capitalism, questioning the Founding Fathers' commitment to a purely secular government and presenting Republican political philosophies in a more positive light" (McKinley). Don't we need to counter such localism with *some* effort toward national standards, more progressively framed? I see Common Core State Standards (CCSS) as one potential step in this direction, albeit a flawed one.

A similar anomaly, which Ravitch does not pursue, is that to insist on "the values and standards" of local communities that are blighted by poverty and illiteracy might amount to acquiescence in their plight. As critics including Henry Louis Gates, Walter Benn Michaels, and John Guillory have suggested, this kind of thinking verges on a travesty of identity politics: "We're poor, and we're proud." (See Gates, "Pluralism and Its Discontents.") Progressives like Lisa Delpit and Jonathan Kozol have also argued that it might be condescending to limit education to identity politics for the poor and minorities, with the implication that they lack the innate intelligence to attain a rigorous level of broader knowledge and critical thinking, given supportive conditions. Kozol, whose position on these matters has been similar to mine going back to *Illiterate America* in 1985, has written more recently about parents he worked with in predominantly black schools in Roxbury, Massachusetts:

> [They] were disturbed when highly privileged young people who had had the benefits of culturally strong, well-balanced, and successful education came into the neighborhoods denouncing lesson plans and any concentrated emphasis on basic skills as "instruments of cultural oppression" and who spoke of "children's independent learning" as if it were incompatible somehow with grown-ups' conscientious teaching. An aversion to giving poor black children difficult work—real work at all, indeed—was one of the familiar attitudes that parents noted with dismay among some of these well-intending but unconsciously quite patronizing intellectuals. (*Shame* 269–70)

Mightn't an alternative here be to push for the kind of standards that would include fostering of knowledge and critical thinking in all students toward political literacy, focusing precisely on teaching the conflicts about issues like socioeconomic and racial inequality? Such progressively conceived standards might, among other aims, serve to introduce more privileged or provincial students to arguments for why they should support reducing national and international inequality, within a concept of schooling like that in CCSS, which "builds knowledge, enlarges experience, and broadens worldviews" (3) and calls for students who "demonstrate the cogent reasoning and use of evidence that is essential to . . . responsible citizenship in a democratic republic" (3)—a tacit rebuke of the Texas Republican platform.

One attempt in the early 1990s to establish such progressive standards met a discouraging fate. A panel of distinguished historians was commissioned by Lynne Cheney as director of the National Endowment for the Humanities to produce a set of national standards for high school history. Drafted by progressives like Gary Nash and Joyce Appleby, the standards were admirably close to the level of European testing in the depth

170

of knowledge covered and in test questions demanding critical thinking and essay-writing skills, as well as being amply multicultural and recognizing the history of women and progressive movements. I do think the drafters should have included more conservative viewpoints, in the mode of teaching the conflicts, and that the controversies they provoked should have been worked out within scholarly circles. However, by the time the standards were published in 1994, Cheney was no longer in office, and the Republican line had shifted from the national perspective of *A Nation at Risk* (which Ravitch defends as being more progressive than most liberals acknowledged) back toward Jeffersonian localism. Cheney led a Republican culture-wars offensive against the standards as an egregious example of PC. They were bizarrely made the subject of a full Senate vote, which was railroaded through with almost no senators having read them—history professor Paul Wellstone being among their few supporters—and overwhelmingly rejected (see Nash).

Fiascos like those recounted above have repeatedly blocked any progress and soured progressives against further initiatives for standards. But bipartisan appeals for their revival have recently appeared in works by Ravitch and Hirsch, Mike Rose, Martha Nussbaum, Gerald Graff and Cathy Birkenstein, and the CCSS. Hirsch says in *The Making of Americans*: "Practical improvement of our public education will require intellectual clarity and a depolarization of this issue. Left and right must get together on the principle of common content" (177). Rose, a leading progressive educator, wrote in 2006, "People leery about calls for standards need to remember their benefits and reclaim them for democratic ends, despite the fact that standards and assessments in the past too often have been used to stratify students into educational tracks based more on economic and racial background than on academic ability" (*An Open Language* 419).

Graff and Birkenstein in an article for the American Association of University Professors' *Academe Online* (May–June 2008), titled "A Progressive Case for Educational Standardization," joined the many scholars who rejected the version of national standards for college education proposed by the Spellings Commission in the Department of Education under George W. Bush, but they took issue with those who argued against any standardization whatever, especially in standards of critical thinking:

> Thus in his response to the report, Lee Shulman, president of the Carnegie Foundation for the Advancement of Teaching, argues that though legislators may seem to agree on the importance of critical thinking as a standard for college-level work, the term is used to mean

so many different things that its usefulness as a standard is undermined. As Shulman puts it, "common educational goals like 'critical thinking' . . . are often invoked for quite different achievements. . . . No single set of measures can do justice to all those variations." . . . Shulman demands that colleges be free to take "many different approaches to higher education" rather than being forced to converge "on the 'one best system.'"

But we need go no further than Shulman's own prose—or that of other Spellings critics—for an example of the critical-thinking skills whose commonality he denies. Even as Shulman claims that the concept of critical thinking is hopelessly diffuse, his writing, like that of Spellings's other critics, shows that it involves such basic moves as identifying and accurately summarizing views to which one wants to respond; selecting, framing, and explaining quotations; exploring claims and explaining their implications; making connections to similar or related claims; offering a cogent argument of one's own; moving between one's own argument and the view to which one is responding without confusing readers; citing evidence and showing how it supports one's own argument and not competing ones; and anticipating and answering counterarguments.

These fundamentals—whose ubiquity in the intellectual world Shulman denies—are precisely those that most students fail to learn. And in our view, students will go on failing to learn these fundamentals unless they are standardized across all domains and levels—that is, are represented with enough redundancy, consistency, and transparency that students can recognize them as fundamentals rather than as one set of arbitrary preferences competing for their attention among many.

Even such a commonsense position as this gains no assent from orthodox pluralists. I can conceive no likely way out of the two fatal stalemates that I have delineated : that progressives' doctrinaire opposition to national standards in the cause of local diversity and multiculturalism tacitly concedes control of much provincial education to the most reactionary political forces, and that, as Ravitch paraphrased the progressive argument, "It would not be fair to expect students to meet high content standards so long as there were glaring inequalities among schools and school districts." As emphasized throughout this book, I fully agree that overcoming those inequalities should be our top priority, yet, as Ravitch suggested, this position can become an excuse for inaction on the grounds that so long as inequalities persist, no other major efforts should be made to raise the present standards in curriculum and teacher education—both of which often have long been abysmal not only in poor districts but in middle-class ones like the one I grew up in. Again, there is a process of cooption here, as conservative local legislators and administrators explicitly or implicitly exploit the ethos of liberal pluralism and fostering of student self-esteem ("The kids are alright") as an excuse for sheer, penny-pinching lassitude in schools.

Common Core State Standards: The Perfect Storm

The most significant recent event concerning the issues I am addressing was the publication in 2010 of the National Governors Association's *Common Core State Standards Initiative* (CCSS), which coordinated guidelines in critical reading, writing, and thinking with disciplinary knowledge in history, social studies, and literature, and which modeled specific texts for reading in those fields at ascending levels from K to 12. In 2013, when it had begun to be implemented, a firestorm of controversy over CCSS belatedly erupted in political, educational, and journalistic circles. (The daily Education section of the online *Washington Post*, edited by Valerie Strauss, has been exemplary in regularly publishing lengthy blogs pro and con by prominent players like Hirsch and Graff, pro, and Ravitch, con, and *Education Week* has been a regular source of criticism.) Much of this controversy has been a rerun of the same opposing arguments in the earlier episodes recounted by Ravitch above. I get the impression that many of the opponents on both the left and right haven't even read the standards but have simply reverted to their previous scripts. Conservatives rail against CCSS as a liberal, big-government takeover of local education; this line has recently become red meat for Republican politicians and fodder for right-wing conspiracy theories. Progressives also take the anti-federal-government line, as well as railing against any national standards as discriminating against the poor and minorities, being implemented by high-stakes, standardized testing, and being a Trojan horse for a corporate takeover of public education. The perfect storm of intransigent opposition on all sides makes it appear likely at this moment that CCSS is doomed. I consider this a tragedy because, although the critical skills and texts in it did not reach the level of analysis of underlying ideological issues and partisanship in current public discourse that I advocate, it at least provided more of a context where such analysis would fit than most such previous standards statements, especially those of NCTE.

Most significantly, in sixty-five pages of text and a monumental, two-hundred-page appendix of exemplary assignments, the standards present a historic shift away from recent privileging of science, technology, engineering, and mathematics (STEM) subjects and closer to other countries discussed in chapter 4 above, in integrating study in English language arts with history, social studies, and science, at succeeding grade levels and consistent with National Assessment of Education Progress (NAEP) reports, culminating at a level and quality equal to or beyond many current college courses. Note how closely their aims match the critical thinking criteria defined in chapter 3, as well as everything that the Citation Project, discussed in chapter 4, has identified as lacking in current first-year writing; they delineate developmental reading, writing, reasoning, and research skills in response to literary, informational, and argumentative texts, including elements of political literacy missing from most recent English standards. Under "Anchor Standards for Writing": "Gather relevant information from multiple print and digital sources, assess the credibility and accuracy of each source, and integrate the information while avoiding plagiarism" (63). More specifically, in the reading standards for informational text at different grade levels, Grade 8 (!) includes:

> Delineate and evaluate the argument and specific claims in a text, assessing whether the reasoning is sound and the evidence is relevant and sufficient; recognize when irrelevant evidence is introduced. . . . Analyze a case in which two or more texts provide conflicting information on the same topic and identify where the texts disagree on matters of fact or interpretation. (39)

The July 2012 *College English* featured a long symposium on the *Framework for Success in Postsecondary Writing*, produced in 2010 by a task force from the Council of Writing Administrators, NCTE, and the National Writing Project, conceived as a counterstatement to CCSS, in which, the authors of the *Framework* complain, "the absence of college writing teachers and researchers from the committees developing the Standards was striking from the beginning" (522). And, "The narrow band in which these concepts are to be developed does not reflect research-based current practices in postsecondary writing instruction." Beginning from this tone of sour grapes, the authors explain that as a preferable model to CCSS, they turned to a 2000 "Outcomes Statement for First-Year Composition from the Council of Writing Program Administrators," modifying it rather vaguely to apply to beginning college students. These two projects continue a long history of outcomes statements from NCTE and allied organizations whose vagueness and blandness seem calculated to avoid offending multicultural sensibilities or to make any exacting demands on teachers and teacher education, thereby also avoiding either controversy or commitment to anything close to specific goals for nationwide student achievement at different levels of study. Indeed,

"Outcomes" echoed prior liberal orthodoxy in rejecting "'standards,' or precise levels of achievement," which "should be left to specific institutions" (1). Specific institutions like those controlled by the 2010 Texas Board of Education and 2012 Texas Republican Party platform?

The vagueness and "narrow band . . . of concepts" in both the CWPA and *Framework* statements, in comparison to CCSS, is epitomized in aims of instruction for critical thinking. Buried in such a list in a subordinate section of the *Framework* is: "Evaluate sources for credibility, bias, quality of evidence, and quality of reasoning" (530). Absent from this list is evaluation of students' own written arguments for these traits. *In fact, the whole subject area of argumentation is nowhere mentioned in either the Framework or "Outcomes."* The Task Force introduction casually mentions that the CCSS "focus on two primary modes (argumentative writing and informational writing) and describe work with these modes at increasing levels of complexity throughout a student's education in K-12" (521)—but it says nothing further about the elaborate treatment of argumentation in CCSS. Thus the *Framework* and "Outcomes" give short shrift to this entire realm of instruction, with no further guidance for the levels of English courses, *in either K-12 or college*, at which it should be incorporated into a sequence of units of study, or for the extensive teacher training and classroom challenges it entails; indeed, these two statements lack *any* developmental concept of either secondary or college writing instruction like Shaughnessy's or CCSS's. In these ways, it predictably reinforces the marginalizing of argument throughout our professional discourse and curricula discussed in chapter 4 above. Incidentally, neither *College English* nor *CCC* to this date has published or planned any articles directly about the CCSS.

Moreover, the failure to expand on "evaluat[ing] sources for credibility . . ." continues the de-emphasis throughout the profession of critical reading of nonfictional prose, reducing it, as the *Framework* advocates, to "craft[ing] written responses to texts that put the writer's ideas in conversation with those in a text" (530). This phrase obviously derives from theorists like Harris and Bartholomae conceiving argumentative writing courses as a "conversation" among student writers or between their home cultures and academic texts, while reducing acquisition and evaluation of factual knowledge, as the *Framework* implies, to emulating the allegedly arbitrary "conventions" of the academic discourse community. (See my critique of Bartholomae on this point in chapter 7).

In Carol Severino's astute critique of the narrow scope of the *Framework* in the *College English* symposium, she argues, "Although we no longer speak of 'cultural literacy,' we can still speak of multicultural and global literacy: knowledge not only of international events and controversies, but also of how to research them if more knowledge is needed." She continues, "Researching in order to describe, analyze, and advocate positions in controversies—the major assignments, for example, in the University of Iowa's rhetoric curriculum—is much more difficult when students are unfamiliar with the geographical and historical contexts for these issues" (536). Having been a guest teacher in that wonderful rhetoric program at Iowa, I can say amen to that.

Public and professional debate over CCSS has been so polluted that I often do not know whom to believe; so I will refrain from passing firm judgments pending further developments. Here are some key criticisms of CCSS by progressives, and my provisional take on them:

Teachers and professional associations, especially in English, were not adequately consulted in drafting and implementing the standards. NCTE has posted several blogs to this effect, and it is repeated in the *Framework* discussed above. This charge is somewhat contradicted in CCSS background statements indicating substantial teacher input. My impression, mainly from articles in NCTE's *Council Chronicle* and the International Reading Association's *Common Core Resources*, is that CCSS has been more widely praised, and fruitfully implemented, among K-12 teachers than allowed for by critics. Some reports also refer to teachers and administrators who are grateful for the standards as being on a higher level than those from either local boards of education or organizations like NCTE and schools of education, although there have been widespread complaints about implementation, discussed below.

CCSS may be admirable in its conception and contents, but without adequate lead time and financial support for its implementation, with supplemental support for poor districts, it will—like prior, inequitably funded standards—inadvertently reinforce established lines of class and racial discrimination. In practice, many teachers and students are finding the level of CCSS so far above what they are accustomed to, they can't handle it. This argument has been made by Ravitch ("Why I Oppose") and American Federation of Teachers (AFT) president Randi Weingarten, who in April 2013 reaffirmed her previous support for CCSS but argued that it was being implemented too hurriedly, so appealed for a delay with increased budgetary support (Strauss, "AFT"). Ravitch concluded, "I hope for the sake of the nation that the Common Core standards are great and wonderful. I wish they were voluntary, not mandatory. I wish we knew more about how they will affect our most vulnerable students. But since I do not know the answer to any of the questions that trouble me, I cannot support the Common Core standards." I find these objections compelling, as expressed by some local schools and parents beginning to implement the standards, who have begged for an extension of time and more resources from federal and local government before proceeding. One can only hope the Obama administration and succeeding ones will be supportive on this problem.

In the English Language standards, the emphasis on critical reading and writing of nonliterary texts crowds out literary study. This is a nonstarter. CCSS does not imply mutual exclusion but only expanded attention in English courses to general-education or journalistic texts including those in the arenas of political literacy I emphasize in this book. Might some English teachers' defensiveness here indicate their sense of inadequacy to teach about a broader range of subjects than strictly literary ones? Graff further argued in a talk at the 2012 MLA convention, in defense of CCSS, that study and practice of argumentation is an essential link between teaching nonliterary and literary works, including criticism and theory ("Trickle-Down Miseducation" 3).

CCSS is culturally biased. NCTE's *Council Chronicle* for September 2013 published a section on "Implementation of the Common Core State Standards," written by the NCTE office of policy research, directed by Anne Ruggles Gere. It cites a sample CCSS essay question: "Analyze seminal U.S. documents of historical and literary significance (e.g., Washington's Farewell Address, the Gettysburg Address, Roosevelt's Four Freedoms Address, King's 'Letter from Birmingham Jail'), including how they address related themes and concepts." The authors comment:

> Here there are recommended texts and implicit themes [awk ss—DL], and the authors represent a narrow definition—in terms of race, language, and gender [not of class?—DL]—of what counts as "seminal US documents." Here teachers will have to take considerably more initiative to introduce a rich range of authors of color and women [not the working class and poor?] to help students become actively engaged with issues raised by texts, and to foreground socially, culturally, critically informed learning while addressing this standard. (14)

Really! Many other sample questions in CCSS are amply multicultural. Must every one be so, with the implication that any expectation that all students be familiar with these particular texts is arbitrary, exclusionary, and onerous? At this late date, isn't the instruction to "analyze . . . how they address related themes and concepts," especially with King as a reference point, sufficient to prompt cultural critique, without laboring the issue in this kind of heavy-handed edict (which for all that reveals a prejudice against class analysis) that exposes us to ridicule as the PC Thought Police?

CCSS is just another Trojan horse false "reform," designed by special interests like the Bill and Melinda Gates Foundation to gain control over American education for their own corporate and ideological benefit. All this *might* turn out to be true, in line with Ravitch's earlier critique of "the billionaire boys' club" self-serving, top-down mode of educational reform. But I at least have seen no definitive evidence so far that it is true. This time *might* be different, and I have seen no sign of corporate or nationalistic indoctrination in the portions of CCSS I have read, such as the call to "demonstrate the cogent reasoning and use of evidence that is essential to . . . responsible citizenship in a democratic republic." Pending clear evidence to the contrary, mightn't we give the benefit of the doubt to the Gateses and other designers for perhaps having transcended the lameness of earlier standards models? I for one at least would rather see Gatesian high-tech, corporate-liberal standards like these than those endorsed by the Texas Republican Party and state board of education, pending better options by progressive forces that have any chance of enactment.

Some progressives claimed to find the smoking pistol that CCSS was a right-wing plot in a *Washington Post* analysis by Lyndsey Layton, "How Bill Gates Pulled Off the Swift Common Core Revolution" (7 June 2014), which traced the origin of the initiative to a meeting in 2008 where Gene Wilhoit, director of a national group of state school chiefs, and David Coleman of the College Board persuaded Bill and Melinda Gates to provide massive financial and political support. Layton gives no indication that Gates sought either to impose an ideological agenda on the schools, to privatize and voucherize them, or to squeeze out liberal arts in favor of technological education. On the contrary, Layton says Gates expressed primary concern for increasing financial support of public schools in poor districts to help them meet the level of CCSS, and he endorsed elements like critical literacy and the math standards that "require students to learn multiple ways to solve problems and explain how they got their answers, while the English standards emphasize nonfiction and expect students to use evidence to back up oral and written arguments." Layton also discounts claims that seeking financial gain for Microsoft in supplying course and testing materials was a strong motivator for Gates, who acknowledges some Microsoft investments but insists that they were only an incidental consideration and have been vetted against conflicts of interest. Gates appears here to be legitimately determined to combat the antagonisms between local and federal control, liberal and conservative politics, which have stymied national standards efforts in the past. He has sought bipartisan cooperation by funding pro-CCSS projects by both conservative educational players and liberal ones like the National Education Association, American Federation of Teachers, and the Center for American Progress. Other sources, however, indicate that pro-privatizing activities by some projects sponsored by the Gates Foundation have contradicted Gates's claims to being above corporate motives. (See Phillips, "Tom Van Der Ark's New York-Area Charter Schools Falter.")

Even if players like Gates had disinterested, benevolent motives, CCSS will be exploited toward the same old business-dominated agenda of high-stakes, standardized testing, with short-answer questions that can be machine-graded. It will be another profitable government subsidy for corporate producers of textbooks, curricular, and testing materials. An entry on testing in a 2012 FAQ section of the CCSS site says only, "States that adopted the Common Core State Standards are currently collaborating to develop common assessments that will be aligned to the standards and replace existing end of year state assessments. These assessments will be available in the 2014–2015 school year" (http://www.corestandards.org/resources/frequently-asked-questions). Other answers to questions in this FAQ section at least indicate the scholarly superiority of CCSS to earlier efforts toward national standards.

Nevertheless, *Education Week* recently reported that a big contract is going to Amplify Insight, which "is a division of Amplify, an ed-tech company whose chief executive officer is Joel Klein, the former New York City schools chancellor. Amplify is the education arm of the media conglomerate News Corporation, led by Rupert Murdoch" (Cavanaugh, "Amplify"). Another big contract went to Partnership for Assessment of Readiness for College and Careers (PARCC). *Education Week* reported, "Pearson and Educational Testing Service won contracts totaling $23 million to design the first 18,000 items in [PARCC'S] test bank" (Gewertz). The text of CCSS (and PARCC's delineation of language arts assessment—see "PARCC Task Prototypes") imply that students should be graded on their essays, not multiple choice exams, and I still cannot imagine machine-grading of essays for "cogent reasoning and use of evidence" or "analyz[ing] a case in which two or more texts provide conflicting information on the same topic." However, Gewertz's 2012 article in *Education Week* noted, "As the contracts were being finalized in late June, PARCC officials heard rumors that one or more of the vendors planned to announce a suite of computer-based formative and summative tests spanning grades 3–11 and designed to measure college and career readiness—similar to what PARCC planned." Some level of corporate profiteering from any such national project is probably unavoidable, whatever modes of assessment are involved. The issue is whether profiteering becomes the tail that wags the dog, and whether conservative executives like Rupert Murdoch and Joel Klein will attempt to control the content or testing of CCSS.

The most distressing information I have received recently came from K-12 teachers in Tennessee who have now seen or used the tests connected to CCSS beginning in 2014 and who say they are the same old high-stakes, short-answer, computer-graded tests *that have no relation to the stated, substantive goals of CCSS*. If this is true, it would seem to confirm a bait-and-switch scheme, although exactly how it was hatched remains a mystery. It seems unlikely that David Coleman and other initiators set out to deceive the public. The more even-handed accounts that I have seen, such as Timothy Murphy's "Inside the Mammoth Backlash to Common Core" in *Mother Jones*, indicate that Coleman's good intentions were betrayed by corporate special interests, although he has refrained from saying this publicly.

By the end of 2014, virtual obituaries for CCSS were being written, such as "Rage against the Common Core," in the *New York Times*, by David Kirp, a veteran authority on education and public policy, who concluded, "Had the public schools been given breathing room, with a moratorium on high-stakes testing that prominent educators urged. resistance to the Common Core would likely have been less fierce. But in states where the opposition is passionate and powerful, it will take a herculean effort to get the standards back on track." We can hope that the problems with CCSS can eventually be ironed out, following the precedent of the Affordable Care Act. But if CCSS dies, it will likely doom any future movement for critical thinking, civic literacy, and everything else praiseworthy in it.

Most of us teachers and scholars would probably at least agree on one alternative to CCSS. Suppose that a program like it was implemented on a similar nationwide scale, but that its aim was not to terrorize schools, students, and teachers through fetishizing high-stakes testing, but rather to set "standards" in the sense of goals for real educational achievement, with government, corporate, and teacher-union support—first, to improve the economic condition of poor neighborhoods, then to upgrade learning and teaching conditions, teacher education, and salaries—toward helping less privileged schools attain those goals through quality instruction, not teaching to the test. In this alternative, setting the bar of expectations high could serve to inspire, not to intimidate and discriminate.

But realistically, no matter what educational reforms along these lines might be initiated, they seem fated to be taken over by the corporate privatizers and producers of model curricula, textbooks, and standardized, high-stakes tests, whose lobbies appear to have both political parties, and officials like President Obama and Secretary of Education Duncan, in their power. Some leftist critics have gone so far as to suggest that the CCSS initiative from its inception was a cynical scheme by the corporate privatizers to sabotage public education through turning it to these uses and failing to provide adequate funding and time for implementation. (For arguments along this line, see FairTest and "The Trouble with Common Core" in *Rethinking Schools*.) On the one hand, it is hard to deny that Obama and Duncan were in league with the corporate educational camp. But on the other hand, it strains credibility that the whole, massive effort to produce and implement CCSS could have been cruelly designed for failure, by all the different parties involved. It will be up to educational historians over the years ahead to sort out the tangle of motives and obstacles to implementation at various levels from the presidential administration and National Association of Governors on down. The large questions remain of exactly when and how this apparent take-over occurred with CCSS, and whether there can ever be, in the foreseeable future, a way of preventing these corporate forces from becoming the tail that wags the dog of American education.

PART 3

PSYCHOLOGICAL AND SOCIOLOGICAL PERSPECTIVES:
AGENDA FOR A REVIVAL

10

WHY DOES ALL THIS STILL MATTER?

We are right to think that the aim of education should not be to destroy working-class culture and substitute for it a universal lower-middle-class culture. But these are not the only options. People do have a right to be offered, to the tops of their bents, what all those of us who engage in educational debates have and value, a grasp of the public use of language which is the essential tool for understanding our own situations and the nature of our society better, and for deciding what we can do to improve matters. To wish less for people is implicitly to hand them over even more firmly to the new social controllers, the low-level mass-persuaders. —Richard Hoggart, *An English Temper*

To reiterate my arguments in parts 1 and 2, the lines of composition and rhetorical theory that I have criticized have tended to neglect at best, or to denigrate and distort at worst, an array of scholarship dating back to the 1950s that I have found valuable for understanding problems in student cognition and critical thinking, especially about politics, in writing and literature courses, and especially among Middle American or lower-middle-class students. As I noted earlier, poststructuralist and postmodernist theories and scholars who have applied them to composition have sweepingly ignored the realms of sociology, social and developmental psychology, which I personally find far more thought-provoking and relevant to our studies. Part 3, then will make a historical-revisionist case for reversing the prejudices of recent theory and re-evaluating, within the political and pedagogical framework I have established, the significance of these fields:

- Historical and social-psychological studies of oral versus literate cultures
- Psychology of cognitive and moral development
- Sociological studies of social class, linguistic codes, political socialization, "the culture of poverty," "the authoritarian personality," and the black English versus standard English debate

- Effects of mass culture, especially television, on cognition and political consciousness

The sources and issues surveyed here occasioned heated, continuous controversy, both within their own disciplines and in their applications to English studies, mainly in the 1960s through 1980s. (Some of my explorations may seem to lead far afield from English, but whenever I am unsure about where I'm going and why, I go back to Shaughnessy's *Errors and Expectations* and am reassured to find most of the connections, explicitly or implicitly, in her text and citations; she is truly the matron saint of composition as a site for rich veins of scholarship.) I will attempt in this survey to delineate the main points of controversy and sort through the many oversimplifications, misunderstandings, and partisan appropriations or misappropriations that have led to denigration of these studies in the last three decades. (Some of the misappropriations caused the theories that were misappropriated to be thrown out along with their misappropriations, as in the case I address in chapter 12 of Basil Bernstein's work being distorted into a basis for notions of "cultural deprivation" and "cognitive deficits" in the poor and minorities.) My own conclusions from this survey, as expressed in previous published versions, have themselves met with some hostile responses from scholars and political partisans on both the right and left, so I will incorporate here additional clarification, support, and rebuttals to my critics.

To begin with, my central aim here is not to evaluate all aspects of these studies for their empirical validity—often a key point of dispute—but rather to mine eclectically from each of them theoretical concepts that provide criteria with common-sense application to English studies. For example, some critics have responded to my use of historical studies of oral and literate cultures by labeling me an advocate of a discredited "great leap theory" of the historical transition from oral to literate societies. I have no stake in defending this theory, and I grant the validity of its critics in the historical realm, but that does not negate the applicability of some of the differences posited between oral and literate culture to present-day society, in terms of cognitive development and critical-thinking skills in our students as well as in terms of the political effects of family socialization patterns or of the oral/visual medium of commercial television. Likewise, many mid-century studies in history of literacy, developmental psychology, and sociology obviously had class, racial, or gender biases that need to be corrected in retrospect, while the very nature of older categories like "middle class" and "working class" has undergone revision in terms of changes in political economy, access to college education, and the homogenizing effects of mass culture.

One of the most valuable contributions of postmodernist theory has been the recognition that concepts like social class are more problematic, complex, and fluid than assumed in earlier eras. Nevertheless, once necessary adjustments are made, I still find some of the psychological and sociological categories defined by these fields of study significant. Once again, some of my critics have missed my ironic point that in my teaching experience, white, middle-class college students display the traits of "restricted-code," "sociocentric," "lower-order," "oral-culture" thinking as much as, or more than, poor and minority students do. Shaughnessy's analysis of the cognitive problems in inner-city basic writing students was just about equally applicable to many of my affluent rural and suburban students in advanced courses at Cal Poly and the other upscale colleges where I have taught. It is precisely their restricted cognitive development that results in writing for courses that is racist, sexist, naively chauvinistic, and biased in adulation of the rich and scorn for the poor. I even speculate that differences in these cognitive patterns have themselves become new criteria in defining class divisions. As C. Wright Mills, Aldous Huxley, and the Frankfurt School theorists plausibly suggested, to the extent that mass culture perpetuates restricted cognitive development, these forces contribute to a "culture of poverty" in millions of people who belong to diverse social classes by other criteria such as income level, education, race, and so on.

All this is to suggest a large agenda for empirical research in English studies, exploring correlations between college students' levels of critical thinking about political issues and their socioeconomic backgrounds, television viewing, etc. A heavy teaching load in a state college through most of my career prevented me from tackling extensive research myself, and my own speculations are based mainly on what students in my writing and literature classes have volunteered about themselves, as well as on anonymous questionnaires on these matters that I distribute at the beginning of each course. (To reiterate an anomaly here, scholars in teaching colleges who are immersed in pedagogical problems that demand a wealth of research do not have the time for research, while those in research universities are pressured to concentrate on more advanced and esoteric topics.)

In brief summary, I will make a case here that the restricted cognitive patterns dominating American socialization (primarily in the lower middle class) and public discourse also induce predominantly conservative attitudes, not in the sense of a reasoned conservative ideology, but in the sense of an uncritical conformity that reinforces the social status quo and precludes oppositional consciousness. The lower stages of cognitive development, basically those of children, are most susceptible to sociocentric appeals to support government, military and police authority, orthodox religion, traditional "family values" and gender roles, one's own country, race, ethnic group, and socioeconomic system (in America, capitalism, especially in the idealized form of it packaged as "free enterprise"), and to fear foreign nations, races, and ideologies. It is much less easy to rally people at this level to international cooperation and pacifism than to war, xenophobia, patriotism, and retribution against alleged atrocities by the enemy Other—currently Muslims and terrorists—and alien hordes of immigrants. Similarly, on issues like seeking revenge on "evildoers" internationally and domestically, the death penalty and "getting tough on criminals," abortion, the (personal) right to bear arms, low taxes and "getting government off our backs," the simplistic conservative position seems intuitively, emotionally appealing, while the liberal and leftist ones take more account of counterintuitive, empirically verified realities, complexities, and ironies. (This is not to deny, though, that the conservative positions may be defensible on a more complex cognitive level.) The most profitable path for corporations, media, and politicians pandering for votes, then, is clearly to exploit and reinforce this conservative socialization—which is also the path of least resistance for educators. In Communist countries, similar "conservative" socialization is used in support of conformity to a leftist status quo, with the difference that exaltation of the wealthy and free enterprise is not part of their status quo. To reiterate a central point throughout this book, conservative ideologues refuse (often with cynical disingenuousness) to acknowledge all these forms of conservative bias, so they succeed in smearing humanistic educators attempting to fulfill their legitimate role of instilling the "liberal" trait of skeptical questioning of the status quo simply as politically correct perpetrators of liberal bias.

My own political leanings are toward democratic socialism, and part of the agenda of this section—by no means a hidden part of it—is a concern that political illiteracy is contributing toward the kind of one-dimensional society that Herbert Marcuse diagnosed, in which the capacity to imagine alternatives to the status quo, especially alternatives of a socialistic nature, has been systematically precluded. In other words, it is justifiable for scholars to posit socialist perspectives as a *cognitive* alternative to the closed universe of capitalist discourse. I do not expect more conservative readers—or even all liberals and leftists—to share this concern or to agree with all of my arguments in its support, but I do hope to gain their assent to the ultimate thrust of my argument, which is that the low level of cognitive development to which American public discourse and education is presently geared is woefully inadequate for the effective functioning of a democracy. The implication of my analysis is not that educators and cultural critics should try to impose a leftist political persuasion on the public or students. They do have a responsibility, however, to help deprogram the public and students from the uninformed conservatism induced by political illiteracy and mass culture, while at the same time striving to raise American public discourse to the higher levels of unconstricted debate between all reasoned ideologies. Part of this responsibility lies in reorienting our theoretical concerns, research, and curricula to include the topics that are surveyed, in a very tentative way, in part 3.

As further preface to this broad survey, I propose that we appropriate Basil Bernstein's binary between "restricted code" (RC) and "elaborated code" (EC) simply as a synonym for the development of critical-thinking skills, as a shorthand, common-sense designation of the cognitive and linguistic development from childhood to adulthood, mediated both by formal education and literacy and by a widening circle of acquaintances, experience, travel, and sources of information. Likewise, RC can also be used to describe the adult experience of the worldwide masses of people throughout most of history who have lived their entire lives in the same small geographical area, whose work lives were endless drudgery, who could not read and thus, before the modern age of mass communication, had little knowledge of the world beyond their immediate experience, and were fixed in cognitive stages termed by psychologists "sociocentric," or "ethnocentric." Neither children nor illiterate adults have factual knowledge of history to compare and contrast with the present, or a firm sense of sequence of events and cause-and-effect between the past and present (beyond oral accounts), acquisition of which is a key component of an EC. (As we will see here, Walter Ong distinguishes between the "primary orality" of preliterate societies, which could be highly elaborated and complex, and the "secondary orality" of illiterate people in literate society, particularly under the influence of television, which leads to more restricted cognition and communication than was common in primary orality.) The vestiges in present social groups of such lack of historical thinking may be related not only to problems of "present orientation" identified by researchers in several fields surveyed here, but to the problems Mina Shaughnessy identified in basic writers' difficulties with tense and syntax—such as the recursiveness and cumulation necessary in the suspended time span of writing or reading a sentence with cogent coordinate and subordinate clauses or phrases, or a paragraph further developing thematic continuity.

Furthermore, both children and adults with extremely limited experience and education have little alternative to unquestioning acceptance of national chauvinism and the authority of their parents, church, rulers, the military, police, and mass culture. So I term as RC-thinkers college students who display the kind of primary certitude resulting from the egocentrism, ethnocentrism, and authoritarianism typical of those whose experience before college has been extremely limited in social and geographical scope, as well as in education in history, geography, etc.—such as many of my students from family farms, provincial towns (like Des Moines when I grew up there), or homogeneous middle-class suburbs. They tend not to have developed the capacity for introspection and critical questioning of their own beliefs or their sources of information. For developmental psychologist William Perry, "The liberally educated man, be he a graduate of college or not, is one who has learned to think about even his own thoughts, to examine the ways he orders his data and the assumptions he is making and to compare these with other thoughts that other men might have" (*Forms* 39). By contrast, Christopher Lasch suggests, "The habit of criticism, from a lower-middle-class point of view, appeared to invite people to be endlessly demanding of life, to expect more of life than anyone had a right to expect" (*True* 493).

This mindset provides a possible key to every kind of resistance to instruction in critical thinking. When my students express dogmatic political opinions and I ask them what their source is, the most common answer by far is, "my father." To the extent that they have gotten opinions from mass media, the strongest influences tend to be those like talk-radio conservatives who pitch their message to precisely this kind of audience. Such students predictably, reflexively defend American foreign policy and war, government authorities (but only those in their own political party), the wealthy and corporate executives, the military, and police, while belittling blue-collar workers, labor unions, and poor people, in the manner of Students A and B in chapter 3. They will rationalize whatever these perceived authorities do, and when the latter are tainted by scandal, they write things like that memorable journal entry, in one of my classes, about a presidential cabinet member when he was under fire for corruption: "I don't know why people are so critical of the Secretary. They fail to realize that he must want what's best for the U.S., that's why he was elected." They just as reflexively denounce critics of these authorities as unpatriotic, "negative thinkers," who are only out for attention or money, and they tend to exaggerate their prevalence. They write statements like, "Anyone who defends President Bush or the Iraq war is viciously attacked"—without acknowledging comparable attacks on critics of the war, especially in its initial stages. Or "The media always gives more attention to bad news and the complainers—the squeaky wheel always gets the oil." Assertions like this are typically made without supporting sources, any recognition for the need to do research on the topic, or acknowledgment of the contrary pressures on media to wave the flag and report good news about wars and other actions by the incumbent administration. They are inclined toward wanting the teacher to convey unambiguous "facts" and clear-cut, authoritative views. (This assumes, of course, that those facts and views do not contradict their previous opinions.) They tend to have a low tolerance level for contradictory views or decentering exercises, and to react defensively against them even when asked just to consider them provisionally, as hypotheses to be considered in an open-minded manner. They may complain about teachers presenting a one-sided viewpoint, without understanding that the viewpoint may only be put forth as an unfamiliar rhetorical counterweight against views that they are fully familiar with and assume as truth already.

RC and authoritarian tendencies are also manifested by students whose accustomed mode of assignments is busywork and rote memorizing rather than critical thinking, who want to be told exactly what to study for and to write every day, who want the course syllabus to be laid out with every assignment in detail the first day of class (and who get upset with any subsequent deviation), and who expect to be graded on a clearly prescribed, quantifiable scale with no subjective latitude; thus they tend to think that grades should be based wholly on how compliantly they have done their busywork, not on the exercise of their intellect. Without daily roll call and quizzes, they are apt to cut class and not do assignments. They are constantly calculating, "Will this be on the exam?" and "How much will this count?"

By contrast, EC-code students are less obeisant to authority in teachers and public figures, more comfortable with flexibility in assignments; they are more oriented toward initiative and autonomy in studying, more motivated toward learning for its own sake rather than jumping through hoops for the grade. I sometimes ask students to invent their own exams synthesizing the material covered with their own understanding. Those who are more adept in EC take this in stride; those who aren't are thrown into high anxiety and beg me to give them clear-cut questions. A necessary qualification here, of course, is that many RC students are less secure financially, and that their insistence on rigid organization of calendars and assignments may be to some extent understandable in light of the pressures on their time imposed by an overwhelming schedule of courses, jobs, and family obligations. Another part of the cause here is what can be called restricted-code educational conditioning, which perhaps determines students' expectations externally, more than any of their innate or developmental capacities. This is another instance of socioeconomic inequities and pedagogical exigencies becoming a vicious circle.

In terms of historical consciousness, the tendency of RC college students is to have only a hazy one if any, not only in their lack of knowledge of specific historical facts but in their sense of the past as a vast blur in which they have no grasp of differences in, and sequences between, events and situations years, decades, or centuries apart. (There may be a chicken-and-egg question here: perhaps knowledge of historical specifics precedes a sense of historical sequence and cause-and-effect, or vice versa. Study of research in historical pedagogy would be useful here.) I have had students refer to works by Martin Luther King or James Baldwin as written "in the days of slavery." More commonly, white students reading Baldwin's *The Fire Next Time*, which I make clear was published in 1963 and refers to the segregated America of the 1950s, charge that Baldwin was "prejudice [*sic*] against all whites" and angrily deny the truth of his account by referring to today's more integrated society, or even to the present "privileged" position of blacks over whites. (Black students and citizens, even those not college educated, tend to have a more clear sense of American racial history, conveyed through their family stories—which indicates an element in whites' thinking of the defense mechanism of denial or willful ignorance, precisely the point made by Baldwin in saying, "They do not know . . . and do not want to know" the historical truth [5], and "It is the innocence that constitutes the crime" [6].)

Even within the lifespan of students who might be quite bright, the awareness of historical sequence is apt to be blurry. In 2006 some of my students wrote research papers based on rhetorical analysis of sources on the tenth anniversary of the reforms in welfare under President Clinton. In the sources they wrote about, they tended not to distinguish between those written before the reforms or about the prior system, and those written after, specifically about the reforms. So in reading their drafts, I had to specify the need to make such distinctions in the final version. In writing about the Iraq War, they had a similar tendency not to distinguish the sequence of the Bush administration's shifting justifications for the war or of developments since the war began, so many uncritically accepted the argument that the presence of Al Qaeda in Iraq, demonstrably the *consequence* of American occupation, confirmed the administration's initial claims that Saddam Hussein harbored Al Qaeda. Their thinking about the Iraq war in general showed an inability to evaluate the rhetoric defending the war in the perspective of similar rhetoric in previous wars, most recently Vietnam, so that the realities of this war were assumed to be unprecedented—which is also the way they were presented in the rhetoric of the government and news media. The historical analogies invoked by conservatives were between Saddam Hussein and Hitler, or Al Qaeda and fascism, as in "Islamo-fascism," but those who made or accepted these analogies tended to use them just as a scare tactic, without examining their accuracy in historical specifics.

All of these factors contribute to the paradox, central to this book, that students and faculty at "elite," upper-class colleges tend more to be liberal or leftist than those at many middle- or working-class colleges. In my experience as a student and teacher, the EC tendencies are more characteristic of students and faculty in private liberal arts colleges and the more selective public universities, while the RC tendencies are more common to students in occupational and technological majors and in less selective private and public colleges. I am thinking mainly of the hierarchy in the California system between the University of California campuses, especially Berkeley, where I did my doctoral study and spent several years as a TA and instructor, the state university ones, where I taught for some twenty-five years, and community colleges, where I have not taught. This is the kind of statement that gets me accused of elitism, but my point in describing these stark realities is not to approve of them but to criticize their role in the reproduction of class and cultural inequities, and to advocate reversing those inequities. (For critical accounts of the way the system was structured under the Master Plan for Higher Education in California, see Lazere, "Stratification" and "Class Conflict.") The correlation here of RC and EC with social class and with liberal or left versus conservative attitudes is a complex, paradoxical one that will be explored through the course of the following sections. Just to reiterate a key distinction, though, when I identify RC thinking with conservatism, I refer to the uninformed, conformist level of conservatism, not to the intellectually informed level, which is marked by a comparable level of EC thinking to that of informed liberalism or leftism.

All of these issues have been muddied by misunderstandings or misapplications by scholars and social critics of Bernstein's ideas as well as those concerning developmental psychology, orality-literacy theory, and "students' rights to their own language"—particularly by many progressive educators in English and other fields. As I will detail in this section, their failure to distinguish between the regressive and progressive aspects of defenses of literacy and higher education has led to the kind of anti-intellectualism on the left that I take issue with throughout this book. In other words, progressive theorists of literacy divide between those who recognize only the oppressive, conformist dimension of intellectual or academic discourse and those who defend the oppositional, liberating dimensions, as I do. Likewise, many progressive theorists have defended left-wing populism against the widespread, undeniably biased antipopulist scholarship, back to the 1950s, that explicitly or implicitly identified populism primarily as right wing; however, in legitimately defending left-wing populism, progressives have tended to underestimate the actual extent of right-wing populism in America, from the 1960s to the present Tea Party variety, including the many college students immersed in that belief system; so among the aims of the agenda surveyed in this section is to garner information useful toward pedagogy that takes realistic account of the mindset of such students. With this introductory perspective, then, let us re-evaluate the scholarship in the fields surveyed here with an eye toward what points may still be applicable to English studies and what lines of theoretical inquiry and empirical research might still be fruitful.

11

ORALITY, LITERACY, AND
POLITICAL CONSCIOUSNESS

Historians of literacy, including Eric Havelock, Walter Ong, Jack Goody, and Ian Watt, have correlated the social origins of written discourse and of analytic reasoning. According to Goody and Watt in "The Consequences of Literacy":

> In oral societies the cultural tradition is transmitted almost entirely by face-to-face communication; and changes in its content are accompanied by the homeostatic process of forgetting or transforming those parts of the tradition that cease to be either necessary or relevant. Literate societies, on the other hand, cannot discard, absorb, or transmute the past in the same way. Instead, their members are faced with permanently recorded versions of the past and its beliefs; and because the past is thus set apart from the present, historical enquiry becomes possible. This in turn encourages scepticism; and scepticism, not only about the legendary past, but about received ideas about the universe as a whole. From here the next step is to see how to build up and to test alternative explanations: and out of this there arose the kind of logical, specialized, and cumulative intellectual tradition of sixth-century Ionia. The kinds of analysis involved in the syllogism, and in the other forms of logical procedure, are clearly dependent upon writing, indeed upon a form of writing sufficiently simple and cursive to make possible widespread and habitual recourse both to the recording of verbal statements and then to the dissecting of them. It is probable that it is only the analytic process that writing itself entails, the written formalization of sounds and syntax, which makes possible the habitual separating out into formally distinct units of the various cultural elements whose indivisible wholeness is the essential basis of the "mystical participation" which Levy-Bruhl regards as characteristic of the thinking of non-literate peoples. (Giglioli 352–53)

Watt, incidentally, was a British literary scholar at Cambridge (and later Stanford), where he collaborated with Goody, an anthropologist, and his best-known book, *The Rise of the Novel*, fruitfully links literary theory and literacy theory. Ong, in *Orality and Literacy* and other works, developed the intriguing hypothesis that the account of historical development from oral to literate society in Goody, Watt, and Havelock is recapitulated through individual cognitive development in childhood. Ong identifies a similar parallel in Vygotsky and Luria's accounts of stages of development in both children and adults; he says that Luria "does not systematically encode his findings expressly in terms of orality differences. But despite the elaborate Marxist scaffolding, Luria's report clearly turns in fact on the differences between orality and literacy" (50).

An important, complementary work in orality-literacy theory is *The Psychology of Literacy* by social psychologists Sylvia Scribner and Michael Cole, published in 1981. Scribner and Cole undertook to test the body of theory that I refer to above in an ethnographic study of a tribe in Liberia that had retained a culture of primary orality. (Ong distinguishes primary orality, the dominant culture in preliterate societies, which can be quite complex cognitively, from the secondary orality of illiterate, marginalized people in literate society.) They confirmed that the people's reasoning and discourse were highly sophisticated for meeting the needs of their particular society, although they encountered predictable problems with the introduction of formal schooling. Kurt Spellmeyer, in our exchange in *CCC* about an earlier version of my survey here, claimed that "Lazere's entire line of reasoning, taken whole-cloth from Basil Bernstein, has been decisively overturned by Scribner and Cole's magisterial work, *The Psychology of Literacy*, which rejects the very notion that literacy imparts critical consciousness, a broadened perspective, or some kind of meta-awareness that non-readers lack" (294). (I presume Spellmeyer meant "wholly" or "wholesale" from Bernstein rather than "whole-cloth," which means "fabricated from thin air.") Spellmeyer, whose confused account indicated no sign of his having actually read either Scribner and Cole or Bernstein, failed to explain exactly how their ethnographic study of adult schooling in a Liberian tribal community, from which they drew the most modest and mixed conclusions, "over-turns" Bernstein's own ethnographic studies of socialization patterns of children in working-class versus middle-class British families. In fact, Scribner and Cole do not discuss Bernstein's work or sociolinguistics at all, beyond one entry in their bibliography. Nor do they make the kind of ridiculously sweeping claims Spellmeyer attributes to them above, which would amount to rejecting truths that are so obvious as to be tautological: that people who can read are enabled to learn more about the world outside their immediate experience than those who cannot, and that mastery of the language of academic discourse and complex syntactic thought suggested by Goody and Watt, and anatomized by Shaughnessy in the context of college basic writing, is necessary (though perhaps not sufficient) for "critical consciousness" toward political rhetoric in today's society. Spellmeyer, along with his former Pittsburgh colleagues like Bartholomae, Petrosky, and Harris, seemed to be captive to a postmodernist version of the Rousseauan myth of the innate wisdom of children, the noble savage in the state of nature, the unschooled in modern society—a mythology that did not cloud the more complicated view of Scribner and Cole's ethnographic research. Incidentally, an article that Cole wrote with his colleague in developmental psychology at Harvard, Jerome Bruner, argues that in the utterly different social context of the United States, exclusive acquisition of language through black dialect and oral culture puts black children at a disadvantage in schools and other realms of society dominated by standard English and written culture ("Cultural Differences").

It is, again, true that a good deal of recent scholarship, as reported by Beth Daniell and others, has damaged the empirical credibility of earlier histories of orality and literacy, but still, it is not necessary for scholars to accept them "wholesale" to apply judiciously in English studies the patterns they traced. Consider the controversial work of Thomas J. Farrell, a graduate student of Ong at St. Louis University, later a close colleague of Shaughnessy at City College of New York, and a specialist in what he calls "Onglish Studies." In early articles like "Literacy, the Basics, and All That Jazz" (1977) and "Developing Literacy: Walter J. Ong and Basic Writing" (1978), Farrell extended to college basic writing students the hypothesis from Ong and Vygotsky about the development of reasoning capacities from those of childhood speech to the more complex ones attainable in writing. Those articles first brought Farrell to my attention, since his explanations confirmed my observations of my own *advanced writing* students, who were overwhelmingly middle class, but whose language is primarily the oral one of television, radio, popular music, social media, and peer conversation.

One of Farrell's most thought-provoking hypotheses about basic writers is their tendency, as in oral cultures and nonliterate speech, to use paratactic language and thinking—that is, placement of phrases or clauses one after the other without logical connectives or sequence. In contrast, literate cultures and written language make more use of hypotactic (subordinate) and syntactic (coordinate or sequential) structures and ideas. (Bernstein makes the same distinction in restricted and elaborated codes, as we will see.) In other words, oral culture tends to be appositional and formulaic, while literate culture tends to be propositional in reasoning, so that writing facilitates a greater degree of abstract and analytic thinking, as described by Shaughnessy and Lunsford. So Farrell suggests various pedagogical methods for making these transitions in basic writing courses. These distinctions again tacitly reflect the traits of oral culture in contemporary mass culture, especially television, advertising, and political propaganda, as identified by critics like Postman, Aronowitz, and Kate Moody.

My Camus-centrism prompts an application of this point to the famous paratactic sentence structure of Meursault's narrative in *The Stranger*, calculated to express a consciousness that is purely sensory, recording a series of verbal snapshots without connection, interpretation of meaning and significance, or moral judgment. Always the dialectical ironist, however, Camus later wrote in his introduction to *The Rebel*, tacitly contradicting *The Stranger* and its essayistic companion piece *The Myth of Sisyphus*, "Any philosophy of non-signification survives on a contradiction in the very fact of expressing itself. Simply by being expressed, it gives a minimum of coherence to incoherence, and introduces consequence where, according to its own tenets, there is none" (*Rebel* 8). (I earlier applied the same principle to the self-contradiction in feminist theorists who denounce "phallocentric" reason while using it themselves.) Even in *The Stranger*, the trick that Meursault's narrative is not actually spoken but written gives it the cogency and permanence of a literary artifice, and the narrative can be interpreted as Meursault's "writing" of his life at the end of it, giving that life an aesthetic unity ironically comparable to Proust's *Remembrance of Things Past* as an aesthetic recreation of an entire life (an analogy that Camus indicated was intentional). Elsewhere Camus refuted critics who charged that his books expressed solipsism and despair, "If he speaks, if he reasons, above all if he writes, immediately the brother reaches out his hand, the tree is justified, love is born. Literature of despair is a contradiction in terms" (*Lyrical* 57). Thus Camus traced the path from self-absorption to sociopolitical responsibility, from solitude to solidarity, through the act of writing—a path also delineated in a passage from Camus I analyze at the end of this chapter.

Farrell ran into a buzzsaw of attacks by cultural pluralists in response to two of his articles that indirectly criticized the 1974 *Students' Right to Their Own Language*, "Differentiating Writing from Talking" in 1978, and "IQ and Standard English" in 1983. The latter, in *CCC*, was accompanied by four harsh rebuttals, and Farrell has continued to be anathematized in rhetcomp ever since, quite unfairly in my opinion. "IQ and Standard English" begins by addressing the low performance of black children in IQ tests, which he attributes to the measurement by such tests of performance in cognitive operations and mastery of syntactic structures intrinsic to standard English as a grapholect, or written language. He goes on to assert that many black students—particularly those from poor backgrounds—have been socialized in the purely oral cognitive patterns of black English, which is essentially a spoken rather than written language, and they therefore lack control of the full panoply of conjugations and coordinating and subordinating syntax that distinguishes standard *written* English and that forms a necessary matrix for abstract and analytic thought, both in testing and academic studies generally. Farrell singles out the incomplete conjugation of the verb "to be" in American black English as the sign of a restricted sense of time and as a handicap to propositional reasoning. He concludes with a proposal for instructional techniques designed to help students bridge the gap between black and standard English, between dialect and grapholect.

It is difficult to make a balanced evaluation of Farrell's article because, beyond his titular subject, he has audaciously attempted to synthesize topics and sources covering nearly the whole range of recent theories of literacy in regard to both linguistics and literature—with very mixed results; valid points are mingled with wildly invalid ones. Many of the criticisms leveled by his four respondents in *CCC*, Karen Greenberg, Patrick Hartwell, Margaret Himley, and R. E. Stratton, are sound, in my admittedly inexpert opinion. They say his exclusive emphasis on black oral culture as the cause of blacks' difficulties in schooling is reductive, isolating matters of oral and written language from matters of vocabulary and subject matter—as well as from the larger social context in which learning does or does not take place. He endorses conventional, authoritarian pedagogy as opposed to interactive literacy of the kind advocated by Shirley Brice Heath and Paulo Freire. Perhaps worst, he accepts Arthur Jensen's and R. A. Figueroa's use of a "digit span" IQ test as a valid measure of abstract reasoning proficiency, although he rejects Jensen's theory of racially inherited IQ. Greenberg and Hartwell effectively refute Farrell's premise that the incomplete conjugation of the verb "to be" in black English indicates a cognitive deficiency in that dialect. John Ogbu, in an article published before Farrell's in 1983, rejects the theory that American black children's problems in school are primarily attributable to their oral culture. He makes a compelling case that different social groups from oral cultural backgrounds vary widely in adapting to literate schooling, and he offers, as an alternate explanation for blacks' problems, an array of more influential factors involving specifically antiblack social and cultural prejudice.

Along with these valid points by Farrell's critics, however, are others that are disputable. Karen Greenberg's response in *CCC* concludes sweepingly about Farrell, "Advocating a separate pedagogy for students because of differences in their genes or in their language is racist" (460). This label has stuck to Farrell over the years, but I think it is unjustified, indeed malicious, on both counts. Farrell explicitly rejects genetic theories like Jensen's. *Racism* also implies overgeneralizations and ignorant misconceptions about an entire race, which Farrell also rejects. He had taught for many years in inner-city black schools. (I wonder how many of his critics have done so.) He expresses full appreciation of the literary and linguistic richness of the black oral tradition in the United States, as well as its roots in African culture. He simply argues that for reasons grounded in the past denial by whites of black access to schooling, black culture has not been strongly attuned to the written word or academic discourse. Farrell also makes it clear that his thesis does not apply to all American blacks, but only uneducated ones: "There are educated blacks who speak ['read and write' would have been more felicitous phrasing] standard English, and their children generally score better than most of their black ghetto peers on IQ tests. This paper is obviously not about them" (479). He might have pursued this point further, to stress that he really is talking more about issues of class than of race; his points could apply to any comparison of working-class or lower-middle-class groups whose culture is oral to groups in higher classes with access to literate culture, with all the implications of Bernstein's theory about restricted working-class versus elaborated middle-class linguistic-cognitive codes.

Farrell's pedagogical strategies for helping students make the transition from oral to written discourse—oral reading of or listening to recordings of texts, French-style *dictées*, etc.—must be considered on the grounds on which he presents them: do they work? (Cultural pluralists take offense at Farrell's recommendation of McGuffey's *Readers* as oral texts for transcription, although this was their original use; if McGuffey's content is culturally biased, many other readings, including those by black authors, would serve as well.)

It would have helped Farrell's case if he had been able to present testimony from his black students or others having undergone similar techniques that they found them beneficial. By the same token, some of Farrell's critics seem more intent on laying down a correct political line than on considering what real black students happen to want. Farrell, after all, does not advocate forcing these techniques on all students, but offering them to those who want to improve their academic reading and writing skills and performance on tests, or who want to learn to use standard English—*in addition to, not instead of*—black dialect. If they judge that McGuffey or any other resource has helped them, who is to deny the legitimacy of that judgment? Incidentally, Farrell's general position received tacit support from

Lisa Delpit, whose *Other People's Children* concludes from her experience teaching black inner-city children that they dislike the current neglect of standard form and mechanics and *want* instruction in the formal skills they need to progress in schooling. Similar conclusions have been reached by progressive psychologists and sociologists of education like Michael Cole and Jerome Bruner, Richard Hoggart and Basil Bernstein, as we will see in the next chapter.

Orality, Literacy, and *Students' Right*

Farrell's general approach to orality and literacy in rhetcomp studies, and in *Students' Right to Their Own Language* in particular, helped me focus my own criticisms of that document, in which I have found multiple confusions and inadvertent false dilemmas that obstruct its worthy intentions. (See Lazere, "Orality," *Class Politics*). Four decades after its publication in 1974, *Students' Right* continues to be a lightning rod of controversy.

The very title *Students' Right to Their Own Language* was misbegotten, with consequences that have multiplied through the years. The word *Language* should have been replaced by *Dialect*, which is virtually the only subject addressed throughout the monograph. Its claims that are incontestably true about dialect have been sweepingly carried over by its adherents to other matters of language and learning that are highly contestable, especially at the college level. Its key opposition between black English and standard English confuses differences among oral dialects with the difference between any oral dialect and grapholect. So while it may be true that all oral dialects are equal in the ways *Students' Right* asserts, it is misleading to call standard written English or Edited American English merely a dialect, analogous to black English. And while, as the statement says, nonstandard dialects pose no intrinsic obstacle to learning to read and write, I have insisted throughout this book that the central point that needs to be addressed is not standard English or even written language *per se*, but the whole greater repertory of vocabulary, syntactic and logical complexity (including Shaughnessy's "vocabulary of logical relationships"), *and factual knowledge* that becomes possible only through the resources of a grapholectic system, particularly in academic discourse, as Shaughnessy amply delineated it.

Students' Right asserts:

If teachers understand that the spoken language is always primary and the written language is a separate and secondary or derived system, they will be able to recognize that students inexperienced in the written system may still have great competence and facility in

> the spoken language. . . . Once a teacher understands the arbitrary
> nature of the oral and written forms, the pronunciation or spelling of
> a word becomes less important than whether it communicates what
> the student wants to say. (15)

And earlier, "Learning to write in any dialect entails the mastery of such conventions as spelling and punctuation, surface features of the written language" (8). Thus all Edited American English is implicitly reduced to such arbitrary "surface features." *Students' Right* labors the obvious truth that no oral dialect in itself poses an obstacle to learning to read or write standard English, although it fails to note that people tend automatically to diminish their dialect as they become more educated. (I do, however, know professors, lawyers, and doctors in Knoxville who have retained their thick East Tennessee accent, without detriment to their career.) However, if the speaker of any dialect (including middle-class white English) has grown up immersed almost exclusively in oral language, not reading or writing much, and not being acclimated to academic discourse and subject matter, those factors—scarcely mentioned in *Students' Right*—are apt to be obstacles in college.

These equivocations in *Students' Right* were compounded by its having been published by the Conference on College Composition and Communication and written by a panel of prominent, college-level rhetcomp theorists like Richard Lloyd-Jones, Elizabeth McPherson, W. Ross Winterowd, and Geneva Smitherman (whose own scholarship on black English dominates the statement). The text, however, has virtually no direct application to college study. It might at least have included a section on its *implications* for college. The authors drew from Chomskyian and other popular linguistic theories of the time, which are surveyed in a bibliographical appendix and which primarily addressed language acquisition in children, instruction at the elementary level, and colloquial speech in children and adults, with little attention to stages of development in reading and writing through K-12 and continuing through college—which hasn't prevented many of its adherents as recent as Paul Butler in 2008 from assuming it can be applied at that level. The few references to college instruction are confusedly formulated, like the claim that students are usually required to take "'developmental' or 'compensatory' English well into college if their native dialect varies from that of the middle class" (2). Is spoken dialect the only, or even the primary, basis for students being placed in basic writing courses?

Or consider this claim about college, which was a veritable manifesto for the excesses of postmodern pluralism:

Many of us have taught as though the function of schools and colleges were to erase differences. Shou ld we, on the one hand, urge creativity and individuality in the arts and sciences, take pride in the diversity of our historical development, and on the other hand try to obliterate all the differences in the way Americans speak and write?

Do all these differences that are to be encouraged in "schools and colleges," without value judgments distinguishing them, include only those of regional or ethnic accents and idioms, or also differences in levels of speaking, reading, writing, and reasoning between college-educated adults and children, between well-informed citizens and ignorant bigots, between readers of Edmund Burke and Rush Limbaugh "dittoheads," or between *The Fire Next Time* and Labov's black youths discussing God on the street?

Students' Right does go so far as to acknowledge, "Schools and colleges emphasize one form of language, the one we called Edited American English (EAE). It is the written language of the weekly newsmagazines, of almost all newspapers, and of most books. This variety of written English can be loosely termed a dialect" (6–7). The implication here that spoken vernacular and the entire universe of edited, published prose are no more than separate but equal dialects then gets further tangled up in an irrelevant paragraph about Chomskyian "deep structure" in reading by children, toward the point that "dialect itself is not an impediment to reading." What, then, *is*?

> Reading difficulties may be a result of inadequate vocabulary, problems in perception, ignorance of contextual clues that aid in the reading process, lack of familiarity with stylistic ordering, interference from the emotional bias of the material, or combinations of these. In short, reading is so complicated a process that it provides temptations to people who want to offer easy explanations and solutions. (7)

Exactly who ever wanted to reduce all reading and writing problems to nonstandard dialects? Did this straw adversary warrant a monograph laboring the subject of dialect for thirty-two pages, while it shrugs off in one sentence the whole scope of larger problems that would soon thereafter be addressed frontally by Mina Shaughnessy and E. D. Hirsch? Hirsch has been pilloried in rhetcomp circles for three decades for merely asking in *Cultural Literacy* what knowledge Americans need to be able to read at the level of the journalistic media cited above. Dogmatic resistance in NCTE circles to any concrete delineation of levels of development in reading and writing, including levels of factual knowledge, recurs periodically, most recently in the fierce reaction against the richly detailed developmental models in the Common Core State Standards.

In sum, the exclusive focus of *Students' Right* on dialect is a distraction from the serious problems of students who are not attuned to written, academic discourse when they reach college, and the role in those problems of oral versus literate culture—not *dialect*—compounded by discrimination in class socialization and access to quality K-12 education. These are daunting problems for many of the middle-class white students I have taught, whose dialect might be described as Television-Texting-Twitter English, as well as for minorities and the poor.

In *The Making of Americans* (2008), Hirsch similarly says about *Students' Right* and its endorsement by NCTE and CCCC:

> The honorable impulse behind the resolution is that teachers should not make students feel that their home speech is somehow unworthy. But that is all it should have said. The rest is simply incorrect, and I am embarrassed that two organizations I once belonged to are still supporting this factually inadmissible and ethically suspect resolution. The leaders of these organizations should check up on these claims, especially the assertion that "language scholars long ago denied that the myth of a standard American dialect has any validity," the most ill-informed public statement by a learned society in many years. . . . Even if one argues (incorrectly) that there is no standard American dialect but only a dialect of "power," to restrict students' mastery of that dialect is to deny them access to power, as Gramsci and others after him have observed. (99)

Nothing that either Hirsch or I say is intended to minimize the depredations resulting from racial and class discrimination—exactly the contrary: I think the adherents of *Students' Right* were more inclined to do that in their overly optimistic view of students' readiness for college studies, absent a sweeping reform in economic equity for college preparation.

The undeniable persistence of American public prejudice against black English was heartbreakingly dramatized in June 2013, in the gaudily televised trial in Florida of George Zimmerman for killing teenager Trayvon Martin. The prosecution's key witness portraying Zimmerman as a racist was Martin's friend Rachel Jeantel, a nineteen-year-old high school student who spoke in black English and whose demeanor fed into the most negative stereotypes of black women, which were instantly made the subject of ridicule through social media. She was mercilessly cross-examined for five hours by the defense attorneys trying to destroy her credibility (by pressing her on understandable faulty recollections and quotidian white lies) and to deflect the charge of racism back onto her and Martin, who she testified told her on his cell phone that he was being followed by "a creepy-ass cracker." An illuminating fact little remarked on by the media pundits was that she was born in Haiti and her first two languages were Creole and Spanish, which might have been factored into her dialect and halting English. It is also tempting to speculate on this as a possible case of courtroom elaborated-code language being exploited to fluster a restricted-code thinker unaccustomed to retrospection and verbal reconstruction of past events— although any such interpretation was complicated by Jeantel's international life experience, which might well have made her thinking more elaborated, and silently shrewder, than the attorneys'—or mine—in survival strategies like silence or playing dumb.

Theories of Cognitive and Moral Development

In developmental psychology, the key names are, at the childhood level, Jean Piaget, Lev Vygotsky, and A. R. Luria, and at the college level, William Perry, Lawrence Kohlberg, Carol Gilligan, and Mary Field Belenky et al. Vygotsky's *Thought and Language* and *Mind in Society* are especially important for rhetoric and composition studies for his research on the development in children from inner speech to oral expression to writing and reading. He and Luria are additionally interesting for having lived in the USSR and incorporated into their work elements of Marxism and other sociopolitical dimensions lacking from much Western scholarship, a point shrewdly developed by Min-Zhan Lu. As noted in chapter 5, Lu's chapter "Importing 'Science': Neutralizing Basic Writing" traces, in the early American appropriations of Vygotsky's work, the suppression of its Marxist dimension and its replacement with a "scientific" framework, a regular feature of the cultural Cold War. She identifies this "amputation" in Jerome Bruner's introduction to the 1962 translation of *Thought and Language*, and notes that it was corrected in a 1986 edition, edited by Alex Kozulin, as well as in a 1978 translation of *Mind in Society* with an introduction by Cole and Scribner (authors of *The Psychology of Literacy*). *Culture, Communication, and Cognition: Vygotskyian Perspectives*, edited by James V. Wertsch, is exemplary as a wide-ranging, interdisciplinary collection, with thorough emphasis on the Marxist dimension of Vygotsky's work. James Zebroski's *Thinking through Theory: Vygotskian Perspectives on the Teaching of Writing* is a thorough, thoughtful survey of Vygotsky's work and the uses and misuses to which it has been put in American scholarship, particularly in composition. A schema toward the end titled "Vygotsky's Influence on Composition" lists American and British sources that have applied Vygotsky toward either conservative or leftist ends, along the same lines that I suggest about the appropriations of

Bernstein's work in chapters 12 and 13. Unfortunately, Zebroski nowhere develops this schema in his text, which shortchanges the dimensions of class and ideological analysis in Vygotsky and Luria.

Piaget is useful for his studies of children's growth from the stages of egocentrism (or narcissism in psychoanalytic terms) to sociocentrism or ethnocentrism to reciprocity, development that is often still in process at the college level. A delightful article by Piaget, "The Development in Children of the Idea of the Homeland," was based on his interviews with Swiss children from age four to ten about their perceptions of Switzerland in relation to other countries. The chauvinism of the younger children is especially ironic because tiny Switzerland is among the least ethnocentric countries due to its multilingual, cosmopolitan, nonmilitary culture and borders with France, Germany, and Italy. A six-year-old is asked, "If you were born without belonging to any country, which would you choose?" He responds, "I'd like to become Swiss." "Why?" "Because." "Say you could choose between France and Switzerland, would you choose Switzerland?" "Yes." "Why?" "Because the French are nasty." "If I asked a little French boy the same question . . . what do you think this child would choose?" "He'd want to be Swiss" (55). When a twelve-year-old is asked the same series of questions, her response to the first is still Switzerland. But when asked why, she says, "Because I was born in Switzerland and this is my home." When asked to compare the Swiss and French, she replies, "Oh, on the whole, they're much the same. There are some very nice Swiss and some very nice French people, that doesn't depend on the country." When asked whether a French boy would prefer France or Switzerland, she says probably France, for the same reason that she said Switzerland. When next asked which would be right, she replies, "You can't tell. Everyone is right in his own eyes. All people have their opinions" (57).

These developmental stages described by Piaget were extended by Perry in *Intellectual and Ethical Development in the College Years*, based on studies of the progression in reasoning of students at Harvard over the course of a four-year liberal arts education; the students were all male, a shortcoming that prompted later revision by Gilligan and Belenky et al. (See Bizzell's "William Perry and Liberal Education," in *Academic* 153–63, for a judicious assessment of his work.) In Perry's summary, his scheme consists of three parts with three positions within each:

> In positions 1, 2, and 3, a person modifies an absolutistic [and socio-centric] right-wrong [or dualistic] outlook to make room, in some minimal way, for that simple pluralism we have called Multiplicity. In positions 4, 5, and 6 a person accords the diversity of human outlook

its full problematic stature, next transmutes the simple pluralism of Multiplicity into contextual Relativism, and then comes to foresee the necessity of personal Commitment in a relativistic world. Positions 7, 8, and 9 then trace the development of Commitments in the person's actual experience. (57)

Kohlberg's stage-developmental scheme of moral reasoning, derived from study of individuals from about the age of seven into adulthood, similarly has three major steps, subdivided into six. The Preconventional stage is egocentric, rule-bound, and compliant to authority. The Conventional stage is more sociocentric and bound to the beliefs or customs of one's community or culture. The Postconventional, or Principled, Stage incorporates Perry's higher stages of relativism and committed relativism, culminating in moral-intellectual autonomy and individuation in forming ethical principles independent of externally imposed norms.

Lunsford's two articles in 1979 and 1980 applied both Perry and Kohlberg in attempting to devise empirical research on stages of cognitive and moral-reasoning development in basic writers. In retrospect, I find nothing in these articles to warrant Bartholomae's put-down of them: "Basic writers . . . are seen as childlike or as uncultured natives. There is an imperial frame to this understanding of the situation of those who are not like us." In fact, Lunsford stated quite clearly:

> In some ways, as Maxine Hairston has suggested to me, the basic writers' prose is more vital, more engaging and more true to the students' experiences than the impersonal, strangely disengaged prose often produced by our more skilled students. The real challenge for us as teachers of basic writing lies in helping our students become more proficient in abstracting and conceptualizing and hence in producing acceptable academic discourse, without losing the directness many of them now possess. ("Content" 287)

Lunsford made this essential point in a more refined manner than the crude dichotomy in *Students' Right to Their Own Language* and in Paul Butler's endorsement of it, quoted in chapter 6 above: "In every class there are examples of writing which is clear and vigorous despite the use of non-standard forms . . . and there are certainly many examples of limp, vapid writing in 'standard dialect'" (*Students'* 8).

What I find in Lunsford is an admirable, early effort toward the kind of emphasis that I advocate, mixed with some of the limitations in our profession's perspectives that still persist. For "Content," in her first faculty position at Simon Fraser, she studied essays written for a British Columbia college English placement test from "a representative cross-section of British Columbia" where "the range of writing ability seems similar to that displayed by incoming freshmen at a typical large state university" (279). She "had the sample group evaluated by three experienced readers trained in holistic scoring in order to identify two groups of essays: those written by basic writers and those written by skilled writers" (279). The students could choose to write on one of several topics, some on the kind of personal topics typical at this level, like "Who is the most memorable person you have known? Why?" Some others, though, dealt with social controversies like the pros and cons of capital punishment and dishonesty in advertising, and one was a historical comparison between the political and cultural characteristics of the 1950s, 1960s, and 1970s. (Interestingly, more students, both basic and skilled, chose these topics than the personal ones.) As noted in chapter 4, the findings on capital punishment strongly supported my contention about uninformed conservative support for it: 71 percent of the basic writers supported it, while 73 percent of the skilled writers opposed it.

Lunsford cited Shaughnessy's precedent in studying another dimension of the students' writing on these subjects, the level of their vocabulary, syntactical and grammatical fluency. She found that

> a basic writer's vocabulary is characterized by a high percentage of personal pronouns, especially those relating to first person, by a relatively low degree of nominalization, and by the use of concrete diction and simple concepts. In contrast, the skilled writers' vocabulary can be characterized by a low percentage of personal pronouns, relatively high degree of nominalization, and by the use of abstract diction and complex concepts" [for example, "derision," "skepticism," "hostility," "distinction," "formality," "impermanence"]. (287)

Along with the excellent beginnings in Lunsford's application of developmental psychology to basic writing, from today's perspective several limitations are evident in them, as she herself has acknowledged—though my reservations differ from the postmodernist critique by Bartholomae and others, who tend to ignore these limitations. One problem is the selection of topics in the Canadian college entrance exam that she studied, which she did not question. It seems evident today that in placement exam questions on capital punishment, dishonest advertising, or cultural history, student writers who had more knowledge of facts and vocabulary about them—say, from previous academic study—would have a large advantage over those who didn't, with the consequent effect on the quality of their writing performance that Hirsch would verify in *Cultural Literacy*. At any level, shouldn't we avoid assigning such topics for student essays, especially placement exams, based purely on personal opinion, when what is needed is "the critical use of textual and historical evidence" (Commission on the Humanities) and evaluation of opposing lines of argument by qualified sources? This comes back to the problem I addressed in chapter 4 about the isolation of American (and apparently Canadian) writing instruction and testing from academic subject matter and discourse, as well as the necessity to delineate stages of subject matter at successive levels of writing courses (as, for example, in the Common Core State Standards).

Lunsford's own privileging of skilled writers' "low percentage of personal pronouns, relatively high degree of nominalization, and . . . use of abstract diction and complex concepts" was the kind of judgment that irked multiculturalists and seemed to go against her qualification that "the real challenge for us as teachers of basic writing lies in helping our students become more proficient in abstracting and conceptualizing and hence in producing acceptable academic discourse, without losing the directness many of them now possess." Perhaps she could have clarified her point by saying that skilled writers become better able to switch styles and modes of thinking, between the personal and the impersonal, concrete and abstract, and so on, according to what is most appropriate to any given writing task.

My aim here is not to single out for criticism, long after the fact, either that Canadian exam or Lunsford's research based on it; on the contrary, my point is that Lunsford's articles raised a wealth of questions, explicitly or implicitly, of exactly the nature that we should have been pursuing then and now, but that we have largely abandoned. It was a sign of the changing times that with the denigration of developmental psychology and agonistic argument in much postmodern-pluralist and feminist theory that became dominant around 1980, Lunsford herself dropped them to turn her attention—very productively to be sure—to women's rhetorical issues and collaborative writing, working with Lisa Ede and others. She would return to write on argumentation in the late 1990s in two textbooks with John Ruszkiewicz and more recently in her research with Karen Lunsford on the role of argument in first-year writing courses.

Women's Ways of Knowing

The new wave of Western feminism since the 1960s (foreshadowed by Simone de Beauvoir's *The Second Sex* in 1954) has produced a revolutionary moment in human consciousness, with the potential to undermine the masculinist foundations of war, personal violence and aggression, the patriarchal family and politicoeconomic hierarchy, capitalistic "winner take all," and the gender prejudices in virtually every realm of culture. (Charlotte Perkins Gilman's utopian novel *Herland* in 1915 dramatized all these themes, emphasizing the ultimate link between feminism and socialism.) *In a Different Voice* and *Women's Ways* remain invaluable syntheses of these key themes. So I obviously admire the lines of thought in Gilligan and Belenky et al., in spite of the reservations I will express here.

In the feminist developmental theory of Gilligan and Belenky et al., the latter's *Women's Ways of Knowing* is most useful here because of its more systematic analysis of stages of development at the college level. (Incidentally, both Gilligan and Belenky et al. frequently draw examples from literature, making their work equally applicable to teaching literature and composition.) *Women's Ways* is far more nuanced and judicious than the work of some feminists (discussed in chapter 6) who have reified its slightly misleading title into a cognitive killer dichotomy between genders. The authors emphasize that the traits they identify often occur in both sexes and within one individual, so in effect they are delineating an ideal of the feminine and masculine in all of us. They reformulate Perry's male-based model in application to female college students, with five developmental stages, which again progress from restricted-code conservative toward elaborated-code liberal positions, both in relation to women's identity and to politics in general:

> *Silence,* a position in which women experience themselves as mindless and voiceless and subject to the whims of external authority; *received knowledge,* a perspective from which women conceive of themselves as capable of receiving, even reproducing knowledge from the all-knowing external authorities but not capable of creating knowledge on their own; *subjective knowledge,* a perspective from which truth and knowledge are conceived of as personal, private, and subjectively known or intuited; *procedural knowledge,* a position in which women are invested in learning and applying objective procedures for obtaining and communicating knowledge; and *constructed knowledge,* a position in which women view all knowledge as contextual, experience themselves as creators of knowledge, and value both subjective and objective strategies for knowing. (15)

The stage of constructed knowledge is also synonymous with "the kind of maturity that we call connected knowing, an orientation toward understanding and truth that emphasizes not autonomy and independence of judgment but a joining of minds" (55). Another word associated with this stage is *understanding,* by which we mean something akin to the German word *kennen*, the French *connaître*, the Spanish *conocere*, or the Greek *gnosis*, implying personal acquaintance with an object (usually but not always a person). Understanding involves intimacy and equality between self and object, while *knowledge* (*wissen, savoir, saber*) implies separation from the object and mastery over it. (100–101)

These concepts are related to psychoanalytic theory of child psychology positing development from a narcissistic or egocentric stage, in which children's identity is undifferentiated from the physical and visual bond with their mother, to the beginning of individuated ego identity. For boys this stage tends to be more pronounced than for girls because of the growing consciousness of their anatomical difference from their mother and of their identification with the father, leading to ambivalence between the need to establish male identity and the anxiety of oedipal conflict. Through adolescence and the college years, then, male identity formation tends (or did tend until late twentieth-century changes in social roles) more than female to continue the process of emotional and intellectual individuation and autonomy, along with social or occupational achievement.

So in effect, Belenky et al. are positing a stage of emotional and intellectual development that transcends male-inflected autonomy toward a higher-level reaffirmation of mother-child bondedness and intuitive mutual understanding. This line of thought has been developed in studies of male and female conversational modes by Robin Lakoff and Deborah Tannen among others, including different patterns in telephone calls, in which men tend to minimize discussion to conveying basic information and making plans, while women tend to share every day's events. The latter activity has exponentially increased in new media like cell phones, texting, and especially Facebook, widely used like a communal diary; as I noted earlier, it all reminds me of the function of daily "visiting" in Middle American small towns when I was growing up. The extent to which use of social media in America has been gender specific would be a good research topic along the lines of Lakoff and Tannen, and an even better one would be a comparison with their use in very different social contexts like the Arab Spring uprisings, in which women's participation was especially striking.

In relation to education, the concluding chapter of *Women's Ways*, "Connected Teaching," directly applies Freire's and Peter Elbow's principles to a distinctively female-oriented pedagogy, in which teachers are "midwives" who "focus not on their own knowledge (as the lecturer does) but on the student's. They contribute when needed, but it is always clear that the baby is not theirs but the student's" (218). Feminist critic Patricia Spacks is para-phrased, "Women can mimic a masculine authority rooted in 'a universal systematic methodology' and therefore speak with certainty, but we can also try to construct a different kind of authority, based on personal individual experience and acknowledging 'the uncertainties implicit in an approach which values the personal'" (221). Likewise, "Marylyn Rands, who teaches in a women's college, encourages students in her innovative social psychol-ogy course to use a variety of formats in making their presentations. Not one student has ever chosen the debate" (221). And, "In a 'woman-centered university,' Adrienne Rich says, more courses would be conducted in the style of community, fewer in the 'masculine adversarial style of discourse,' which has dominated much of Western education" (223).

My main reservation about connected teaching and learning, as indi-cated in chapter 5 about the "safe house" and "contact zone" models, is that it can be disabled in any classroom with know-it-all students set on browbeating everyone else, who in my experience are women as often as men, or when it runs up against the belligerent rhetoric that dominates public discourse in general. Republican spokeswomen like Ann Coulter and Sarah Palin mimic macho posturing, hectoring us to "man up" or describing themselves as "mama grizzlies" and "tiger mothers." Classes like Rand's and Rich's above, or Elizabeth Ellsworth's described in chapter 6, which are turned into laboratories for feminist ways of learning, undoubtedly have their merits, but seem somewhat cloistered from real-life conflict or even debate. I have not seen extensive efforts by scholars like these to devise application of their ideas to actual political conflict resolution, say, through nonviolent resistance in the mode of Gandhi, Martin Luther King, Dorothy Day, Simone Weil, A. J. Muste, Sojourners, the Berrigan brothers, or Camus in his pacifist pamphlet *Neither Victims nor Executioners*, written amid the rubble following World War II in 1946 and the impending Cold War:

> Little is to be expected from present-day governments, since these live and die according to a murderous code. Hope remains only in the most difficult task of all: to reconsider everything from the bottom up, so as to shape a living society inside a dying one. . . . The peace move-ment I speak of would base itself, inside nations, on work-commu-nities and, internationally, on intellectual communities; the former, organized cooperatively, would help as many individuals as possible to solve their material problems, while the latter would try to define the values by which this international community would live, and would also plead its cause on every occasion.

More precisely, the latter's task would be to speak out clearly against the confusions of the Terror and at the same time to define the values by which a peaceful world may live. The first objectives might be the drawing up of an international code of justice whose Article No. 1 would be the abolition of the death penalty, and an exposition of a sociable culture (*"civilisation du dialogue"*). . . .

Let us suppose that certain individuals resolve that they will consistently oppose to power the force of example; to authority, exhortation; to insult, friendly reasoning; to trickery, simple honor. . . . Let us suppose they devote themselves to orienting education, the press, and public opinion toward the principles outlined here. Then I say that such men would be acting not as Utopians but as honest realists. (19–20)

Perhaps the best provisional resolution of the agonism-cooperation dilemma is to teach students to defend themselves in agonistic argument when necessary, while simultaneously maintaining the ideal of a culture committed to transcending it, such as that voiced by Camus. Rhetoric and composition scholars who have admirably attempted to reconcile feminist sensibility with agonistic argument include Patricia Roberts-Miller, Susan Jarratt, bell hooks, Lynn Worsham, Karen Fitts, and Patricia Bizzell. And the many recent feminist scholars or artists who have also been political activists include Adrienne Rich, Toni Morrison, Barbara Kingsolver, Elaine Scarry, Lani Guinier, Elizabeth Warren, Carolyn Forché, and Judith Butler (in her Middle East interventions). To recapitulate, the immense value of women's way of knowing lies in its serving as a complement to men's way, not as posing a mutually exclusive, killer dichotomy.

Gendered Cognitive Development in Camus

The discussion in *Women's Ways* of the binaries of individuation versus connectedness and of reason versus comprehension in gender identity were especially thought-provoking for me in relation to my studies of Albert Camus. His early lyrical essay "Between Yes and No," published when he was twenty-five, voiced his lifelong ambivalence between feminine and masculine identity. The piece hinges on the memory of discussions with his mother about his father, who died when Albert was two: "His head was split open in the battle of the Marne. Blinded, it took him a week to die" (*Lyrical* 38–39). At one point in the remembered dialogue, she says Albert is "the spitting image" of his father (38). Albert was raised in a French-Algerian slum by his mother, an illiterate, half-deaf cleaning woman who spoke little. The essay shifts from a present-tense narration in the first person to a reminiscence of various memories of his mother, in which he creates distance by referring to himself in the third person: "And so it was not long ago . . . when a son went to see his mother" (37). He describes "the ties attaching him to his mother" in "the tender and despairing image of two people's loneliness together" (36). In the most recent memory, when he has visited her as an adult, "They sat down facing each other, in silence. But their eyes met. . . . And though her lips do not move, her face lights up in a beautiful smile. It's true, he never talked much to her. But did he ever need to? When one keeps quiet, the situation becomes clear. He is her son, she is his mother. She can say to him, 'you know'" (37–38). His identification with her traits of nearly autistic detachment, indifference, and silence is echoed in *The Stranger*, where Meursault shares the same traits with his recently deceased mother, toward whom he was tacitly affectionate—significantly complicating his famously cryptic indifference to her death.

However, it becomes clearer throughout this reminiscence that Camus also feared the danger that excessive identification with his silent mother presented to development of his autonomy, individuated identity, and articulation of language, necessary in order "to be a man" (34). At the end of the essay, he breaks out of nostalgic merging of identity with his mother: "I no longer want to make such dangerous descents. . . . I must break this too limp and easy curve. I need my lucidity" (39). Note the contrasting of his often-expressed insistence on lucid vision ("clairvoyance") to his father's blinding, and of clear language (as discussed above in chapter 6 and here in *Neither Victims nor Executioners*) to his mother's silence. These connections are all synthesized in the concluding paragraph: "Don't let them say about the man condemned to death: 'He is going to pay his debt to society,' but 'They're going to chop his head off.' It may seem like nothing. But it does make a little difference. There are some people who prefer to look their destiny straight in the eye" (39).[1]

Camus's assertions of male identity and lucidity were defined specifically in his becoming a politically engaged intellectual, writer, and public speaker. At the same time, though, his politics were based on the feminine principles of universal compassion and "solidarity" (contrasted to "solitude"), of "a civilization of dialogue" rather than monologue, applied to communitarian socialism, trade unionism, human rights, world peace, nonviolent resistance, and opposition to capital punishment. (His great 1956 polemic "Reflections on the Guillotine"—anticipated in the above allusions in "Between Yes and No" and *Neither Victims nor Executioners*, and in the plot of *The Stranger*—was influential in the abolition of the death penalty in France.) He did conceive of solidarity in the same key word of *Women's Ways*, *la compréhension*, in its two senses of (mutual) understanding and inclusiveness, but solidarity was more male inflected in his psyche (formed in phallocentric times, to be sure), where commitment to universal "fraternity" marks a stage of Piagetian reciprocity that transcends his personal bond to his mother.

Beyond its relation to gendered cognitive development, "Between Yes and No" is an extraordinarily complex prose poem, with more dimensions than have been addressed here. Among those dimensions is its being a paradigm of the ways Camus integrated personal with political writing, emotion with reason, literary artistry with social commitment—as in the tacit linking of his father's fate here to his polemics against war and capital punishment.

12

SOCIOLINGUISTICS, POLITICAL SOCIALIZATION, AND MASS CULTURE

The British scholarship in sociology of education and culture that emerged in the 1950s was a crucial source for the issues and viewpoints addressed in this book. Its two early leading figures were Basil Bernstein and Richard Hoggart. Bernstein's concepts of restricted and elaborated codes were most controversial, but perhaps Hoggart remains more timely today in having articulated a broader, more profound critical perspective. In his studies of the clash between mass culture and traditional working-class culture, Hoggart became a mentor, along with Raymond Williams, of the Birmingham Centre for Contemporary Cultural Studies, a major base for the cultural studies movement. Hoggart is best known in recent American studies through Richard Rodriguez's identification with his term "scholarship boy" in Rodriguez's memoir *Hunger of Memory*, although as I noted in chapter 7 about its inclusion in *Ways of Reading*, Bartholomae and Petrosky's gloss on it discussed the term, through typical American avoidance of class issues, in relation to his family and ethnic identity rather than, as in Hoggart, in relation to crossing class lines. (Rodriguez in his subsequent career has become a brilliant political journalist and cultural critic in print and on PBS.)

Hoggart's classic *The Uses of Literacy: Changing Patterns in English Mass Culture* (1957) draws from his own working-class background and later socialization as a scholarship boy into the codes of academic discourse. Like the Frankfurt School, he emphasizes the corrosive, flattening effects of mass culture on family life, literacy, and indigenous cultural traditions, especially in the working class, for "working-class people are in some ways more open to the worst effects of the popularisers' assault than are some other groups" (145). In a chapter titled "Living in the Present and 'Progressivism,'" he discusses the present-tense cognitive orientation reinforced by the conditioning of consumerism and mass culture always to be "up to date":

> This particular pattern of assumptions is reinforced, among working-class people in particular, by the fact that they are substantially without a sense of the past. Their education is unlikely to have left

them with any historical panorama or with any idea of a continuing tradition.... Similarly, there can be little real sense of the future.... Such a mind is, I think, particularly accessible to the temptation to live in a constant present. (159)

However, in a later essay titled "The Uncertain Criteria of Deprivation" in *An English Temper: Essays on Education, Culture and Communications* (1982), Hoggart repudiates the version of the cultural deprivation theory that "blames on the shortcoming of the home ills which arise much more from both the short-sightedness of the teachers themselves and from the whole drive of society, its uses and misuses of the educational system" (33). After affirming the values in working-class language and culture studied in his own writing and that of Bernstein, Raymond Williams, and E. P. Thompson in England and William Labov in the United States, he goes on (in the passage just before the above epigraph):

Working-class people, even the most deprived, can be verbally more skillful than we have been used to thinking; their ways may be as dignified and humane as those of the genteel. Nevertheless, there are many people from deprived homes whose language shows no trace of traditional vigour, who are indeed locked into restricting forms of speech, who have virtually no command of language for activities outside the home or neighbourhood, of those types of speech which will allow them to move with reasonable effectiveness through the public situations—elections, applications for public assistance, medical needs, educational questions, shopping itself day by day—which complex societies increasingly present to all of us. They are not used to handling concepts even in their own kinds of speech; they are neither numerate nor really literate. Their lives do not give them the opportunity or the habit of planning forward, of making long-term choices between options. Their children seem therefore destined to become the new hinds [peasants—DL] of twentieth-century industrial society.... (31)

Hoggart's subsequent comments bear more broadly on our recent disputes over Hirschian cultural literacy versus cultural pluralism:

An understanding of the strengths of working-class culture and of the powers and limits of its available language may well affect the way teachers set about their work, help to define starting points, suggest qualities to connect with and build upon; and all that can be useful. But such knowledge does not in itself define what is to be done, does not provide basic educational aims. (38)

He in effect strikes a middle position on this issue, on which he says he agrees with Raymond Williams "when he argues for a common culture, but one which can best be acquired by starting from strong and differentiated social experiences. . . . It is important to stress again the value of starting and indeed the absolute need to start from where people are" (39).

Hoggart also attempts to reconcile a Freirean critical literacy with more traditional academic values, in recommending that teachers "shape teaching around issues which bear upon their pupils day by day, but which they at present see only in an immediate, on-the-pulses way, without having the tools with which to make larger sense of what is happening to them. . . ." (41). The last sentence echoes a passage in *Reproduction in Education, Society, and Culture* by Pierre Bourdieu and Claude Passeron saying that schools manage to "convince the disinherited that they owe their scholastic and social destiny to their lack of gifts or merits, because in matters of culture absolute dispossession excludes awareness of being dispossessed" (210).

Hoggart concludes:

> [Teaching] would deal with issues in the environment—the pressures of urban life on the individual and the family, the role of the mass media, racism, the increasing gap between the developed and the underdeveloped world. . . . All this can lead to some exciting and inspiring new teaching. But, like all new modes, it can be unwisely used. Some teaching in Britain which is inspired by this outlook is sloppy; there is still a case for teaching the major intellectual disciplines as we have habitually known them. (41)

The Bernstein Controversy

The early work of Bernstein in the 1950s became an indirect source for concepts in American educational theory including "compensatory education," "cultural deprivation," or "cognitive deficits," "the disadvantaged child," "working class authoritarianism," and "the culture of poverty." Each of these terms has become a political battleground from the early 1960s to the present, as has the application of Bernstein's opposition between restricted and elaborated codes to linguistic and cultural differences between speakers of standard English and black English. Whether one agrees or disagrees with these controversial aspects of Bernstein's work, they remain a fascinating source of theoretical speculations that I personally find more stimulating than the poststructuralist theory that has received far more attention, and as such they are certainly due for a revival of interest, and for a wealth of new research, in rhetcomp theory.

In brief, Bernstein, who died in 2000, was, like Hoggart, a committed socialist whose studies sympathetically addressed problems in socialization that often impede both children and adults in the working class and in poverty from thinking autonomously and being receptive to progressive political policies that could benefit them. Along with Bourdieu, his colleague in France (they collaborated at the École Pratique des Hautes Études in Paris), he emphasized the ways in which workplace roles are reproduced in both family socialization and education—such as the restricted codes of blue-collar workers under strict supervision and doing fixed routines tend to carry over to authoritarian family structure and child rearing.

The following, sketchy synopsis of key passages from Bernstein scarcely hints at the scope and provocativeness of his thought, although his prose can be cumbersome and his unqualified labeling of working class versus middle class traits is apt to strike readers today as crude and biased. He did make extensive qualifications of these labels elsewhere, but his terms certainly call for more refinement than he ever provided. For our purposes here, these passages are useful primarily in their definitions of certain cognitive-linguistic traits and their possible relation to modes of socialization *in whatever class they may occur,* so I suggest that readers just substitute "restrictive code socialization" for "working class" and "elaborated code socialization" for "middle class." Another problem in reading Bernstein today is the sexism in his own language use and assumptions about family gender roles; I leave it to readers to make their own critique or corrections of such passages.

Among the key chapters in volume 1 of *Class, Codes, and Control,* the first, "Some Sociological Determinants of Perception" (1958), has been most frequently cited. There he suggests that in EC, parents explain things to children and engage with them in dialogue. In RC, parents tend more to just give orders, as in "Shut up" and "Because I say so, that's why." Christopher Lasch reports a corroborating account by psychologist Robert Coles of an interview with a white, Catholic housekeeper from Somerville, Massachusetts, who worked for a professional family in Cambridge: "I tell my kids to obey the teacher and listen to the priest; and their father gives them a whack if they cross him. But it's different when I come to fancy Cambridge. In that house, the kids speak back to their parents, act as fresh and snotty as can be. I want to scream sometimes when I hear those brats talking as if they know everything" (*True* 494). Lasch, however, sides with this woman as a victim of the hidden injuries of class and the arrogance of the professional-managerial class.

According to Bernstein, in RC, "The content of the speech is likely to be concrete, descriptive, and narrative rather than analytical and abstract" (78). This point coincides with various National Assessment of Educational Progress findings as well as, more recently, the premises of the Common Core State Standards, that students who are proficient in narrative reading and writing often have difficulties moving to abstract and analytic discourse. More precisely, EC facilitates integrating the concrete and the abstract, while RC tends toward lurching irrationally—often with doublethink self-contradictions—between concrete realities and what Ray Kytle calls *unconcretized abstractions*, in unquestioning sociocentrism, patriotism, religious or ideological dogmas, and in literal-minded reification of symbols like the flag, the Pledge of Allegiance, (including "under God"), the National Anthem, the Bible, and religious rituals. (Thus in the 2008 presidential campaign, Barack Obama was chastised by conservatives for not wearing an American flag lapel pin, and finally started doing so.).

Bernstein identifies individuation and differentiation as traits defining personal and social identity that develop earlier and stronger in EC childhood cognitive and linguistic development—terms that relate to similar phases in Piagetian, psychoanalytic, and Vygotskian developmental schema—from the egocentric to the reciprocal stage, from the narcissistic to the ego-formation and object-relations stage, and from the oral to the literate stage. Thus children raised in restricted codes are apt to speak with "egocentric-sociocentric signals" (114), and "these children are less likely to learn to cope with problems of role ambiguity and ambivalence" (155). . . . "An educationally induced change of code from a restricted code (object) to an elaborated code (person) involves a shift in organizing concepts from authority/piety towards one of identity" (165). Also,

> One of the aims of the middle-class family is to produce a child oriented to certain values but individually differentiated within them. The child is born into an environment where he is seen and responded to as an individual with his own rights, that is, he has a specific social status. . . . The greater the differentiation of the child's experience the greater his ability to differentiate and elaborate objects in his environment (27–28). . . . Change in habitual speech codes involves changes in the means by which object and person relationships are realized. (176)

In later chapters Bernstein extends this process of differentiation to development from a "we" to an "I" identity, with obvious parallels to developmental psychology and implications for reader- versus writer-based prose.

(Bernstein draws explicitly from Vygotsky and Luria, although the only place I have found where he relates his ideas directly to orality-literacy theory is in a review of a book on the oral lore of children and adolescents in England, on pages 71–75.) For example,

> [In the elaborated code] difference lies at the basis of the social re-lationship, and is made verbally active. . . . Meanings which are dis-crete to the speaker must be offered so that they are intelligible to the listener. Communalized roles have given way to individualized roles, condensed symbols to articulated symbols. Elaborated speech variants of this type realize universalistic meanings in the sense that they are less context-tied. Thus individualized roles are realized through elaborated speech variants which involve complex editing at the grammatical and lexical levels and which point to universalistic meanings. (178)

"Individualized roles" here does not refer to individualism in the sense of narcissism or selfishness; quite the contrary, it refers to the sense of differen-tiation of individual from familial or communal consciousness, along with Piagetian awareness of the viewpoint of groups other than our native one. "The type of social solidarity realized through a restricted code points to-ward mechanical solidarity, whereas the type of solidarity realized through elaborated codes points towards organic solidarity (147)." Bernstein's point might seem to clash with "women's ways of knowing" that privilege com-munity identity, associated with female values over autonomous, male-as-sociated identity; however, his point is that development of individuated consciousness, in both females and males, is necessary to expand our sense of community and solidarity beyond the tribe or family.

Also note that *differentiation* in Bernstein means quite the opposite of *difference/différance* in Derrida and postmodernist theories of infinite mul-tiplication of differences, "a fluid, shifting sense of identity which flies in the face of what Harris calls 'the myth of the autonomous, essential self'" (Horner and Lu 133). Perhaps the clash between that notion and Bernstein's of the value of development of differentiation toward autonomous ("essen-tialized," if you will) identity lies at the center of the controversies I have traced throughout this book. I agree with Irvin Peckham that being in a po-sition to formulate or endorse the very notion of fluid, shifting identity may itself be an upper-middle-class luxury; those who formulate it are inclined either to ignore or facilely denigrate the notion that social-psychological and sociological determinants tend to impose an essentialized, restricted identity on the poor or lower-middle class.

Other concepts in Bernstein concerning perception of time, space, and causation are also significant for all aspects of literacy theory:

> The child in the middle-class and associative levels grows up in an environment which is finely and extensively controlled; the space, time, and social relationships are explicitly regulated within and outside the family group. The more purposeful and explicit the organization of the environment with reference to a distant future, the greater the rationality of the connections and inter-relations between means and distant ends, the greater the significance of objects in the present. Objects in the present are not taken as given, but become centres for enquiry and starting points for relationships. . . . An orientation toward structure [of time and space] allows many interpretations or meanings to be given to any one object. (29)

In RC, however,

> The stress on the present in the *means* of communication precludes the understanding of the meaningfulness of a time continuum other than of a limited order. Necessarily, the child lives in the here-and-now experience of his world, in which the time-span of anticipation or expectancy is very brief, and this is reinforced by the lack of a rigorous working out of connections between means and distant ends. . . . One important consequence of this patterning of perception is that it produces a descriptive cognitive process, e.g., the recognition of events A, B, C, D as separate unconnected facts or, at best, crude causal connections are made. (33)

Bernstein connects this restricted sense of time not only to faulty causal analysis and other aspects of logic but to both semantic and syntactic aspects of language:

> The working class boy [*sic*] is often genuinely puzzled by the need to acquire vocabulary or use words in a way that is, for him, peculiar. It is important to realize that his difficulties in ordering a sentence and connecting sentences—problems of qualifying an object, quality, idea, sensitivity to time and its extensions and modifications, making sustained relationships—are alien to the way he perceives and reacts to his immediate environment. The total system of his perception, which results in a sensitivity to content rather than the structure of objects, applies equally to the structure of a sentence. . . . (35)

Other passages further relate the two kinds of codes to various aspects of logic, criteria of critical thinking, and modes of discourse. In the restricted code,

> The rigid range of syntactic possibilities leads to difficulty in conveying linguistically logical sequence and stress. The verbal planning function is shortened, and this often creates in sustained speech sequences a large measure of dislocation or disjunction. The thoughts are often strung together like beads on a frame rather than following a planned sequence. A restriction in planning often creates a high degree of redundancy. . . . Restricted codes draw upon metaphor, whereas elaborated codes draw upon rationality. (134, 176)

The image of "thoughts strung together like beads on a frame" anticipated Farrell's point that the language of oral culture is more paratactic that syntactic, and it also could apply to Camus's intended effect of the narrative in *The Stranger*.

The connection between RC versus EC family socialization and success in school becomes increasingly central in Bernstein's later studies, which explore in detail the way socialization is reinforced by the structuring of time and space in curriculum and pedagogy:

> The school is an institution where every item in the present is finely linked to a distant future, consequently there is not a serious clash of expectations between the school and the middle-class child. The child's developed time-span of anticipation allows the present activity to be related to a future, and this is meaningful. . . . The school aims at assisting the development of cognitive and emotional differentiation or discrimination, and develops and encourages mediate relationships. There is in the child a desire to use and manipulate words in a personal qualifying or modifying way and, in particular, a developing sense of tense (time) which together combine to reduce the problem of the teaching of English: reading, spelling, writing. (29–30)

Bernstein's Refinements

The foregoing synopsis of the traits that Bernstein associated with restricted and elaborated codes needs to be considered within the contexts and qualifications he provided. To begin with, "Restricted codes are not necessarily linked to social class. They are used by all members of a society at some time" (128). And,

> A restricted code will arise where the form of the social relation is based upon closely shared identifications, upon an extensive range of shared expectations, upon a range of common assumptions. Thus a restricted code emerges where the culture or sub-culture raises the "we" above the "I." Such codes will emerge as both controls and transmitters of the culture in such diverse groups as prisons, the age group of adolescents, army, friends of long standing, between husband and wife. (146–47)

Everyone, then, uses restricted codes in certain situations, but some social groups are more able than others to switch to another code in other situations, and this code-switching capacity is itself a defining characteristic of the elaborated code; for instance, "The middle-class child is capable of manipulating the languages—the language between social equals (peer groups), which approximates to a public language, a formal language which permits sensitivity to role and status. This leads to appropriateness of behaviour in a wide range of social circumstances" (30). This essential point in Bernstein, often overlooked by his critics, confirms that EC does not signify a rigid, self-absorbed mentality but, on the contrary, one with maximum flexibility. Anyone who is adept in EC and who has a modicum of common sense switches into RC discourse in any number of situations, as those of us with higher educations do, with greater or lesser grace, with our less educated family and acquaintances. But those with only access to RC cannot do the opposite.

Another qualification:

> Clearly social class is an extremely crude index for the codes. . . . Variations in behavior found within groups who fall within a particular class (defined in terms of occupation and education) within a mobile society are often very great. It is possible to locate the two codes and their modes more precisely by considering the orientation of the family-role system, the mode of social control and the resultant linguistic relations. (135–36)

He might also have studied these factors in families of different nationalities, ethnicities, and father-mother roles.

Unlike the conservative social scientists who preempted his ideas, and contrary to the accusations of some of his critics, Bernstein does not deny that restricted codes have their own intrinsic value:

> It is important to realize that a restricted code carries its own aesthetic. It will tend to develop a metaphoric range of considerable power, a simplicity and directness, a vitality and rhythm; it should not be disvalued. Psychologically, it unites the speaker to his kin and to his local community. . . . (136)

> In a fundamental sense, a restricted code is the basic code. It is
> the code of intimacy which shapes and changes the very nature of
> subjective experience, initially in the family and in our close personal
> relationships. (253)

And, after an enumeration of the limiting aspects of restricted-code communication,

> To say this about a communication system is not to disvalue it, for
> such a communication system has a vast potential, considerable meta-
> phoric range and a unique aesthetic capacity. A whole range of diverse
> meanings can be generated by such a system of communication. It
> happens, however, that this communication code directs the child to
> orders of learning and relevance that are not in harmony with those
> required by the school. (143)

Conversely, Bernstein does not consider the elaborated code as superior
in every sense; he considers it as necessary for more complex thought and
communication, but not sufficient: "It cannot be assumed that because a
person moves toward an elaborated code, the meanings he is signaling
are of any great significance. A lot of nonsense can be signaled in this
code" (251).

Again in contrast to some scholars and politicians influenced by him,
Bernstein's point in delineating the social disadvantages of restricted codes
in the working class is not to make a negative judgment on that class in itself
but to criticize the structures of capitalist class society that put the working
class at disadvantage and to identify ways in which educators should attempt
to prevent schooling from reproducing this disadvantage—some of which
ways anticipate recent, radical educational theory in the United States:

> For the child limited to a restricted code the school experience is one
> of symbolic and social change [in contrast to children socialized in
> the elaborated code, who are already attuned to the school environ-
> ment]. . . . A change of code involves changes in the *means* whereby
> social identity and reality are created. This argument means that
> educational institutions in a fluid society carry within themselves
> alienating tendencies. To say this is not to argue for the preservation
> of a pseudo-folk culture but is to argue for certain changes in the
> social structure of educational institutions; it is also to argue for
> increased sensitivity on the part of teachers toward both the cultural
> and cognitive requirements of the formal educational relationship.
> The problem goes deeper than this. It raises the question of a society

which measures human worth, accords respect and grants significance by means of a scale of purely occupational achievement. . . .

    I am suggesting that if we look into the work relationships of
this particular group, its community relationships, its family role
systems, it is reasonable to argue that the genes of social class may
well be carried less through a genetic code but far more through a
communication code that social class itself promotes. (136–37, 143)

And in conclusion,

We must ensure that the material conditions of the schools we offer, their values, social organization, forms of control and pedagogy,
the skills and sensitivities of the teachers are refracted through an
understanding of the culture the children bring to the school. After
all, we do no less for the middle-class child. The problem does not
stop there. Housing conditions must be improved, social services
extended and pre-school education developed. (152)

Provocative though Bernstein's suggestions are about the reproduction
of work roles in family socialization and linguistic codes, he never gets
around to developing or supporting them in much detail. Melvin Kohn
did a more extensive study in the United States, in *Class and Conformity:
A Study in Values*. (Some fruitful research might be done in English studies
on correlations between college students' own, or their parents', work experience and their cognitive-linguistic patterns in English courses.) What
Bernstein does focus on increasingly, in the later essays in volume 1 and those
in volume 3, is broader issues in the sociology of education and knowledge.
Under the influence of Bourdieu, he emphasized a structural approach to the
reproduction of the general socioeconomic and class system in pedagogy,
curriculum, and physical spaces in schools. The last chapter in volume 3,
"Aspects of the Relations Between Education and Production," relates his
ideas to those of Bourdieu and other Marxist educational theorists like Louis
Althusser, Samuel Bowles, and Herbert Gintis.

    Bernstein devotes a good deal of attention to the subtle ways in which
both family socialization and educational theory and practice shift in ac-
cord with society's changing economic needs. Here elaborated codes gain
distinctive significance as the discourse mode increasingly fostered by (and
in) middle- and upper-class families and schools in the late twentieth century as formation for the kind of autonomous work roles of the expanding
professional-managerial or "new" class. Alvin Gouldner picks up this theme
from Bernstein in "The New Class as a Speech Community," in which he

substitutes for Bernstein's "elaborated code" the phrase "the culture of critical discourse" as the definitive characteristic of the New Class.

One of the most significant aspects of this analysis, explored in "Open Schools—Open Society" and "Class and Pedagogies: Visible and Invisible" in volume 3, is Bernstein's hypothesis that the open classroom experiments of the 1960s, advanced mostly by radical educators in an attempt to enable working-class children to overcome the effects of restricted-code, authoritarian socialization, inadvertently have had the opposite effect, since such experiments have been received most favorably by middle-class children and most resisted by those of the working class, for whom the cognitive dissonance of middle-class educational codes has simply been compounded by the open classroom. (This analysis ties in with my recurrent arguments that upper-class colleges and universities often nurture left politics and critical pedagogy more than those lower on the social scale.) Indeed, Bernstein suggests that open-classroom theory itself may have come into being (unaware though its advocates may have been of it) indirectly out of the dictates of the evolving capitalist economy for socialization and schooling patterns producing the expanded professional-managerial class. In general, progressive educators are caught in the dilemma that reforms in schooling often end up counterproductively, being twisted into new means of reinforcing the established power structure: "On the one hand, they stand for variety against inflexibility, expression against repression, the interpersonal against the interpositional; on the other hand, there is the grim obduracy of the division of labor and of the narrow pathways to its positions of power and prestige" (volume 3, 126).

Bernstein's hypothesis about the drawbacks of the open classroom and Hoggart's reservations about progressive pedagogy were supported and applied to American composition theory by Myron Tuman in his 1988 *CCC* article "Class, Codes, and Composition: Basil Bernstein and the Critique of Pedagogy"—one of the very few articles on Bernstein or disputes in sociolinguistics to appear in English professional journals in the past three decades.[1] Tuman criticizes the political naiveté of process-oriented and other theories aimed at development of individual expressiveness without sufficient regard for the larger sociopolitical forces constricting or channeling individual consciousness:

> Thus, any reform movement such as process pedagogy, by making the entire educational enterprise seem fairer, more open, and more relevant to success outside school, while not altering the relative disadvantage of different groups within the overall class structure of

society, may work to the detriment of those groups by legitimating the efforts of those best positioned to succeed. We are, alas, too eager to confuse an "open" classroom with an open society, and the ease with which we can reshape the world within our classroom walls with the "grim obduracy" of the world without.... Ultimately, what looks like reform, both in and out of the classroom, is often only a new form of control. (49–50)

These arguments are confirmed by Lisa Delpit, who says in *Other People's Children: Cultural Conflicts in the Classroom* that she has concluded from her experience teaching black inner-city children that they are far less receptive to open-classroom and other progressive pedagogy than middle-class students, that they dislike the current emphasis on encouraging students' natural expression in writing to the neglect of standard form and mechanics because they want instruction in the formal skills they need to progress in schooling; in other words, it is the teachers bending over backward to avoid patronizing such children who are in fact patronizing them.

Tuman draws a further conclusion from Bernstein questioning the limits of nonauthoritarian, interactive, peer-oriented educational theory from the open classroom to the recent approaches of theorists like Shirley Brice Heath and Paulo Freire:

Changes in the writing curriculum may thus well be subject to the same criticism that Marxist critic Christopher Lasch made about changes in traditional family life: "Instead of liberating the individual from external coercion . . . [the breakdown of traditional structure—MT] subjected him to new forms of domination, while at the same time weakening his ability to resist them." (91)

Tuman earlier says:

Traditional family practices, for example, not only conditioned us to obey authority but, as Lasch goes on to explain, drawing from the work of German social theorist Max Horkheimer, they also nurtured within us "The dream of a better condition for mankind." A certain form of authoritative family practice, in other words, may have a crucial role to play in developing within individuals or groups the ideal sense of justice that seems to be a concomitant part of sustained social criticism and protest. Thus, by extension, we should not summarily dismiss the possibility that certain traditional, seemingly authoritative aspects of writing instruction—for example, an emphasis on product over process or teacher as authority rather than facilitator—while perhaps not serving [perhaps rather than serv-ing?—DL] to extend the structures of professional family life in ed-ucating and in socializing future workers, may have a similar role to play with our students, awakening within them both the aspirations for a better world and lingering suspicions of this one. (50)

The Culture of Poverty and the Authoritarian Personality

Two related topics of scholarship in political socialization have had a sim-ilar history of being contested terrain between—and within—the left and right: the culture of poverty and the social psychology of authoritarianism. The term "the culture of poverty" is associated primarily with the work of anthropologist Oscar Lewis studying poverty in Mexico, Puerto Rico, and the urban Latino communities in the United States, in his books *Five Families: Mexican Case Studies in the Culture of Poverty* (1959), *The Chil-dren of Sanchez* (1961), and *La Vida: A Puerto Rican Family in the Culture of Poverty* (1966).

In his introduction to *La Vida*, Lewis writes:

The culture of poverty is both an adaptation and reaction of the poor in their marginal position in a class-stratified, highly individuated, capitalistic society. It represents an effort to cope with feelings of hopelessness and despair which develop from the realization of the improbability of achieving success in terms of the values and goals of the larger society. . . . Once it comes into existence it tends to per-petuate itself from generation to generation because of its effect on the children. By the time slum children are age six or seven they have usually absorbed the basic values and attitudes of their subculture and are not psychologically geared to take full advantage of chang-ing conditions or increased opportunities which may occur in their lifetime. (xliv–xlv)

Among the psychological effects of this culture,

Other traits include a high incidence of maternal deprivation, of oral-ity, of weak ego structure, confusion of sexual identification, a lack of impulse control, a strong present-time orientation with relatively little ability to defer gratification and plan for the future, a sense of resignation and fatalism, a widespread belief in male superiority, and a high tolerance for psychological pathology of all sorts. People with a culture of poverty are provincial and locally oriented and have very little sense of history. They know only their own troubles, their own local conditions, their own neighborhood, their own way of life. Usually they do not have the knowledge, the vision or the ideology to see the similarities between their problems and those of their counterparts elsewhere in the world. They are not class-conscious, although they are very sensitive indeed to status distinctions. (xlviii)

Lewis does add the qualifier:

When the poor become class-conscious or active members of trade-union organizations, or when they adopt an internationalist outlook on the world, they are no longer part of the culture of poverty, although they may still be desperately poor. Any movement, be it religious, pacifist or revolutionary, which organizes and gives hope to the poor and effectively promotes solidarity and a sense of identification with larger groups, destroys the psychological and social core of the culture of poverty. In this connection, I suspect that the civil rights movement among the Negroes in the United States has done more to improve their self-image and self-respect than have their economic advances, although, without doubt, the two are mutually reinforcing. (xlviii)

Lewis, like Bernstein, protested against the way his formulation of the culture of poverty has been turned to conservative political uses, since his own sympathies were leftist, as indicated in the above quotes and in his praise for the success of the Castro regime in Cuba in overcoming the culture of poverty there, and of Frantz Fanon's view of the revolutionary potential of the Third World lumpenproletariat in *The Wretched of the Earth*. Lewis concludes, "I suspect that the culture of poverty flourishes in, and is generic to, the early free-enterprise stage of capitalism and that it is also endemic in colonialism" (l).

In scholarship on authoritarianism, *The Authoritarian Personality* by Theodor W. Adorno, Else Frenkel-Brunswick, Daniel J. Levinson, and R. Nevitt Sanford (1950) was the germinal work. In *The Authoritarian Specter*, Robert Altemeyer notes the common but mistaken association of this study primarily with Adorno, as in citations of "Adorno et al." The authors were listed alphabetically, but Sanford, a Berkeley sociologist, was the primary author and Adorno came into it late and marginally (Altemeyer 317n). Still, the association with Adorno is fitting to the extent that he was a leading figure of the Frankfurt School, which beginning in Germany in the 1920s and continuing in the United States when its members became refugees from Nazism, was centrally concerned with the mass appeal of twentieth-century authoritarianism, primarily in the fascist countries of Europe but also in the United States and other democratic countries. (See, for example, the powerful chapter on authoritarianism in Erich Fromm's 1941 *Escape from Freedom*, as well as his widely read 1961 afterword to the Signet edition of Orwell's *1984*, which linked O'Brien with Dostoevsky's Grand Inquisitor, the prophet of twentieth-century authoritarianism.)

The leftist viewpoint of *The Authoritarian Personality* is clear from the book's nearly exclusive emphasis on right-wing authoritarianism. Thus, the four categories of questionnaires used in interviews with the subjects of this research project attempted to measure anti-Semitism, ethnocentrism, political and economic conservatism, and authoritarianism itself, as measured by what the authors called the "F scale"—"F" standing for tendencies toward fascism. Unlike Bernstein, the authors did not focus centrally on social class differences in relation to authoritarianism, possibly for reasons dealing with postwar leftist intellectuals' increasing ambivalence toward the working class. Thus the authors assert that "the crucial role in the struggle against increasing concentration of economic power will have to be played by the working people, acting in accordance with their self-interest," but they also added that it was "foolhardy . . . to underestimate the susceptibility to fascist propaganda within these masses" (267).

In the 1950s and 1960s, *The Authoritarian Personality* was largely discredited on methodological grounds and attacked in its politics from both the right and left. Conservatives charged that it ignored left-wing authoritarianism, and this lack was compensated for by several subsequent books that postulated more of an equation between fascist and communist authoritarians; these books included *Political Man* by Seymour Martin Lipset, *The Open and Closed Mind* by Milton Rokeach, and *The True Believer* by Eric Hoffer. Another prominent book in this vein, Gordon Allport's *The Nature of Prejudice* (1954), was closer to Adorno et al. in finding right-wing prejudices more prevalent in American society than left-wing ones. (It is noteworthy for rhetcomp studies that Allport and Rokeach were associated with the International Society for General Semantics.) To my mind, Allport's book remains a less dated guide than *The Authoritarian Personality* to research and pedagogically applicable aspects of critical thinking. One of its distinctive elements is a rare discussion of middle-class prejudices in favor of the rich and against the poor, here in relation to race (320–25). For example,

> One little girl, five years of age, cried when she saw the Negro family next door moving away. "Now," she wailed, "there is no one that we are better than." At a somewhat older age, children are inclined to

ascribe all sorts of virtues to upper-class individuals and sorts of defects to members of the lower classes. An experiment with fifth-and sixth-grade children, for example, asked them to give the names of schoolmates whom they considered "clean," "dirty," "good-looking," "not good-looking," "always having a good time," and the like. For every desirable quality the children of higher social classes in the school were given higher ratings. Children from lower social classes were given lower ratings. It seems that the youngsters were not able to perceive their classmates as individuals, but only as representatives of class. To them children from the upper classes seem to be good-in-general; from the lower classes, bad-in-general. Since these fifth and sixth graders are "thinking ill without sufficient warrant" we conclude that they are manifesting class prejudice. (322)

Lipset's *Political Man*

The book that is perhaps most emblematic of postwar American social science was Seymour Martin Lipset's *Political Man* (1960, revised in 1962 and 1981; my page references are to the last). Lipset cited Bernstein, Hoggart, Adorno et al., C. Wright Mills and other leftists in support for his best-known chapter, titled "Working Class Authoritarianism." (He was then in the sociology department at Berkeley, which had been home to the research project producing *The Authoritarian Personality*.) In his introduction to the 1962 edition, Lipset, a former Marxist and national chair of the Young People's Socialist League, responded to critics of the first edition from both the right and left: "I should state at the outset that I consider myself a man of the left, but, I must add that I think of the United States as a nation in which leftist values predominate.... And since I feel that inequality though inevitable is *immoral*, I support all measures that would serve to reduce its extent" (xxi–xxii). Lipset goes on to argue, along similar lines as Daniel Bell's *The End of Ideology*, that in the system of capitalism under democratic government in America, political stability has been provided through peaceful struggle among pluralistic interests rather than by violent class conflict, and that economic prosperity has achieved gradual improvement for most of the population, basically through the trickle-down process; as his political hero John F. Kennedy put it, "A rising tide lifts all boats." Thus he concludes that this system has actually come closer to overcoming inequality than any previous society and contains more potential for gradually resolving the admittedly large residue of poverty and injustice than revolutionary socialism, which has fostered, in the cause of drastic state redistribution of wealth, authoritarian dictatorship in communist countries similar to that under fascism.

Moreover, Lipset's argument goes, there is a social-psychological tendency within the working class toward either right-wing authoritarianism, such as in American supporters of McCarthyism, or leftist varieties such as in the Communist Party and some labor union hierarchies. The latter were both far more powerful when Lipset was writing than now, so that the left-right equivalency argument has lost its force, except as a rhetorical ploy by conservatives to exaggerate the power of the far left. In 2012, future senator Ted Cruz of Texas claimed in a campaign speech that in the early 1990s when he and Barack Obama were students at Harvard Law School, "There were fewer declared Republicans in the faculty when we were there than Communists! There was one Republican. But there were twelve who would say they were Marxists who believed in the Communists overthrowing the United States government" (quoted in Mayer, "Is Senator Ted Cruz Our New McCarthy?").

Bernstein's influence on Lipset, emphasizing the right-wing variety of authoritarianism, is evident in many passages like, "A number of elements contribute to authoritarian predispositions in lower-class individuals. Low education, low participation in political or voluntary organizations of any type, little reading, isolated occupations, economic insecurity, and authoritarian family patterns are some of the most important" (100–101). And,

> This emphasis on the immediately perceivable and concern with the personal and concrete is part and parcel of the short-time perspective and the inability to perceive the complex possibilities and consequences of actions which often result in a general readiness to support extremist political and religious movements, and a generally lower level of liberalism on noneconomic questions. (112)[2]

The last phrase refers to those members of the working class who, then and now, are inclined to be liberal on issues of economic inequality but conservative on "noneconomic questions" or social issues such as abortion, religion, patriotism, civil liberties, gun control, racial and gender bias, or homosexuality; one label for this grouping in America has become "Reagan Democrats."

Lipset does also find right-wing authoritarian tendencies in certain sectors of the middle class, especially (and most significantly for my arguments) the lower-middle class:

> The rural population, both farmers and laborers, tends to oppose civil liberties and multi-party systems more than any other occupational

group. Election surveys indicate that farm owners have been among the strongest supporters of fascist parties.... The groups which have been most prone to support fascist and other middle-class extremist ideologies have been, in addition to farmers and peasants, the small businessmen of the small provincial communities—groups which are also isolated from "cosmopolitan" culture and are far lower than any other nonmanual labor group in educational attainment. (105)

In all the socioeconomic groups that Lipset and his sources studied, he concluded that the strongest deterrent to authoritarianism was higher education and cosmopolitan culture, for which the preconditions are greater economic security through both personal employment and governmental support. Lipset assumed that these preconditions could best be achieved through economic, governmental, and educational policies—for example, compensatory education—aimed at integrating workers and the poor into middle-class status and values. At the time Lipset wrote, those policies were increasingly being managed not from the bottom up, by organized labor or broad segments of the populace at large, but from the top (or, more precisely, the professional-managerial middle class, or New Class) down.

In one of the most provocative sections in *Political Man*, titled "Upper Class Liberalism," Lipset appropriates the oxymoronic term "Tory radicalism" from nineteenth-century English history, designating members of the aristocratic or intellectual classes who supported, out of conscientiousness or *noblesse oblige*, egalitarian social reforms seemingly against their own class interests. Lipset applies this concept to American history:

Recent research by sociologists and historians has clarified some aspects of American politics which do not seem to fit a "class" interpretation of American history, like the fact, already noted, that the wealthier classes and their parties, the Whigs and Republicans, were more antislavery than the Democrats who were supported by the lower classes.... The fundamental factor in noneconomic liberalism is not actually class, but education, general sophistication, and probably to a certain extent psychic security. But since these factors are strongly correlated with class, noneconomic liberalism is positively associated with social status (the wealthier are more tolerant).... [However,] within the conservative strata it has not been the wealthier classes in general which have led the political struggle for noneconomic liberalism, but rather those of established "old family" background as differentiated from the *nouveaux riches*. (320)

Liberal members of the upper classes in American history would also include Jefferson and other Revolutionary leaders, Ivy League–educated supporters of women's and workers' rights, and opponents of the Mexican-American and Spanish-American Wars, World War I, and the Cold War (as exploited by demagogues like Joe McCarthy). "Old family" conservatives for non-economic liberalism would include the now nearly extinct "Rockefeller Republicans."

Lipset concludes this section with a celebration of Democrats: "The true party of Tory radicalism in America is the Democratic party. It has achieved Disraeli's objective of a party based on the working class but led by the responsible 'squires'—first Roosevelt of Groton and Harvard, and currently Adlai Stevenson of Choate School and Princeton, . . . John F. Kennedy of Choate and Harvard" (320–21). (Al Gore, John Kerry, John Dean, and Jay Rockefeller would be recent examples.) *Political Man* goes on to make a case that many such scions of the upper class, elite university graduates, and middle-class intellectuals have been leaders of leftist movements—as much as indigenous working-class representatives—throughout American history up to the 1950s when Lipset was writing. In his 1981 afterword, he makes the same case in praising upper-class New Left activists in the 1960s, including in the civil rights movement (in alliance with many grassroots activists, to be sure), campus protest, opposition to the Vietnam War, environmentalism, and women's liberation. An entire book might be devoted to the role in the New Left of heirs of old family wealth—like William Sloan Coffin, Kingman Brewster, Emma Rothschild, and Adam Hochschild—or holders of doctoral degrees like Martin Luther King, graduates and faculties of Ivy League and other elite universities like many of the leaders of Students for a Democratic Society, the Student Non-Violent Coordinating Committee, and prominent opponents of the Vietnam War such as Noam Chomsky and Daniel Ellsberg. (Edward Said came from an upper-class Palestinian family and held degrees from Princeton and Harvard.)

Also in the 1981 edition of *Political Man*, addressing participation in and support of, or opposition to, the protest movements of the 1960s (which Lipset generally supported—except for the excesses of antiwar and campus protest), he asserted, "A consistent and continuing research literature has documented relationships between low levels of education and racial and religious prejudice, opposition to equal rights for women, and support of, and involvement in, fundamentalist religious groups" (478). And, "Education was a strong correlate of attitudes toward protest. . . . And although in most cases education was the strongest factor, lower socioeconomic status and income were also associated with antagonism to protest actions" (482).

Political Man has faded into obscurity over recent decades, but perhaps it is time to undertake a balanced reappraisal of what is, whatever its flaws, a monumental, clearly written survey and evaluation of the sociology and history of class, education, and intellectuals worldwide and in the United States. A contemporary updating with Lipset's scope could be invaluable for scholarship in rhetoric and composition as well as social science. Lipset raised a host of issues that can still provoke intense debate—his rebuttals to New Left critics in the 1981 edition are worth extensive review in themselves—but here I will only pursue a few that are directly related to my themes. (Other related points are pursued in my next chapter and conclusion.) First, he and other prominent social scientists in the 1960s were savaged by New Leftists for painting an overly rosy portrait of corporate liberalism and the role in it of New Class intellectuals, a portrait that may have also been self-serving to the extent that many of the same social scientists and other intellectuals had become prestigious policy advisors to top Democrats like President Kennedy. (See, for example, the pamphlet by James Jacobs, published by Students for a Democratic Society, titled "S. M. Lipset: Social Scientist of the Smooth Society," and David Halberstam's *The Best and Brightest*, a devastating take-down of the policy intelligentsia that engineered the Vietnam War debacle). I think this line of criticism was largely accurate then, and still is in relation to the corporate liberalism (or neoliberalism) of the Clinton and Obama Democratic Party. Such criticisms explain a lot about why Lipset and other liberal social scientists became neoconservatives when 1960s radicals rejected their authority and reaffirmed left populism. Lipset left Berkeley in the wake of the Free Speech Movement—one of whose targets of criticism was faculty corporate liberals like Lipset—moving first to Harvard, then to the Hoover Institution, a conservative think tank. As far as I know, though, he never lurched as far to the right as other neoconservatives like Irving Kristol, his son William, and Norman Podhoretz, who became unabashed apologists for the Republican right wing. He died in 2006.

And yet, from today's perspective, I believe the alliance of New Class intellectuals like Lipset with Democratic leaders, despite all their financial corruption and false façade of populism, has been justified as an alternative to the ever more virulent anti-intellectualism of the Republicans. (See my account in chapter 13 of Alvin Gouldner's validation of the progressive elements in intellectuals of the New Class.) I also think the widespread repudiation of Lipset's ideas sometimes went too far in denying any validity in his notion that upper- or middle-class intellectuals can play, and have historically played, a significant role in progressive politics—and education— benefiting workers, the poor, minorities, women, and other disfranchised people who often have lacked the power or voice to speak and act forcefully for themselves. (Nothing is to be gained by quibbling over who played the greater role in, say, the civil rights movement or protest against the Vietnam War; most important is that the two groups were able to work together, each according to their abilities, in an ideal Gramscian moment of a progressive role for "organic intellectuals.") The same left anti-intellectualism has carried over into the recent variety of rhetoric and composition studies that depicts as monolithic agents of oppression elite universities, academic discourse (as in Horner and Lu's encouragement of "discursive voices which conflict with and struggle against the voices of academic authority"), and teachers who would maintain some degree of intellectual authority over students—even toward progressive, liberatory ends.

Authoritarianism Revisited

Recent years have seen a movement by social scientists to redeem the reputation of *The Authoritarian Personality* by Adorno et al., at least in its general project, and to correct its methodological flaws with more sophisticated research tools. This movement has been prompted by the rise to political dominance of the New Right from Barry Goldwater's 1964 presidential bid to George W. Bush's presidential administration, and most recently movements such as the Tea Party and its corporate backers like the Koch brothers, Richard Armey, and Rupert Murdoch. In a 2005 column titled "The 'Authoritarian Personality' Revisited," in the *Chronicle of Higher Education*, political scientist Alan Wolfe wrote,

> Before anyone was talking about the radical right in America—the John Birch Society, the most notorious of the new conservative groups to develop in the postwar period, wasn't founded until 1958—*The Authoritarian Personality* seemed to anticipate the fervent crusades against communism and the attacks on Chief Justice Earl Warren, the United Nations, and even fluoridation that would characterize postwar politics in the United States. The fact that the radical right has transformed itself from a marginal movement to an influential sector of the contemporary Republican Party makes the book's choice of subject matter all the more prescient.

Wolfe continues, "Many of the prominent politicians successful in today's conservative political environment adhere to a distinct style of politics that the authors of *The Authoritarian Personality* anticipated." He singles out John Bolton, Tom DeLay, and Senator John Cornyn, citing statements by them exemplifying attitudes from the F-Scale such as "There are some activities so flagrantly un-American that, when responsible officials won't take the proper steps, the wide-awake citizen should take the law into his own hands," "When you come right down it, it's human nature never to do anything without an eye to one's own profit," and "Too many people today are living in an unnatural, soft way; we should return to the fundamentals, to a more red-blooded, active way of life."

Responding to those who savaged the book for downplaying left-wing authoritarianism in the United States, Wolfe argues,

> If one could find contemporary "authoritarians of the left" to match those on the right, the authors of *The Authoritarian Personality* could rightly be criticized for their exclusive focus on fascism. Yet there are few, if any, such examples; while Republicans have been moving toward the right, Democrats are shifting to the center. No liberal close to the leaders of the Democratic Party has called for the assassination of a foreign head of state; only a true authoritarian like Pat Robertson, who has helped the Republicans achieve power, has done that.

Direct echoes of *The Authoritarian Personality* can also be heard in several recent general-circulation books such as linguist George Lakoff's 2002 *Moral Politics: How Liberals and Conservatives Think* (whose analysis of the opposing family models of conservatives and liberals is classic Frankfurt School), clinical psychologist Drew Westen's 2007 *The Political Brain* (which attributes Republicans' recent electoral dominance to their appeal to emotions of the authoritarian variety, as opposed to Democrats' appeals to reason, science, and wonkish policy positions), and especially John W. Dean's 2006 *Conservatives without Conscience*.

Dean, famous for his testimony as President Nixon's White House counsel during the Watergate affair and still a professed Goldwater conservative, has nevertheless recently written two books harshly critical of the Republican Party in the past three decades—beginning with the ruthless circle around Nixon and particularly since 2000—for replacing responsible conservative ideology with proto-fascistic authoritarianism in both leaders and their mass base. He specifies figures like Newt Gingrich, Rush Limbaugh, Richard Cheney, Tom DeLay, Karl Rove, and Jack Abramoff. For a trade book, *Conservatives without Conscience* presents a surprisingly well-documented, up-to-date survey of scholarship on the authoritarian personality, with primary emphasis on the books of social psychologist Robert Altemeyer, *Right-Wing Authoritarianism*, *Enemies of Freedom*, and *The Authoritarian Specter*. Dean summarizes one research study indicating "people become or remain political conservatives because they have a 'heightened psychological need to manage uncertainty and threat.'" More specifically, the study established that the various psychological factors associated with political conservatives included (and here I am paraphrasing) fear, intolerance of ambiguity, need for certainty or structure in life, overreaction to threats, and a disposition to dominate others" (30). Also, "They seem to have little facility for self-analysis" and they "are not aware of their illogical, contradictory, and hypocritical thinking. If made cognizant of it, they either rationalize it away, neglect to care, or attack those who reveal their weaknesses" (30). This account was reminiscent of the Nixon White House dirty trickster Roger Stone, whose credo was: "Politics is not about uniting people. It's about dividing people. . . . Attack, attack, attack—never defend." And "Admit nothing, deny everything, launch counterattack" (quoted in Toobin). In a point that I have seen confirmed over and over again in my attempts to question conservative polemicists about errors or inconsistencies in their writing, Dean notes, "Not surprisingly, the very conservatives who love to hurl invective against the ranks of their enemies prove to have the thinnest of skins when the same is done to them" (26).

Dean further related these doublethink traits in authoritarians to the mental trait of projection, whether as an unconscious state of mind or as a deliberate tool for obfuscation, as in Roger Stone's "Admit nothing, deny everything, launch counterattack." Nixon's vice president Spiro Agnew famously raged in the early 1970s against "the liberal elite," which consisted of "the raised eyebrow cynics, the anti-intellectual intellectuals, the pampered egoists who sneer at honesty, thrift, hard work, prudence, common decency, and self-denial" (quoted in Nobile 5). In 1973 Agnew was indicted for taking bribes and evading taxes as governor of Maryland and as vice president. He pleaded no contest and resigned the vice presidency, shortly before the reality of Nixon's own moral double standards was exposed in the Watergate scandal. Nixon's secret private tape recordings later revealed his constant rationalization that he was only fighting fire with fire, since in his mind the Democrats were equally unscrupulous or more so. In *Blinded by the Right*, former self-confessed, journalistic "right-wing hit man" David Brock says he and other Republican propagandists rationalized their unscrupulousness by assuming the Democrats had a similarly powerful and unscrupulous machine, but he eventually came to realize this was a false assumption: "I unconsciously projected onto the liberals what I knew and saw and learned of the right wing's operations" (114). In his 2011 memoir *Capital Crimes*, disgraced lobbyist Jack Abramoff recounted his presidency of the national College Republicans in the 1980s, when he already formed part of a triumvirate with Grover Norquist and Ralph Reed, who all took equal pride in their unscrupulous attack apparatus. Abramoff says, "To us, politics was war without the benefit of armed forces. 'Kill or be killed' became an unspoken mantra, contrary to all I believed and was raised to believe [as an orthodox Jew]" (30). According to Nina Easton's portrait of Reed in *Gang of Five*, he required College Republican recruits to memorize George C. Scott's bloodthirsty lines in *Patton*, substituting "Democrats" for "Nazis": "The Democrats are the enemy. Wade into them! Spill *their* blood! Shoot *them* in the belly!" (Easton 143). Obviously Democratic Party operatives have been far from angelic over the same decades, but, as Brock admits, no conservative polemicist among the many I have read has been able to document a comparable catalogue of authoritarian aggression and projection by them. (For more in this vein, see my chapters "The Conservative Attack Machine" and "Right-Wing Deconstruction: Mimicry and False Equivalences" in *Why Higher Education*.)

Also among the significant points that Dean surveys in Altemeyer and other sources is a distinction between authoritarian leaders or rulers and their followers. The former are characterized as "social dominators" who believe equality is "a sucker word in which only fools believe" and that "there really is no such thing as 'right' and 'wrong'; it all boils down to what you can get away with . . . Basically, people are objects to be quietly and coolly manipulated for your own benefit" (57–58). Dean suggests that there is often a strain of doublethink in authoritarian followers who vacillate between an idealized image of their authority figures and craving for iron-fisted, domineering rule. In *Escape from Freedom*, Fromm diagnosed this relationship as sadistic in the dominators, masochistic in the dominated.

Dean's account here reminds me of a student in my argumentative writing course at Cal Poly, from a small town and majoring in automotive technology, who after studying assigned readings about recent concentration of corporate ownership in America, wrote in a paper,

> It seems a small handful of corporations are in control of just about everything in America, and it is a good thing. The average one of the masses could hardly run his own life correctly if someone wasn't looking after him. These corporations are responsible for the economic and social well-being of the nation, hence it is logical to assume that they know what is best.

I always regretted not asking him whether he considered himself one of those destined to look out after the masses or one of those who could hardly run his own life—and in either case, what that indicated about his sense of self-esteem. This is another instance of a stage of cognitive development that lurches into distant abstractions without relating them to the concrete circumstances of one's own life. (Was he perhaps slyly exercising resistance and transgression against my imposition of leftist arguments? Perhaps, but doubtful in light of students' infamous calculations to tell professors what they want to hear.)

In recent composition studies, Patricia Roberts-Miller is among the few scholars who have been drawing from social-psychological scholarship on authoritarianism, in her articles "Dissent as 'Aid and Comfort to the Enemy'" and "Democracy, Demagoguery, and Critical Rhetoric," whose works cited sections include further recent sources in the field. Her stated point is "to persuade scholars in rhetoric that this scholarship provides a richer and more productive way to think about the real experience of public persuasion than does our own (too heavy) reliance on traditional explanations of expertise and authority" (172). She calls for more attention to the psychological dimensions of belief and argumentation, especially in the authoritarian, ethnocentric traits of in-group versus out-group, or us-versus-them rhetoric. Thus "Dissent" addresses the ages-old pattern of conservatives stereotyping and tarring dissenters against war—in the case under study, the Iraq War—as traitors giving aid and comfort to the enemy.

13

SHIFTING CRITICAL PERSPECTIVES
ON LANGUAGE AND CLASS

The cluster of sociological concepts surveyed in chapter 12—restricted and elaborated codes, the culture of poverty, and the authoritarian personality—has generated intense intellectual and political debate from the mid-1960s to the present. Beginning with RC and EC, what Bernstein intended as a critique of the class bias of industrial capitalism and of what Richard Sennett and Jonathan Cobb called the hidden injuries of class, got preempted by American conservative educational theorists in the 1960s "blaming the victim," in William Ryan's term, for supposedly innate and intractable cognitive deficits. This view has continued to the present in conservative sociologists like Charles Murray and Republican politicians who blame the persistence of poverty on poor people's bad attitudes—perhaps genetically engrained—toward education and family values. Bernstein strongly objected to this misuse of his ideas (see his introduction to *Class, Codes and Control Volume 3* in 1975), but when New Leftists in the late 1960s waged a counteroffensive against the conservative misappropriations, many lumped Bernstein with the conservatives. Even Noam Chomsky, in a rare intellectual lapse, fell into this confusion in a 1977 interview, part of *Language and Responsibility*, deriding a straw-man Bernstein with no indication of having read him: "The work of Bernstein may very well be reactionary in its implications, and perhaps hardly worth discussing as a specimen of the rational study of language" (56).

The general critical injustice toward Bernstein has been corrected little by little. So in *Rewriting English: Cultural Politics of Gender and Class*, a 1989 collection of essays by progressive educators in England, the authors first strongly condemn the appropriations by conservatives of Bernstein's concepts, but then stipulate:

> "Invisible pedagogies" is Bernstein's phrase (Bernstein 1975); and in this respect it is possible that his work, first welcomed and then harshly repudiated by progressives, and even denounced for helping

to reinforce the linguistic subordination of working-class children, may now be coming to be seen only to enjoin a necessary realism. Even that notorious distinction between restricted and elaborated codes, despite the valuable work that it prompted, by way of refutation, on the expressiveness and structural complexity of non-standard language, can be understood as an attempt to grasp the relations of linguistic power within the school, relations embedded in the deep structures of the curriculum and the school system. (39)

In other words, Bernstein's work has now come to be regarded more as he and Bourdieu conceived it, as a critique of the way scholastic language systematically reinforces middle- and upper-class hegemony. Their own critique, however, tends to evade the issue of the intrinsic value that elaborated codes may have for critical thinking and progressive politics, beyond being mere class markers—a value not denied by Bernstein, Bourdieu, and especially Hoggart and Labov, the latter as indicated below.

Bernstein's undeservedly bad reputation among progressive American educators was reinforced in 1974 by the tacit repudiation of his ideas in *Students' Right to Their Own Language*, in favor of the views of Labov, which, like those of Scribner and Cole, were widely, erroneously presumed to have "decisively overturned" Bernstein, as Kurt Spellmeyer put it. But what did Labov actually say about Bernstein? In "The Logic of Nonstandard English," he condemned the distortion of Bernstein's ideas in conservative American educational theorists (198). In *The Study of Nonstandard English*, after respectfully summarizing Bernstein's main ideas, Labov concluded:

> Clearly, then, the verbal skills which characterize middle class speakers are in the area which we have been calling "school language" in an informal sense, which speakers confined to a nonstandard dialect plainly do not control. There is no reason to presuppose a deep semantic or logical difference between nonstandard dialects and such an elaborated style. Some aspect of the formal speech of middle class speakers may very well have value for the acquisition of knowledge and verbal problem solving. But before we train working-class speakers to copy middle class speech patterns wholesale, it is worth asking just which aspects of this style are functional for learning and which are matters of prestige and fashion. (38)

Indeed, that is the question evaded in English studies in recent decades, and that I am trying to revive throughout this book.

Mueller and Gouldner in Support of Bernstein

Two important books by leftist scholars supporting Bernstein's and Lewis's ideas were Claus Mueller's *The Politics of Communication* in 1972 and Alvin Gouldner's *The Future of Intellectuals and the Rise of the New Class* in 1979. Mueller, a German-American sociologist of communication, drew from Bernstein, the Frankfurt School, and a host of related sources in theory and empirical research to make a leftist case that the working class in the United States and western Europe has regrettably been disarmed of any revolutionary potential through the mind-deadening effects not only of the work conditions Bernstein identifies as the prime source of restricted codes, but by "the closed universe of discourse" and "one-dimensional language," in Marcuse's terms, of political propaganda and mass culture. Mueller, surveying a body of empirical research on these matters, emphasizes the interaction between these external forces and family socialization in the working versus the middle class:

> To the extent that the official language, as expressed in mass media, educational institutions, and advertising, infringes upon the primary socialization process, external influence over private language is exerted. For middle-class families, however, the realm of private language appears to be relatively broad since the capacity to manipulate symbols inherent in an elaborated speech code combined with a focus on self-direction allows for a defense system against the influence of extra-familiar socialization agencies. Possession of an elaborated code equals political as well as cultural capital. . . .
>
> Conformity and allegiance to established authority as well as resistance to change were found to be political predispositions of individuals brought up in the lower classes. Empirical research also demonstrates that class-specific factors such as conformity, reception to one-sided arguments, and the absence of skepticism correlate with the susceptibility to persuasion and manipulation. (71–72, 100)

Concerning the role of mass media, Mueller cites a study of the relatively liberal *New York Times* and conservative *New York Daily News*: "The simplified wording and sentences of the *Daily News* correlated, as would be expected, with the class background of its readership, which tends toward a restricted code, while the more complex vocabulary of the *Times* correlated to the generally elaborated code of its middle-class readers." A similar study in Germany found stylistic elements in a mass-circulation newspaper "typical of the restricted code, such as concrete metaphors, dichotomized statements, simplified sentence structures, typified formulations, an undifferentiated vocabulary, and stereotypifications" (98).[1]

The reference to stereotypification recalls T. W. Adorno's great 1954 essay "Television and the Patterns of Mass Culture":

> The more stereotypes become reified and rigid in the present setup of culture industry, the less people are likely to change their preconceived ideas with the progress of their experience. The more opaque and complicated modern life becomes, the more people are tempted to cling desperately to clichés which seem to bring some order into the otherwise un-understandable. (Rosenberg and White 484)

Implicit in Adorno and explicit in Mueller was that in the United States, stereotyping and clichés in politics, media, and individual thought serve primarily the authoritarian political right—though the opposite is doubtlessly true in Communist countries.

Mueller sees cognitive and communicative obstructions to oppositional working-class consciousness closing out the possibility of social policies that might be in workers' own interests:

> Today's working class symbolism has become so opaque that it is impossible for the worker to link his situation to an ideological framework with which he could understand, and more importantly, act upon the deprivation he experiences.... The concept of alienation, for example, can hardly be made operative politically because a semantic barrier built of a restricted language code excludes it from the worker's ideational world. This sort of difficulty was encountered by West German trade unions which tried to make the symbol "participation" a meaningful one for the workers. (115)

In Mueller's concluding chapters, his pessimism about this closed linguistic universe is slightly mitigated by a turn in the direction of *The Legitimation Crisis* by Habermas: "In advanced capitalist societies riddled by affluence and poverty, the absence of effective legitimating rationales constitutes a problem to which the political system has no answer. It is precisely this problem that undermines a political system tenuously held together by material benefits" (182). And, "To date, the cultural strata including the professional intelligentsia appears to be the only groups whose opposition to the political system is of consequence. The withdrawal of cooperation by the cultural strata erodes the normative basis required for the cohesion and operation of advanced industrial society" (181).

Mueller's point about the "professional intelligentsia" was more fully developed in Marxist political sociologist Alvin Gouldner's *The Future of Intellectuals*, which in my opinion presented a brilliant, insufficiently recognized perspective on our topics here. Central to the book is the notion of "the culture of critical discourse," Gouldner's acknowledged elaboration on Bernstein's "elaborated code." A chapter titled "The New Class as a Speech Community," applying sociolinguistic concepts, begins:

> The culture of critical discourse (CCD) is an historically evolved set of rules, a grammar of discourse, which (1) is concerned to *justify* its assertions, but (2) whose *mode* of justification does not proceed by invoking authorities, and (3) prefers to elicit the *voluntary* consent of those addressed solely on the basis of arguments adduced. CCD is centered on a specific speech act: justification. It is a culture of discourse in which there is nothing that speakers will on principle permanently refuse to discuss or make problematic. . . . The culture of critical discourse is characterized by speech that is *relatively* more *situation-free*, more context or field "independent." (28)

Gouldner further identifies the CCD as the defining trait of the New Class—a grouping synonymous with what other social scientists call the professional-managerial class, but with emphasis by Gouldner on the academic intellectuals within it, as a speech community: "*The shared ideology of the intellectuals and intelligentsia is thus an ideology about discourse*" (28). Gouldner's position is different from critics of the New Class on both the political right and left in his defense of intellectuals as the last best hope for the political left, and (more pertinent to our concerns) his case for the CCD as the basis for politically progressive education.[2]

Gouldner is among the many modern leftists who have reluctantly lost hope in the revolutionary possibilities of the working class, for reasons including Bernstein's and Lewis's accounts of the cognitive and linguistic restrictions that are imposed on the poor and blue-collar workers. It is up to progressive educators and other intellectuals, then, to maintain a critical consciousness of, and opposition to, the social forces perpetuating those restrictions, and to enable students and other citizens (of any class, I would add) to evolve from restricted to elaborated codes. In his introductory chapter, Gouldner states:

> The new school system becomes a major setting for the intensive linguistic conversion of students from casual to reflexive speech, or (in Basil Bernstein's terms) from "restricted" linguistic

codes to "elaborated" linguistic codes, to a culture of discourse in which claims and assertions may *not* be justified by reference to the speaker's social status. This has the profound consequence of making all *authority-referring* claims potentially problematic. (3)

In a chapter titled "Education and the Reproduction of the New Class," Gouldner cites a survey of research in Howard R. Bowen's *Investment in Learning: The Individual and Social Value of American Higher Education* confirming—along similar lines to Kohlberg and Perry—the growth in critical thinking skills among students over the course of a liberal education, including "the recognition of unstated assumptions, . . . increments in abstract reflective thought and theoricity . . . a decline in religiosity, a reduction in rigidity, authoritarianism, dogmatism, and ethnocentrism while increasing autonomy and complexity" (46). Bowen's sources also found

dramatic differences in gains for those who attended college four years as compared to those who dropped out of college, worked or became housewives. These findings remained valid when controls for student ability levels and socioeconomic status were introduced . . . gains in intellectual tolerance are greater for students of the arts and sciences than among those in such professional fields as business and engineering. (47)

Gouldner adds, still referring to Bowen, "Finally, a propos of the *reflexivity* that is critical for CCD, it is notable that findings indicate that . . . 'people with more education seem to be more introspective about themselves, more concerned about the personal and interpersonal aspects of their lives . . . both the positive and negative aspects. . . . '" (47). The last, essential point, recalls Patricia Bizzell's gloss on William Perry's higher developmental stages, "Many theorists in composition studies have argued that writing is a unique mode of learning precisely because it fosters this kind of distancing. . . . Learning to write, then, can be seen as a process of learning to think about one's own thinking, a process which may well be unfamiliar to students in their home communities" (*Academic* 162).

Gouldner argues that the New Class contains both conservative and progressive wings, but that the latter is unique in human history in the nature of its class interests. According to the Marxist theory of ideology, throughout history the ideas that serve the interests of every ruling class have been imposed on subordinate classes and assumed to be the natural, common-sensical way things are. In other words, those in power would have those beneath them believe that what is beneficial for them is beneficial for everyone: "What's good for General Motors is good for America." While not denying an element of self-interest in the New Class's thinking, Gouldner in effect argues that what is good for the New Class *is* good for everyone. Critical thinking and the CCD happen to be the codes of that speech community, and reproducing them in students might thus happen to serve New Class interests, but acquiring them is also in the self-interest of everyone who does so. The CCD and the intellectuality it accompanies are by their intrinsic nature not only ideologically neutral but also defenses against ideological domination by *anyone*. "It subverts all establishments, social limits, and privileges, including its own. The New Class bears a culture of critical and careful discourse which is an historically emancipatory rationality" (84). And,

> CCD is radicalizing partly because, as a relatively situation-free speech variant, it experiences itself as distant from (and superior to) ordinary languages and conventional cultures. A relatively situation-free discourse is conducive to a *cosmopolitanism* that distances persons from local cultures, so that they feel an alienation from all particularistic, history-bound places and from ordinary, everyday life. . . .
>
> From the standpoint of the culture of critical discourse, all claims to truth, however different in social origins, are to be judged in the same way. Truth is democratized and all truth claims are now equal *under* the scrutiny of CCD. . . . Traditional authority is stripped of its ability to define social reality, and, with this, to authorize its own legitimacy. (59)

Thus if the CCD were attainable through education and cultural media to everyone in society, the New Class would in effect become a "universal class," a new basis for Marx's classless society, facilitated through the common interests of the working class, middle class, *and* intellectuals, against capitalist society, made manifest to all through critical thinking (specifically, I would append, applied to a curriculum for civic literacy). As Gouldner acknowledges, his arguments are akin to those of Jürgen Habermas, who Gouldner says seeks "a new institutional framework—the 'ideal speech situation'—within which not only technical means might be chosen, but which would also revitalize morality" (39).

Gouldner is not blind to the many faults of the New Class pointed out by countless critics on both the right and left, and he concludes that it is at present "the flawed universal class." Among the drawbacks of EC speech: "In its negative modality, however, self-editing also disposes toward an unhealthy self-consciousness, toward stilted, convoluted speech, and inhibition of play, imagination, and passion, and continual pressure for expressive discipline" (84). (Although these tendencies are undeniably latent in EC discourse, Gouldner might have mentioned that they can be mitigated by Bernstein's point that mastering EC also includes the capacity to switch from it on occasion back to the more positive traits of RC.) Still, compared to either the present capitalist class, the unintellectual middle class, or the working class and poor, Gouldner judges intellectuals to be the best remaining hope for progressive politics, a view I share. And he mounts a powerful, leftist defense of intellectuals against anti-intellectual, or antiacademic leftists like Chomsky. Along similar lines to mine in chapter 5, he refutes leftists who depict universities as monolithically conservative:

> To understand modern universities and colleges, we need an open-ness to contradiction. For universities both reproduce and subvert the larger society. . . . While the school is designed to teach what is adaptive for the society's master institutions, it is also often hospitable to a culture of critical discourse by which authority is unwittingly undermined, deviance fostered, the status quo challenged, and dis-sent systematically produced. (45)

He notes the obvious anomaly that some of the harshest critics of intellec-tuals and university scholars are themselves prominent members of both groups (he mentions Chomsky and Christopher Lasch), who are vilified by the anti-intellectual right. Finally, Gouldner points out the many middle- or upper-class intellectuals who have been leading figures in revolution and rebellion throughout history (along similar lines to Seymour Martin Lipset's history of "Tory radicals" in *Political Man*), from Marx and Engels to Trotsky to Castro, culminating in the student rebellions of the 1960s.

In progressive literacy theory too, many leading teachers, scholars, and theorists have come from New Class backgrounds and/or gone to elite uni-versities. Paulo Freire came from a middle-class Brazilian family, studied law and philosophy at the University of Recife, and is said by friends to have had expensive tastes. Jonathan Kozol's father was a professor at Harvard, from which he also graduated. Richard Ohmann's father was a teacher, and he went to Oberlin and Harvard. Mina Shaughnessy, though a miner's and elementary-school teacher's daughter from Lead, South Dakota, was a "scholarship girl" who studied theater at Northwestern and literature at Columbia. She was known at CUNY for her elegant personal style and upper-class social and political connections, such as with the Rockefeller Foundation, which funded her research; a photo in Jane Maher's marvelous biography shows her and her husband in formal attire on their way to a dinner at Gracie Mansion with New York mayor John Lindsay, for whom he worked as an aide (92). Her colleague Marilyn Maiz discusses Shaughnessy's friendship at CUNY with Irving Howe, a socialist from a working-class immigrant background:

> Irving Howe used to tell a wonderful story about Mina. When she met him one day at the graduate center having come directly from teaching a class, he commented upon her beautiful outfit; she was wearing an exquisite cape that her friend Maggie Lane had brought her from Africa. When Howe asked if Mina's students were put off by her fancy clothes, she replied: "But Irving, my students know I dress up for them." (Quoted in Maher 167)

None of this is meant in the least to disparage these personalities, who are among the contemporaries I most revere, but simply to reiterate two of my points. First, class and cultural differences impede rapport between progressive professors and both working-class and lower-middle-class students. Second, middle-class intellectuals—in spite of the painful, inescapable anomalies of their/our marginal identity—have played important roles in the political and cultural left, especially education, in ways that contradict not only a strict Marxist view of class conflict and self-interest, but also many educational populists' anti-intellectualism and denigration of academic discourse, as surveyed in previous chapters.

Left Anti-Intellectualism in Ehrenreich and Lasch

Of the many critics who have explored the pros and cons of the theories discussed in the foregoing chapters, Barbara Ehrenreich and Christopher Lasch are among the most skeptical toward such theories, from a leftist perspective. (For a survey of conservative critical perspectives on these theories, see my chapter "Neoconservatives as Defenders of Intellectual Standards: From *Partisan Review* to *Fox News*" in *Why Higher Education*.) Ehrenreich grew up in a Butte, Montana, family that moved up from working class to professional-managerial class (a term she helped coin in her journalism). She has prodigiously combined academic studies in science (she has a BA in electrochemistry from Reed College and PhD in cellular immunology from Rockefeller University) with superb, New Left political journalism and activism, being one of the few openly socialist journalists who have gained access to mainstream media like *Time*, the *New York Times*, and the *New Yorker*.

Fear of Falling: The Inner Life of the Middle Class (1989) surveys a body of empirical research indicating that restricted codes, authoritarianism, jingoism and prejudice are no more common in the working class than in the middle and upper classes; for instance, "The late sixties saw the most severe strike wave since shortly before World War II, and by the early seventies the new militancy had swept up automobile workers, rubber workers, steelworkers, teamsters, city workers, hospital workers, farmworkers, tugboat crewmen, gravediggers, and postal employees" (121).

Thus she refutes "the old sociological prejudice that the 'lower classes' are limited and parochial in their utterances, or not worth listening to." She counters against the "we" who hold that view:

> We tend to think of the problem, if we think of it at all, as simple *lack* on the part of the "lower" classes—most likely, a simple lack of vocabulary. Stereotypes of verbally deprived workers come to mind: Archie Bunker with his malapropisms, Ed Norton braying dumbly on *The Honeymooners*. But usually it is the middle class that is speaking the strange language—something sociologist Alvin Gouldner called "critical discourse." . . . Relative to the vernacular, critical discourse operates at a high level of abstraction, always seeking to absorb the particular into the general, the personal into the impersonal. This is its strength. But the rudely undemocratic consequence is that individual statements from "below" come to seem almost weightless, fragmentary, unprocessed. Since ordinary speech does not aspire to universality and does not hide the speaker in a gauze of impersonal rhetoric, it is easily dismissed as limited and "anecdotal." Meanwhile, even a truly "limited" idea, when expressed in the impersonal mode common to the middle class, becomes grander than the utterance of an individual person—larger in implication, more consequential.
>
> The way across the language barrier lies, first, through awareness of the middle-class assumptions that automatically denigrate "ordinary" styles of speech. In the longer term, we need a critique of critical discourse itself. Is there a way to "re-embody" the middle class's impersonal mode of discourse, so that it no longer serves to conceal the individual and variable speaker? For we may need to find ourselves in the language of abstraction, if we are ever to find the "others" in the language of daily life. And finding the "others"—not as aliens, not as projections of inner fear—is essential to the revival of middle-class conscience. (259–60)

With all the virtues of *Fear of Falling*, I find it glosses over some of the problems addressed in this section and is yet another instance of the *either-or* fallacy. Her accounts of Lipset and Gouldner are slanted, as in her derisive reduction of Gouldner's "culture of critical discourse" to excessive, scholastical, or bureaucratic abstraction, while somewhat sentimentalizing the consciousness of poor workers. Neither exclusively abstract nor concrete thinking and language is desirable; the key element of critical discourse/ critical thinking is to *connect* the two, just as Ehrenreich does in *Nickel and Dimed* in experiencing herself the concrete conditions of low-wage work while using her elaborated intellectual and linguistic skills to place those conditions within a broader political analysis that uneducated workers may not be able to articulate.

In her chapter "The Blue Collar Stereotype," Ehrenreich is particularly snarky toward Lipset's and kindred sociologists' theories about working-class authoritarianism. Some of her accounts of Lipset are unfair; for example:

> Fascism had put authoritarianism, understood as a personality trait, on the sociological agenda. Anti-communism kept it alive as an issue in the fifties, especially for scholars like Lipset who saw fascism and communism as two manifestations of the same slavish predilection on the part of the masses. In his analysis, the working class was responsible for totalitarianism of all varieties, at all times, because working-class people were inherently narrow-minded, intolerant, and most of all, "authoritarian." (109–10)

On the next page, however, she fudges in her account of Lipset, from claiming he implies the working class is "inherently" authoritarian to acknowledging that he attributes authoritarianism to "the working-class social environment" (111). The distinction here between hereditary and environmental causation was, and still is, a crucial source of dispute between the conservative and liberal or leftist camps, in which Lipset clearly sided with Bernstein, Hoggart, Adorno et al., Mueller, and others on the left, myself included, who look for solutions in alleviating the external socioeconomic inequities degrading the working-class social environment. Lipset clarified this position in his 1981 edition's "second thoughts" on his earlier chapter (476–77).

More particularly, Ehrenreich's claim that Lipset portrays fascism and communism as "two manifestations of the same slavish predilection on the part of the masses," by which the working class was "responsible for totalitarianism" of all varieties, is a crude oversimplification of what in Lipset is a vast, complex survey of empirically based, international studies over the whole stretch of modern history, with highly qualified conclusions from it about the responsibility for fascism in different European classes. Ehrenreich fails even to mention that Lipset's chapter on working-class authoritarianism, and its role in communist parties and organizations like labor unions, is followed by another, fifty-two page chapter titled "'Fascism'—Left, Right, and Center." In his 1981 postscript to that chapter, Lipset summed it up with an uncharacteristically broad statement: "Politically, working-class authoritarianism is communism, and to a lesser extent Peronism, just as middle-class authoritarianism is fascism" (488).

In the above passages and elsewhere, both Lipset and Ehrenreich are dismayingly equivocal in definitions of social classes and segments, intermingling terms like *working class*, *lower class*, and *masses*, while casually tossing in references to "middle-class authoritarianism" or "the small businessmen of the small provincial communities" who support fascism. Lipset and Ehrenreich are equally vague here on delineating political attitudes among diverse segments including whites versus minorities, females versus males, blue-collar versus white-collar workers, unionized versus nonunionized labor, employed workers versus the poor (with gradations among the partially or temporarily employed, the working poor, and those in dire poverty—the "underclass")—though Ehrenreich has written powerfully about these delineations in other books. These differences surely would have colored attitudes on the topics in the empirical studies surveyed. In Ehrenreich's sweeping defense of working-class Americans as actually being farther to the left than depicted by sociologists, news and entertainment media, or by politicians who insist that America is a center-right country, much of her evidence is convincing, but it is tendentiously selected to leave out the more conservative class segments above. For example, she ridicules the case in Lipset's 1981 edition that much working-class opposition to the Vietnam War was of the "win or get out" variety, but doesn't directly refute his sources. More extensive study is certainly warranted to evaluate the conflicting empirical evidence and lines of argument in Lipset and Ehrenreich, as well as to factor in historical changes since they wrote—above all, the cataclysmic disruptions of class lines and consciousness by the global economy and neoliberal ideology, which have produced a grim reconfirmation of Marx's account of immiserization of the proletariat and proletarianization of the middle class.

More pertinently to the argument of my book, neither Lipset nor Ehrenreich foregrounds the distinctive presence of the lower-middle class in America. So "the middle class" in her title actually is limited to the professional-managerial class, to the neglect of the LMC, with its social identity between the working class and higher classes and with its members' inclination to be more prejudiced against those below them and more admiring of those above them than members of the PMC are. ("Fear of falling" into poverty is certainly more characteristic of the LMC than the PMC.) Her derogatory, anti-intellectual analysis of the PMC is further restricted to its more conservative segments, to the neglect of that segment of it to which she herself belongs, the intellectual left. So she tends to denigrate by omission those in the PMC who share her political values and commitments, like her comrades in Democratic Socialists of America including Michael Harrington, Irving Howe, Ellen Willis, Stanley Aronowitz, and Noam Chomsky, or the student leaders of the New Left, whom she gives too little credit for their role in the civil rights and antiwar movements or community-organizing projects.

However, the concluding passages of Ehrenreich's book do make an exemplary call for an alliance—political, economic, and linguistic—of middle-class intellectuals with low-wage workers in common cause against the ever-increasing hegemony of the wealthy and corporations. As a journalist she has subsequently provided a fine model for this alliance in her books like *Nickel and Dimed* and *Bait and Switched*, in which she gives voice to the harsh experience of the working poor and lower-middle class who have in large numbers since the 1970s indeed fallen into poverty.

From today's perspective, Lipset and Ehrenreich do not actually appear to be that far apart, especially in their mutual revulsion against the resurgence of the American New Right, which then as now eclipsed such divisions on the left in its virulent antagonism toward *everyone* on the left—the poor, labor unions, public schools and teachers in them, government officials with their social engineering, scholars and intellectuals. After all, *Political Man*, like *The Authoritarian Personality*, was prompted more by the rise of the right-wing authoritarianism epitomized in Senator McCarthy than by the power of the American Communist Party or autocratic labor bosses. As late as 1977, Lipset coauthored with Earl Raab *The Politics of Unreason: Right-Wing Extremism in America*. Indeed, Ehrenreich and many other leftists who had objected to the distorted stereotypes of the working class in sociologists like Lipset have subsequently joined in similar stereotyping of Republican right-wing demagogues and their mass base—generally with good cause, in my opinion, since so many present-day conservatives, including the college students I have discussed, unabashedly parade that stereotype.

In *The True and Only Heaven*, Lasch (the eminent cultural historian who wrote sympathetically about *The Agony of the American Left*), is even harsher than Ehrenreich on the PMC, particularly social scientists, and of their elaborated codes. Following an undeniably devastating survey of the more class-biased sociology of the postwar period, he concludes:

Blind to their own prejudices, the children of light could not see that their own world was in many ways just as narrowly circumscribed as the worker's. . . . Their educated jargon had lost touch with everyday spoken language and no longer served as a repository of the community's common sense. . . . Academic English—the abstract, uninflected, colorless medium not only of the classroom but of the boardroom, the clinic, the court of law, and the government bureau—had discarded most of the earthy idioms that betrayed its Anglo-Saxon past, and the spoken form of this English no longer betrayed any hint of regional accent or dialect. . . .

Exemption from manual labor deprived them of any appreciation of the practical skills it requires or the kind of knowledge that grows directly out of firsthand experience. Just as their acquaintance of nature was limited to a vacation in some national park, so their awareness of the sensual, physical side of life was largely recreational, restricted to activities designed to keep the body "machine" in working order. Nor did open-mindedness make up for the absence of strongly held convictions. The educated classes overcame fanaticism at the price of desiccation. (467)

Despite some degree of truth here, Lasch stereotypes and overgeneralizes about members of the PMC as sweepingly as he accuses them of doing about lower classes. Lasch disagrees with Ehrenreich over what he considers her sentimentalized view of the working class: "She counters one stereotype of the worker with another, the image of Archie Bunker with the image of revolutionary solidarity enshrined in the annals of the left. The second image bears no closer relation to reality than the first" (525). But Lasch is no less sentimental and distant in championing the LMC as an alternative to the PMC as the best hope for a return to a premodern society of limited expectations, ecological balance, localism, and rejection of consumer consumption as the driving force of the economy and culture; he conveys little sense of personal experience of the more reactionary tendencies in the LMC. In relation to our pedagogical concerns here, in Lasch's and Ehrenreich's animus toward the PMC, they fail to acknowledge the efforts of contemporary progressive scholars and teachers, as members of the PMC, to overcome cultural gaps and to promote critical thinking in students and the public. Ehrenreich and Lasch could have enriched their critique by a fair-minded consideration of those like Paulo Freire and his followers, along with Mina Shaughnessy, Shirley Brice Heath, Deborah Meier, Lisa Delpit, Jonathan Kozol, Mike Rose, and Herbert Kohl, who have devoted their lives to empowering poor students.

Ohmann on Class and Language

Among the most incisive surveys of the broad issues addressed here are two articles by Richard Ohmann, "Questions about Literacy and Political Education" in *Radical Teacher* (1978) and "Reflections on Class and Language," first published in *College English* in January 1982 and reprinted in Ohmann's *Politics of Literacy* in 1987 (cited here). In "Questions," Ohmann initially presents a sympathetic review of Bernstein, Mueller, and others who "clearly write from a left perspective, and identify their interests with those of workers" (25). He begins by affirming a Gramscian concept of the ideal "organic" relation between progressive intellectuals and the working class, then asks what forces inhibit mutual communication, education, and cooperation.

> Suppose the barrier to political education of workers is not just their deprivation of critical, radical, or socialist ideas, but a deeper cognitive deprivation? Suppose that deprivation is rooted in working class language itself, and thus passed on in the home from infancy, rather than just brought about by schools and television? Suppose the problem is not just in the unfamiliarity and social unacceptability of what we want to teach workers, but also in the form itself of what we want to teach them, and in the language we use to talk about it?
>
> To focus these questions a bit more: a number of studies . . . suggest that only a few people—those sharing in power or influence, by and large—have ordered and relatively abstract understandings of society. (This is not to say, of course, that their understandings are right, or that workers are not in many ways more sensible.) Workers' belief systems tend to be less conceptual, more fixed on concrete things, more centered in the local and particular. Their ideas on specific issues also tend to be more fragmented and inconsistent than the ideas of the more highly educated and privileged. Finally, the American working class as a whole lacks a consensus in beliefs and values, compared to the ruling class and the professional and managerial strata. (24)

Ohmann continues to say that this research "does imply that a totalizing system of ideas such as marxism would be uncongenial, by virtue of its form, to workers." In "Questions About Literacy and Political Education," he concludes,

> If Bernstein and Mueller are right, those who have available only a restricted code can do little more than passively observe the shaping of the future. Worse, there is probably as much potential for fascism

as for democracy in the working class, since people raised by rule and nurtured in restricted codes tend "to abide by the prescriptions of external authorities." (283)

While conceding the "hypnotic power" of these arguments, Ohmann goes on to give several reasons he finds them faulty. First, he asks about the researchers: "But does their work reflect a common bias of intellectuals, in favor of understanding the world abstractly?" And he concludes,

> When we try to communicate to workers a socialist understanding of things, must we think of our task as, in part, making up a cognitive and linguistic deficit? Or should we take it that the problem is more in the ways we talk and write, and attempt somehow to translate marxism into more concrete and immediate terms than the ones we ordinarily use? (25)

In my view, it is unquestionably imperative that leftists seek more accessible modes of communication, but how far can they do so without debasing the irreducible complexities of socialist thought and duplicating the oversimplifications of capitalistic propaganda or vulgar Marxism?

Concerning the working class in general, Ohmann concludes:

> Mueller's political pessimism is justified only if we assume, as many leftists do (myself included at the time I first addressed these questions), that political consciousness is fixed, either at home in infancy and childhood or, even more deeply than that, by gross structural features of the society—if we assume that workers cannot become equal communicators and political participants step by step, and through action, but only by understanding, in a kind of conversion experience, the fundamental concepts of marxism. Movements toward worker self-management, co-ops, progressive credit unions, consumer movements, union organizing, populist movements of many kinds, are all fertile soil in which elaborated codes . . . may grow along with the habit of democracy. (293)

Likewise concerning education, Ohmann's Freirean conclusion is that it is mistaken to draw the inference from Bernstein "that we should teach elaborated codes to working-class kids, within the customary social relations of the school." Instead:

> I think the educational moral is roughly that of the 1960s reform movements, now much condemned: students should have as much

responsibility as possible for their own educations. The habits of expressive power come with actual shared power, not with comput-
erized instruction in sentence-combining or with a back-to-basics
movement that would freeze students' language into someone else's
rules, imposed from without. Respect the linguistic resources students have; make language a vehicle for achievement of real political
and personal aims. (293)

In retrospect, Ohmann's recommendations for local community empowerment have been fruitfully applied in the wealth of projects studied
by scholars like those surveyed in chapter 8 and others reported on in
Radical Teacher. But not so much on the national and international level,
as he has acknowledged in subsequent writings lamenting the suppression
of national and international organization on the left by the reactionary
forces of neoliberalism. And, as I argued previously, Ohmann's proposals
had questionable application to students from the lower middle class like
those I have taught, whose own language, political and personal aims are
often quite reactionary, a point to be continued in my concluding chapter,
where I reiterate the value of teaching elaborated codes to working-class,
and LMC, kids, "within the customary social relations of the school."

Classroom Applications: Durst and Peckham

Two welcome applications of the issues surveyed here directly to composition pedagogy appeared in Russel K. Durst's *Collision Course* (1999) and
Irvin Peckham's *Going North Thinking West* (2010). As noted in chapter
1, the program Durst directed at the University of Cincinnati featured a
commendable first-year-writing sequence from a conventional first-quarter
course to "English 102, which shifts the focus from writing about primarily
personal experience and knowledge to reading and writing about larger
cultural and political issues that help to shape contemporary thought. There
was also a research-writing component in this course. The course was based
on a cultural studies and critical pedagogy framework . . . [applying] critical
thinking and analytic reasoning" (16). His book presented "an extended
empirical analysis of classroom work in first-year composition classes" (1),
especially in students' transition between the two terms, in a case study
of one second-term course taught by a graduate student. So this course
sequence, and Durst's study of it, were one of the few instances in recent
comp theory positing such a developmental sequence both of courses and
of students' psychological, sociolinguistic, and political responses to the
higher level, thus addressing head-on the crucial dilemmas in the relation

between higher order reasoning and progressive politics. Durst also basing a project in empirical research on this material was exemplary of the kind of scholarly study I am calling for.

In a section on "Ground Rules and Social Class," Durst indicated that students in writing courses at Cincinnati came from "a fairly wide range of socioeconomic backgrounds, from upper-middle-class to poor, though the majority of students are in the mid-range of the middle class" (71). Moreover, "The majority of students appeared to be fairly or very conservative" (2) and "I soon realized that many of our students clung tenaciously to the belief that authority was to be respected and accepted, not questioned" (131). Durst focused on the ethnographic and psychological factors in conservative students' resistant readings of texts in the popular anthology *Rereading America* (Colombo et al.). What Durst, and later Peckham in discussing Durst's book, get at here in incisive specificity (in contrast to the vagueness of Horner and Lu's similar efforts) is the incomprehension and resentment that restricted-code conservative students express toward the complex level of vocabulary, syntax, and thought in the readings—what Lu terms "talking analytically"—and toward the leftist politics seemingly yoked to them. Durst reports that the graduate student who taught the class under study concluded, "The related problems of dealing with complex questions for which no easy answers exist would prove perhaps even more debilitating to students' work than the accompanying political differences" (129).

Durst continues, "The required textbook, *Rereading America*, immediately set many students' teeth on edge by calling into question a number of their basic beliefs. Some said that "they disliked the title itself, professing no need or desire to 'reread' their country" (130). One section in the book that provoked intense resistance was "Harmony at Home: The Myth of the Model Family," and especially the essay "The Paradox of Perfection," by sociologist Arlene Skolnick, which argues that

> the image of the so-called ideal, happy, problem-free family of two parents, a few children, a comfortable income, and a house in the suburbs, has never been as common in the United States as people typically think it has; but its pervasiveness as a media image makes the vast majority of us who are from less-than-ideal families feel bad about their own situations. (134)

Durst comments,

> First of all, a number of students seemed to misunderstand the essay in an almost fundamental sense. Given the piece's complexity

and level of abstraction, and given students' lack of familiarity with reading texts that are meant to convey an argument, such a lack of comprehension is perhaps to be anticipated. . . . Students' misunderstandings mainly entailed their thinking that the author was herself taking the positions that she was actually attempting to characterize and, in some cases, to critique. . . . [Some] believed she was "making fun" of the family. (136)

So this was an example of students being put off and led into misunderstanding simultaneously by complex ideas and by unfamiliar leftist cultural critique. The lesson I draw from this account is that the use of cultural-studies readers like *Rereading America* needs to be preceded or at least accompanied by an introductory study of elements of critical thinking and reading as well as of argumentation.

Durst focuses on statements recorded in an interview about the course by one student, Louise, "a returning student who was politically conservative and Christian. . . . She was the mother of three school-aged children and a housewife in her mid-thirties who had taken a vocational curriculum in high school and who was coming to college . . . with the ambition of completing a nursing degree." Durst says she "objected to the content and arguments of the vast majority of the liberally oriented readings. She was also extremely resistant to and confused by the demands of the critical analysis required in the assignments" (129). In a long section of Peckham's book reflecting on Durst's account of Louise, he characterizes her hostility toward the very language of the course objectives in the syllabus, with reference to *Rereading America*, which sought "to explore, with a challenging eye, the cultural forces that have shaped you . . . [to] analyze, argue, and ponder perspectives regarding the individual, the family, progress, and opportunity, race, gender, education, media, and democracy." According to Peckham, this terminology must "seem strained to a working-class student used to straightforward syntax and diction," and Louise regarded the notion of studying perspectives other than her accustomed one an unwelcome distraction from her career-oriented studies (Peckham 116). Louise especially detested Skolnik's essay; the very notion in it of casting "a challenging eye" on the cultural myths of family, compounded by the implicit prompt for student readers to cast that eye on their own families, was likely to make a student like her doubly defensive and in denial about possible problems in her parents' family or those in her own marriage, to the point of horror over being asked to write about her family for a college class, which she should not have been.

In Durst's concluding chapter, "Reflective Instrumentalism and the Teaching of Composition," he sympathizes with both critical teachers and the conservative students who resist them in their pursuit of "instrumental," or career-oriented, education. He proposes a middle path for the second-term course, in which a research-paper project "asks students to investigate their intended major through examining documents relating to the course of study (such as the department's description of the major), reading about the field, interviewing a professor as well as a professional in the area, and conducting field observations at a work site" (178). Readings for the course "present students with diverse points of view on many of the central issues that have shaped contemporary thought about higher education" 177–78). Durst continues, "While not attempting to position students as opponents of inequities in higher education or society as a whole, neither should the course be viewed as supporting an oppressive status quo. . . . The very idea of success can itself be critically examined and complicated as part of an analysis of school and career issues" (179). This model, further described in Durst's *You Are Here*, would seem to present a reasonable, nonthreatening means of applying a quasi-Freirean generative theme and my rhetorical schema for teaching the political conflicts. I can well imagine Louise being enthusiastic about gaining a broader perspective on her chosen career through reading a variety of perspectives on, and through on-site study of, the vexed social-class situation of the nursing profession.

Peckham's perspective on these issues, in contrast to both Durst's and mine, is that of a working-class background and of a writing program director at Louisiana State University, which has many working-class students. He deserves praise for giving far more attention to class analysis, critical thinking, and conservative students than most recent theorists, even Durst, and he shares my aversion to theoretical jargon and abstractions, while his own writing is lucid, modest, and generous toward those he disagrees with (undoubtedly more than mine). He frames his criticism of critical-thinking pedagogy in a well-informed chapter on the history of the discipline, with somewhat the same scope as my chapter 3; thus he is among the few recent composition theorists who have studied models of critical thinking based in philosophy and developmental psychology. He differs somewhat from Durst in two ways here. First, having delineated a more thorough account of the discipline of critical thinking, he can identify in precise terminology the cognitive difficulties Durst's students encounter (such as recursion and cumulation, multiple viewpoints and levels of meaning, irony). Second, Peckham draws more from Bernstein and Bourdieu in suggesting explicit connections between students' cognitive or political resistances and the class-inflected codes of political socialization and communication. I take issue with him on some key points, but we are definitely in the same ballpark.

Although a brief summary cannot do justice to Peckham's meticulously developed and documented arguments, I see two main lines. First, he criticizes equivocations between teaching writing (including for instrumentalist, "job skills" aims) and teaching thinking, whether under the rubric of critical thinking or of critical pedagogy and cultural studies. Like Durst, he makes clear that he identifies with progressive politics—he spent a stretch in Berkeley during the 1970s teaching in the National Writing Project and was one of the editors of the *College English* special issue on working-class studies in 2004 (Linkon); he is only questioning their imposition on required writing courses. Second, he asserts, along similar lines to Bourdieu, that acquisition of critical thinking and academic discourse serves primarily as an arbitrary marker of class and power elevating the middle class over the working class, and that proponents of critical pedagogy, who smugly believe they are empowering students, are typically in denial about their own complicity as enforcers of that marker. Along the same line as Durst, he says working-class students tend to be further alienated from the study of critical thinking, both because of its elaborated-code vocabulary and cognitive complexities and because it appears to them to be used by teachers mainly to coerce them into liberal/left political views. Peckham goes so far here as to devote a chapter to suggesting that even access to the cognitive-communicative know-how to engage in argument beyond the home, playground, or bar similarly excludes the working class; ergo, college-level argumentation is intrinsically class biased. (His position here resembles that of the antirational feminists I discussed in chapter 6, but is grounded in class terms more demonstrable than theories of *l'écriture féminine*.) These points are crucial in their larger implications about the complex of anomalies in American society posed by the widespread, simplistic association of intellectual discourse with both cultural and politicoeconomic elitism, even when that discourse champions left populism—an issue I return to in the next chapter.

Although Peckham supports these arguments with ample and persuasive classroom examples, I think both lines need some qualification. First, in posing a dichotomy between writing and thinking instruction, he does not distinguish clearly—as Durst does—between BW or FYW (if we suppose that they should address fundamental levels of writing) and more advanced courses like those I taught and write about, focusing on writing based on critical reading and analysis of sources. Students are somewhat less inclined to complain about inappropriate subject matter if they are in a program with this clearly delineated sequence.

On Peckham's second point, the thought-provoking case that critical-thinking instruction has often been used as a Trojan horse for liberal/left political indoctrination, this is certainly sometimes true. However, I have argued here and in *Why Higher Education* that critical thinking (aka elaborated code, literate versus oral, higher order reasoning, the culture of critical discourse) is by definition virtually congruent with liberal-to-left politics, in the sense of being based on thinking that is open-minded, reciprocal (as opposed to sociocentric), cosmopolitan, complex, and cognizant of multiple viewpoints—in obvious contrast to left-wing indoctrination in Communist countries and the most prominent strain of American conservatism, which both appeal to the lowest common denominator of cognitive development. Yet again, I distinguish restricted-code conservatism from the higher level of conservative thought incorporating critical thinking and applying it to liberal/left abuses of it, so that my pedagogy aims toward raising debate to that higher cognitive level, which is a precondition, for many students, ever to be exposed extensively either to any left views or to intellectual conservative ones. On Peckham's corollary argument that critical thinking serves primarily to exclude the working class and enhance the power of the middle class, this is much the same line followed by the postmodern adversaries of academic discourse that I have refuted throughout part 2, so my arguments there about the intrinsic value of acquiring academic discourse and critical thinking, for those of any class, are equally applicable here.

Peckham sympathizes almost wholly with students like Durst's Louise and thinks we should accommodate more to them, mainly by avoiding partisan, personal disputes. I disagree to the extent of suggesting that we do have a responsibility (at least in advanced writing courses) to challenge these students' preconceptions, not initially in the cause of progressive politics, but simply that of Kytle's maxim, "One of the things education is all about is learning to question our assumptions" (49)—which echoes Socrates's injunction to "know thyself," at the heart of the Western humanistic tradition. Going back to Durst's description of Louise as having been on a vocational-ed track beginning in high school, maybe the root cause of these problems is the long-running failure of American secondary education to provide grounding in liberal education and critical citizenship for *all* students, prior to any subsequent tracking, as in Europe and elsewhere—in turn an effect of broader socioeconomic class discrimination.

Discretion is the better part of critical pedagogy, so our challenge is to prompt self-questioning by students, not through intimidation but through the kind of dialogic understanding of their viewpoint that Peckham and Durst so helpfully demonstrate, followed by discreet prompts toward readings or experiences that differ from theirs, with help in understanding unfamiliar aspects of them and in revealing information that they might well find to their advantage. After all, many of the working-class students and adults I have known deeply regret having been deprived of college education, critical-thinking instruction, and the broadened intellectual vistas they provide, and are eager for any opportunity to access them.

I am also curious about how Peckham would accommodate my distinction between students from the working class, lower middle class, new rich, and professional-managerial class. I attribute to LMC students attitudes that are frequently those stereotypically attributed to the working class, but turned toward prejudice against the working class, combined with authoritarian awe toward the rich, as in students A and B in my chapter 3, or as in Durst's Louise, whose viewpoint seems to me more typical of the LMC in its unquestioning faith in the social and familial status quo than of many blue-collar workers and the poor, whose visceral experience tends more toward skepticism about such faith. Peckham's account of working-class students indicates their tendency to support labor unions, but the prevailing attitude in my students has been strongly anti-union, as noted in chapter 2. In any case, my concluding chapter explores, as a tacit response to Peckham's general line of critique, possible ways of turning critical pedagogy toward teaching students who are neither the oppressed nor the oppressor, but are prone to support the latter.

In his conclusion, Peckham admits that he is on uncertain, constantly shifting ground in these dilemmas. "I have understood that as writing teachers, we need to teach students not only how to write in academic genres, but we also need to teach them to evaluate other discourses, in order to enter intelligently into any serious public discussion." And, "If it is possible to interweave critical thinking in the cognitive and social strands with the more focused instructional objective, as I have described it, I am all for it" (161). But beyond saying that teachers should be more self-critical, he does not leave us with any specific prescriptions for dealing with the painful situations he delineates. But then, neither I nor any of the other theorists I have surveyed have been able to provide much more extensive prescriptions, beyond my long-range goal of reducing the socioeconomic inequities that discriminate against the poor and minorities from birth.

However, I do believe that several of the problems delineated by Peckham, Durst, and other opponents of critical pedagogy can be bypassed through my model for a second-term course based on direct study of elements of critical thinking and argumentative rhetoric, applied to understanding opposing ideological positions and lines of argument in public disputes that impinge directly on students' lives. In that model, the cognitive problems that Durst's students encountered with *Rereading America* themselves become a subject for objective study, in an impersonal manner that poses less of a threat to them. For instance, their resistance against challenges to their acceptance of social conformity and authority can be examined through basic study of some social psychology and the critical-thinking topic of where to draw the line, applied to the definition of fascism as acceptance of authority pushed to a totalitarian extreme, or to *1984*'s dramatization of loving Big Brother in an equally totalitarian socialist state. I have seen students—without being prompted toward a personal response—burst into tears with the shock of recognizing themselves in Fromm's description of the authoritarian personality in *Escape from Freedom.*

CONCLUSION: THEORIZING THE LOWER MIDDLE CLASS, AND PEDAGOGY OF THOSE WHO SUPPORT THE OPPRESSOR

I have argued throughout this book that many recent rhetcomp studies have had a blind spot in fixating on diverse groups mainly within the working class—which are also concentrated in big cities with heterogeneous student and community identities—to the near-total neglect of students from the lower middle class, who are more prevalent in small towns and cities, homogeneous suburbs, and universities in those areas. Indeed, the LMC is the classic student body base in universities like those attended by most of my family and friends from Iowa and those where I have taught, renowned as football factories, party schools, and occupational diploma mills. Those of us devoted to critical pedagogy in English courses face distinctive difficulties in teaching students from the LMC. Students from that base are more likely to resist general-education requirements and critical-thinking instruction—especially critical pedagogy—than students in either liberal arts colleges, elite universities, or working-class schools. So I will survey the distinctive traits of this class segment in general, then conclude with some suggestions for pedagogy addressing those traits in students.

The lower middle class has been undertheorized, as it were, in American academic and intellectual discourse, as indicated in previous chapters. So I think it is a useful prelude to piece together a theory of that class from diverse sources, especially in reference to its current resurgence in the guise of Tea Party conservatism. The Tea Party may be an amorphous entity in organization and affiliations, but its driving ideology is unmistakably similar to earlier historical manifestations described in Rita Felski's paraphrase of historian David Blackbourn:

> Both the pre-industrial, independent lower middle class and the modern white-collar class have been cast as the natural prey of the extreme right, the easily alarmed and defenseless victims of demagogues who have played successfully on the "classic" lower middle-class weaknesses of economic insecurity, status anxiety, parochialism and conservative social morality. (Felski 44–45)

Let us return, then, to Felski's *PMLA* article "Nothing to Declare: Identity, Shame, and the Lower Middle Class," in which Felski calls for more attention in cultural studies to this class and wittily speculates on causes for its neglect—one being that scholars like her who themselves come from it generally aren't eager to call attention to it.

> Being lower middle class is a singularly boring identity, possessing none of the radical chic that is sometimes ascribed to working-class roots. In fact, the lower middle class has generally been an object of scorn for intellectuals, blamed for everything from exceedingly bad taste to the rise of Hitler. . . . At the same time, lower-middle-classness is not so much an identity as a nonidentity. . . . No one ever describes himself as belonging to the lower middle classes. (34)

Felski continues, "Petit bourgeois subjects have nothing to declare: their class origins cannot be assimilated into a discourse of progressive identity politics" (46). The very fact that so many scholars and other intellectuals come from this class might fuel their need to distance themselves from it; alluding to Bourdieu, Felski notes: "Within the elaborate minuet of distinction, the intelligentsia may choose to align itself with the culture of the most oppressed but must constantly differentiate itself from the culture closest to it" (47).

Certainly in English studies, the key words in recent decades have been "margins" and "diversity," while as Felski notes, "The petite bourgeoisie is peculiarly resistant to the romance of marginality" (47), and it is the most un-diverse of groupings. (An exception here is the recent influx of immigrant shopkeepers, taxi drivers, and artisans from all over the world in America and Europe.) The LMC is still the putative, "unmarked" norm. Every politician poses as the champion of "ordinary Americans," "Middle America," "the real majority," and "the American heartland." (Sarah Palin added "real Americans.") It is the primary target audience of mass culture and consumerism. Barbara Ehrenreich sardonically traces the introduction of "Middle Americans" into the American political and media vocabulary to the late 1960s, prompted by a combination of blue-collar and white-collar reaction against the protest and countercultural movements of that decade:

> The Middle Americans that the media discovered were, of course, a far larger category than the blue-collar working class [a class whose more progressive elements, Ehrenreich argues, are habitually unreported on by the media]. In fact, in their haste to get away from the no-longer-newsworthy blacks, hippies, radicals, and poor people,

most media analysts were content to define Middle Americans as almost anybody but the members of those disturbing groups. (*Fear* 103)

By the time of the 2008 presidential election, both Barack Obama and John McCain substituted the trope of the struggling "middle class" for what historically has been defined as the working class, a move that enabled both to evade discussing their positions on issues like labor unions, poverty, minimum or living wage. It merits more attention than the media have granted that this widespread semantic ploy might really signal that much of the vaunted American middle class has regressed to working class penury in the age of the global economy.

Many scholars concur about the LMC as the historic American norm, at least in idealized images. Felski quotes a 1975 article by historian Arno J. Mayer with the

> intriguing thesis that the United States is a quintessentially lower-middle-class nation. In the first half of the nineteenth century, the country was primarily composed of independent small producers and property owners. While this old petite bourgeoisie has largely disappeared, contemporary American society, made up of white-collar workers, has become "a uniquely lower-middle-class nation whose labor force is preeminently nonmanual, modestly salaried and totally dependent." (47)

The empirical accuracy of these stereotypical images of Middle America is disputable, to be sure, but their mythic force undeniably persists in the attitudes of my students who cling fiercely to them—perhaps ever more fiercely as they experience the declining odds of maintaining even LMC social status in the age of the global economy.

In taking on the tricky task of defining the LMC, Felski describes it as "a messy, contradictory amalgam of symbolic practices, structures of feelings, and forms of life. It usually includes both the traditional petite bourgeoisie of shop owners, small businesspeople, and farmers and the 'new' lower middle class of salaried employees such as clerical workers, technicians, and secretaries" (36). I would add from my family background salespeople, local-level accountants, insurance and real estate agents, midlevel functionaries in the private and public sectors, and skilled laborers. Felski goes on to survey the traits of conformity and "other-direction" preeminently associated with this class by writers like Sinclair Lewis, David Riesman, and George Orwell in his early novels: "The lower middle class is driven by the fear of shame, tortured by a constant struggle to keep up appearances on a low income. . . . It inhabits a world that is almost completely lacking in spontaneity, sensuality, or pleasure," inhibited by "guilt about money, anxiety about status, and fear of the neighbors' disapproval." (41). I know people like this who hire house-cleaners but spend hours themselves cleaning up before they come to avoid *their* disapproval. Other defining stereotypes include obsessive "cleanliness, respectability, and distance from the perceived grubbiness and disorder of working-class life" (44), as well as "irremediably bad taste (kitsch is often seen as quintessentially petit bourgeois)" (45). Christopher Lasch adds to the stereotypical traits (in the course of challenging them), "It clung to outworn folkways—conventional religiosity, hearth and home, the sentimental cult of motherhood—and obsolete modes of production" (*True* 458).

Felski notes that LMC jobs "often pay little more and often less than blue-collar industrial jobs. The lower middle class often feels itself to be culturally superior to the working class, however, while lacking the cultural capital and the earning power of the professional-managerial class" (36). Lasch similarly describes the LMC (at least as it is regarded by intellectuals in the Marxist tradition): "It resented social classes more highly placed but internalized their standards, lording it over the poor instead of joining them in a common struggle against oppression" (*True* 459).

Such views were anticipated by C. Wright Mills in *White Collar,* a book whose comprehensive analysis of the mid-twentieth-century LMC and its relation to mass society remains stunningly undated in many ways since its publication in 1950. In a chapter on "The Small Business Front," Mills addresses the anomaly of small business owners and other members of the LMC identifying their interests with national and multinational corporations and the super-wealthy, who in multiple ways—for instance, the Wal-Mart syndrome—are dedicated to squeezing them out. The main perceived common interests are opposition to high taxes, government regulation, and labor unions. This shared set of antipathies

> makes it possible for big business to use small business as a shield. In any melee between big business and big labor, the small entrepreneurs seem to be more on the side of business. It is as if the closer to bank-ruptcy they are, the more they cling to their ideal. . . . Small business's attitude toward government, as toward labor, plays into the hands of big-business ideology. In both connections, small businessmen are shock troops in the battle against labor unions and government controls. (52–53)

I see this pattern again and again in my students, as in the way those at Cal Poly whose families owned farms, ranches, or other small businesses raged against the inheritance tax, or "the death tax," which they had been led to believe, by talk radio and other right-wing sources, entitled the government to confiscate their inheritance—though very few of their families' holdings were large enough to be subject to it.

Historians have long noted the authoritarian, reactionary tendency of the LMC. D. B. Wyndham Lewis's 1928 biography of poet François Villon describes a fifteenth-century student riot at the Sorbonne: "The Provost [police chief] seems to have let his men get completely out of control, as the police often do; and there is naturally conflict between the University and the police evidence. . . ." An innocent bystander was beaten by the police. "On taking refuge in a harness-maker's shop he was driven out again by a number of the lower bourgeoisie, who are always on the side of the big battalions" (105). Living in Berkeley in the 1960s, I read this passage with the shock of recognition as trashing of shops by protesters on Telegraph Avenue understandably drove the merchants to side with the big battalions commandeered by Governor Ronald Reagan, who called for a "blood bath" against protestors.

Lipset's chapter on working-class authoritarianism includes this:

> The groups which have been most prone to support fascist and other middle-class extremist ideologies have been, in addition to farmers and peasants, the small businessmen of the small provincial communities—groups which are also isolated from "cosmopolitan" culture and are far lower than any other nonmanual labor group in educational attainment. (105)

And in a later chapter,

> In recent decades the control of large corporations by college-educated men and scions of established wealth rather than by the relatively uneducated *nouveaux riches* has created an alliance between economic power and traditional status. But this alliance has not meant that the Republican party has easily become the expression of sophisticated conservatism. Rather large sections of it have continued to express the reactionary sentiments of the small-town provincial middle classes. Since its centers of electoral strength, particularly during periods of Democratic dominance, are in the "provinces" rather than the large metropolitan cities, the Republican party can be more properly accused of being the agent of the small-town *bourgeoisie* than of big business. (320–21)

I think Lipset should just have refined the last sentence along Mills's line: "Small business's attitude toward government, as toward labor, plays into the hands of big-business ideology," which has become increasingly more true over subsequent decades. Republican big business elitists (mostly new rich) from Richard Nixon and Ronald Reagan to George W. Bush, Mitt Romney, the Koch brothers, Rush Limbaugh, and Rupert Murdoch have posed as champions of the small-town *bourgeoisie* and have been taken at their word by evangelical Christians and LMC college students like mine described in chapter 3 who avow that corporate executives "work hard and deserve to keep every dollar they earn." Thomas Frank's books *One Market under God* and *What's the Matter with Kansas?* amply document the growth in worship of big business authoritarianism (under the disguise of free-market libertarianism) by "the Republican base."

The LMC and the New Rich

From my own familiarity with my family and many other people in the LMC, including the kind of students I have quoted, I would say that being petit bourgeois is more a state of mind than a strict designation of socioeconomic situation. Those from families with this mind-set might make good money—say, net worth of their businesses or farms in the million-dollar range—and attain high status in their local communities, while still not acquiring either the cultural capital and cosmopolitanism that can accompany higher, humanistic education and Gouldner's culture of critical discourse. Nor do they typically acquire the political and social power of large-scale corporate executives, but tend to remain politically inactive and uninformed, beyond the level of power over their own employees and perhaps lobbying for Chamber of Commerce boosterism and their companies' interests in their community. One of my relatives from Iowa, a self-made millionaire entrepreneur, did complain to me that President Reagan had betrayed him, after his years of being a campaign contributor, by capping the amount he could deduct from his income tax for entertaining clients at his country club, but he did not hobnob personally with Reagan or any other politicians. Among those I have known well, they tend to remain uncritical consumers of commodities and mass culture—just on a more ostentatious scale. They acquire the taste level associated with terms like "philistine," "Babbittry," or "new rich." To spin Hemingway, the *nouveaux riches* are different from the LMC only in having more money. In a class discussion when I was teaching at one upscale private college, I used the words *sophisticated* and *cosmopolitan* in describing the value of expanding our intellectual horizons beyond our own ethnocentrism of community, class, race, and country; one student, however, insisted she was sophisticated because she bought expensive brand names.

The cultural poverty of the new rich is a classic theme in drama, novels, and film, from Molière's *The Bourgeois Gentleman* to Woody Allen and Tracey Ullman's hilarious turn in *Small Time Crooks*. My affluent relatives' concept of "high-class" culture is hotel spectacles in Las Vegas and its clones like Branson, Missouri. (My own low opinion of these venues is not based on snobbery but on my years working in celebrity journalism and observing their tawdry operations, their producers' and performers' contempt for their audience.) My country-club-conservative relative, a Rush Limbaugh fan, constantly fulminates against "yuppies" and the wine-sipping liberal cultural elite. (Similarly, former Republican lobbyist Jack Abramoff fulminates repeatedly in his memoirs against Ivy League alumni lobbyists who court Democratic politicians at "wine and brie" cocktail parties—as though their Republican rivals serve nothing but Budweiser and Velveeta.) He and his wife have traveled abroad, but they stay in upscale American chain hotels and complain about any encounter with locals who do not speak English or fulfill every American expectation. They remind me of the apocryphal story about the American arriving in a European airport and, upon seeing a sign saying "Foreigners This Way," bursts out, "But *you* are the foreigners."

Among the anomalies in American class structure, then, is the mistaken perception that higher education and high culture are congruent with wealth and power; likewise, the cultural term "highbrow" is often misunderstood to mean rich. On a recent Iowa visit with yet another relative, the well-to-do widow of a local business executive, my wife told her about my several recent publications of scholarly books and articles. She replied approvingly, "Oh, he must be making a lot of money, then." Well, that may be so for star professors at prestige universities, but for teachers of undergraduates at state colleges receiving little or no reward for scholarly publication, not so much. My top salary at Cal Poly was about $65,000 in the late 1990s.

It is obvious that wealth, status, and power in one's family facilitate access to higher education and culture, that scholarship boys and girls *can* also gain initial access to that wealth, status, and power, and that this access almost inevitably has some conservatizing influence on liberals and even leftists. Yet intellectual members of the PMC are still more likely to have liberal or leftist political views than either the unintellectual new rich or the less affluent members of the LMC. I think the key explanation is a form of Lipset's "Tory radical" syndrome: that people who have the financial and cultural background (or scholarships) to attain access to liberal education in elite colleges, to high culture and extensive travel, are more apt to have the secure status that allows one to see beyond immediate survival, self-interest, and a restricted, sociocentric community toward a disinterested, cosmopolitan vision, with its liberalizing effect and access to the culture of critical discourse. Graduates with this mind-set, many of whom become professors, tend to be satisfied with the status of what Orwell called "the shabby genteel class" rather than pursuing wealth. (This phrase is central to Orwell's classic delineation in *The Road to Wigan Pier* of the subtle cultural markers impeding a united front between socialist intellectuals and the working class.) This is not, of course, to overlook the Ivy League legacy admissions who party their way through school with Gentleman's C's, benefit mainly from the social networking at these colleges, and are bred for the old upper-class establishment. Some other PMC students at elite universities might also harbor political attitudes that are as retrograde as my LMC ones, but they are apt at least to have absorbed enough of the protocols of academic discourse not to broadcast their racial, sexual, or class biases. However, for serious students there, especially scholarship boys and girls like Mina Shaughnessy, Richard Rodriguez, and me, high-caliber liberal education frequently is a gateway to cosmopolitan viewpoints and progressive politics.

By contrast, the LMC students at the colleges where I have taught tend to be fixated on occupational education. As noted in chapter 2, many say they would rather not be in college at all, and certainly not have to take any general education courses, but have been pressured by their parents and peers. I suspect that this mentality is especially prevalent in students whose family could afford elite colleges, but who are in a state college or second-tier private one (of the kind that is financially dependent on such students) because they could not get into a more academically demanding one. These circumstances predictably contribute to anti-intellectualism and hostility toward "the liberal cultural elite."

If students destined for the PMC are likely to be more liberal than those in the LMC or new rich, so (in my teaching experience) are those from poor, working-class, and minority backgrounds, who often are thirsty for the liberal education that they have been denied but which tends to be taken for granted by LMC students, whose attitude toward high school and college is typically bored endurance and cynical calculation for grades. I regularly compare teaching notes with Alan Hausman, my childhood friend from Des Moines, who after many years as a philosophy professor at Ohio State and Southern Methodist, has been at Hunter College in New York for the past decade, teaching a popular, interdisciplinary lecture course introducing students to the culture, codes, and controversies of higher education, including many of the same issues I am addressing here. His students include many working-class adults in the New York area, with an incredible mix of ethnic, national, and class backgrounds. In contrast to his experience with LMC and new-rich students in his previous positions, who resembled mine in taking high school and college education for granted to the point of bored disengagement, he has been overjoyed at having classes filled with students whose extra-academic life experience prompts enthusiasm for ideas and impassioned debates on issues immediate to their diverse identities. Needless to say, the proportion of conservative to liberal or leftist students is the opposite of mine.

While I have always had a smaller number of poor, working-class, and minority students than Alan does, my experience with them also confirms that most have led less sheltered lives than LMC students, with more hard experience of the world that provides a skeptical shield against the credulity of the LMC toward government, military, police, and corporate authority, or the virtues of the rich. Living among those who are most likely to be fighting in Iraq or Afghanistan, they are more resistant to the patriotic rationalizations for war and sentimentalizing of "our boys" common among LMC students who know they can avoid military service. The harshness of their lives also tends to make them more immune to the upscale consumerism and glamorized world projected by TV and other mass media.

Shifting Class and Cultural Lines

Of course, any broad, theoretical discussion of class differences like that I have broached here is subject to endless debates over complexities, qualifications, refinements, exceptions to the rule, and historical shifts. (So add these debates to an agenda for studying and teaching the conflicts in composition and rhetoric.) One important qualification in my analysis is the need to acknowledge changes in class position and cultural capital over people's lifetimes and from generation to generation (although generational mobility is most restricted among the poor). In Iowa, the emergence of the influential presidential caucuses has put the state on the national political map and has energized many more people there, both young and old, into political activism, which is all to the good. Several of my Iowa childhood friends in the 1950s attained a higher level of education than our parents and were the first in our families to become professionals and intellectuals, while many of our children and grandchildren have become still more cosmopolitan. One young cousin's grandparents and parents, who did not go to college, built up a small manufacturing business in Des Moines until it was bought out by a national corporation in the 1980s, and they were Republicans. He went to George Washington University, majored in political science, and was most recently a middle manager at a Wells Fargo headquarters in India. For what it's worth, he is a liberal Democrat, which is the tendency in the younger generation of the New Class with high-tech education and cosmopolitan experience, even (or especially?) when they become agents of the neoliberal global order.

An amusing spin on class, higher education, and the blurring of earlier ideological divides appeared in conservative journalist David Brooks's 2000 book, *Bobos in Paradise: The New Upper Class and How They Got There*. The theme—formulated with a direct nod to postwar sociological studies and developed with a satirical touch—was that by the 1990s, the culture wars of recent decades were waning as American society (or at least the middle class) became permeated by Boboism—a merging of bourgeois (conservative) and bohemian (liberal) politics through the rise of the cosmopolitan lifestyle of higher education, the professional-managerial class of both parties, and the trickling down of that lifestyle through Middle America. (Unfortunately, President Clinton's impeachment scrape and the presidency of George W. Bush, especially after 9/11, the recession beginning in 2008, then the election of President Obama and the right-wing backlash following it, marked at least a short-term regression from the Bobo paradise, reigniting all the old cultural animosities. Brooks's whole social picture also shamefully ignored the poor, minorities, and blue-collar workers.) Brooks's best-known section, on the rise of "Latte Towns," used latte as a signifier for the Bobo culture of university towns like Burlington, Vermont, one of Brooks's sites of study—a signifier that has also been picked up by conservative populist polemicists to tar the liberal elite with. Thus Berkeley linguist Geoffrey Nunberg's spin in his 2006 book *Talking Right: How Conservatives Turned Liberalism into a Tax-Raising, Latte-Drinking, Sushi-Eating, Volvo-Driving*, New York Times-*Reading, Body-Piercing, Hollywood-Loving, Left-Wing Freak Show*.

Brooks's anatomy of Bobo food and beverage preferences highlighted the fact that taste in, and education about, food and nutrition are obviously class markers in the United States, where Middle American eating habits have long been a source of satire and some serious social criticism, as in Baldwin's use in *The Fire Next Time* of packaged white bread as a metonymy for whites' sensual repression: "It will be a great day for America, incidentally, when we begin to eat real bread again instead of the blasphemous foam rubber that we have substituted for it" (43). My Iowa family's food tastes indeed consisted of Wonder Bread, Sanka, macaroni and cheese, tuna casserole, overcooked meat and vegetables, plus, after the 1950s, frozen foods and TV dinners. In German director Percy Adlon's 1987 film *Bagdad Café*, a delightful comedy of cultural contact zones, a German *hausfrau* who has broken up with her husband while touring in the Mojave Desert incongruously takes up residence at a truck stop/motel with the equally incongruous name of Bagdad Café—and teaches the locals to appreciate strong European coffee instead of American "brown vatah," while she in turn is won over by American working-class culture, spiced up by Southwestern multiculturalism.

It is true that in recent decades, more refined tastes in food have spread through the American heartland, accompanied to some extent by more liberal politics—though the phenomenon is preeminently a middle-class one, bypassing the poor, whose class afflictions often include unhealthy diet, obesity, and heavy smoking. From the 1970s to the 1990s, when I was living there, the provincial California area of San Luis Obispo, Paso Robles, and environs went from being cow towns to latte (and French bistro, Trader Joe) towns as the area became a great wine-producing center, with a corresponding shift from Republican to Democratic politics. On the other hand, my Berkeley leftist friends lament that upscale food culture (albeit environment-friendly in the mode of 1960s Berkeley icon Alice Waters) has replaced politics there—as they hang out at Chez Panisse Café, Peet's Coffee, or Acme Bakery. Even our local Kroger market in Appalachian Knoxville now sells arugula and Peet's Coffee. There are also many good wine stores in Knoxville, though they are closed on Sunday, and alcohol can't be sold in supermarkets or mail-ordered—policies probably continued less by religion than marketing turf wars, and trending toward being overturned. The good old boy who tends my yard was a moonshiner and segregationist in his youth, but now he joins me in wine-tasting and avidly supports President Obama, especially because of having access to health insurance for the first time in his life through Obamacare.

I do not think it is too frivolous, then, to suggest that encouraging our students to develop more elaborated-code taste in food—literally, as well as in consciousness of the politics of nutrition, agricultural ecology, food processing, and marketing—can be a legitimate part of courses in cultural studies, critical thinking, and civic literacy. Books like Marion Nestle's *Food Politics*, Eric Schlosser's *Fast Food Nation*, and Michael Pollan's *The Omnivore's Dilemma* can be effective texts here.

To reiterate, the cultural shifts I have discussed here have mostly taken place within segments of the middle class, and I have not intended in this chapter or anywhere else to imply that for individuals to attain higher education and cosmopolitan tastes in itself is the solution to the basic evil: endemic, growing economic inequality, with the class and cultural lines it inevitably produces. The constant focus on cultural issues in American politics, media, and education (including multicultural issues) serves as a smokescreen distracting attention from the gross economic disparities throughout American history and compounded with a vengeance since the 1970s. (For this line of argument, see John Marsh, *Class Dismissed: Why We Cannot Teach or Learn Our Way out of Inequality*, Ohmann's review of it in *Radical Teacher* no. 94, and Walter Benn Michaels's *The Trouble with Diversity*.) All I am suggesting is that as lower-middle-class students acquire a more cosmopolitan worldview, they are more likely to overcome their prejudices idolizing the rich and despising the poor.

My favorite story from my Iowa background is that of my distant cousins the Bucksbaum family, Jewish immigrants from rural Russia at the turn of the twentieth century who settled in tiny Marshalltown as peddlers, then started a grocery store. The three second-generation sons (only one of whom, Matthew, went to college, at the University of Iowa) expanded the store into a small chain, then started Iowa's first shopping mall, in Cedar Rapids, in 1955. The subsequent growth of a chain of malls throughout Iowa and nationally, named General Growth Properties, landed them in the Forbes 400 in 2007, with family assets of $4.1 billion. Matthew's wife Carolyn, known as Kay, who came from a more affluent Jewish family than mine in Des Moines and was several years ahead of me at Roosevelt High, was an honors student in English and Journalism at nearby Grinnell College. After the family fortune grew, she initiated numerous philanthropic, liberally oriented cultural activities, largely under the auspices of the Matthew and Carolyn Bucksbaum Foundation, including endowments for universities and museums as well as trusteeships and memberships on the board of directors for several colleges, symphonies, ballet companies, and National Public Radio, on which the Bucksbaum Foundation sponsors Chicago Lyric Opera broadcasts. (Melva Bucksbaum, Martin's widow, has been equally active in cultural philanthropy and prominent in the New York art world.) Matthew and Carolyn's daughter Ann also graduated from Roosevelt, in 1973, but went to Stanford, where she graduated Phi Beta Kappa in three years, majoring in economics and history. She then received a master's degree at the London School of Economics in international relations and worked for investment bankers in Chicago, New York, London, and Beirut. In Beirut she met, and eventually married, Thomas Friedman of the *New York Times*. (Media accolades to Friedman rarely ask whether his neoliberal worldview might be skewed by his wife being a billionaire.) My relatives in Cedar Rapids, lifelong acquaintances of the elder Bucksbaums, attest that they remain plain folks, not at all "stuck up"—in other words, intellectual. So there are always the exceptional stories like this to show that the American Dream still lives and to give sustenance to LMC students' faith that "anyone can get rich in America," even if the odds are increasingly astronomical.

Adapting Critical Pedagogy to Lower-Middle-Class Students

I want to use the Bucksbaums' story to come back in conclusion to my central question of how critical pedagogy might be adapted to teaching LMC or new-rich, conservative students. What is called for is not pedagogy of the oppressed but pedagogy of those who support the oppressor—exposing them to arguments for why they perhaps should stop worshipping the rich and socioeconomic policies that oppress the poor while widening the gap between the rich and those like themselves in the LMC.

Suppose we accept the principle agreed upon by virtually all the theorists surveyed in this book: start where the students are at, in this case their faith that anyone can get rich in America and that unbounded wealth is to be admired, as it is attained through hard work and managerial wisdom, and is socially beneficial—then make that a Freirean generative theme throughout an argumentative writing course that includes critical thinking and evaluating reading and research sources. The Bucksbaums' story might well serve as such a theme, with several dimensions. To take that story a step further, in an arc that has become familiar in American big business, as the family business grew and accumulated surplus capital over the years, the role of the brothers (and Matthew's son John, who became CEO) shifted from hands-on management of each mall—indeed requiring much hard work, risk, and skill—to speculative buyouts of other mall corporations, through heavily leveraged loans, in a booming period of the national real-estate market based largely on bonds consisting of bundled, often overvalued, subprime mortgages; these activities were what vaulted them into the billionaire ranks. But when the bottom dropped out of the real-estate market in the crash of 2008, their General Growth Properties lost most of its value and declared bankruptcy. John and other top executives were charged with mismanaging investments, and the Bucksbaums were forced out. They lost 97 percent of their family fortune at its peak, though they were still left with net worth of over $100 million. (See Frank and Hudson, "Dark Days for Mall Dynasty" in the *Wall Street Journal* and "General Growth Properties" in *Wikipedia*.)

At this point, conservative students might argue that it is exactly the risk of losing your entire investment and all the work and skill you've put into it that justifies being allowed to profit as much as you can. Those words might well have been applicable to the Bucksbaums' early years building up their chain of malls, but as they acquired a large surplus of capital, their efforts turned increasingly away from direct management to more speculative, and riskily leveraged, buying and selling of previously established malls and other companies. Conservatives will argue that the latter activities still necessitate much work, skill, and risk, but liberals will reply that there has been a semantic equivocation here in the meaning of these three words, which do not apply any more to directly managing one's own business but rather to buying and selling impersonal investments in stock or bond markets, with the risk of general market decline that is not necessarily influenced by any single, personal holding. Indeed, one of the most significant developments in the American and world economy over recent decades has been a massive shift in the center of financial activity from single companies to "too big to fail" investment banks, "hedge" and "equity" funds, buying low and selling high whole bundles of companies and their assets. The similarity of their enterprises to that of sheer gambling has given rise to the term "casino capitalism." But, the liberal argument goes, few of us understand the arcane workings of institutions like investment banks or hedge funds, and Americans do not generally regard gambling as an admirable model of entrepreneurial hard work, skill, and risk, benefitting society at large. So conservative propagandists must distract attention from the reality of casino capitalism by continuing to sell the gullible members of the LMC on Horatio Alger myths like the (early) Bucksbaum story.

Other dimensions of the Bucksbaum story that might be pursued in student research and debate include critical studies like *The Malling of America* by William Severino Kowinski, about the history of American malls, their effects on local communities and small businesses (including desertion of central cities in favor of automobile-dependent suburbs); their local labor practices and selling of products made by sweatshop labor abroad; or the role in the increasing American wealth gap of the rapid accumulation of inconceivable wealth by families like the Bucksbaums exercising oligopolistic concentration of corporate ownership. Conservative students are encouraged in my course to find evidence and arguments refuting these last points.

The case study concluding chapter 3 above suggests a related generative starting point: student readings of the section in Giroux's "The Age of Irony?" about the growing economic squeeze on the majority of Americans since the 1970s, and the responses to it by Students A and B, comparing executives and rank-and-file employees to diamonds and rocks, arguing that executives work hard and deserve to keep every dollar they earn, and that they (as well as the student) should not have to pay taxes to support all those who have chosen to drop out and live off the dole (Mitt Romney's infamous 47 percent of Americans). The better part of a course might well be devoted to debating the logic in such arguments and researching evidence on opposing sides of the issues. On one key point of logic, defined in chapter 3 as "predicting probable consequences," neither Student A or B was able, or willing, to predict the probable consequences for American democracy or for themselves of the exponential widening of the gap of wealth and corporate ownership between the rich and everyone else. In other words, their consciousness was that of Basil Bernstein's and Oscar Lewis's "present orientation" and failure to make cause-effect connections.

Such arguments are precisely the subject of an extended outline that I devised, in *Reading and Writing* and *Thinking Critically*, titled "An Outline of Conservative and Liberal or Leftist Arguments on the Rich, the Poor, and the Middle Class" (developed from the earlier version in Fitts and France's *Left Margins*), which provides students with prompts for opposing lines of argument and topics for research. The outline is incorporated in my culminating textbook chapter, "Analyzing Economic Arguments and Statistical Trickery."

Yet another apt prompt for studies along these lines is provided by Ehrenreich in her conclusion to *Fear of Falling*, calling for an alliance of PMC intellectuals with low-wage workers—politically, economically, and dialogically—in common cause against the ever-increasing hegemony of the wealthy and corporations. Her formula for intellectuals to find the "others" is for cultural-studies scholars to turn from their abstract theories of commodity consumption to "read" commodities in another way:

> ... not only as statements about the status of their owners, but as the congealed labor of invisible others. Whatever it is, someone manufactured it, packed it, trucked it to market, and stood behind a counter until it was sold. When we are prepared to listen, the computerized appliance speaks of Asian women straining their eyes on a distant assembly line; the gourmet take-out food speaks of immigrant workers chopping food in a sweltering kitchen; the towering condominium building speaks of lives risked at high altitude; and everything speaks of the tense solitude of the over-the-road truck driver. Learning to read things this way is a step to breaking out of the middle class's own lonely isolation. (258)

Ehrenreich's formula (reminiscent of John Berger's Marxist art criticism in *Ways of Seeing*) is equally applicable as a subject of study in undergraduate argumentative writing: students can research evidence about these situations in a variety of sources—academic, journalistic, literary and cinematic, or experiential, in the mode of Ehrenreich's *Nickel and Dimed* and *Bait and Switch*. The liberal or leftist implications in each of these situations can be balanced by students researching conservative justifications for such situations.

Ehrenreich's final phrase about breaking out of the middle class's own "lonely isolation" suggests another, broader avenue of study here—the large body of influential writing in the 1950s and 1960s on social alienation, especially in the middle class. My hunch is that many of today's LMC students who profess to be happy with the American status quo would experience the shock of recognition if they were to read those works with titles like *Growing Up Absurd, The Lonely Crowd, Man Alone: Alienation in Modern Society, Escape from Freedom,* and *The Sane Society,* along with SDS's "Port Huron Statement" and Mario Savio's speeches in the Berkeley Free Speech Movement, such as:

> Many students here at the university, many people in society, are wandering aimlessly about. Strangers in their own lives, there is no place for them. . . . The university is well structured, well tooled, to turn out people with all the sharp edges worn off, the well-rounded person. . . . This means that the best among the people who enter must for four years wander aimlessly much of the time questioning why they are on campus at all, doubting whether there is any point in what they are doing, and looking toward a very bleak existence afterward in a game in which all of the rules have been made up, which one cannot really amend. (Cohen 332)

Surely it is strange that the whole concept of alienation has dropped off the radar of American public consciousness. Perhaps one explanation is that the economic squeeze on Middle Americans has made consciousness of alienation a luxury, that the young have become, in Norman Mailer's phrase, "alienated beyond alienation," that they have been forced into resigned acceptance of the reality, in Savio's words, that "the 'futures' and 'careers' for which American students now prepare are for the most part intellectual and moral wastelands. This chrome-plated consumer's paradise would have us grow up to be well-behaved children" (333). Most LMC students would probably be baffled by Savio's peroration, "But an important minority of men and women coming to the front today have shown that they will die rather than be standardized, replaceable, and irrelevant" (333). This rhetoric today sounds hyperbolic, though its immediate context was the civil rights movement, especially in that deadly summer of 1964, in which Savio had been active in Mississippi a few months earlier. In today's world, however, students might make connections with protest movements of the young in the Arab Spring, in European resistance to economic austerity measures, and elsewhere, and they might discuss why so little protest of this kind has taken place here, beyond short-lived movements like Occupy Wall Street, or study the similarities and differences between the conservative Tea Party and left-wing protest movements. Among social critics, the Girouxs and Stanley Aronowitz have perhaps been most forceful in reiterating the theme of alienation among young Americans. At the least, turning LMC student study back toward the subject of alienation would be an interesting experiment, and I would welcome reports from any teachers who have been trying it. It could certainly be incorporated in a course like the one Russell Durst proposes that problematizes students' career paths.

This chapter is followed by an epilogue, "A Core Curriculum for Civic Literacy," applying my approach to an entire, ideal undergraduate curricular segment. But I also want to refer here to one more application of my teaching principles in this chapter, on a different topic from economics, though one closely related to the economic disputes addressed here. A section titled "A Historical-Causal Analysis of the White Problem" comes at the end of an early chapter on elements and techniques of argumentation in *Reading and Writing.*) It is deliberately phrased to illustrate the vocabulary of critical thinking, reasoning, and argumentative rhetoric surveyed in chapter 3, along with use of supporting evidence and sources, while marginal notes indicate the organization of the essay with steps in the causal analysis and points of refutation. Its intended audience is conservative white, mostly LMC, students who have repeatedly in my courses made the arguments it refutes, and I assigned it as a class reading, so teaching it applies the banking model, which I think is justified in this kind of case to introduce students to factual knowledge, vocabulary, and extended lines of argument that many were unfamiliar with. But it is also presented as a prompt for students to research rebuttals to its liberal lines of argument by conservative writers on "the Negro problem" like Charles Murray, Thomas Sowell, and David Horowitz, so it provides another example of arguments on which there is never a "last word." It begins:

> White Americans used to talk about "the Negro problem," but during the 1960s, writers like James Baldwin argued that this very phrase indicated the kind of doublethink mentality that obscured the fact that what we have always had in this country is "the White problem," and that the kind of rationalizations that whites have concocted amount to mass delusion. The most common white rationalizations are the following: "Slavery and discrimination against blacks were all in the past. Why do they keep complaining now, when they have all the advantages?" "My family never had slaves, and I don't discriminate, so why should I feel guilty or responsible?" "Other immigrant groups

have come to this country and overcome adversity. Why haven't the blacks?" And, "Blacks have a high rate of crime and immorality, which causes legitimate fears and disapproval by whites."

A historical perspective on this problem begins with the question, "When did the past end, and the present begin?" William Faulkner wrote, with specific reference to the persistent after-effects of slavery in the South, "The past is never dead. It isn't even past" (*Requiem* 229). Specifically, since exactly what date has discrimination against blacks been a thing of the past? Let us look at the chain of historical causation.

In closing, I hope this and my other suggested topics for study in this chapter will confirm that "conventional" academic study can well be turned toward critique, not enforcement, of the social status quo. And I hope it will make salient the gaping absences in the approaches to teaching favored by the postmodern theorists I have criticized, as well as their state of denial in failing to acknowledge the reality of the attitudes in many of our students that I have at least tried to address frontally.

EPILOGUE:
A CORE CURRICULUM
FOR CIVIC LITERACY

The past few years have seen an outpouring of books and reports deploring Americans' civic ignorance, with titles like *Just How Stupid Are We?*, *The Dumbest Generation*, *The Age of American Unreason*, and *Tuned Out: Why Americans Under 40 Don't Follow the News*. This is a problem that everyone seems to complain about but no one tries to solve through any coordinated, nationwide effort.

To be sure, a beginning has been made by the formation of several national organizations including the Campaign for the Civic Mission of Schools, the Carnegie Foundation for the Advancement of Teaching's Political Engagement Project, and Campus Compact and its Research University Civic Engagement Network. These organizations have published important interdisciplinary books, such as *Educating for Democracy* by Anne Colby et al. (Jossey-Bass, 2007), and *Civic Engagement in Higher Education* by Barbara Jacoby et al. (Jossey-Bass, 2009). To this date, however, all these efforts have remained disparate and limited in influence.

Many campus programs have also been exemplary, as surveyed in Charles Muscatine's *Fixing College Education* (University of Virginia Press, 2009). In *The Assault on Reason* (Penguin Press, 2007), Al Gore praised the American Political Science Association for starting a Task Force on Civic Education. That should prompt similar task forces in the Modern Language Association (my discipline) and other professional associations, along with a unifying interdisciplinary organization for secondary and postsecondary education, a National Commission on Civic Education.[1] Liberal and conservative educators and politicians should collaborate in hammering out their differences on what should constitute a core curriculum for civic literacy. We can hope for sponsorship in this effort by both conservative and liberal foundations, as well as for support from the U.S. Department of Education and National Endowment for the Humanities.

Adapted from a column in the *Chronicle of Higher Education*, 31 Jan. 2010.

One way to prompt deliberation here is to spin E. D. Hirsch's much-debated agenda for what every American needs to know to be culturally literate: What does every American need to cont to be a civically literate, critically conscious, responsible citizen? And, as a corollary, what role should the humanities play in a renewal of education for civic literacy? My agenda would give priority to the factual knowledge and analytic skills that students need to make reasoned judgments about the partisan screaming matches and special-interest propaganda that permeate political disputes. One source for such knowledge and skills can be the disciplines of critical thinking and argumentative rhetoric. Unfortunately, few high schools or colleges require courses with that focus, a problem that has been shamefully ignored by government initiatives like No Child Left Behind and Race to the Top. The Governors' Commission of the States' Common Core State Standards Initiative does commendably go so far as to advocate instruction to "demonstrate the cogent reasoning and use of evidence that is essential to . . . responsible citizenship in a democratic republic," but without getting very specific about where in the curriculum that instruction belongs.

We have all by necessity been thinking a lot lately about one particular branch of civic literacy: economic knowledge. How many among us understand how or why our personal economic fates—mortgages, retirement pensions, and our colleges' financing and endowments—are captive to booms and busts in the stock market and the occult realm of national and international high finance? In the prophetic words of the "corporate cosmology" revealed by the arch-capitalist Arthur Jensen in Paddy Chayefsky's 1976 film, *Network*, "The totality of life on this planet" is now determined by "one vast and immane, interwoven, interacting, multivariate, multinational dominion of dollars."

What a tragic gulf lies between most citizens' understanding of economic forces and their power over each of our daily lives and livelihoods. And what an enormous hole there is, in both K-12 and college curricula, in teaching about those forces as an integral part of general education. I am not talking about courses in formal economics, but in thinking critically about the rhetoric of economic issues at the everyday level of political debates and news and opinion—although those studies would identify oversimplifications at that level that could certainly be pursued in economics classes.

The term "core curriculum" has sadly become a culture-war wedge issue, with conservatives preempting it in the cause of Eurocentric tradition and American patriotism, thus provoking intransigent opposition from progressive champions of cultural pluralism and identity politics. Surely, however, we should urge the opposing sides to seek common ground in a core curriculum for critical citizenship that transcends—or encompasses— ideological partisanship.

My own immodest proposal models a core curriculum that centrally includes critical thinking about, and analysis and practice of, public rhetoric, at the local, national, and international levels. Far from being a radical proposal, it is a conservative one in returning to something like the eighteenth-century rhetoric-based curriculum in American education. That curriculum, as the historian of rhetoric S. Michael Halloran describes it, "address[ed] students as political beings, as members of a body politic in which they have a responsibility to form judgments and influence the judgments of others on public issues." Halloran and other historians have lamented the modern diffusion of studies in forensics, literature, composition, and other humanistic fields, as a result of the hegemony of disciplines and departments oriented toward specialized faculty research, which have become the tail that wags the curricular dog. Those forces and a depressing array of others have caused the study of political rhetoric to fall between the cracks of most current curricula, almost to the disappearing point.

So let's envision how a revived curriculum for civic literacy might be embodied in a sequence of undergraduate courses that would supplement, not supplant, basic courses in history, government, literature, and other humanist staples. These could be interdisciplinary offerings, with at least a partial component of English studies. Within English, they would follow, not replace, first-year writing—which in recent decades has focused on generating students' personal writing rather than critical analyses of readings or public rhetoric—and a second term in critical thinking and written and oral argumentative rhetoric.

The following headings correspond to chapters in my textbook for such a second-term course, but my own and other instructors' experience in using the book is that for any single course or textbook to "cover" what really demands a full curriculum is an impossible expectation. So I will break that material down, more appropriately, into four courses.

Course 1: Thinking Critically about Political and Economic Rhetoric
This would begin with a survey of semantic issues in defining terms like *left wing, right wing, liberal, conservative, radical, moderate, freedom, democracy, patriotism, capitalism, socialism, communism, Marxism, fascism,* and *plutocracy.* It would explore their denotative complexity and the ways in which they are oversimplified or connotatively slanted in public usage.

Study would then focus on defining ideological differences between and within the left and right, nationally and internationally, and on understanding the relativity of political viewpoints on the spectrum from left to right. For example, the *New York Times* is liberal in relation to Fox News but conservative in relation to the *Nation*; the Democratic Party is liberal in relation to the Republicans but conservative in relation to European social-democratic parties. Principles of argumentative rhetoric would then be applied to "reading the news" on political and economic issues in a range of journalistic and scholarly sources and from a variety of ideological viewpoints, with emphasis on identifying the predictable patterns of partisan rhetoric in opposing sources.

Course 2: Thinking Critically about Mass Media

Key questions would include: Do the media give people what they want, or condition what they want? Are news media objective and neutral, and should they be? The debate over liberal versus conservative bias in media would be approached through weighing the diverse influences of employees (editors, producers, writers, newscasters, performers); owners, executives, and advertisers; external pressure groups; and audiences. Research on the cognitive effects of mass culture would be applied to such issues as the impact of electronic media on reading, writing, and political consciousness. Implicit political ideology in news and entertainment media would be studied through images of corporations, workers, and unions; the rich, poor, and middle class; gender roles, ethnic minorities, and gays; military forces and war; and immigrants, foreigners, other parts of the world, and Americans' international presence. A final topic of study would be how the Internet has altered all of those issues.

Course 3: Propaganda Analysis and Deception Detection

Study here would begin with problems in defining and evaluating propaganda. A survey of its sources would include government and the military, political parties, lobbies, advertising, public relations, foundations, and sponsored research in think tanks and elsewhere. The role of special interests, conflicts of interest, and special pleading in political and economic rhetoric would be examined, along with propagators' frequent resort to deceptive modes of argument or outright lying—especially with statistics. This course (or another entire one) would include topics in critical consumer education: reading the fine print in contracts, like those for student loans, credit cards, rental agreements, and mortgages;

examining health and environmental issues in consumer products; and seeking out the often hidden facts of the production and marketing of food and pharmaceuticals.

Course 4: Civic Literacy in Practice

This would connect these academic studies with service learning, community or national activism, or work in government or community organizations, journalism, and elsewhere. One good model here is suggested in Ellen Cushman's "Rhetorician as Agent of Social Change."

Two possible objections:

"What you are proposing is that English and other humanities courses take on the impossible burden of remediation for the failures of the entire American education system in civic literacy."

You betcha. It's a dirty job, but someone has to do it, and I don't see any likelier disciplines jumping into the breach, especially ones with courses that are conventionally general education and breadth requirements. (Some communication and speech departments are in schools of liberal arts, but others are not; many offer courses in political rhetoric and media criticism, but those are mostly advanced ones for majors.) An ideal solution would be for these to be offered as interdisciplinary core courses, in which humanities faculty members would collaborate with those in the social sciences, communication, and so on. If civic education at the secondary level ever picks up the slack that it should, the college humanities involvement in such instruction can be phased out.

"Mightn't your proposals just be a Trojan horse for dragging in the academic left's same old agenda and biases?"

The courses could be conceived in their specifics and taught by instructors with varying ideological viewpoints—or best of all, through team teaching by liberal and conservative instructors. In principle, this framework would "teach the conflicts," on Gerald Graff's model, not through advocacy or the monologic perspective of any teacher's own beliefs, but through enabling students to identify and compare a full range of opposing ideological perspectives (including those of the instructor and the students), their points of opposition, and the partisan patterns and biases of their rhetoric. I have found it easy to grade students on the basis of their skill in articulating those points, without regard to my political viewpoints or theirs.

To be sure, this conception runs up against the near impossibility of anyone even defining terms and points of opposition between, say, the left and right with complete objectivity and without injecting value judgments. That problem itself, however, can become a subject of study within these courses and in advanced scholarly inquiry. Indeed, the courses could prompt a wealth of related research and theoretical explorations, creating a fruitful arena for bridging the gap between advanced scholarship and undergraduate teaching.

NOTES

1. Marginality as the New Orthodoxy

1. This book is a companion piece to four of my previous ones: *American Media and Mass Culture: Left Perspectives*; *Reading and Writing for Civic Literacy: The Critical Citizen's Guide to Argumentative Rhetoric*; *Thinking Critically about Media and Politics*; and *Why Higher Education Should Have a Leftist Bias*. There are also some snippets from *The Unique Creation of Albert Camus*, mainly concerning Camus's views on the political responsibilities of intellectuals and artists—foremost the defense of clear, truthful public language—which anticipated Noam Chomsky's "The Responsibility of Intellectuals," plus my analysis of the theme of gender identity and language in his work, in chapter 11. I have pulled bits and pieces from those books and my published articles listed in the works cited, but have recombined and updated them without duplicating any in their original form, except for the epilogue, "A Core Curriculum for Civic Literacy," which is virtually the same as the version published as a column in the *Chronicle of Higher Education*. *Reading and Writing for Civic Literacy* (2006, 2009) applied the scope of my studies systematically in a textbook format; a short, interdisciplinary spin-off titled *Thinking Critically about Media and Politics* was published in 2013. I hope readers will not view these citations just as plugs for my books but as cross-references for how they supplement this one and as a prompt for others to improve on my versions toward expanding such efforts into a major part of composition and rhetoric studies.

2. In a preemptive reaction strike against the common objection to the quotation from Marcuse, that he is saying the people are morons (or that I am saying this), I insist to the contrary that our object of criticism is the demagogic politicians and mass media producers who *treat* the people like morons in dragging public discourse down to that level. (I will be addressing variations on this point throughout the book.) As Dwight Macdonald, one of my personal mentors as a teacher at Northwestern, argued in "Masscult and Midcult,"

> Whenever a Lord of Masscult is reproached for the low quality of his products, he automatically ripostes, "But that's what the public wants, what can I do?" A simple and conclusive defense, at first glance. But a second look reveals that . . . to the extent the public "wants" it, the public has been conditioned to some extent by his products. . . . The technology of

producing mass "entertainment" (again, the quotes are advised) imposes a simplistic, repetitive pattern so that it is easier to say the public wants this than to say the truth which is that the public gets this and so wants it.... For some reason, objections to the giving-the-public-what-it-wants line are often attacked as undemocratic and snobbish. But it is precisely because I do believe in the potentialities of ordinary people that I criticize Masscult. (9–11)

3. Such disagreements are typified by clashes between postmodernists and Marxists, in which I broadly side with the latter, like Eagleton in *The Illusions of Postmodernism*; Mark Wood in "Another World Is Possible" (Rosendale and Rosendale); and Zavarzadeh, Ebert, and Morton, *Post-Ality, Marxism, and Postmodernism*.

2. My Teaching Story

1. The basic writing course at Berkeley was called Subject A and was housed in an excellent interdisciplinary program for teaching and research that was the origin of the Bay Area Writing Project and later the National Writing Project. Jane Stanley's *The Rhetoric of Remediation* presents an illuminating history of Subject A and of efforts to modify or replace it over the years, in the context of her argument that at Berkeley, "The rhetoric of remediation regulates the tension between the demand for access and the demand for status, the tug of democracy and the lure of elitism" (137).

2. Charles came from a lower-middle-class background, but was a scholarship boy as an undergraduate and graduate student at Yale. For over forty years at Berkeley, he was revered not only as a scholar and teacher but as a champion of academic freedom (in the 1950s he was fired for refusing to sign a loyalty oath, but later reinstated), curricular reform, and students' rights. He was a staunch supporter of the students in the Free Speech Movement, later being the lead author of a book endorsing the reforms FSM called for, popularly known as "The Muscatine Report." He published *Fixing College Education: A New Curriculum for the Twenty-First Century* in 2009, shortly before he died at eighty-nine. We were long-time allies in advocating education for political literacy, and I was privileged to have appeared on two MLA panels with him devoted to this subject.

3. A reviewer of an earlier draft indignantly disputed my account of the lack of student diversity at Cal Poly, San Luis Obispo, which the reviewer said is only 65 percent white. A 2014 study in the *Chronicle of Higher Education*, "Student Diversity at Nearly 1,800 Universities," confirmed the 65 percent white claim but showed 0.7 percent African American (that is, less than 1 percent) and 12.1 percent Latino—among the lowest enrollments in these two groups of any Cal State or UC campus. The 35 percent minority referred to is skewed upward by 10.4 percent Asian American students (many of whom at Cal Poly come from middle-class backgrounds and are high achievers in science), plus 3.6 percent

"Multiracial" and 7.9 percent listed as "Unknown/Other" (B28). In response to my inquiry, Linda Halisky, dean of arts and sciences, confirmed "the university's current efforts to deal with our historic problems attracting and retaining underrepresented students" (e-mail 26 Jan. 2011).

4. Savio, a multitalented student with a genius IQ, later taught math, poetry, and—yes—critical thinking at Sonoma State, where he continued to fight the bureaucratic power until dying from a heart attack at fifty-three. *Freedom's Orator* by Robert Cohen is a wonderful biography and collection of Savio's speeches, which confirms that he was one of the great orators of our time. Of interest to rhetoric scholars, Savio avidly studied classical oratory and practiced public speaking, partly to overcome a stutter, which is slightly audible in the film clips of his speeches in Mark Kitchell's documentary *Berkeley in the Sixties*.

4. What Ever Happened to Critical Thinking?

1. "Redefining the Legacy" first appeared in the *Journal of Basic Writing*, then was reprinted in Lu's book *Representing the Other*, coauthored with Bruce Horner but including some of their separate articles. That is the source I cite here. The article also was reprinted in the second edition of Tate and Corbett's *The Writing Teacher's Sourcebook*.

5. Degrees of Separation from Academic Discourse

1. In *Going North Thinking West*, Irvin Peckham shrewdly observes of notions like Lu's and Harris's here, "The postmodern assumption of evanescent subject positions presents an additional unacceptable framework for the working-class student.... For the working-class person raised in circumscribed environments, identify is fixed" (73).

2. See: Kampf and Lauter, eds., *The Politics of Literature*; Ohmann, *English in America: A Radical View of the Profession*, *Politics of Letters*, *Selling Culture*, and (as editor) *Making and Selling Culture*; Lauter, *Canons and Contexts* and *Heath Anthology of American Literature* (for which he was chief editor); O'Malley, Rosen, and Vogt, eds. *Politics of Education: Essays from* Radical Teacher; Entin, Rosen, and Vogt, eds. *Controversies in the Classroom: A* Radical Teacher *Reader*; Rosen, ed., *Class and the College Classroom: Essays on Teaching*.

6. Down with "Clear, Logical Prose"?
Ceding Reason to Conservatives

1. In Cheney's 1995 book *Telling the Truth*, she asserted, primarily in reference to college English studies, "One of the characteristics of postmodern thought is that it is usually asserted rather than argued, reasoned argument being rejected as one of the tools of the white male elite" (18). My "Ground Rules for Polemicists: The Case of Lynne Cheney's Truths" acknowledged the grains of truth in Cheney's claims, as I reiterate in this chapter, while I used reasoned argument

to anatomize the factual inaccuracies and fallacious reasoning throughout her book—most glaringly in the selective vision piling on instances of irrationality and dishonesty on the left while white-washing those on the right. Also see my chapter "Conservative Scholarship: Seeing the Object as It Really Isn't," in *Why Higher Education*.

7. Bartholomae and Petrosky's Depoliticized Ways of Reading

1. One partial exception, in *WOR*, is the excellent sequence of the reading from *Hunger of Memory* in which Richard Rodriguez identifies as a high-achieving Chicano, followed by sociologist Hoggart's classic description of the upwardly mobile British "scholarship boy" in *The Uses of Literacy*, the text of which follows in the exercises. Even here, though, the editorial glosses frame this sequence more in terms of personal "stories" than of Hoggart's sociological perspective on class lines.

2. See Mattelart, "Cultural Imperialism, Mass Media, and Class Struggle," and Mattelart and Sieglaub, eds., *Communication*.

3. This chapter in Poirier's *Poetry and Pragmatism* is about Emerson, and this passage tacitly echoes a famous section in "The American Scholar": "He plies the slow, unhonored, and unpaid task of observation. . . . Worse yet, he must accept—how often!—poverty and solitude" (73). But neither Poirier nor Bartholomae note Emerson's following, and perhaps contradictory, proviso:

> It is a shame to him if his tranquility, amid dangerous times, arise from the presumption that like children and women, his is a protected class; or if he seek a temporary peace by diversion of his thoughts from politics or vexed questions. . . . What deafness, what stone-blind custom, what overgrown error you behold is there only by sufferance—by your sufferance. See it to be a lie, and you have already dealt it its mortal blow. (74–75)

Emerson's passage in turn was echoed in Noam Chomsky's Vietnam/Watergate-era manifesto, "The responsibility of intellectuals is to tell the truth and to expose lies" (1).

4. *WOR* was first published in 1987; I will discuss and cite its third edition (1993) and ninth, (2011). (A tenth edition was published in 2014, but it is not much different from the ninth.)

5. Still, as noted in chapter 3, I have used several episodes from Proust in teaching basic critical thinking. As is typical of younger readers, when I first read each of these episodes, I only registered their events literally and in isolation (as Proust's narrator does at the moment of their occurrence); it required more life experience, a more mature rereading and the guidance of an expert teacher to understand how the variations on the same themes added up to a symbolic pattern. One of Proust's wonderful similes for this process is photographic images becoming progressively clearer as a negative is developed. Initial explanation by

a teacher of this process at the time of a first reading might at least prime the pump toward fuller understanding later.

8. Acting Locally, Thinking Locally:
The Shrinking of the Public Sphere

1. It strikes me that in its most fruitful forms, the current movement of localism evokes anarcho-communitarian political thought from the late 1940s to early 1960s, expressed by Arendt and other writers like Albert Camus, Paul Goodman, Dwight Macdonald, and Tom Hayden (in Students for a Democratic Society's "Port Huron Statement"), and its fruition in community organizing projects undertaken by Dorothy Day, Saul Alinsky, SDS's Economic Research and Action Project, and above all the civil rights movement. (See Gitlin's *The Sixties* on all these sources). These writers and movements, however, combined local activism with equally active resistance against super-power politics nationally and internationally. Current activists might well benefit from study of these sources on this combination.

11. Orality, Literacy, and Political Consciousness

1. In chapter 4 of *The Unique Creation of Albert Camus*, I develop this interpretation into a psychoanalytic reading of "Between Yes and No" and *The Stranger*, emphasizing Camus's subliminal association of blinding and decapitation with fear of castration, and the related, Lacanian imagery of eyes and the dominating, gendered "gaze." In this reading, the "between yes and no" refers to his unconscious mix of love and fear toward his mother and all the female traits he associated with her, but also refers to the larger emotional balance he sought between the masculine and feminine in himself and in the values he affirmed as a writer.

12. Sociolinguistics, Political Socialization, and Mass Culture

1. Tuman develops his defense of Bernstein in *A Preface to Literacy*.

2. I have argued throughout this and my other books that the kind of restricted language and reasoning that Lipset describes here is also characteristic of much mass political and corporate media discourse, especially in television and advertising, which is aimed at the lowest level of cognitive development in audiences by its propagators to manipulate, stupefy, and profit from those audiences. Lipset was well aware of the leftist scholars who had made these arguments, including Hoggart, Mills, Horkheimer, Adorno, Marcuse, and Lipset's Berkeley colleagues in sociology Leo Lowenthal and William Kornhauser. Indeed, he cites them all, but in a perfunctory manner in omnibus footnotes, without pursuing this aspect of their thought. When he does talk about media corporations, he considers them only as one among many influences in his pluralistic model of political power. This liberal-pluralist view prevailed in the early 1960s, serving to discredit works in the mode of the above authors, such as Mills's *The Power Elite* and Kornhauser's *The*

Politics of Mass Society, but this view was largely discredited in turn by the New Left's critique of corporate dominance and one-dimensional society—which in yet another turn has come under attack by postmodern pluralists, who in anomalous ways could be seen as reviving Lipset's liberal pluralism. This was exactly Ellen Willis's point in her 2005 critique of "the multiculturalists who have reinvented liberal pluralism, celebrating 'diversity' and 'inclusiveness' within a socioeconomic system whose fundamental premises are taken for granted" (445–46) My point here is to reaffirm the need for a concerted effort in composition studies to counteract the dominant corporate restricted-code discourse.

13. Shifting Critical Perspectives on Language and Class

1. At the time Mueller wrote, the other major New York daily tabloid, the *Post*, was equally restricted code in literacy level but had the liberal viewpoint of its owner Dorothy Schiff and editor James Wechsler—a rarity at that time and even more since then, in this period when Rupert Murdoch owns the *Post* and has imposed his conservative views on a chain of tabloids worldwide, as well as on Fox News. Likewise, the conservative *Wall Street Journal* was as elaborated code as the liberal *Times*, at least until it was bought by Murdoch, who to his credit also founded the elaborated-code-conservative *Weekly Standard*.

2. Whereas New Leftists focused their criticism of the intellectual New Class on its self-described liberal members who became administrators of or advisors to conservative governmental, corporate, and military forces (or on apologists for this class like Lipset), conservatives like Irving Kristol in the 1970s criticized the segment who supported leftist or progressive policies, allegedly with the self-serving motive of replacing the capitalist establishment with their own class rule. That negative image has become the staple of massive conservative antagonism toward "the liberal cultural elite." These opposing lines of attack against the New Class merged in critics like Ehrenreich and Lasch.

Epilogue: A Core Curriculum for Civic Literacy

1. A worthy step in this direction was the publication in 2012 of *A Crucible Moment: College Learning and Democracy's Future*, published by the National Task Force on Civic Learning and Democratic Engagement, a project of the Association of American Colleges and Universities.

WORKS CITED

Abraham, Matthew. "Developing Activist Rhetorics on Israel-Palestine: Resisting the Depoliticization of the American Academy." Kahn and Lee, 115–24.

Ackerman, John. "Rhetorical Engagement in the Cultural Economies of Cities." Ackerman and Coogan, 76–97.

Ackerman, John, and David J. Coogan, eds. *The Public Work of Rhetoric: Citizen-Scholars and Civic Engagement.* Columbia: U of South Carolina P, 2010.

Adorno, Theodor W. "Television and the Patterns of Mass Culture." *Mass Culture: The Popular Arts in America.* Eds. Bernard Rosenberg and David Manning White. New York: Free P, 1957. 474–78.

Adorno, T. W., Else Frenkel-Brunswik, Daniel J. Levinson, and R. Nevitt Sanford. *The Authoritarian Personality.* New York: Harper and Row, 1950.

Allport, Gordon. *The Nature of Prejudice.* 25th anniversary ed. Reading, MA: Addison-Wesley, 1979.

Altemeyer, Robert. *The Authoritarian Specter.* Cambridge: Harvard UP, 1996.

Altick, Richard. *A Preface to Critical Reading.* 5th ed. New York: Holt, Rinehart, 1969.

American Academy of Arts and Sciences. *The Heart of the Matter: The Humanities and Social Sciences for a Vibrant, Competitive, and Secure Nation.* Cambridge: 2013.

American Council of Trustees and Alumni. "Mission." *goacta.org*, n.d. Web. 27 March 2015.

Anderson, Elizabeth. "Affirmative Action Is About Helping All of Us." *Chronicle of Higher Education*, 29 May 2011. Web.

Anzaldúa, Gloria. *Borderlands/La Frontera: The New Mestiza.* San Francisco: Aunt Lute, 1987.

Arendt, Hannah. *The Human Condition.* Chicago: U of Chicago P, 1958.

Aronowitz, Stanley. *How Class Works: Power and Social Movements.* New Haven: Yale UP, 2003.

———. "Mass Culture and the Eclipse of Reason: The Consequences for Pedagogy." *The Crisis in Historical Materialism.* New York: Praeger, 1991, 281–88.

———. *The Politics of Identity.* New York: Routledge, 1992.

Aronowitz, Stanley, and Henry Giroux. *Postmodern Education: Politics, Culture, and Social Criticism.* Minneapolis: U of Minnesota P, 1991.

Artz, Lee. "Speaking Power to Truth: Observations from Experience." Kahn and Lee, 47–55.

Arum, Richard, and Josipa Roksa. *Academically Adrift: Limited Learning on College Campuses.* Chicago: U of Chicago P, 2011.

Baldwin, James. *The Fire Next Time.* New York: Dial, 1963.

Barber, Benjamin R. *An Aristocracy of Everyone.* New York: Oxford UP, 1992.

Barnard, Ian. "The Ruse of Clarity." *College Composition and Communication* 61.3 (2010): 434–51.

Bartholomae, David. *Writing on the Margins.* Boston: Bedford-St. Martin's, 2005.

Bartholomae, David, and Anthony Petrosky, eds. *Facts, Artifacts, and Counterfacts.* Portsmouth: Boynton/Cook, 1986.

———. *Ways of Reading: An Anthology for Writers.* 3rd ed. Boston: Bedford 1993. 9th ed., 2011.

Batsleer, Janet, Tony Davies, Rebecca O'Rourke, and Chris Weedon. *Rewriting English: Cultural Politics of Gender and Class.* London; Methuen, 1985.

Bauer, Dale M. "The Other 'F' Word: The Feminist in the Classroom." *College English* 32 (1990): 385–96.

Bazerman, Charles. "The Work of a Middle-Class Activist: Stuck in History." Kahn and Lee, 37–46.

Belenky, Mary Field, Blythe McVicker Clincy, Nancy Rule Goldberger, Jill Mattuck Tarule. *Women's Ways of Knowing: The Development of Self, Voice, and Mind.* New York: Basic, 1986.

Bell, Daniel. *The Cultural Contradictions of Capitalism.* New York: Basic, 1978.

Berlin, James A. "Composition Studies and Cultural Studies." Gere, 99–116.

———. *Rhetorics, Poetics, and Cultures: Refiguring College English Studies.* Urbana, IL: NCTE, 1996.

Bernstein, Basil. *Class, Codes, and Control: Theoretical Studies toward a Sociology of Language.* New York: Schocken Books, 1971.

———. *Class, Codes, and Control, Volume 3: Towards a Theory of Educational Transmission.* London: Routledge, 1975.

Berrett, Dan. "Freshman Composition Is Not Teaching Key Skills in Analysis, Researchers Argue." *Chronicle of Higher Education* 30 March 2012, A29.

Berthoff, Ann. *The Making of Meaning: Metaphors, Models, and Maxims for Writing Teachers.* Montclair: Boynton/Cook, 1981.

Bizzell, Patricia. *Academic Discourse and Critical Consciousness.* Pittsburgh: U of Pittsburgh P, 1992.

———. "Marxist Ideas in Composition Studies." Harkin and Schilb, 52–68.

———. "Power, Authority, and Critical Pedagogy." *Journal of Basic Writing* 10.2 (Fall 1991): 54–70).

Botton, Alain de. *How Proust Can Change Your Life.* New York: Pantheon, 1999.

Bourdieu, Pierre, and Jean-Claude Passeron. *Reproduction in Education, Society, and Culture.* Trans. Richard Nice. London: Sage, 1997.

Bowen, Howard R. *Investment in Learning: The Individual and Social Value of American Higher Education*. San Francisco: Jossey-Bass, 1977.

Bracher, Mark. "Teaching for Social Justice: Reeducating the Emotions through Literary Study." *Journal of Advanced Composition* 26 (2006), 464.

Brock, David. *Blinded by the Right: The Conscience of an Ex-Conservative*. New York: Crown, 2002.

Brooks, David. *Bobos in Paradise: The New Upper Class and How They Got There*. New York: Simon and Schuster, 2000.

Bruner, M. Lane. "The Public Work of Critical Political Communication." Ackerman and Coogan, 56–75.

Bryson, Bill. *The Lost Continent: Travels in Small-Town America*. New York: Harper and Row, 1989.

Butler, Paul. "Revisiting the Evidence: Reply to Donald Lazere." *Journal of Advanced Composition* 31 (2011): 314–22.

———. "Style and the Public Intellectual: Rethinking Composition in the Public Sphere." *Journal of Advanced Composition* 28 (2008): 44–84.

California State Department of Education. *Curriculum Guidelines 8–12*. Sacramento: State Board of Education, 1984.

Camus, Albert. *Essais*. Paris: Gallimard, 1965.

———. *Lyrical and Critical Essays*. Trans. Ellen Conway Kennedy. New York: Knopf, 1968.

———. *Neither Victims nor Executioners*. Trans. Dwight Macdonald. Berkeley: World without War Council, 1961.

———. *The Rebel*. Trans. Anthony Bower. New York: Knopf, 1968.

———. "Reflections on the Guillotine." *Resistance, Rebellion, and Death*. Trans. Justin O'Brien. New York: Knopf, 1958.

———. "Speech of Acceptance upon the Award of the Nobel Prize for Literature." Trans. Justin O'Brien. *Atlantic Monthly*, May 1958.

———. *State of Siege. Caligula and Three Other Plays*. Trans. Stuart Gilbert. New York: Knopf, 1958.

———. *The Stranger*. Trans. Stuart Gilbert. New York: Vintage, 1946.

Cavanaugh, Sean. "Amplify Insight Wins Contract from Common-Core Testing Consortium." *Education Week* 14 Mar. 2013. Web.

Chaput, Catherine. *Inside the Teaching Machine: Rhetoric and the Globalization of the U.S. Public Research University*. Tuscaloosa: U of Alabama P, 2008.

———. "The Role of Communism in Democratic Discourse: What Activist Rhetoricians Can Learn from the World Bank." Kahn and Lee, 81–90.

Chomsky, Noam. *Language and Responsibility*. New York: Pantheon, 1977.

———. "The Responsibility of Intellectuals." *New York Review of Books* 23 Feb. 1967, 1.

Cintron, Ralph. "Democracy and Its Limitations." Ackerman and Coogan, 98–116.

Cohen, Robert. *Freedom's Orator: Mario Savio and the Radical Legacy of the 1960s.* New York: Oxford UP, 2009.

Colapinto, John. "The Young Hipublicans." *New York Times Magazine* 25 May 2003. 30–35.

Cole, Michael, and Jerome Bruner. "Cultural Differences and Inferences about Psychological Processes." *Culture and Cognition: Readings in Cross-Cultural Psychology.* Eds. J. W. Berry and R. Dasin. London: Methuen, 1974.

Coleman, David. "Bringing the Common Core to Life." New York State Department of Education. 28 Apr. 2011. Web.

Common Core State Standards Initiative. *Common Core State Standards for English Language Arts and Literacy in History/Social Studies, Science, and Technical Subjects.* Washington: National Governors Association, 2010. Web.

———. *Appendix B: Text Exemplars and Sample Performance Tasks.* N.d. Web. 25 Oct. 2012.

Coogan, David. "Sophists for Social Change." Ackerman and Coogan, 157–74.

Cooper, Marilyn. "Rhetorical Agency as Emergent and Enacted." *College Composition and Communication* 62.3 (2011): 420–49.

Corbett, Edward P. J. *Classical Rhetoric for the Modern Student.* 2nd ed. New York: Oxford UP, 1971.

Council of Writing Program Administrators. "WPA Outcomes Statement for First-Year Composition." Apr. 2000, amended July 2008. Web. 7 Oct. 2012.

Crews, Frederick, and Orville Schell, eds. *Starting Over: A College Reader.* New York: Random House, 1970.

Crowley, Sharon, and Debra Hawhee. *Ancient Rhetorics for Contemporary Students.* New York: Pearson Longman, 2004.

Crowley, Sharon. *Composition in the University: Historical and Polemical Essays.* Pittsburgh: U of Pittsburgh P, 1998.

Curtis, Marcia, and Anne Herrington. "Writing Development in the College Years: By Whose Definition?" *College Composition and Communication* 55 (2003): 69–90.

Cushman, Ellen. "The Public Intellectual, Service Learning, and Activist Research." *College English* 61 (1999): 328–36.

———. "The Rhetorician as an Agent of Social Change." *College Composition and Communication* 47 (1996): 7–28.

Daniell, Beth. "Narratives of Literacy: Connecting Composition to Culture." *College Composition and Communication* 50 (1999): 393–410.

Dean, John. *Conservatives without Conscience.* New York: Viking, 2006.

Deblassis, Shelley, and Teresa Grettano. "Breaking News: Armchair Activists Access Their Power." Kahn and Lee, 170–88.

Delpit, Lisa. *Other People's Children: Cultural Conflicts in the Classroom.* New York: The New P, 1995.

DeMott, Benjamin. *Created Equal: Reading and Writing about Class in America.* New York: Harper Collins, 1996.

———. *The Imperial Middle: Why Americans Can't Think Straight about Class.* New York: Morrow, 1990.

Dieterich, Daniel, Ed. *Teaching about Doublespeak.* Urbana, IL: National Council of Teachers of English, 1976.

Dumke, Glenn. *Chancellor's Executive Order 338.* Long Beach: Chancellor's Office, California State University, 1980.

Durst, Russel K. *Collision Course: Conflict, Negotiation, and Learning in College Composition.* Urbana, IL: NCTE, 1999.

———. *You Are Here: Readings on Higher Education for College Writers.* Needham Heights, MA: Simon and Schuster Custom Publishing, 1999.

Eagleton, Terry. *Illusions of Postmodernism.* New York: Wiley, 1996.

Easton, Nina. *Gang of Five: Leaders at the Center of the Conservative Crusade.* New York: Simon and Schuster, 2000.

Ebert, Teresa. *The Task of Cultural Critique.* Urbana: U of Illinois P, 2009.

Ehrenreich, Barbara. *Bait and Switch: The (Futile) Pursuit of the American Dream.* New York: Henry Holt, 2005.

———. *Fear of Falling: The Inner Life of the Middle Class.* New York: Pantheon, 1989.

———. *Nickel and Dimed: On (Not) Getting By in America.* New York: Henry Holt, 2001.

Elbow, Peter. *Writing without Teachers.* New York: Oxford UP, 1974.

Ellsworth, Elizabeth. "Why Doesn't This Feel Empowering? Working through the Repressive Myths of Critical Pedagogy." *Feminisms and Critical Pedagogy.* Ed. Carmen Luke and Jennifer Gore. New York: Routledge, 1992. 90–119.

Emerson, Ralph Waldo. *Selections from Ralph Waldo Emerson.* Ed. Stephen E. Whicher. Boston: Houghton, 1960.

Ennis, Robert. *Critical Thinking.* Englewood Hills: Prentice Hall, 1996.

Entin, Joseph, Robert C. Rosen, and Leonard Vogt, eds. *Controversies in the Classroom: A Radical Teacher Reader.* New York: Teachers College P, 2008.

Escholz, Paul, Alfred Rosa, and Virginia Clark, eds. *Language Awareness.* 6th ed. New York: St. Martin's, 1994.

Faigley, Lester. *Fragments of Rationality: Postmodernity and the Subject of Composition.* Pittsburgh: U of Pittsburgh P, 1992.

FairTest. "Common Core Myths and Realities." National Center for Fair and Open Testing, 3 Sept. 2013. Web.

Farrell, Thomas J. "IQ and Standard English," *College Composition and Communication* 34 (1983): 470–84.

———. "Literacy, the Basics, and All That Jazz," *College English* 38 (1977): 448–49.

———. "Developing Literacy: Walter J. Ong and Basic Writing," *Journal of Basic Writing* 2.1 (1978): 30–51.

Faulkner, William. *Sanctuary and Requiem for a Nun.* New York: Signet, 1954.

Felski, Rita. *Doing Time: Feminist Theory and Postmodern Culture*. New York: New York UP, 2000.

Fish, Stanley. *Save the World on Your Own Time*. Oxford: Oxford UP, 2008.

Fisher, Stephen L., and Barbara Ellen Smith, eds. *Transforming Places: Lessons from Appalachia*. U of Illinois P, 2012.

Fishman, Stephen M., and Lucille Parkinson McCarthy. "Teaching for Social Change: A Deweyan Alternative to Radical Pedagogy." *College Composition and Communication* 47 (1996): 342–66.

Fitts, Karen, and Alan W. France, eds. *Left Margins: Cultural Studies and Composition Pedagogy*. Albany: State U of New York P, 1995.

Fleming, David. "Finding a Place for School in Rhetoric's Public Turn." Ackerman and Coogan, 211–28.

Flower, Linda. *Community Literacy and the Rhetoric of Public Engagement*. Carbondale: Southern Illinois UP, 2008.

Fox-Genovese, Elizabeth. "American Culture and New Literary Studies." *American Quarterly* 42.1 (1990): 15–29.

——. "The Claims of a Common Culture: Gender, Race, Class, and the Canon." *Salmagundi* 72 (Fall 1986): 131–43.

France, Alan W. *Composition as a Cultural Practice*. Westport, CT: Bergin and Garvey, 1994.

——. "Theory Cop: Kurt Spellmeyer and the Boundaries of Composition." *College Composition and Communication* 48 1997): 284–87.

Frank, Robert, and Chris Hudson. "Dark Days for Mall Dynasty." *Wall Street Journal* 9 Dec. 2008. Web.

Frank, Thomas. *What's the Matter with Kansas? How Conservatives Won the Heart of America*. New York: Metropolitan, 2004.

Freire, Paulo. *Pedagogy of the Oppressed*. New York: Continuum, 1970.

Fromm, Erich. *Escape from Freedom*. New York: Rinehart, 1941.

Gates, Henry Louis, Jr. "Pluralism and Its Discontents." *Profession 2009*. New York: Modern Language Association, 2009.

Geertz, Clifford. *Local Knowledge: Further Essays in Interpretive Anthropology*. New York: Basic Books, 1983.

"General Growth Properties." *Wikipedia*, n.d. Web.

Gere, Anne Ruggles, ed. *Into the Field: Sites of Composition Studies*. New York: Modern Language Association, 1993.

——, et al. "Implementation of the Common Core State Standards." *NCTE Council Chronicle* Sept. 2013: 13–15.

Gewertz, Catherine. "Questions Dog Common-Test Development." *Education Week* 31 July 2012. Web.

Giglioli, Pier Paolo, ed., *Language and Social Context*. New York: Penguin, 1972.

Gilbert, Sandra, and Susan Gubar. *No Man's Land. Volume 1: The War of the Words*. New Haven: Yale UP, 1988.

Gilligan, Carol. *In a Different Voice: Psychological Theory and Women's Development*. Cambridge: Harvard UP, 1982.

Gilman, Charlotte Perkins. *Herland*. New York: Pantheon, 1979.

Giroux, Susan Searls. "The Age of Irony?" *Journal of Advanced Composition* 22.4 (2002): 960–76.

Giroux, Henry A. *Youth in Revolt: Reclaiming a Democratic Future*. Boulder: Paradigm, 2013.

Giroux, Henry A. and Susan Searls Giroux. *Take Back Higher Education*. New York: Palgrave Macmillan, 2004.

Gitlin, Todd. *The Sixties: Years of Hope, Days of Rage*. New York: Bantam, 1987.

———. *The Twilight of Common Dreams*. New York: Metropolitan, 1991.

Gleason, Barbara. Contribution to "Symposium on Basic Writing, Conflict and Struggle, and the Legacy of Mina Shaughnessy." *College English* 45.8 (1993): 886–89.

Gomstyn Alice. "Nation Faces a College-Access Crisis, Education-Policy Group Warns." *Chronicle of Higher Education* 2 Oct 2003. Web.

Goodman, Kenneth. "Standards, NOT!" *Education Week* 7 Sept. 1994: 39.

Goodman, Paul. *Growing Up Absurd*. New York: Random House, 1960.

Gouldner, Alvin. "The New Class as a Speech Community." *The Future of Intellectuals and the Rise of the New Class*. New York: Seabury, 1979. 28–42.

Graff, Gerald. *Beyond the Culture Wars: How Teaching the Conflicts Can Revitalize American Education*. New York: Norton, 1992.

———. *Clueless in Academe: How Schooling Obscures the Life of the Mind*. New Haven: Yale UP, 2003.

———. "Trickle Down Miseducation." Modern Language Association convention, 2013.

Graff, Gerald, and Cathy Birkenstein. "A Progressive Case for Educational Standardization." *Academe Online* (May–June 2008). Web.

Gramsci, Antonio. *Selections from the Prison Notebooks*. Trans. and ed. Quinton Hoare and Geoffrey Nowell Smith. New York: International Publishers, 1991.

Grossberg, Lawrence. *We Gotta Get Out of This Place: Popular Conservatism and Postmodern Culture*. New York: Routledge, 1992.

Habermas, Jürgen. *The Structural Transformation of the Public Sphere*. Cambridge: MIT P, 1989.

Hairston, Maxine. "Diversity, Ideology, and the Teaching of Writing." *College Composition and Communication* 43.3 (1992): 178–93.

Halloran, Michael. "From Rhetoric to Composition: The Teaching of Writing in America to 1900. *A Short History of Writing Instruction*. James Murphy, ed. Davis, CA: Hermagoris, 1990.

———. "Rhetoric in the American College Curriculum: The Decline of Public Discourse." *PRE/TEXT* 3 (1982): 245–69.

Harkin, Patricia, and John Schilb, eds. *Contending with Words: Composition and Rhetoric in a Postmodern Age*. New York: Modern Language Association, 1991.

Harris, Joseph. "Revision as a Critical Practice." *College English* 65 (2003): 577–92.

———. *A Teaching Subject: Composition since 1966*. Upper Saddle River: Prentice-Hall, 1997.

Harvard University Committee on General Education. *Guide to the Core Program*. Cambridge, 2008. Web.

Hasbrook, Melissa Day. "Intervention and Rhetorics of War." Kahn and Lee, 62–73.

Hatcher, D. L., and L. A. Spencer. *Reasoning and Writing: From Critical Thinking to Composition*. 3rd ed. Boston: American P, 2004.

Hayakawa, S. I. *Language in Thought and Action*. New York: Harcourt, 1941. 3rd ed. 1972.

Heath, Shirley Brice. *Ways with Words: Language, Life, and Work in Communities and Classrooms*. Cambridge: Cambridge UP, 1983.

Herman, Edward, and Noam Chomsky. *Manufacturing Consent: The Political Economy of the Mass Media*. New York: Pantheon, 1988.

Hirsch, E. D., Jr. *Cultural Literacy: What Every American Needs to Know*. Boston: Houghton Mifflin, 1987.

———. *The Making of Americans: Democracy and Our Schools*. New Haven: Yale UP, 2009.

———. "Reading Test Dummies." *New York Times* 22 Mar. 2009. Web.

Hoggart, Richard. *An English Temper: Essays on Education, Culture, and Communications*. New York: Oxford UP, 1982.

———. *The Uses of Literacy*. Boston: Beacon, 1961.

Horkheimer, Max, and Theodor W. Adorno. *Dialectic of Enlightenment*. New York: Seabury, 1972.

Horner, Bruce, and Min-Zhan Lu. *Representing the "Other": Basic Writers and the Teaching of Basic Writing*. Urbana, IL: NCTE, 1999.

Horton, Myles, and Paulo Freire. *We Make the Road by Walking: Conversations on Education and Social Change*. Philadelphia: Temple UP, 1990.

Hoyles, Martin, ed. *The Politics of Literacy*. London: Redwood Burn, 1977.

Huxley, Aldous. *Brave New World and Brave New World Revisited*. New York: Harper, 1960.

Huyssens, Andreas. *After the Great Divide: Modernism, Mass Culture, Postmodernism*. Bloomington: Indiana UP, 1989.

International Reading Association. *Common Core Resources*. N.d. Web. 17 March 2015.

Jacobs, James. "S. M. Lipset: Social Scientist of the Smooth Society." Boston: New England Free P, n.d.

Jarratt, Susan. "Feminism and Composition: The Case for Conflict." Harkin and Schilb, 105–23.

Jarratt, Susan, and Lynn Worsham, eds. *Feminism and Composition Studies: In Other Words*. New York: Modern Language Association, 1998.

Jefferson, Thomas. "To John Adams: *The Natural Aristocracy*." *Writings*. Ed. Merrill D. Peterson. New York: Library of America, 1984. 1304–10.

Johnson, Nicholas. *How to Talk Back to Your Television Set*. New York: Little Brown-Bantam, 1970.

Jones, David R. Letter: "Diversity at CUNY." *New York Times* 21 Oct. 2012. Web.

Kahane, Howard. *Logic and Contemporary Rhetoric: The Use of Reason in Everyday Life*. Belmont, CA: Wadsworth, 1971.

Kahane, Howard, and Nancy Cavender. *Logic and Contemporary Rhetoric: The Use of Reason in Everyday Life*. 12th ed. Belmont, CA: Wadsworth, 2013.

Kahn, Seth, and Jonghwa Lee, eds. *Activism and Rhetoric: Theories and Contexts for Political Engagement*. New York: Routledge, 2011.

Kampf, Louis, and Paul Lauter, eds. *Politics of Literature: Dissenting Essays in the Teaching of English*. New York: Random House, 1972.

Kaye, Harvey. *Why Do Ruling Classes Fear History?* New York: St. Martin's, 1997.

Kilbourne, Jean. *Killing Us Softly: Advertising's Image of Women*. DVD. Northampton, MA: Media Education Foundation, 1979.

Kirp, David L. "Rage against the Common Core." *New York Times* 27 Dec. 2014. Web.

Knoblauch, A. Abby. "A Textbook Argument: Definitions of Argument in Leading Composition Textbooks." *College Composition and Communication* 63 (2011): 244–68.

Kohlberg, Lawrence. *The Philosophy of Moral Development: Volume One*. San Francisco: Harper and Row, 1981.

Kohn, Melvin. *Class and Conformity: A Study in Values*. Chicago: U of Chicago P, 1977.

Kozol, Jonathan. *Illiterate America*. New York: Doubleday, 1985.

———. *Savage Inequalities: Children in America's Schools*. New York: Crown, 1991.

———. *The Shame of the Nation*. New York: Viking, 2005.

Kowinski, William Severino. *The Malling of America*. New York: Xlibris, 2002.

Kristol, Irving. *Neoconservatism: The Autobiography of an Idea*. New York: Free P, 1995.

Kytle, Ray. *Clear Thinking for Composition*. New York: Random House, 1969.

Labov, William. "Academic Ignorance and Black Intelligence." *Atlantic* July 1972. Web. Excerpt from *The Logic of Nonstandard English*. Washington, DC: Georgetown University Institute of Language and Linguistics, 1969.

———. *The Study of Nonstandard English*. Urbana, IL: NCTE, 1969, 1978.

Lakoff, George. *Moral Politics: How Liberals and Conservatives Think*. 2nd ed. Chicago: U of Chicago P, 2002.

Lakoff, Robin Tolmach. *The Language War*. Berkeley: U of California P, 2000.

Langstraat, Lisa R. "'Hypermasculinity' in Cultural Studies and Composition: Mapping a Feminist Response." *Composition Forum* 7.1 (Winter 1996): 1–16.

Lasch, Christopher. *The Agony of the American Left*. New York: Vintage, 1969.

———. *The True and Only Heaven: Progress and Its Critics*. New York: W. W. Norton, 1991.

Lauter, Paul. *Canons and Contexts*. New York: Oxford UP, 1991.

———, et al., eds. *Heath Anthology of American Literature*. New York: Heath, 1990.

Laurence, Patricia. Contribution to "Symposium on Basic Writing, Conflict and Struggle, and the Legacy of Mina Shaughnessy." *College English* 45.8 (1993): 879–82.

Layton, Lyndsey. "How Bill Gates Pulled Off the Swift Common Core Revolution." *Washington Post* 7 June 2014. Web.

Lazere, Donald, ed. *American Media and Mass Culture: Left Perspectives*. Berkeley: U of California P, 1987.

———. "Back to Basics: A Source of Oppression or Liberation?" *College English* 54 (1992): 1–16.

———. "Butler Unclarifies the Issues." *Journal of Advanced Composition* 31 (2011): 308–13.

———. "Critical Thinking in College English Studies." *ERIC Digest*, 1987.

———. "Ground Rules for Polemicists: The Case of Lynne Cheney's Truths." *College English* 59 (1997): 661–85.

———, ed. "Mass Culture, Political Consciousness, and English Studies." Special issue of *College English* 38 (1977).

———. "Orality, Literacy, and Standard English." *Journal of Basic Writing* 10.2 (1991): 87–98.

———. "Postmodern Pluralism and the Retreat from Political Literacy." *Journal of Advanced Composition* 25 (2005): 257–91.

———. *Reading and Writing for Civic Literacy: The Critical Citizen's Guide to Argumentative Rhetoric*. Boulder: Paradigm, 2006. Brief edition, 2009.

———. Rev. of *Class Politics: The Movement for the Students' Right to Their Own Language*, Stephen Parks. *Journal of Advanced Composition* 21.3 (2001): 698–704.

———. Rev. of *Arts of Living*, Kurt Spellmeyer. *Journal of Advanced Composition* 23 (2003).

———. "Spellmeyer's Naive Populism." *College Composition and Communication* 48 (1997): 288–91.

———. "Stratification in the Academic Profession and in the Teaching of Composition." *Humanities in Society* 4 (1981): 379–94.

———. "Teaching the Conflicts about Wealth and Poverty." Fitts and France, *Left Margins*, 189–205.

———. "Teaching the Political Conflicts: A Rhetorical Schema." *College Composition and Communication* 43 (1992): 194–213.

———. *The Unique Creation of Albert Camus*. New Haven: Yale UP, 1973.

———. *Thinking Critically about Media and Politics*. Boulder: Paradigm, 2013.

———. *Why Higher Education Should Have a Leftist Bias*. New York: Palgrave Macmillan, 2013.

Lears, Jackson. Contribution to Symposium, "Intellectuals and Their America." *Dissent*, Winter 2010. Web.

Leavis, F. R. *The Great Tradition*. New York: New York UP, 1960.

Lemann, Nicholas. *The Promised Land: The Great Black Migration and How It Changed America*. New York: Knopf, 1991.

Lewis, Oscar. *Five Families: Mexican Case Studies in the Culture of Poverty*. New York: Basic, 1959.

Lewis, D. B. Wyndham. *François Villon*. Garden City: Doubleday, 1958.

Linkon, Sherry, Irving Peckham, and Ben Lanier-Nabors, eds. "Social Class and English Studies." Special issue of *College English* 67 (2004).

Lipset, Seymour Martin. *Political Man: The Social Bases of Politics*. New York: Doubleday, 1960. Anchor edition, 1963. Expanded edition, Baltimore: Johns Hopkins UP, 1981.

Lu, Min-Zhan. "From Silence to Words: Writing as Struggle." *College English* 49 (1987): 437–48.

Lunsford, Andrea. "Cognitive Development and the Basic Writer." *College English* 41 (1979): 449–59.

———. "The Content of Basic Writers' Essays." *College Composition and Communication* 31.3 (Oct. 1980): 278–90.

Lunsford, Andrea, and Karen Lunsford. "Mistakes Are a Fact of Life." *College Composition and Communication* 59.4 (2008): 781–806.

Luria, A. R. *Cognitive Development: Its Cultural and Social Foundations*. Trans. Martin Lopez-Morillas and Lynn Solotaroff. Ed., Michael Cole. Cambridge: Harvard UP, 1976.

Lutz, William, ed, *Beyond Nineteen Eighty-Four: Doublespeak in a Post-Orwellian Age*. Urbana, IL: NCTE, 1989.

Lyotard, Jean-François. *The Postmodern Condition: A Report on Knowledge*. Minneapolis: U of Minnesota P, 1984.

Macdonald, Dwight. *Against the American Grain*. New York: Random House, 1962.

MacDonald, Heather. "Why Johnny Can't Write." *The Public Interest* 120 (1995): 3–13.

Maher, Jane. *Mina P. Shaughnessy: Her Life and Work*. Urbana, IL: NCTE, 1997.

Moody, Kate. *Growing Up on Television—The TV Effect*. New York: Times Books, 1980.

Mahoney, Kevin. "You Can't Get There from Here: Higher Education, Labor Activism, and Challenges of Neoliberal Globalization." Kahn and Lee, 147–58.

Mailer, Norman. "The White Negro." *Advertisements for Myself*. New York: Putnam, 1959.

Malcolm X. *The Autobiography of Malcolm X*. New York: Grove P, 1965.

Marcuse, Herbert. *An Essay on Liberation*. Boston: Beacon, 1969.

———. *One-Dimensional Man*. Boston: Beacon, 1964.

Marsh, John. *Class Dismissed: Why We Cannot Teach or Learn Our Way out of Inequality*. New York: Monthly Review P, 2010.

Martin, Harold, James Wheatley, and Richard M. Ohmann. *The Logic and Rhetoric of Composition*. New York: Holt, Rinehart, and Winston, 1969.

Marx, Leo. *The Machine in the Garden: Technology and the Pastoral Ideal in America*. London: Oxford UP, 1964.

Mattelart, Armand. "Cultural Imperialism, Mass Media, and Class Struggle: An Interview." *Insurgent Sociologist* 9 (1980): 69–79.

Mattelart, Armand, and Seth Siegelaub, eds. *Communication and Class Struggle*. Vol. 1: *Capitalism, Imperialism*. New York: International General, 1979.

Mayer, Jane. "Is Senator Ted Cruz Our New McCarthy?" *New Yorker* 22 Feb. 2013. Web.

McKinley, James C. "Texas Conservatives Win Curriculum Change." *New York Times* 12 Mar. 2010. Web.

Medina, Ken, Elissa McBride, Lane Windham, eds. *Faculty@Work: Inspiring Activism and Supporting Working Families*. Washington: AFL-CIO Organizing Institute, 1998.

Michaels, Walter Benn. *The Trouble with Diversity: How We Learned to Love Identity and Ignore Inequality*. New York: Metropolitan Books, 2006.

Mills, C. Wright. *White Collar: The American Middle Classes*. New York: Oxford UP, 1951.

Modleski, Tania. *Loving with a Vengeance: Mass-Produced Fantasies for Women*. New York: Methuen, 1984.

Mueller, Claus. *The Politics of Communication: A Study in the Political Sociology of Language, Socialization, and Legitimation*. New York: Oxford UP, 1973.

Murphy, Timothy. "Inside the Mammoth Backlash to Common Core." *Mother Jones* September–October 2014. Web.

Muscatine, Charles. *Report on Education at Berkeley*. Berkeley: U of California P, 1966.

———. *Fixing College Education: A New Curriculum for the Twenty-first Century*. Charlottesville: U of Virginia P, 2009.

Muscatine, Charles, and Marlene Griffith. *The Borzoi College Reader*. New York: Knopf, 1965.

National Assessment of Educational Progress. *Reading, Thinking, and Writing: Results from the 1979–80 National Assessment of Reading and Literature*. Denver: Education Commission of the States, 1981.

National Council of Teachers of English. "Resolutions on Language." Urbana, IL: NCTE, 1971, 1975. Cited in Dieterich, ix, x.

———. *Standards for the English Language Arts*. Urbana, IL: NCTE, 1996.

National Endowment for the Humanities. *National Tests: What Other Countries Expect Their Students to Know.* Washington, DC: National Endowment for the Humanities, 1991.

National Task Force on Civic Learning and Democratic Engagement. *A Crucible Moment: College Learning and Democracy's Future.* Washington, DC: Association of American Colleges and Universities, 2012.

Nestle, Marion. *Food Politics.* Berkeley: U of California P, 2002.

Nicotra, Jodie. "Dancing Attitudes in Wartime: Kenneth Burke and General Semantics." *Rhetoric Society Quarterly* 39 (2009): 331–52.

Nobile, Philip. *Intellectual Skywriting.* New York: Charterhouse, 1974.

Nunberg, Geoffrey. *Talking Right: How Conservatives Turned Liberalism into a Tax-Raising, Latte-Drinking, Sushi-Eating, Volvo-Driving,* New York *Times–Reading, Body-Piercing, Hollywood-Loving, Left-Wing Freak Show.* Boston: PublicAffairs: 2006.

Nussbaum, Martha. *Not for Profit: Why Democracy Needs the Humanities.* Princeton, NJ: Princeton UP: 2010.

Ohmann, Richard. *English in America: A Radical View of the Profession.* New York: Oxford UP, 1976. Rev. ed., with foreword by Gerald Graff, Wesleyan UP, 1996.

———. *Politics of Letters.* Middletown: Wesleyan UP, 1987.

———. "Questions about Literacy and Political Education." *Radical Teacher* 8 (May 1978): 24–25.

———. Rev. of *Class Dismissed: Why We Cannot Teach or Learn Our Way out of Inequality,* John Marsh. *Radical Teacher* 94 (Fall 2012): 63–72.

Olson, Gary A. "Jacques Derrida on Rhetoric and Composition: A Conversation." *(Inter)views: Cross-Disciplinary Perspectives on Rhetoric and Literacy.* Ed. Gary A. Olson and Irene Gale. Carbondale: Southern Illinois UP, 1991. 121–41.

Olson, Gary A., and Lynn Worsham, eds. *Education as Civic Engagement: Toward a More Democratic Society.* New York: Palgrave Macmillan, 2012.

O'Malley, Susan Gushee, Robert C. Rosen, and Leonard Vogt, eds. *Politics of Education: Essays from Radical Teacher.* Albany: SUNY P, 1990.

Ong, Walter J. *Orality and Literacy: The Technologizing of the Word.* New York: Methuen, 1992.

Orwell, George. *Orwell's Nineteen Eighty-Four: Text, Sources, Criticism.* Ed. Irving Howe. 2nd ed. New York: Harcourt, Brace, Jovanovich, 1982. 248–58.

———. *The Road to Wigan Pier.* New York: Harcourt Brace Jovanovich, 1958.

Parks, Stephen, and Eli Goldblatt. "Writing beyond the Curriculum: Fostering New Collaborations in Literacy." *College English* 62 (2000): 584–606.

Partnership for Assessment of Readiness for College and Careers. "PARCC Task Prototypes and New Sample Items for ELA/literacy." N.d. Web. 17 March 2015.

Patterson, James, and Peter Kim. *The Day America Told the Truth*. New York: Prentice Hall, 1991.

Paul, Richard. *Critical Thinking*. Rohnert Park, CA: Sonoma State U Center for Critical Thinking and Moral Critique, 1990.

Peckham, Irvin. *Going North Thinking West: The Intersections of Social Class, Critical Thinking, and Politicized Writing Instruction*. Logan: Utah State UP, 2010.

Perry, William, Jr. *Forms of Intellectual and Ethical Development in the College Years*. New York: Holt, Rinehart, and Winston, 1970.

Phillips, Anna M. "Tom Van Der Ark's New York-Area Charter Schools Falter." *New York Times* 14 July 2011. Web.

Piaget, Jean. "The Development in the Child of the Idea of the Homeland." *Piaget Sampler*. Ed. Sarah Campbell. New York: Wiley, 1976.

———. *The Language and Thought of the Child*. New York: New American Library, 1955.

Poirier, Richard. *Poetry and Pragmatism*. Cambridge: Harvard UP, 1992.

Pollan, Michael. *The Omnivore's Dilemma*. New York: Penguin, 2006.

Possin, Kevin. "A Field Guide to Critical Thinking Assessment." *Teaching Philosophy* 31.3 (2008).

Postman, Neil. *Amusing Ourselves to Death*. New York: Viking Penguin, 1985.

———. *Teaching as a Conserving Activity*. New York: Delacorte, 1981.

Proust, Marcel. *Remembrance of Things Past*. Trans. C. K. Scott Moncrieff. Two vols. New York: Random House, 1932. Sub-volume *The Past Recaptured*. Trans. Frederick A. Blossom.

Rank, Hugh. *Persuasion Analysis: A Companion for Composition*. Park Forest, IL: Counter-Propaganda P, 1988.

———. *The Pitch: How to Analyze Ads*. Park Forest, IL: Counter-Propaganda P, 1982.

Ravitch, Diane. *The Death and Life of the Great American School System*. New York: Basic Books, 2010.

———. *National Standards in American Education: A Citizen's Guide*. Washington, DC: Brookings Institution, 1995.

———. *Reign of Error: The Hoax of the Privatization Movement and the Danger to America's Public Schools*. New York: Knopf, 2013.

———. "Why I Oppose the Common Core Standards." Posted by Valerie Strauss, *Washington Post* 26 Feb. 2013. Web.

Ravitch, Diane, and Chester Finn. *What Do Our 17-Year-Olds Know?* New York: Harper and Row, 1987.

Report of the Commission on the Humanities. *The Humanities in American Life*. Berkeley: U of California P, 1980.

Republican Party of Texas. "2012 Platform." Web.

Rethinking Schools. "The Trouble with Common Core." Summer 2013. Web.

Rhodes, Jacqueline, and Jonathan Alexander. "Reimagining the Social Turn: New Work from the Field." *College English* 76.6 (July2014): 48–87.

Richards, I. A., and C. K. Ogden. *The Meaning of Meaning*. Cambridge: U of Cambridge P, 1923.

Riedner, Rachel, and Kevin Mahoney. *Democracies to Come: Rhetorical Action, Neoliberalism, and Communities of Resistance*. Lanham, MD: Lexington Books, 2008.

Roberts-Miller, Patricia. *Deliberate Conflict: Argument, Political Theory, and Composition Classes*. Carbondale: Southern Illinois UP, 2004.

———. "Democracy, Demagoguery, and Critical Rhetoric." *Rhetoric and Public Affairs* 8.3 (2005): 459–76.

———. "Dissent as 'Aid and Comfort to the Enemy': The Rhetorical Power of Naïve Realism and Ingroup Identity." *Rhetoric Society Quarterly* 39.2 (2009): 170–88.

Rodriguez, Richard. *Hunger of Memory: The Education of Richard Rodriguez*. New York: Bantam, 1983.

Rogers, Carl. *On Becoming a Person: A Therapist's View of Psychotherapy*. London: Constable, 1961.

Rose, Mike. *An Open Language: Selected Writing on Literacy, Learning, and Opportunity*. New York: Bedford St. Martin's, 2006.

Rosen, Robert C., ed. *Class and the College Classroom: Essays on Teaching*. New York: Bloomsbury, 2013.

Rosendale, Laura Gray, and Steven Rosendale, eds. *Radical Relevance: Toward a Scholarship of the Whole Left*. Albany: State University of New York P, 2005.

Ross, Alex. "The Naysayers: Walter Benjamin, Theodor Adorno, and the Critique of Pop Culture." *New Yorker* 15 Sept. 2014: 88–94.

Ryan, William. *Blaming the Victim*. New York: Pantheon, 1971.

Saltman, Kenneth J. *The Failure of Corporate School Reform*. Boulder: Paradigm, 2012.

Savio, Mario. "An End to History." Cohen, 329–32

Schilb, John, and Patti Harkin, eds. *Contending with Words: Composition in a Postmodern Era*. New York: MLA, 1991. 105–25.

Schilb, John. "Reconsiderations. 'Inventing the University' at 25: An Interview with David Bartholomae." *College English* 73 (2011): 260–82.

Schildgen, Brenda Deen. "Reconnecting Rhetoric and Philosophy in the Composition Classroom." Gere, *Into the Field*, 30–43.

Schlosser, Eric. *Fast Food Nation*. New York: Harper Perennial, 2002.

Schutz, Aaron, and Anne Ruggles Gere. "Aaron Schutz and Anne Ruggles Gere Respond." *College English* 61 (1999): 356–59.

———. "Service Learning and English Studies: Rethinking 'Public Service.'" *College English* 60 (1998): 129–49.

Scott, Peter Dale. *Coming to Jakarta*. New York: New Directions, 1988.

Scott, Tony. *Dangerous Writing: Understanding the Political Economy of Composition*. Logan: Utah State UP, 2009.

Scribner, Sylvia, and Michael Cole. *The Psychology of Literacy*. Cambridge: Harvard UP, 1981.

Sennett, Richard, and Jonathan Cobb. *The Hidden Injuries of Class*. New York: Free Press, 1966.

Shaughnessy, Mina P. *Errors and Expectations: A Guide for the Teacher of Basic Writing*. New York: Oxford UP, 1977.

———. "Some Needed Research on Writing." *College Composition and Communication* 28 (1977): 320.

Shor, Ira. *Critical Teaching and Everyday Life*. Boston: South End, 1980.

———, ed. *Freire for the Classroom*. Portsmouth, NH: Boynton/Cook, 1987.

Smitherman, Geneva. *Talkin and Testifyin: The Language of Black America*. Detroit: Wayne State UP, 1977.

Sokal, Alan. "Transgressing the Boundaries: Towards a Transformative Hermeneutics of Quantum Gravity." *Social Text* 46/47 (1996): 217–52.

Spellmeyer, Kurt. *Arts of Living: Reinventing the Humanities for the Twenty-first Century*. Albany: SU of New York P, 2003.

———. "Culture and Agency." *College Composition and Communication* 48 (1997): 292–96.

———. "Out of the Fashion Industry: From Cultural Studies to the Anthropology of Knowledge." *College Composition and Communication* 43 (1996): 424–36.

———. "Saving the Social Imagination: The Humanities at the Present Time." *College English* 74 (July 2012): 567–87.

Stanley, Jane. *The Rhetoric of Remediation: Negotiating Entitlement and Access to Higher Education*. Pittsburgh: U of Pittsburgh P, 2010.

Stone, Wilfred, and J. G. Bell. *Prose Style: A Handbook for Writers*. New York: McGraw-Hill, 1968.

Strauss, Valerie. "AFT's Weingarten Calls for Moratorium on High Stakes Linked to Common Core." *Washington Post* 30 Apr. 2013. Web.

"Student Diversity at Nearly 1,800 Institutions." *Chronicle of Higher Education* 31 Oct. 2014. B28-46.

Students for a Democratic Society. "The Port Huron Statement." James Miller, *Democracy Is in the Streets: From Port Huron to the Siege of Chicago*. New York: Simon and Schuster, 1987. 329–77.

Students' Right to Their Own Language. Special issue of *College Composition and Communication* 25 (Fall 1974).

"Symposium on the *Framework for Success in Postsecondary Writing*." *College English* 74 (2012): 420–53.

Tannen, Deborah. *You Just Don't Understand: Women and Men in Conversation*. New York: Morrow, 1990.

Thompson, E. P. *The Poverty of Theory and Other Essays*. London: Merlin, 1978.

Thoreau, Henry David. *Walden and Other Writings*. Ed. Brooks Atkinson. New York: Modern Library, 1957.

Tompkins, Jane. "Pedagogy of the Distressed." *College English* 52 (1990): 653–60.

———. *Sensational Designs: The Cultural Work of American Fiction 1790–1860*. New York: Oxford UP, 1985.

———. *West of Everything: The Inner Life of Westerns*. New York: Oxford UP, 1992.

Toobin, Jeffrey. "The Dirty Trickster." *New Yorker* 2 June 2008. Web.

Trotsky, Leon. *Art and Revolution*. Ed. Paul Siegel. New York: Pathfinder, 1970.

Tuman, Myron C. "Class, Codes, and Composition: Basil Bernstein and the Critique of Pedagogy." *College Composition and Communication* 39.1 (1988): 42–51.

———. *A Preface to Literacy*. Tuscaloosa: U of Alabama P, 1987.

Vygotsky, L. S. *Mind in Society: The Development of Higher Psychological Processes*. Ed. Michael Cole et al. Cambridge: Harvard UP, 1978.

———. *Thought and Language*. Ed. Alex Kozulin. Cambridge: MIT P, 1986.

Watt, Ian. *The Rise of the Novel*. Berkeley: U of California P, 1957.

Walsh, Deborah, and Richard Paul. *The Goal of Critical Thinking: From Educational Ideal to Educational Reality*. Washington, DC: American Federation of Teachers Educational Issues Department, 1985.

Wander, Philip C. Foreword. Kahn and Lee, 21–32.

Weisser, Christian R. *Moving Beyond Academic Discourse: Composition Studies and the Public Sphere*. Carbondale: Southern Illinois UP, 2002.

Welch, Nancy. *Living Room: Teaching Public Writing in a Privatized World*. Portsmouth, NH: Heinemann, 2008.

Wells, Susan. "Rogue Cops and Health Care: What Do We Want from Public Writing?" *College Composition and Communication* 47 (1996): 325–41.

Wertsch, James V., ed. *Culture, Communication, and Cognition: Vygotskyian Perspectives*. Cambridge, UK: Cambridge UP, 1985.

Whorf, Benjamin Lee. *Language, Thought, and Reality*. Cambridge: MIT Press, 1956.

Wilde, Oscar. *The Soul of Man under Socialism*. *Selections from the Works of Oscar Wilde*. Ed. Graham Hough. New York: Dell, 1960. 270–305.

Willis, Ellen. *The Essential Ellen Willis*. Nona Aronowitz Willis, ed. Minneapolis: U of Minnesota P, 2014.

Willson, Meredith. *The Music Man*. Columbia LP, 1960.

Wolf, Naomi. *The Beauty Myth*. New York: Anchor, 1992.

Wolfe, Alan. "'The Authoritarian Personality' Revisited." *Chronicle of Higher Education* 7 Oct. 1995, B12–13.

Zavarzadeh, Mas'ud, Teresa Ebert, and Donald Morton, eds. *Post-Ality, Marxism, and Postmodernism*. Washington, DC: Maisonneuve P, 1995.

In six scholarly and text books, as well as many scholarly and journalistic articles, **DONALD LAZERE** has written on the politics of higher education, literacy, media, literature, composition, and rhetoric. He is a professor emeritus of English at Cal Poly, San Luis Obispo, and currently lives in Knoxville, where he has taught at the University of Tennessee.